D1594755

BASTARDS & BROTHERS

BASTARDS & BROTHERS

MARINES AND THE FIGHT FOR AL-QAIM, IRAQ

ROGER 'AJAX' TRUEBLOOD

SEMPER FI!
--AJAX

Deeds Publishing | Athens

Published by Deeds Publishing in Athens, GA
www.deedspublishing.com

Printed in The United States of America

Cover design by Mark Babcock.

ISBN 978-1-950794-87-4

Books are available in quantity for promotional or premium use. For information, email info@deedspublishing.com.

First Edition, 2022

10 9 8 7 6 5 4 3 2 1

For Kevin, Larry, and Adam

"Iraq veteran and former CIA officer Ajax Trueblood has written a detailed, finely-researched account not just of one battalion, but of the complex, grueling nature of the post-Saddam insurgency. He clearly demonstrates that the Marine efforts to win over the Sunni tribes had succeeded many months before the famed "surge" in 2007. He does a great service to the grunts who persisted for years far, far from Baghdad. They turned the tide of the war, although all publicity has been focused upon American generals who came later."

—Bing West, bestselling author of
No True Glory: A Frontline Account of the Battle for Fallujah

"This book should be required reading for NCO's, junior officers and senior leaders. Ajax Trueblood describes in compelling detail tactical level actions and tough decisions that had strategic consequences. Our troopers of the 3rd Armored Cavalry Regiment in Ninewa Province, fought adjacent to Marines of Third Battalion, Second Marines and Regimental Combat Team 2. We monitored each other's operations and situation reports. Our cavalry troopers and the Marines of 3/2 took the offensive against a brutal and determined enemy. The author brings readers into the command post for campaign planning and into the streets for house-to-house fighting in Western Iraq. This is a study of command and combat leadership at all levels. And it is a fitting tribute to those who fought and sacrificed for the mission and their fellow Marines."

—H.R. McMaster, 71st Colonel of the Third U.S. Cavalry and author of *Battlegrounds: The Fight to Defend the Free World*

"Ajax has written a detailed history that is critical to understanding the Marine victory in Iraq's toughest province—Anbar. What is exceptional about Bastards and Brothers is its relentless narrative pace. It's top notch history that is simultaneously hard to put down. That's a rare combination. Trueblood nails both the details and, more impressively, the Marine warfighting culture."

—Owen West, award-winning author of
The Snake Eaters: Counterinsurgency Advisors in Combat

CONTENTS

FOREWORD

This is a story worth telling and a story worth reading. When Ajax told me he was writing a book about the battalion I commanded back in 2005, I was skeptical. It seemed odd that an Air Force veteran would care to tell a Marine story that had been essentially ignored.

Of course, I was immensely proud of the toughness and professionalism of the Marines I led and what they accomplished in Al-Qaim, out west along the Syrian border. Especially since almost everyone thought Iraq was a lost cause at the time. Most histories of the war have focused on the initial invasion in 2003 or the successes that came much later in 2007 with the arrival of General Petraeus and the surge of U.S. forces. Not many have been interested in, or even been aware of, the part my Marines contributed to the story.

Great credit goes to Ajax for working so diligently to finally tell that story (and erasing all traces of my initial skepticism). He has crafted a gripping account of desperate battles in western Anbar Province, fought against a merciless enemy led by foreign terrorists. He has expertly pulled together individual stories from different levels, from private to colonel, describing the valor and skill of so many. It is a moving story told by and about men who would never claim to be heroes. They will always say they were just doing what we expect of them: being professionals, fighting with tenacity, living up daily to the adage, "no better friend, no worse enemy." Yet many of their actions were heroic. It was a great honor and one of the highlights of my career to prepare them for combat in this environment, be their commander, and witness their compassion, courage, and professionalism.

I was fortunate to be where I could see what these amazing Marines could accomplish in the most challenging circumstances. Our junior officers, NCOs, and Marines in the ranks started a rising wave of change by earning the trust of local Iraqis; showing them we cared for them far more than the murderous fanatics we were fighting. By the end of our combat tour, I had witnessed the beginning of a massive turn-around that would spread far beyond Al-Qaim, growing into what would be called The Awakening. The Betio Bastards went into the black hole that was Iraq in 2005 and made a difference.

Through good planning and execution, we suffered fewer casualties than some other units, so in many people's eyes our efforts didn't stand out. But the Marines of 3/2 deserve to have their story told, especially those who paid the ultimate sacrifice. I am extremely grateful that Ajax has captured this account for history. He has brought this important and long-hidden story to light, describing it with great care, deep research, and amazing detail. The result is an outstanding book that Marines, their families, and all Americans should read to understand a vital missing piece of the Iraq War story.

—Timothy S. Mundy
Colonel, United States Marine Corps (Retired)

PREFACE

I am an unlikely, unworthy even, chronicler of a Marine infantry battalion at war. I am not a Marine and have not experienced frontline combat. To Marine infantrymen, who proudly call themselves "grunts", I am a "person-other-than-grunt" (POG or "pogue"). In fact, my POG-ness runs even deeper. As an Air Force intelligence officer (now retired), and a reservist to boot, my status on the spectrum of warrior merit is very low. To be honest, I struggled with that as I began this journey. Internal questions would arise; *What makes you think you can write this story? Wouldn't someone else be more qualified?* But time and again, another question would come; *If not you, who?*

In more confident moments, I realized I brought a unique mix of strengths to the effort. First, long experience as an analyst prepared me to see the larger patterns and pull together pieces of fragmentary information into a coherent narrative. I also have on-the-ground experience in Iraq, though not in Al-Qaim or Anbar. Deployments in both 2004 and 2007 gave me valuable first-hand perspectives on the war, first from the strategic and operational level and then from a more tactical viewpoint.*

Additionally, for an Air Force officer, I am atypically familiar with ground combat operations. Part of that passionate interest stems from having a son in the U.S. Army who has deployed multiple times to Iraq and Afghanistan at the very tip of the spear. As father to a warrior son, I am intimately familiar with the stresses combat veterans and their families face. I have learned much from him, both in concrete and intangible ways. Much of that very personal knowledge relates directly to the experiences of the Marines I write about here.

In a strange way, then, this combination has made me a rare breed of "insider-outsider" and perhaps an ideal teller of this story. As an outsider, I bring a wider perspective on the war and the campaign to stabilize Anbar. And as an Iraq War veteran myself, I hold certain insider perspectives and attitudes that no journalist or academic researcher could tap into.

CIRCLES

What started as an intellectual exercise evolved into something much more personal. As I reached out to veterans one by one and they shared their experiences with me, the feelings behind the facts became the real substance of the book. For some, talking about those days was a release, a chance to open up about things they'd pushed down deep. Some had never shared them with

* In 2004/2005, the author was stationed at Al-Udeid Airbase in Qatar and deployed forward several times into Iraq for short periods. In 2007, he was attached to the U.S. Army's 3rd Infantry Division in Iraq and worked on forward operating bases south of Baghdad in Babil and Wasit Provinces.

anyone. Often, a call I thought would be a short introduction stretched late into the night.

Others were reluctant at first, even suspicious. These combat veterans still maintain close-knit, battle-forged circles of brother warriors. For those circles, I was, will always be, an outsider. And that is as it should be. In most cases, I was granted the honor of conditional, temporary access. Once I'd earned a measure of trust, one Marine would introduce me to others in his circle. But not always. Some remained guarded. And there are some who prefer to keep the past in the past. Their choices must be respected.

Usually though, when these men opened up, they wanted their story to be heard. Some pointedly told me to be accurate, to be fair. Most often there were no demands, just a gracious thank you for my efforts. But even when not explicitly stated, a charge was silently assumed; the charge to "get it right." I have endeavored mightily to do so.

FORGETTING AND REMEMBERING

The sacrifices and accomplishments of the 3rd Battalion, 2nd Marine Regiment during 2005 were either unknown or quickly forgotten. The same goes for the entire Iraq War for that matter. Reaching back now, years later, is to uncover what is ancient history in today's Twitter-fueled hyperworld. Those events have been covered by windblown dunes, layer upon layer of tragedy, and blithe forgetfulness that settled over a nation eager to move on. Which is a tragedy all its own.

The war began badly, with many questionable political, strategic, and military decisions. Too often it takes time for the world's most successful democracy, and the military which serves it, to find what it takes to prevail in a new conflict. Sadly, that learning curve imposes steep costs. This was certainly true in Iraq. Opportunities were missed, resources squandered, precious lives lost, as we learned the hard lessons. But, in fact, even during the darkest days of Operation Iraqi Freedom (the Pentagon's official name for the conflict in Iraq), there was rapid learning taking place.

When seen in full perspective, the American military in Iraq adapted quickly to a new type of warfare and a baffling array of new enemies. In a surprisingly short time span, tactics improved, strategy became aligned with reality, better leaders arose, and units got smarter. The mass "flipping" of Sunni tribes to our side in 2006 and implementation of the Bush/Petraeus surge in 2007 eventually led to amazing success. But the foundations of that success were laid by those who labored through the dark days.

By 2009, Anbar Province, previously the hotbed of insurgency, was peaceful and American troops sipped chai in the marketplaces. Meanwhile, deprived of high casualty counts, media headlines at home were dominated by the latest iPhone release and Michael Jackson's funeral. Paradoxically, success in Iraq only accelerated America's collective amnesia. Still more cognizance was buried as a new administration announced, then executed an ill-advised withdrawal, completed by 2011. Afghanistan became Obama's "good war." Iraq was Bush's "bad war," the stepchild rejected by both left and right.

Then, in 2014, came a layer of hot volcanic ash blasting out of the desert. It swept across the entire landscape as the black shroud of ISIS descended. The Islamic State of Iraq and Syria was the hyper-violent reincarnation of a previous extremist group, al-Qaeda in Iraq (AQI), that U.S, troops had fought and defeated on the battlefield. For veterans who had served in Iraq, especially those who'd been part of the campaigns to pacify Anbar, it was painful to watch enemies they'd once vanquished return to infest large swathes of the country. Each city that fell to the raving killers brought memories of sacrifices made, of friends lost, of blood spilt, all now seemingly in vain.

My own reaction was to psychologically turn away. It was hard to deal with what I felt was a massive betrayal that was unfolding as ditches filled with corpses and roads were lined with severed heads. Other veterans I've spoken with had similar feelings. It was hard to fathom how America could let the progress we'd made, and yes, the victories we'd won, slip away.

And so multiple strata of forgetfulness settled over Anbar, over Al-Qaim (one of the first areas to fall under ISIS rule) and hid the battlegrounds where U.S. Marines fought just a few years before. In a way, then, my task has been akin to that of an archeologist, carefully brushing back layers of sediment to reveal the forgotten truths below.

But the Marines of 3/2 remember. It is time that many others remember as well. I have a deep respect for these men, for what they went through and in too many cases what they continue to endure, and for the sacrifice they offered up for all of us. I now count several of them as friends. Many of them helped me piece together this book, guiding me, providing facts, images, and even their personal journals. Without their help, I could never have written an account of this clarity, depth, and accuracy. To them and the other warriors who assisted me in ways large and small, I am grateful beyond words. This is my humble attempt to tell their story. If there are errors or oversights—inevitably there will be some—they are my own.

SOURCES & METHODS

As I began writing, I felt prepared for a long, tough road. But it was even tougher than I thought. I soon realized that to tell the story faithfully while putting it into the right context would take far longer than I'd anticipated. Available written sources were cursory and fragmented. Just determining correct locations was a challenge. And the decentralized, distributed nature of counter-insurgency operations in Iraq made understanding the relationships between certain events difficult. It required a kind of cognitive percolation process that just took time.

There are published volumes, mostly official histories published by the U.S. Marine Corps, Army, or Department of Defense, providing the outlines of major operations in and around Al-Qaim. But they lack fine-grained descriptions and details. There are also a handful of books with eye-witness accounts of events in far west Anbar during 2004 and 2005. For my purposes, the most important of these were written by men who served either in 3/2 or units that supported them. Naturally, however, these provided a very personalized and limited view.

By far the most useful documentary source was the multi-volume study, conducted and published by the Institute for Defense Analysis (IDA), entitled Al-Sahawa—The Awakening. Sponsored by the Marine Corps, IDA's "Awakening Project" is a remarkable work of scholarship which presents a rich tapestry of the many events, personalities, and currents that culminated in the Sunni Awakening and a key turning point in the Iraq War. I owe Dr. Bill Knarr (Colonel, retired) and his associates a debt of gratitude.

I am also grateful to the Marine Corps University's History Division for giving me access to a valuable collection of recorded interviews conducted in Anbar during the summer of 2005 by a Marine field historian, Lieutenant Colonel David Benhoff. These unique interviews provided an unmatched window directly into the contemporaneous thoughts and perspectives of key participants.

Moving beyond this required exhaustive searches for anything on Al-Qaim and the struggle that raged there from 2003 through 2007. Many press articles from those days were confused and inaccurate but revealed important details when placed properly into the mosaic. Surprisingly, videos turned out to be highly useful. Online documentaries, media clips, B-rolls and footage from Marines' own handheld cameras gave me unfiltered details and vital visual context.

The other irreplaceable online sources were mapping applications, which feature open-source satellite imagery of surprising clarity. Without these tools, I would likely have remained forever confused on topography, place names, and the physical relationship between key locations. I have spent countless hours virtually roving across the terrain where 3/2 operated, zooming into city streets, even identifying individual buildings.

Without a doubt, though, my most valuable sources were the Marines themselves. This book is the product of over two hundred personal interviews, conducted mostly by phone or online chat sessions, with men who were there. The first 3/2 veterans I reached out to had been junior enlisted Marines in 2005. This was because of my own inexperience and lack of contacts, not by design. A seasoned military history author would probably have started by interviewing the top of the chain of command, not the lance corporals. I did eventually make contact with much of the battalion's leadership. They were open and amazingly helpful, providing the bigger picture and absolutely vital operational understanding.

But the bottom-up approach I took by first talking with Marines from the ranks yielded a richness, an emotional depth to the story that could not have come any other way. Laced throughout these pages are stories from the guys who manned the posts, ate dust on patrol, and kicked the doors with God-knows-what behind them. These are the grunts, the heart and soul of the Corps. They're really who this book is about and ultimately who it's for.

The book was reviewed by the Defense Office of Pre-Publication and Security Review at the U.S. Department of Defense and the Central Intelligence Agency's Prepublication Classification Review Board. Minor changes were made to alleviate security concerns. All statements of fact, opinion, or analysis expressed are those of the author and do not reflect the official positions or views of the Department of Defense or the U.S. Government. Nothing in the contents should be construed as asserting or implying U.S. Government authentication of information, factual accuracy, or endorsement of the author's views.

LANGUAGE WARNING

For Marines in their natural habitat, swearing is as natural as breathing. As an example, the following excerpt is from a recording of a young corporal in 3/2 briefing his squad of about a dozen men just before they assault dug-in, well-armed insurgents during Operation Spear. None of them know if they'll survive the day:

> *I'm not gonna give you a moto speech, 'cause I don't do that. But uh, fuck, just listen to your team leaders... If you're in doubt, fuckin' ask somebody. If you have no-shit ID, take the shot. Worry about it later, alright? Fuck. Just make sure you know where everybody's at. If you don't know, ask your team leader. Ask me, I'll tell ya. Alright? Fuck.*

Granted, the grunts' salty vocabulary is a genuine and essential part of their being. But after careful thought, I have scrubbed the harshest profanity (particularly the F-word) from their quotes. In the end, it came down to consideration for their own families. Some Marines may disagree with me on this point, preferring to have their verbal alacrity portrayed for posterity in its full and earthy glory. I hope they will forgive me.

I also hope the general reader will forgive what may seem like a heavy barrage of acronyms and unfamiliar terms. Even for those fluent in "milspeak", the Marine Corps has its own terminology that may need to be deciphered. Most acronyms and unique terms are therefore expanded or explained the first time they appear and there is an extensive glossary at the back of the book.

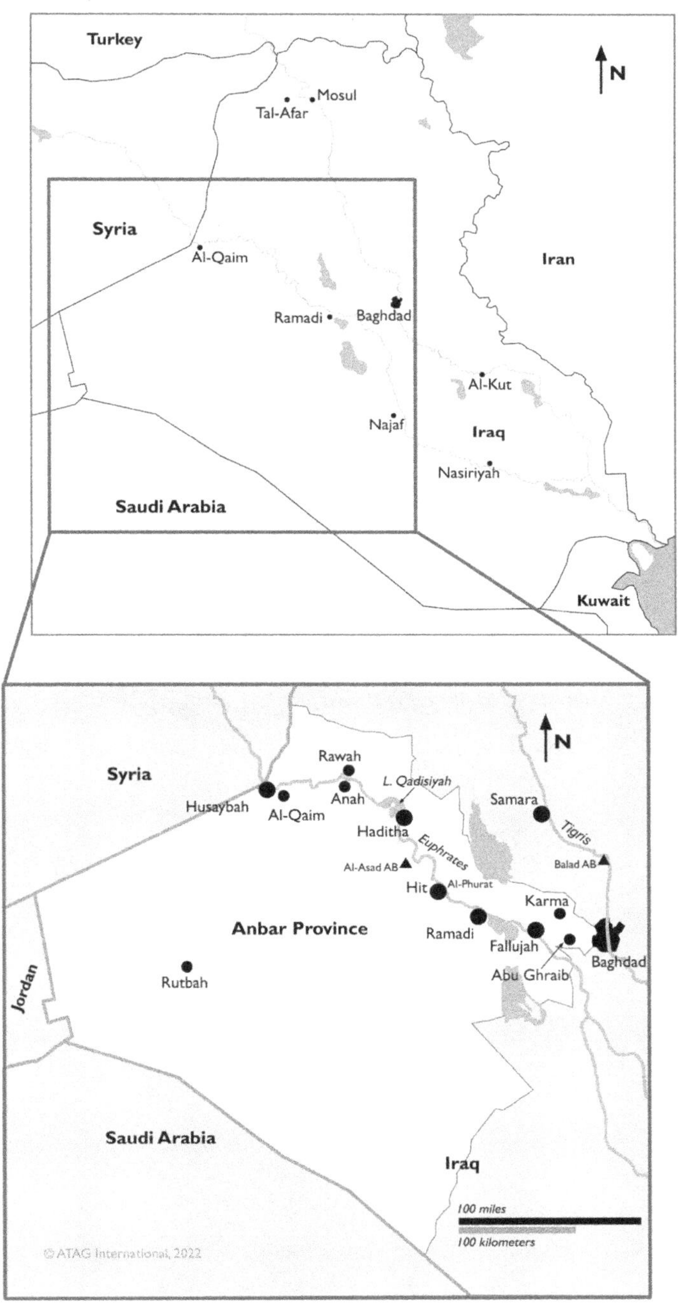

Turkey
N
Mosul
Tal-Afar
Syria
Al-Qaim
Iran
Ramadi
Baghdad
Al-Kut
Najaf
Iraq
Nasiriyah
Saudi Arabia
Kuwait
N
Rawah
Syria
L. Qadisiyah
Anah
Samara
Husaybah
Al-Qaim
Haditha
Tigris
Euphrates
Al-Asad AB
Balad AB
Hit
Al-Phurat
Karma
Anbar Province
Ramadi
Fallujah
Baghdad
Abu Ghraib
Rutbah
Jordan
Saudi Arabia
Iraq
100 miles
100 kilometers
© ATAG International, 2022

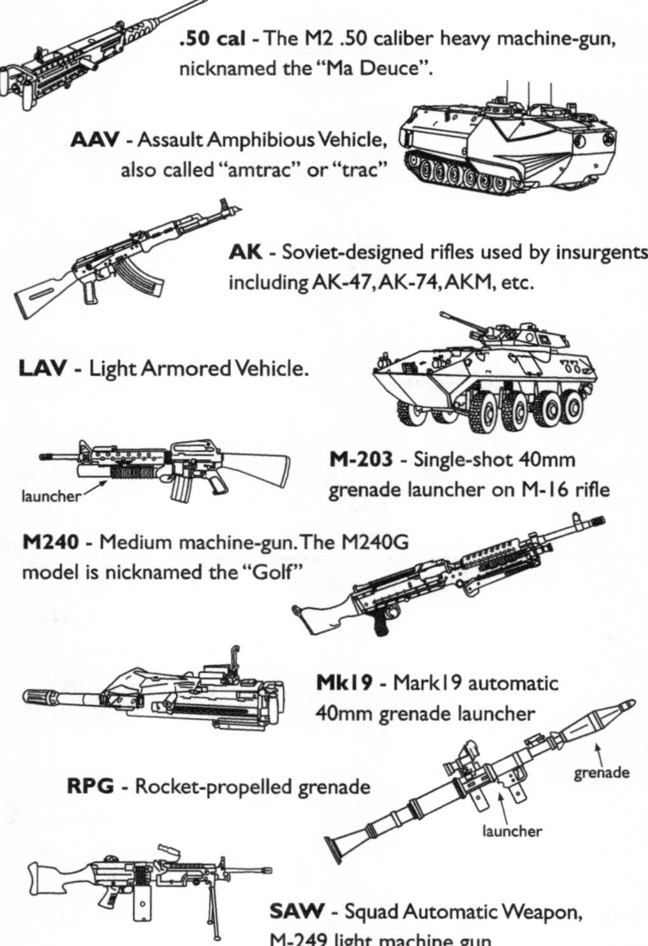
.50 cal - The M2 .50 caliber heavy machine-gun, nicknamed the "Ma Deuce".
AAV - Assault Amphibious Vehicle, also called "amtrac" or "trac"
AK - Soviet-designed rifles used by insurgents, including AK-47, AK-74, AKM, etc.
LAV - Light Armored Vehicle.
launcher
M-203 - Single-shot 40mm grenade launcher on M-16 rifle
M240 - Medium machine-gun. The M240G model is nicknamed the "Golf"
Mk19 - Mark19 automatic 40mm grenade launcher
RPG - Rocket-propelled grenade
grenade
launcher
SAW - Squad Automatic Weapon, M-249 light machine gun

Military units & command levels

Corps (MEF)	Lieutenant General (3 stars) 2+ division equivalents (20,000-45,000 personnel)
Division	Major General (2 stars) 2-4 brigade/regiment equivalents (10,000-15,000 personnel)
Brigade or Regiment	Colonel 2-4 battalions (3,000-5,500 personnel)
Battalion	Lieutenant Colonel 3-4 companies (800-1200)
Company	Captain 3-4 platoons (120-200)
Platoon	1st or 2nd Lieutenant 2-3 squads (20-40)
Squad	Sergeant or Corporal 2-3 fire teams (6-13)
Fire Team	Corporal or Lance Corporal (2-4 men)

Note: Highly situationally dependent. Ranks & numbers of personnel are approximate.

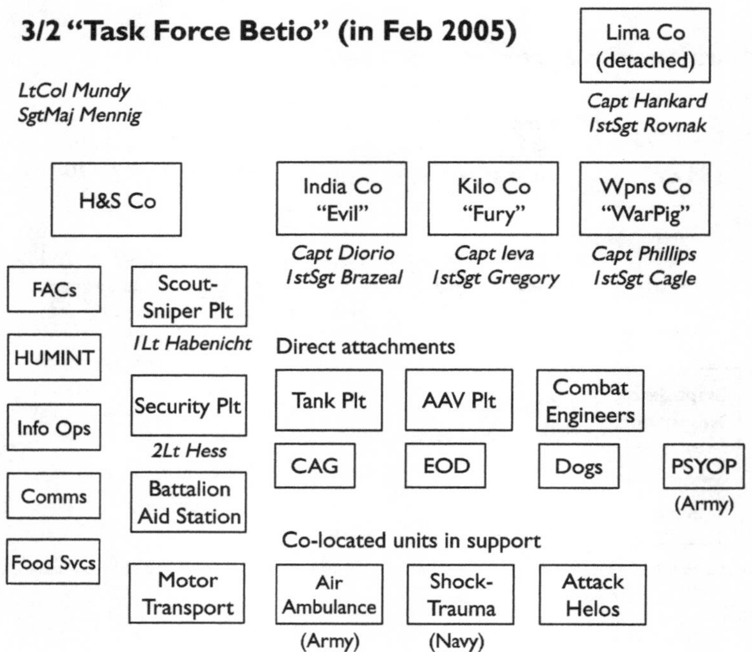
3/2 "Task Force Betio" (in Feb 2005)
LtCol Mundy
SgtMaj Mennig
Lima Co (detached)
Capt Hankard
1stSgt Rovnak
H&S Co
India Co "Evil"
Capt Diorio
1stSgt Brazeal
Kilo Co "Fury"
Capt Ieva
1stSgt Gregory
Wpns Co "WarPig"
Capt Phillips
1stSgt Cagle
FACs
HUMINT
Info Ops
Comms
Food Svcs
Scout-Sniper Plt
1Lt Habenicht
Security Plt
2Lt Hess
Battalion Aid Station
Motor Transport
Direct attachments
Tank Plt
AAV Plt
Combat Engineers
CAG
EOD
Dogs
PSYOP (Army)
Co-located units in support
Air Ambulance (Army)
Shock-Trauma (Navy)
Attack Helos

INTRODUCTION

As he navigated through the cramped hallways of the battle-scarred Government Center in Ramadi, Iraq, award-winning photographer John Moore tried to stay out of the way of gruff U.S. Marines hustling from one room to another. For months, the Government Center had been ground zero in the fight to win back control in the most important city in Anbar Province. Moore lifted his camera as his practiced eye glimpsed a hand-written note on a whiteboard. There, in a careful, cursive script (rare in military settings) some anonymous bard-in-camo had written:

America is not at war.
The Marine Corps is at war;
America is at the mall.

Moore took the photo in January 2007.[1] It was published in U.S. newspapers, then circulated around the blogosphere for a few weeks, but faded quickly from America's collective consciousness—which ironically proved the nameless author's point. No doubt his words were quickly erased as well, as such cutting cynicism is not the message the Marine Corps wants to project to the public.

But for those who had fought vicious battles to secure Ramadi in late 2006, known then as the Sunni insurgency's "heart of darkness", the cynic's lines perfectly captured their mood. It was a hard-edged sentiment, with equal parts pride and disgust. Pride at what they'd endured and accomplished. Disgust and disillusionment that it was so casually disregarded, even actively devalued, by most of their countrymen at home.

Today, that same bitter mixture still circulates in the veins, synapses, and buried memories of those who have served in our nation's most recent wars. Take the time to really talk to a veteran of Iraq or Afghanistan about his or her experiences there, and you will likely hear some version of "America is at the mall."

AWAKENINGS

In the summer of 2007, Wasit Province was the last place anyone thought the Sunni-led, Marine-fostered tribal "Awakening" would reach. South and west of Baghdad, the province's population was predominantly Shiite and operated under an entirely different dynamic than the Sunni areas. Iranian puppets were basically in charge of the provincial capital, Al-Kut. Large parts of the city were controlled by armed militia groups, primarily the *Jaysh al-Mahdi* (Mahdi Army) or JAM. The government and police there were heavily infiltrated or co-opted by JAM or other groups backed by Iran.

Through a convoluted assignment process, I was an Air Force officer working at Camp Delta, just outside Al-Kut. I was attached to an Army staff loosely coordinating a mixed bag of units and personnel. Our mission was ambiguous at best, defined as "interdicting accelerants", which meant keeping weapons, money, and deadly Iranian-made IEDs from transiting into Baghdad and the "belts" of suburban and rural communities surrounding the capital. It was an economy-of-force operation, at the margins of the surge of U.S. forces under command of General David Petraeus.

There was some violence in the area, but not much. A few times a week a rocket or two would impact inside Camp Delta, to little effect. Inside the city, a Police Training Team composed of Army Military Police soldiers had a shootout with Shiite militiamen but escaped casualties. A few weeks later, two private security contractors weren't as lucky. They were killed when their vehicle was struck by an explosively-formed penetrator (EFP), exactly the kind of accelerant we were trying to interdict.

Part of my job was to support a Provincial Reconstruction Team (PRT) as they engaged local tribal leaders and found surprising willingness among them to join the burgeoning "Sons of Iraq" program. I attended a few of these meetings with the sheikhs. We didn't know how legitimate they all were, but it was clear they wanted to support the government and form legal security forces in their areas. Things were changing.

It was an exciting time to be in Iraq. I could sense the momentum shifting every day as the surge and active partnering with Iraqi forces started to take effect. But it was the Awakening movement that had really swung the needle, and it had finally reached Al-Kut and Wasit Province. That experience was the genesis of this book. I was already keenly interested in the phenomenon that went by several names—Anbar Salvation Council, Sons of Iraq, Concerned Local Citizens, or in Arabic, *Harakat al-Sahwah al-Sunniyah,* "Sunni Awakening Movement." I'd been reading up on it since 2006 and at that point, my understanding matched the standard narrative.

TURNING RAMADI

The typical account of the Awakening starts in 2006, when Ramadi, the capital of Anbar Province, was the most violent city in Iraq and the central battleground against the rabid jihadists of al-Qaeda in Iraq (AQI). The foreign-led extremists and their allies declared Ramadi the capital of their Islamic "caliphate." U.S. Marine and Army units battled every day against increasingly brazen, black-clad insurgents, flitting through the blasted ruins of the downtown area to attack checkpoints and patrols. It was an apocalyptic scene that only seemed to be worsening.

But unappreciated by most (particularly the press), that summer Sunni tribes in and around Ramadi began to turn decisively against al-Qaeda and the radicals. Influential tribal leaders recognized the hopelessness and destruction brought by the extremists. And when the sheiks withdrew their support for the terrorists and foreign fighters, the killers of AQI targeted them and their families.

In August, a prominent tribal leader was assassinated for encouraging his kinsmen to join the Iraqi security forces (ISF). The killers then hid his body in a field, denying him the swift burial called for by Islamic belief. This was a catalyst. In the wake of the outrage, 35-year-old Sheikh Abdul Sattar Abu Risha stepped to center stage. He had lost his own father and three brothers to AQI and had had enough. On August 21st, Sattar declared "The Awakening", an alliance of Sunni tribes willing to take up arms against al-Qaeda in Iraq. As he told a reporter:

> *We held a meeting and agreed to fight those who call themselves mujahadeen. We believe that there is a conspiracy against our Iraqi people. Those terrorists claimed that they are fighters working on liberating Iraq, but they turned out to be killers. Now all the people are fed up and have turned against them.*
>
> **—Sheikh Sattar**[2]

He quickly reached out to other sheiks and together they started cooperating with U.S. forces, recruiting members of their tribes to serve as policemen and sending their own fighters to battle the jihadists head-on. Soon hundreds of police recruits were signing up and neighborhood "emergency response units" were formed, an early iteration of the Sons of Iraq. Within just a few months the situation in Ramadi changed dramatically. By early 2007, attacks were down substantially, and weeks would pass with no U.S. casualties. Rubble was being cleared from the streets. Families and businesses were coming back. And as AQI's bloodthirsty grip on the city slipped, the tribal rebellion against them accelerated and spread.

There is an unfortunate tendency in many accounts of the Iraq War to conflate the Awakening with the surge, superimposing them on the timeline. But this obscures important realities. The open rebellion against AQI was underway months before the surge was announced, nearly a year before all five "surge brigades" were on the ground executing General Petraeus' campaign. The Awakening was a precursor to the surge and was probably a prerequisite.

When John Moore snapped his photo of the whiteboard in the Government Center, the corner had been turned in Ramadi. By the time President Bush's surge of American forces to Iraq began, the Awakening had multiplied across most of Anbar and places that had been no-go areas for U.S. and Iraqi troops were amazingly peaceful. And by the time I put my own boots on the ground in May, 2007, the waves of positive change were spreading further into Baghdad and beyond.

BEGINNINGS

But like almost everything in Iraq, it's not that simple. The origins of the turnaround in Ramadi can be traced further back to before 2006. The full history of the Awakening involves multiple layers of intermeshed personalities and factors that are often shrouded in hazy memories, the fog of war, conflicting claims, and sometimes intentional deception. As I finished my 2007 tour and returned to the States, I began a long search to understand the fuller picture of what I'd experienced.

The currents and passions that led to Sheikh Sattar's formation of the Anbar Salvation Council, and the Americans' willingness to support Sunni tribes, did not spring from a vacuum. They were a product of several interconnected trendlines: American overtures to prominent tribal sheikhs, political maneuvering in Baghdad, more imaginative U.S. military leaders, better counter-insurgency techniques, the desperation of everyday Iraqis, and the compounding cruelty of the jihadists.

Moreover, Sheikh Sattar was following in the footsteps of other tribes, in other places, that had previously turned against the extremists. There were awakenings before the Awakening.

The available record of these is fragmentary, often vague, and usually provides just a few tantalizing clues. But as early as 2004, there were stirrings among certain Anbari tribes, a visceral dissatisfaction with outsiders bringing radical Islamist ideology and disruption to their lives.

One of the first instances of tribal forces actively turning against the jihadists came in the villages along the eastern bank of the Euphrates opposite the city of Hit. In early 2004, a small U.S. Army Special Forces team, or Operational Detachment-Alpha (ODA), forged a tight relationship with a branch of the Albu Nimr tribe in the Al-Phurat area. In classic Green Beret fashion, ODA 555 formed, funded, and trained a "provisional company" of tribesmen that began to challenge the foreign-led jihadists for control of their local area.

But the larger political picture doomed this promising early effort. In June of that year, the funding for the provisional company in Al-Phurat was stopped. By the Fall of 2004, all Special Forces ODAs were withdrawn from Anbar and this type of tribal engagement ceased. The Green Berets, the U.S. military's recognized experts in training and advising foreign indigenous forces, were taken off the case.

Even so, throughout 2004 and early 2005, there were scattered instances of what U.S. troops called "red-on-red"* violence. A mysterious exchange of mortar fire would erupt in an area where no coalition forces were operating. Or soldiers on

* Enemy forces are typically referred to or shown on maps as "red" and friendly forces as "blue". Thus "red-on-red" refers to suspected engagements between enemy elements.

night watch would see an unexplained firefight break out in a neighborhood, with a flurry of tracers arcing back and forth, but none towards their position. Such outbreaks added to other evidence of a growing split between Iraqi "nationalist" insurgents and the foreign-led jihadist groups.

The first place where that split became an open fissure was the district of Al-Qaim, in the far west along the border with Syria. Tribal forces there had initially sided with the jihadists to fight against the coalition, seeing the foreign fighters as allies in a battle against invaders. But as the foreigners imposed draconian rules, beating men for not having a sufficiently Islamic beard, cutting smokers' fingers off, taking local "wives" through intimidation, the tribesmen began to chafe. When the interlopers started skimming off a lion's share of profits from their long-established smuggling operations, the most prominent border clan decided to fight back.

PIVOTAL TIME, PIVOTAL PLACE

As I began studying the early years of the Iraq War, 3/2's first deployment to Al-Qaim did not stand out. To a writer's eye, other stories seemed more dramatic. Certainly, Marine units in other times and other places performed magnificently in the legendary battles for Fallujah, Najaf, Ramadi, and elsewhere. In the context of 3/2's own history, the battalion's 2006/2007 tour in Habbaniyah, located between Ramadi and Fallujah, seemed perhaps more notable as it coincided with the momentous events of Sattar's Awakening movement and the beginning of the surge.

Even examining the fight for Al-Qaim, there were worthy

contenders for attention. Two other Marine battalions, 3/7 and 1/7, fought bitter struggles there and paid a heavy price in casualties. There is also much to tell about 3/6, which replaced 3/2 in late 2005 and enjoyed great success in stabilizing the area. I certainly acknowledge the accomplishments and sacrifices of those units. But as I continued to dig into the record, I realized the Marines of 3/2 were sent to a pivotal place at a pivotal time. They arrived during the dark days when the U.S.-led coalition was struggling to find a successful strategy and the body counts were rising. America was losing. Nowhere was that more obvious than Anbar.

1. BLOODY ANBAR

Buddy Miller held his rifle at the low-ready and braced himself for the explosion. Tucked in right behind him was his friend and fire team leader, Joe Poulter. Both were corporals in Kilo Company of 3rd Battalion, 2nd Marines (3/2) and were executing a pre-dawn raid to capture a key insurgent. When the breaching charge blew, it shattered the desert night's calm and the door's hinges while the stack of infantrymen flowed into the house, muzzles up, ready to engage.[1]

It was August 17th, 2005, and 3/2 had been in Iraq for six months. Leading the raid was First Lieutenant Marc Bullock, commander of Kilo's 1st Platoon. Even though this was Bullock's first wartime deployment, in those few months he had seen intense action and had become a seasoned combat leader. That night's objective was a bombmaker on the battalion's list of high-value individuals or HVIs.[2] By this time, many 3/2 Marines had witnessed the horrific results of the devices such men assembled. Just two weeks earlier, a buried bomb had flipped an armored vehicle, killing 15 men from another battalion.

As they entered the house, Miller and Poulter crossed the main room and headed for a stairway. While others cleared the ground floor, they were rushing to get to the roof. During the oppressively hot summer nights, many Iraqis slept in the open air of their enclosed rooftops. The bombmaker might well be found there. Miller reached the stairs first and started up while Poulter paused to cut the lights shining in the stairwell so they wouldn't be silhouetted at the top. But by the time Poulter stepped onto the darkened rooftop seconds later, there was already a serious problem. "When I got up there, Miller was brawling with a guy," says Poulter. "They were both standing up, having a fist fight in the dark."[3]

Miles away, Marines in 3/2's Combat Operations Center (COC) tensed as they watched the rooftop struggle unfold on their glowing computer screens. Orbiting far above was a drone, or unmanned aerial vehicle (UAV) in military parlance, with an infrared camera to see through the night and the ability to transmit full-motion video. The UAV was supporting Bullock's mission, scanning for threats, and feeding live video into the COC. Captain James Keller, the battalion's assistant operations officer, remembers the scene vividly. "Just before our guys got up there, I could see this figure moving furtively on the rooftop," he says. As he watched, he saw Miller emerge onto the roof and within seconds he was grappling with the other individual. "It was one of those 'aw-shit!' moments."[4]

An instant later, Poulter joined the fray, grabbing the insurgent from behind. The three grunting men lurched and scuffled near the edge of the roof. "I was on the man's back," says Poulter, "trying to pin his arms. Then he grabbed Miller's rifle." A muzzle flash abruptly punctuated the night, and a single shot rang out. Frustration surged through the COC as they saw one of the Marines fall backwards. "We're watching all this in black and white, with no sound," says Keller. "There's nothing we can do. You have this helpless feeling. It looked like one of our Marines was pushed back, falling off the roof."

The desperate rooftop wrestling match that night was emblematic of the wider war. In countless small-unit skirmishes across western Iraq that summer, U.S. troops were slugging it out amid the shadows, fighting determined enemies ready for their own destruction if they could pull an American into oblivion with them.

THE WILD WEST

Over two thousand years ago, an ancient ruler built grain storage facilities at the end of the fabled Silk Road along the banks of the Euphrates River. The area took its name from a pre-Islamic word for warehouse and flourished through agriculture and trade. Today Al-Anbar* is the largest of Iraq's provinces, covering almost a third of the country but has only 1.5 million people, just four percent of Iraq's population of 37 million. Yet between 2004 and 2007, the country's most sparsely populated province became the very fulcrum of the Iraq War, the hinge on which so much depended.

On the province's eastern side, the cities of Abu Ghraib, Fallujah, and Ramadi intertwine with their surrounding suburban communities (see map on page xxiii). From there, a slender green ribbon winds north and west, dotted with more cities, towns, and villages. It then extends upstream from Ramadi, north through Hit and Haditha to the man-made Lake Qadisiyah.

* In Arabic grammar, the definite article "Al" precedes place names such as Anbar. For clarity, however, in this book Anbar and many place names appear without "Al" or "Ar."

From the lake, it winds westwards back to the Syrian border. The U.S. military called this the WERV, an inartful acronym for the Western Euphrates River Valley. Outside this narrow, populated strip stretches the vastness of the desert, carved by rugged ridges and deep ravines known as *wadis*. Despite the inhospitable terrain, the seemingly vacant desert is punctuated by dusty trading towns, fueling stations, isolated mining facilities, and military sites.

Unlike most other parts of the country, the province is ethnically monolithic. Nearly 95 percent of its inhabitants are Arabs and Sunni Muslims. Anbar is the heartland of Iraq's Sunnis, their communal strategic depth. Under the rule of Saddam Hussein and the Ba'ath Party, the Sunnis were the officially favored minority. In the forty plus years after a Ba'athist-led coup assumed control of the country in 1963, the Arab Sunnis in Iraq (just 15-20% of the population) enjoyed primacy over the other two major ethno-religious groups, the Shiites (60-65%) and Kurds (15-17%).

Saddam and his regime leaders funded large industrial and civic projects in Anbar, built lavish estates there for themselves and their families, and rewarded their supporters. Sunni men were given elevated positions in government, the military, and business. By 2003, many Sunnis considered this privileged standing to be their birthright.

Of the many significant errors American leaders made at the beginning of the war, one was the scant attention paid to Anbar. The invasion bypassed western Iraq and the coalition's focus in mid-to-late 2003 was on the hunt for Saddam, rounding up his cronies (the deck of cards), and stabilizing Baghdad. Anbar was far down on the priority list.

In those early months, the U.S. Army's 82nd Airborne

Division assumed responsibility for what was named Area of Operations West (AO West) and moved into Anbar's larger cities. The province's western reaches were patrolled by the Army's 3rd Armored Cavalry Regiment (3rd ACR), but they could accomplish little of permanence. This began a pattern that continued through the early years of the war. Coalition forces were stretched thin while the seeds of insurgency germinated and grew.

MARINE COUNTRY

In March of 2004, the 1st Marine Expeditionary Force (1st MEF) under Lieutenant General James Conway, assumed command of the AO. The battlespace was renamed AO Atlanta and for the next six years Anbar was Marine country. While Army units would also operate there, they would do so under a Marine command structure.

Initially, the Marines were confident they could soon bring stability. During his assumption of command, General Conway boasted, "Although Marines don't normally do nation-building, they will tell you that once given the mission, nobody can do it better."[5] This was a not-so-subtle jab at the outgoing 82nd, which had a reputation for overly harsh treatment of Iraqi civilians and being quick on the trigger. A notorious incident had occurred under their watch in Fallujah when the paratroopers felt threatened by hostile protestors and fired into the crowd, killing 17 civilians.[6]

With their long tradition of operating in small wars around the world, the Marines felt they could more adroitly handle what were called Stability and Support Operations (SASO).

They intended to build rapport with locals, gain their confidence, and use force judiciously. The Corps had widely espoused the concept of the Three Block War emphasizing awareness, poise, and discernment among junior Marines. Corporals and lieutenants were being trained to instantly shift from handing out school supplies to engaging in full-on combat.

But facts on the ground soon pushed the Marines into a bitter, very intense struggle. The enemy in Anbar was hardened and willing to fight and most coalition casualties were occurring there. In Ramadi, Hit, Haditha, Karma, and a host of other hardscrabble towns, Sunni insurgents were establishing strongholds. They ambushed coalition patrols, intimidated locals, and laced streets and highways with IEDs. There was little chance to win hearts and minds when kids accepting soccer balls from U.S. troops could have their hands cut off. Anbar was Iraq's wild west.

UPRISING

The pressure-cooker blew on March 31, 2004, after four American security contractors passing through Fallujah were murdered by gunmen. An angry mob then gathered, set their bodies on fire, and hung them grotesquely from a bridge. The incident triggered a wave of violence that swept the country. Not only Sunni areas were affected, but Baghdad and Iraq's southern cities as well. Well-armed Shiite militias took to the streets and coalition leaders were caught off guard by this two-front conflagration. For several weeks in April, it seemed the country would completely unravel. Fallujah became the epicenter and symbol of the uprising. There the most radical insurgents coalesced, led by cells of foreign-born jihadists, and declared the city to be under their rule.

The 1st Marine Division moved quickly to retake Fallujah, commencing Operation Vigilant Resolve on April 4. This reversed the initial emphasis on civil affairs and building schools. Now the Marines took the gloves off. An embedded journalist observed a telling moment. Just before what became known as the First Battle of Fallujah, a battalion commander told his Marines to shave off the culturally-sensitive mustaches he'd asked them to grow just a few months before. As he bluntly explained, "Gents, let me tell you what this is really about. It's about killing shitheads."[7]

The assault began with two infantry battalions pushing into the city. But just days later, on the 9th, politics intervened and the operation was called off, to great frustration up and down the ranks. The media's images of combat and destruction in the city were too hard for both Iraqi and American politicians to endure. Their indecision only set the stage for even more violence down the road.

Simultaneously, serious fighting broke out in other parts of Anbar. While press coverage was focused on Fallujah and the Shiite slums of Sadr City in Baghdad, the mayhem was much more widespread. Hundreds of insurgents coalesced in Ramadi and from April 6 to April 10, 2004, intense combat raged in and around Anbar's provincial capital, claiming 16 Marines and an estimated 250 insurgents killed.

Out on the western border in Al-Qaim District, insurgents launched a series of bold attacks. On April 14, the commander of 3/7 was caught in an ambush in the city of Husaybah. As a platoon rushed to assist, one of its squad leaders, Corporal Jason Dunham was mortally wounded. He had intentionally jumped on a grenade to save his men and subsequently died of his injuries.[8] A few days later on 17 April, Husaybah erupted again. Gun battles echoed up and down the streets for hours as 3/7's Lima Company battled fanatical fighters. During the heat of that combat, the company commander, Captain Richard Gannon, rushed into an insurgent-held room and was killed in a furious gunfight.[9]

Both men were honored for their selfless bravery, becoming permanent parts of the Marine Corps' legacy. Credited with heroically saving the lives of his fellow Marines, Jason Dunham was posthumously awarded the Congressional Medal of Honor, the first awarded to a U.S. Marine since Vietnam. Richard Gannon was posthumously promoted to Major and awarded the Silver Star. The stark border outpost in Husaybah manned by his Marines was named after him.

All through April of that year, the coalition struggled to control the outbreak. American combat units saw heavy action, racing from one flare-up to another. Through strenuous diplomatic and military efforts, the uprising was tamped down and the coalition held together. Then out of a dank corner came a withering blow—from within.

At the end of a terrible month, Major General James Mattis, then commanding the 1st Marine Division, noticed a cluster of men intently watching CNN and asked them what the coverage was about. A junior Marine summed up tersely, "Some assholes just lost us the war."[10] It was April 28 and the story of detainee abuse at Abu Ghraib had exploded onto TV screens and front pages around the world.

Lurid photos, taken by a small group of U.S. Army guards at the notorious prison, were sickening proof of what had occurred. The American public was disgusted and shocked, as was the military. "This is wrong. This is reprehensible," said Brigadier

General Mark Kimmitt in a TV interview. "Don't judge your army based on the actions of a few."[11]

But those few had done tremendous damage. Their actions, and the inattention of their leaders, had far-reaching negative effects. The Abu Ghraib scandal fueled more violence at an already precarious juncture. Extremist groups enjoyed a recruiting surge and Iraqis of all sects and political leanings were outraged, undoing much of the progress made to that point. Among the American public, support for the war slid into negative territory and kept on sliding.

On the battlefield, Shiite militias in Baghdad and southern Iraqi cities had been contained, but barely. After coalition troops fought and killed hundreds of militiamen allied with the militant cleric Moqtada al-Sadr, a tentative ceasefire was reached with his Mahdi Army. But Sadr's stature as a leader grew, and the Mahdi Army reorganized and rearmed.

A key political milestone was reached at the end of June as the Coalition Provisional Authority (CPA) handed control of the country over to an Iraqi-led interim government. This was a crucial step, formally ending the military occupation and turning sovereignty back to Iraqis in preparation for nationwide elections. Ideally, the day would have been marked with pomp, circumstance, and positive publicity. Instead, to foil the very real threat of suicide bombers, the CPA shut its doors and quietly transferred control two days early on June 28, 2004. As he left Iraq, Paul Bremer, the CPA Administrator appointed by President Bush, had to surreptitiously switch planes due to concerns for his safety. The American Viceroy in Iraq had to sneak out of the country.[12]

Meanwhile, Sunni militants and jihadists still controlled Fallujah and boasted of a victory over the vaunted American military. The insurgency continued to fester there while U.S. units across Anbar operated in an increasingly hostile and deadly environment. Between March and September of 2004, over 120 Marines were killed in the province. In Ramadi, Echo Company of the 2nd Battalion, 4th Marines, suffered 22 killed out of 185 men, which sadly was only a precursor.

In July, insurgents brazenly drove to the Ramadi home of Anbar's governor, set it on fire and kidnapped three of his sons. None of the police guarding the house fired a shot, and later the Police Chief himself was arrested for complicity in the attack. The governor negotiated the release of his sons then fled with his family to Jordan. Similar events occurred elsewhere. Insurgent groups, usually instigated by foreign fighters, were assassinating, or driving out local Iraqi officials.

On the 5th of August, the fight against Shiite insurgent groups flared up again in the southern city of Najaf. Marine and Army units battled for over two weeks among the shrines and ancient tombstones of that city's vast cemetery. Once again, the Mahdi Army lost hundreds of fighters, but a negotiated ceasefire ended the fight and Sadr was allowed to leave. Tellingly, several newly formed Iraqi National Guard (ING) units accompanying U.S. troops collapsed or refused to fight.

On September 7th, the number of American servicemen killed in action in Iraq reached one thousand, a fact the media marked, remarked, and marked again with photos of flag-draped coffins.[13] Senator John Kerry, the Democratic Party's challenger to George Bush in the U.S. presidential race, called the day "a tragic milestone." He had famously been for the war before he was against it, but constantly repeated his campaign soundbite that Iraq was the "wrong war in the wrong place at the wrong time."

SECOND FALLUJAH

As summer turned to fall, coalition leaders prepared for the upcoming Iraqi national elections, moving to clean out insurgent sanctuaries. The largest of these was Fallujah. The "city of one hundred mosques" had become the nexus of the Sunni insurgency. April's aborted assault had only emboldened the extremist cells that ruled its streets. Black banners hung from the mosques and foreign radicals preached holy war over the loudspeakers.

By October, 2004, Iraqi politicians were no longer squeamish about cleaning out Fallujah. Jihadists and extremists of all stripes had flocked to the city, while they proliferated suicide bombings and other terror tactics throughout Iraq. Many Fallujah residents were brutalized, and most had fled. Politics in the U.S. had changed as well. American voters re-elected George W. Bush on November 2nd, giving his administration more maneuver room regarding the war.

Four days after Bush's reelection, Iraq's Prime Minister Allawi approved a major assault to retake the insurgent-held city. When told the operation would be named Phantom Fury, he said, "that doesn't tell the Iraqi people why we're fighting this epic fight," and changed it to Operation "Al-Fajr" (New Dawn). As top U.S. generals briefed Allawi on their plans, Lieutenant General John Sattler, who had recently taken command of 1st MEF, was direct. "Once we get going, we're going to have to go all the way," said Sattler intensely, looking the Prime Minister in the eye. Allawi responded firmly, "I understand. When I tell you 'Go', we will accomplish the mission, we will complete the mission."[14]

Like a whirlpool in a current, the lead-up to the Second

Battle of Fallujah sucked resources, attention, and energy into its churn. Units were pulled from other areas and plugged into the buildup of forces. Some 13,000 American, British, and Iraqi troops surrounded the city in early November. About 6,500 Marines and 1,500 Army soldiers would carry out the actual assault. Inside were an estimated 4,000 hard-core insurgents from multiple groups and countries, many ready to fight to the death.[15] This would be the biggest fight since the invasion, dominating news coverage and military planning both in and out of Iraq.

The assault began the night of November 7, 2004, and by morning the battle was in full fury, grinding forward street by street, house to house, room by room. Some Marine units actually fixed bayonets. Fallujah quickly entered Marine Corps lore as the most intense urban fight since the 1968 siege of Hue in Vietnam. The worst of it lasted a week, but the operation didn't officially end until 23 December.

Clearing the enemy stronghold came at a high cost. While nearly 2,000 insurgents were killed, 70 Americans paid the ultimate price, including 57 Marines. Over 600 U.S. personnel were wounded. When the shooting stopped, the city lay in ruins with the majority of its residents displaced for months afterwards.

Second Fallujah fundamentally changed the nature of the war. It was now painfully clear that the end was not around the corner. It had been a year and a half since President Bush had proclaimed "mission accomplished" in Iraq. Yet U.S. troops were still fully engaged in high-intensity operations, fighting for control of major cities, while patience for the war was waning at home.

Meanwhile, the push to have coalition troops stand down as Iraqi forces stood up was still not succeeding. Despite all the effort and money expended, when crunch time came in Fallujah, Ramadi, and Najaf, freshly formed Iraqi units were not ready. Instead, it had been American boots kicking in the doors and those boots still had lots of work to do.

The battle also highlighted that the most dangerous threat was centered in Iraq's Sunni heartland, made up of home-grown insurgent groups combined with jihadist foreign fighters. Many had scattered before the assault, and the focus of coalition combat operations would follow them west into Anbar.

Finally, the violent, no-quarters aspect of the fighting changed base-line attitudes among Marine units in Iraq. In the opening phases of the war, many had adopted General Mattis' motto, "No better friend, no worse enemy." But after Fallujah, there was much less emphasis on the "no better friend" part. Having the grunts shave off culturally-sensitive mustaches and actually fix bayonets set a tone that percolated across the force. In the months to come, the Marines in Anbar were ready and eager to be the insurgents' worst enemy.

Elsewhere, the fighting went on and the grim statistics continued to climb. While attention was focused on Fallujah, insurgents made a concerted push in Mosul and seized large portions of Iraq's second-largest city. The police and Iraqi security forces there evaporated. Just outside the city, on December 21, 2004, an insurgent slipped onto Forward Operating Base Marez wearing an ING uniform and entered the dining facility. Standing in the chow line among Christmas decorations and American troops, he detonated a suicide vest studded with ball bearings, killing 21 others and wounding 75. It was the single deadliest attack against U.S. troops since the invasion.[16]

TWISTS AND TURNS

Despite the carnage, there were some encouraging signs. Iraq's first democratic elections in fifty years were held on January 30, 2005, to select a new constitutional assembly. In much of the country, election turnout exceeded projections and long lines formed at the polling places, despite threats from terrorists. For a euphoric moment, the world stood in awe as Iraqis emerged from the voting centers to proudly show their purple-stained fingers. At the political level, there was cautious optimism in those first months after the election. There was a pathway forward to national parliamentary elections, and more Iraqi politicians were stepping into leadership roles.

But out in Anbar, things were different. Only two percent of the province's eligible voters had cast ballots, highlighting the Sunni-Shia split.[17] The power brokers in Anbar, favored by Saddam's regime for decades, saw newly-empowered Shiites as illegitimate pretenders and a future threat. Moreover, in a perverse twist, the climactic battle in Fallujah had only served to widen the Sunni insurgency and make it more virulent. For the most hard-core insurgents, it had been a martyr's victory. They could not match the world's most powerful military, but they could make the infidels pay dearly. Meanwhile, their key leaders and hundreds of others had escaped and scattered into the Sunni heartland.[18]

Another ominous development had also unfolded in late 2004 and was expanding into monstrous form. In October, the Jordanian-born terrorist known as Abu Musab al-Zarqawi formally declared allegiance to Osama Bin Laden, thus uniting the world's two most violent jihadist networks on the battlefields of Iraq. In the wake of the coalition's apparent victory in Fallujah and amid the post-election glow of early 2005, the insurgency was metastasizing in dangerous and deadly ways.

2. DEPLOYMENT

The 3rd Battalion of the 2nd Marine Regiment began its legacy in the Pacific during World War II. The battalion was in the first wave at Tarawa on 24 November 1943, landing directly into the teeth of Japanese defenses. The atoll's most important island was named Betio (pronounced like "ratio") and the Marines paid dearly for every yard. That forlorn cluster of coral earned its title "Bloody Tarawa" and with sheer tenacity and ferocity the men of 3/2 earned the battalion's nickname; "Betio Bastards". Today, current and past members of the battalion still embrace the name as a badge of honor.

After the shock of 9/11, the entire U.S. military shifted abruptly into a wartime footing. Marine infantry battalions began an extended cycle of training up, deploying, recovering, then preparing for the next deployment or "pump" in the Global War on Terror. In the spring of 2003, 3/2 was part of the invasion of Iraq, known as Operation Iraqi Freedom, Phase I (OIF I).

Advancing north towards Baghdad in what Marines call "the march up", 3/2 was part of the force that ran into unexpected resistance in the southern city of Nasiriyah. This was the first major battle of the war, fought on 23-27 March. As Marines pushed to secure bridges over the Euphrates, they were doggedly opposed by Iraqi soldiers and irregular fighters in civilian clothes. Some of these *fedayeen* fighters ambushed an Army supply convoy, notably capturing a young American soldier, Private Jessica Lynch. While 3/2 played a supporting role in Nasiriyah, many of its men had their first taste of combat there. Two years later, veterans of "The Naz" would leaven the battalion with their experience.

During 2004, elements of 3/2 deployed on anti-terrorism duty to Kabul, Afghanistan, Guantanamo Bay in Cuba, and Djibouti in East Africa. By the time they returned stateside, the battalion had again been given orders to Iraq as part of Operation Iraqi Freedom III. Workup training started in the fall at Camp Lejeune, building up the Marines' tactical skills at local ranges.

In late November 2004, the entire battalion flew out to California and the Marine Corps Training Center at Twentynine Palms, California, with its expansive live-fire ranges. During an intense combined arms exercise, 3/2's commander, Lieutenant Colonel Tim Mundy, emphasized small-unit tactics. "The focus [was on] a squad leader and platoon commander's fight," he recalled. "I wanted them proficient with their Marines."[1]

Then came ten days at March Air Reserve Base, just outside Riverside, California. An old housing area there had been converted into a simulated Iraqi village, complete with Arabic-speaking role-players, where units would experience scenarios representative of a counter-insurgency environment. The training was useful but didn't accurately reflect conditions they would soon encounter. "It was more oriented to units going to cities that had already been subdued," remembered Mundy. "But I was reading the daily situation reports from the battalion I was replacing, 1/7, and their fight out west was still highly kinetic."[2]

Following the California training came Christmas leave. Both before and after the break, the battalion was busy packing up all the gear needed and learning about current conditions in the area they'd soon be responsible for. "There were key leader meetings, where we got information on what was happening over there," recalls Brian Hogancamp, the gunnery sergeant for India Company. "It was good info, but it was hard to really take it in with all the other stuff we were doing to get ready."[3]

ADVANCE ECHELON

Gunny Hogancamp was part of the battalion's advance team that would enter Iraq before the battalion main body to link up with 1st Battalion, 7th Marines (1/7), the unit they would replace. This was the first step in the established Relief in Place/Transfer of Authority (RIP/TOA) process. About thirty officers and NCOs were on the advance team, departing Camp Lejeune in mid-February, 2005.

The battalion's turnover with 1/7 was one part of a massive turnover of Marine forces in western Iraq during early 2005. The 1st Marine Expeditionary Force (1st MEF) was being replaced by the 2nd MEF, along with the corresponding air wing and logistics command. Many other Marine units were flowing into Anbar that spring, including three regimental combat teams (RCTs) and multiple subordinate battalions and squadrons.[4]

The advance team arrived in Iraq on or about 30 January. After initial orientation briefings at Al-Asad airbase, the team helicoptered out to Camp Al-Qaim, where they joined up with their counterparts in 1/7. For the next several weeks, they would absorb the knowledge 1/7 had gained through many firefights, mortar attacks, and IED strikes.

First Lieutenant Mike Mike Hodd, the executive officer (XO) of India Company, accompanied Gunny Hogancamp and Gunnery Sergeant John Harmon of Weapons Company on the next leg of their journey out to the beleaguered forward base known as Camp Gannon. Hogancamp remembers his first meeting with the battle-hardened Marines of 1/7's Baker Company.* "They were like the no-frills, combat-hardened Marines from WWI and WWII," he describes. "Baker Company was part of a long Marine legacy, and I knew I needed to learn as much as I could from them."[5]

CLOSE CALL

On 18 February, Hodd, Hogancamp, and Harmon joined a mounted patrol to begin familiarizing themselves with the area. As they trundled along the unpaved border road, Syrian territory just meters away, their Assault Amphibious Vehicles (AAVs) churned up a billowing cloud that marked their passage and direction of travel. After a twenty-minute stop and a foot recon, they mounted up again for the return trip. Lieutenant Hodd noted that the drivers were extremely careful to follow exactly in the same tracks, to minimize the danger of running over a hidden mine or improvised explosive device (IED).

* Because of its Korean War legacy, 1/7 is the only Marine battalion that designates its Company B as "Baker Company" instead of "Bravo."

Tracs out of water

The Marine Corps began using amphibious, tracked vehicles for beach assaults during WWII. These first amphibious tractors were called "amtracs" and that name has stuck, often shortened to just "trac". Modern variants are called Assault Amphibious Vehicles (AAVs), although they are used in many roles and environments, not just for amphibious landings.

In Iraq and Afghanistan, operating far from any beaches, AAVs were essentially used as oversized infantry fighting vehicles. Carrying up to 25 combat-loaded troops or five tons of supplies, and mounting heavy weapons, AAVs were capable and flexible. But their slab-like sides and relatively thin armor could be penetrated by direct fire weapons. In particular, their large, flat bottoms made them notoriously vulnerable to IEDs.

In the number 2 vehicle, Hodd and the two gunnery sergeants were standing on the interior benches of the AAV, head and shoulders facing outboard to scan for threats. The next thing the lieutenant knew, he was picking himself up, ears ringing. The AAV had struck a mine, which blew a jagged hole in the metal floor. "The mine blast came up about 13 inches from my right foot. Just a little closer, and I'd have been hit," says Hodd. "I don't remember the actual blast. One second I'm standing, the next I'm lying on the bottom of the trac, not knowing how I got there."[6] The effects inside the vehicle were dramatic and violent, as Hogancamp later described:

It exploded right under where we were standing... The entire AAV was filled with black smoke, and I had no orientation on how to exit the vehicle. The handguards on my weapon were blown off and my magazine was blown apart.

—Brian Hogancamp[7]

All three of the advance team members were treated for concussive injuries, scrapes, and bruises, but fortunately no one was killed or seriously hurt. It was a close call, the first of many. "That event made us realize we were in a no-shit combat environment," says Hodd. "Even us Nasiriyah vets realized it would be a different kind of fight this time."[8]

It was also sobering to realize that whoever had placed the mine had intentionally targeted the patrol. On the trip out, the drivers had stayed in the established tracks. They'd been equally careful on the way back. Almost certainly, insurgents had watched the AAVs pass, then quickly placed the mine exactly where they would roll over it on the return trip.

INTO THE SANDBOX

Deployment of the main body was a multi-phase process to move over 1,000 Marines and sailors from Jacksonville, North Carolina into Iraq. In the chilly pre-dawn hours of Friday, 18 February 2005, 3/2 assembled under the glare of lights at the sports fields on Camp Lejeune.[9] In the days leading up to their departure, they'd had some touching moments with their families. John Schneekloth, a squad leader in Kilo Company, remembers a serious talk with his pregnant wife.

There was this surreal moment when we started discussing the possibility of me not coming back. We decided I should record a video for my unborn son, just in case. So, I went into a back room and spent about 45 minutes alone talking to a video camera, giving him sort of a summary of my life's worth of knowledge.

—John Schneekloth[10]

After it was light, a long line of buses arrived to shuttle the men to Marine Corps Air Station Cherry Point. Wives, girlfriends, and family members gathered there too. The men shared one more hug, one more kiss with loved ones, then loaded their duffels and boarded. It was a scene that has played out for millennia, as families sent their warriors into the unknown.

For many, emotions ran high. "I remember boarding the bus and sitting there as my son was outside playing on the grass," recalls Chris Ieva, Kilo Company's commander. "That tore me up. I was convinced I would be KIA on that tour. I just had this feeling. My Dad and I had even talked about it, and he had promised to help raise my kids if I didn't come back."[11] Some family members had traveled long distances to see their Marine off. Leesa Philippon had flown down to Lejeune from the family's home in Connecticut to spend time with her son, Larry:

They moved us out to the sports field, and it was really cold. Everyone's breath was hanging in the air. As he lined up with the others to board the buses, it was like watching my little boy get on that school bus not so long ago. But now he was a man, and this wasn't school. They were going to war. I prayed to be calm, and a tremendous peace came over me. I looked into my son's eyes and told him I loved him and that I would pray him safely home. I remember that last hug vividly. I stood by that bus and Larry waved me a goodbye kiss as they drove away.

—Leesa Philippon[12]

Lieutenant Colonel Mundy was in a pensive mood, quietly experiencing a range of emotions as his battalion made ready to depart. "We knew we were heading into serious business," he remembers. "I was watching Marines saying goodbye to their families and couldn't help but think, 'How many will we bring back?' That weighed heavy, but you just have to focus on the task at hand. Then, as I checked my notebook for something, I found a photo of me walking with my six-year-old son that my wife had placed in there without telling me. That choked me up."[13]

As the buses pulled out, the families could hear the exuberant sounds of young Marines singing "Bye Bye, Miss American Pie."[14] The notes lingered for a moment in the chill North Carolina air.

At Cherry Point, the men boarded several civilian airliners chartered for the transatlantic flight. Hours later, they arrived in Germany, where they waited again. Soon they were back in the air heading to the sandbox. They landed at a base in Kuwait, then boarded military transport aircraft for a long, loud, and uncomfortable flight, sitting on nylon-web jump seats, foam plugs jammed in their ears to muffle the incessant droning of the engines. Finally, they arrived at Al-Asad airbase in Iraq, stepping down the ramps almost 24 hours after assembling at Camp Lejeune.

Just a few miles from the verdant Euphrates River, Al-Asad was one of the American-run mega-bases in Iraq and home to the forward headquarters for 2nd MEF and several of its major components, including the air wing and logistics group.*

* The MEF's other major component, 2nd Marine Division, was headquartered on Camp Blue Diamond near Ramadi.

Almost all Marines coming into or out of Iraq spent time at Al-Asad, which was known for the amenities it offered, including Burger King, Pizza Hut, a swimming pool, and movie theater. Grunts derisively called it "Camp Cupcake."

The battalion main body spent several days in Al-Asad, hooking into the command structure and logistics chain, zeroing weapons at the range, and training in small unit tactics. There was time to enjoy the amenities, but the odd juxtaposition of stateside luxuries inside a war zone could be distracting. Lance Corporal Schneekloth told his squad, "Keep focused. Don't let any of this stuff faze you, cause where we're going, we won't have any of this."[15]

Finally, on 27 February 2005, around 800 personnel from 3/2 boarded several waves of massive CH-53 helicopters for the trip to Camp Al-Qaim. The CH-53s caused a cyclone of dust each time they touched down on the landing zone. The Marines struggled off the birds, pulled off their gear, then hoofed the last hundred meters into their new home for the next seven months.

See **bastardsandbrothers.com** for notes, photos, maps, etc.

3. ECONOMY OF FORCE

Soon after 3/2 arrived, the battalion became part of Regimental Combat Team 2 (RCT-2), headquartered at Al-Asad. Two other battalions fell under the RCT's modular structure; 2nd Light Armored Reconnaissance Battalion (2nd LAR) and a Marine Reserve unit, 3rd Battalion, 25th Marines (3/25). Rounding out the force were attachments of engineers, Assault Amphibious Vehicles (AAVs), Alpha Company from the 1st Tank Battalion and the 1st Force Reconnaissance Company. The commander of RCT-2 was Colonel Stephen W. Davis, a straight-talking, streetwise New Yorker from the Bronx. He had cut his teeth as a Recon Marine and had pulled assignments in the special operations world.

Davis and RCT-2 had responsibility for the massive swathe of territory known as Area of Operations Denver (AO Denver). The area stretched from the borders with Jordan and Syria to north of the Euphrates, then east to the outskirts of Ramadi, encompassing about 30,000 square miles; roughly the size of South Carolina. Unlike the battalions, Colonel Davis and his RCT staff would stay in Iraq for a full year to provide command continuity.

For Davis, the biggest challenge was covering such a huge

area with just 3,200 personnel overall. He characterized his situation as commanding "a little RCT, with a division-sized mission, in a MEF-sized (Corps-sized) battlespace."[1] Moreover, he would start out with just four available rifle companies. Because of decisions up the food-chain, both 3/2 and 3/25 would each give up a company to provide security for Al-Asad. Both battalions would be operating at reduced strength during early 2005. Davis' response was to stress adaptability and flexibility. As he told a Marine historian: "My mission [is] an economy-of-force mission…Interrupt and disrupt…Doing much more with much less and killing the enemy every chance we get. We have got [to] be able to turn and move, turn and move."[2]

POWER SWEEP

Davis and his operations staff, led by his ops officer or S3, Lieutenant Colonel Chris Starling, defined three distinct problem-sets in AO Denver and tasked a battalion to each one. Most of 3/25 was based at the massive hydroelectric dam outside Haditha with one company in the town of Hit. Together they would cover the Hit-Haditha corridor, a key avenue of approach into Ramadi. The 2nd LAR, with its speedy Light Armored Vehicles (LAVs), set up in Rutbah to patrol the vast desert along the Jordanian and Syrian borders. And 3/2 went to Al-Qaim to cover the strategic border crossing area and growing insurgent stronghold there. Each fight would be separate but interconnected. Davis and Starling were well aware that the enemy would flow into the gaps. To conduct these interwoven, overlapping fights, they developed a campaign plan dubbed Power Sweep.[3]

The plan's top priority was the Hit-Haditha corridor. "That's my focus of effort," stated Davis. "Key infrastructure is there and everything there impacts on Ramadi, which is the division's center of gravity…My job is to keep insurgents away from that center of gravity."[4] The effort to secure the border and the fight for Al-Qaim were important but were seen as supporting the RCT's main effort.

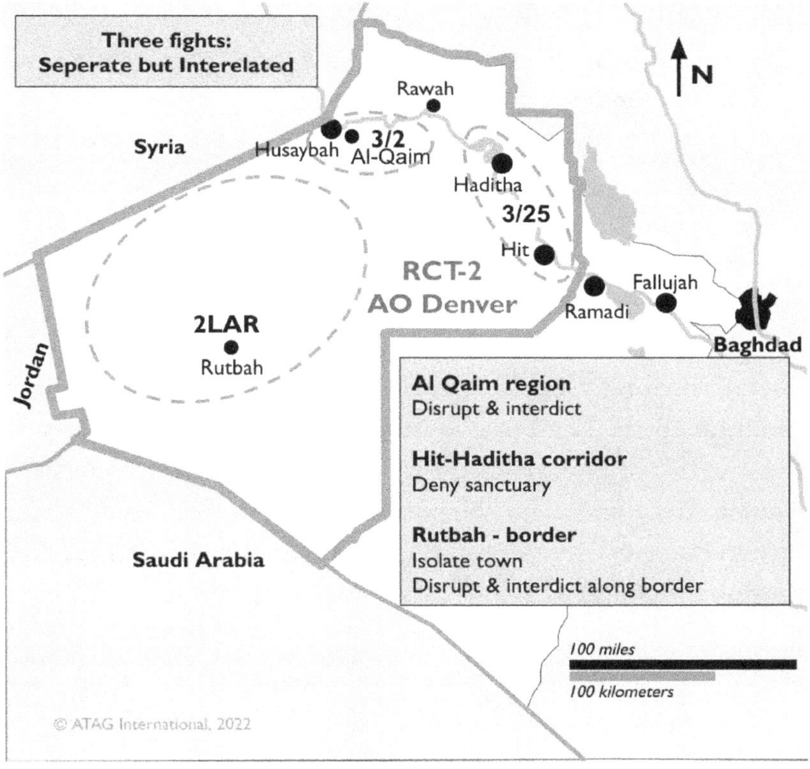

The Colonel knew his RCT would be painfully short on combat power. His task would be to keep the enemy off-balance through a series of operations up and down the river valley, rapidly concentrating when an insurgent stronghold was located then shifting focus to another area:

> *I was trying to create the illusion of a greater force structure by showing up everywhere but nowhere… not setting a pattern… We got criticized a great deal in the press about doing "whack-a-mole."… When people say, "You didn't understand," well, we did understand… We understood that we couldn't make any real progress until we could establish a combined, permanent, persistent presence with Iraqis in the lead.*
>
> —**Stephen Davis**[5]

TEAM BALL

Another characteristic of RCT-2 was its linkage with special operations forces (SOF). The SOF units, also known as "other coalition forces," had a separate chain of command. Early in the war, this often produced friction between conventional Marine or Army units and the special operators that would insert into their areas with minimal coordination. Davis and his RCT, however, established a good relationship with SOF:

> *We came up with a concept we called "team ball" [which was]: 1. Focus on the mission. 2. Leave all egos at the door. 3. Don't worry about who is getting credit. We got along famously from that point. We started fusing these different sources… All of a sudden you get a whole different picture… They were very open in sharing with us, which was helpful.*
>
> —**Stephen Davis**[6]

This approach would pay many dividends throughout the year as the Power Sweep plan progressed. Conventional and special ops forces would need to work together effectively in the key battleground of far western Anbar.

BASTARDS TAKE OVER

The Betio Bastards were on the ground in Al-Qaim even before Colonel Davis took command of AO Denver on 17 March. The advance team had arrived in late January to begin the Relief in Place (RIP) process, which continued into February as the battalion's main body arrived. The RIP included handover of vehicles, larger weapons, equipment and supplies. Newly arriving Marine units didn't bring heavy equipment with them but used vehicles and equipment already there. Thousands of individual items had to be inventoried and transferred, as well as files, digital records, databases, and standard operating procedures (SOP). Area familiarization briefings were held and right-seat/left-seat rides conducted, with 3/2 Marines going on missions alongside their 1/7 counterparts.

The formal Transfer of Authority (TOA) occurred on 9 March 2005 when 1/7's commander, Lieutenant Colonel Chris "Woody" Woodbridge, passed the flag to Lieutenant Colonel Mundy. Upon accepting that flag, Mundy became responsible for one of the most violent areas in Iraq. The battalion area of operations measured about 50 miles east-to-west and 20 miles north-to-south, encompassing cities and towns along the Euphrates, a chunk of desert to the south and a smaller strip of terrain north of the river. Mundy knew it would be a big job, demanding life-and-death decisions and requiring all his energies and experience.

Born into a prominent Marine Corps family, Timothy S. Mundy was the son of Carl E. Mundy, Jr., a Vietnam combat veteran who rose to four-star rank and became Commandant of the Marine Corps. He also looked up to his older brother, who commanded an infantry battalion during the invasion of Iraq and became a general. But it was the Marine Corps itself, not his family, that had prepared Tim Mundy to command a battalion. Commissioned in 1987, he was first a rifle platoon commander then advanced to be company XO during the 1991 Gulf War. As a Captain, he commanded a weapons company which placed him on a path to greater responsibility. In 2003 he pinned on Lieutenant Colonel oak leaves and took command of 3/2 in the summer of 2004.

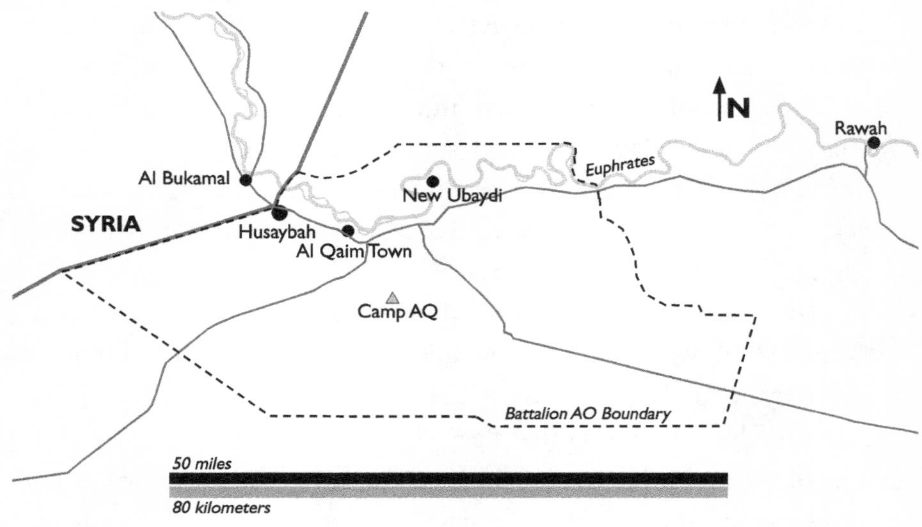

As he took over the AO, Mundy knew he and his men

would soon be in a real scrap. A few months before, he'd been to Al-Qaim on a site survey to see what was happening for himself. Everything he saw confirmed that "1/7 was really in a dogfight."[7] Now his battalion was entering that same arena.

UNITS AND ATTACHMENTS

The force Mundy would command was technically a battalion-minus, since one of its companies was stripped away at the outset. Besides the units organic to 3/2, it included several other attached Marine elements, Navy personnel, and some Army soldiers. In planning documents and official communications it was often referred to as Task Force Betio. The core of its available combat power lay in two rifle companies, Company I or "India" and Company K or "Kilo", and the Weapons Company. A fourth unit, Headquarters and Service (H&S) Company was responsible for maintenance, medical, messing, facilities, and administrative support. However, two smaller combat elements also fell under H&S Company; the scout-sniper platoon and the security platoon.

Task Force Betio also included several attached units and sections. A platoon of four M1A2 Abrams tanks added their considerable firepower. Mobility and more fire support was added with a platoon of AAVs and their crews. A combat engineer platoon and an explosive ordnance disposal (EOD) section brought critical capabilities. Other specialized sections for information operations (IO), human intelligence (HUMINT) collection and civil affairs were integrated as well. The AAV crews, the combat engineers, and the civil affairs team were reservists. Navy and Army units were also assigned to support

3/2, making it a joint force. Navy doctors and corpsmen, and Army medics and helicopters, provided medical support while an Army Psychological Operations (PSYOPS) team was also attached.

Which Al-Qaim?

Many accounts about Al-Qaim are muddled by a fundamental misunderstanding. They frequently confuse the district of Al-Qaim (sometimes called a region) with the town that shares the same name. The town of Al-Qaim, with only about 15,000 residents, is not the district's economic or demographic hub. That honor goes to the city of Husaybah, population 100,000, seven miles to the west. The confusion is only worsened since Husaybah is often called Al-Qaim, even by Iraqis. Yet another problem emerges in U.S. military reports and histories. The main coalition base in the district, several miles south of the town of Al-Qaim, was named Camp Al-Qaim. Because of this, articles and even official histories are often vague about what happened where. In this book, "Al-Qaim" refers to the administrative district. The town itself is referred to as "the town of Al-Qaim" or Al-Qaim town". The Marine base is called "Camp Al-Qaim" or "Camp AQ".

Fortunately, Mundy could rely on an excellent staff to control and direct the force. Major John Reed was the XO, the commander's right hand. Sergeant Major Arthur Mennig, a stocky, barrel-chested bundle of compressed energy, was the senior enlisted advisor and guardian of morale and discipline.

Major John Day was 3/2's operations officer. Tall and wiry with a Texas drawl, he had been the commander of Weapons Company and had great tactical expertise and instincts. Chief Warrant Officer 3 (CW3) Nick Vitale was another key leader as the battalion's Marine Gunner, or weapons employment expert.

Each of 3/2's company commanders were promising officers with proven leadership abilities. These young captains would bear a huge responsibility and would have room to exercise it. Lieutenant Colonel Mundy's leadership style was to trust his subordinates, allowing them autonomy and letting them use their judgment. "I tried to live what the Marine Corps taught in our foundational doctrine," he says. "I always preferred to let them do their job, let them develop the situation."[8]

INTERDICT AND DISRUPT

Echoing RCT-2's mission description, 3/2's main job in Al-Qaim was to interdict and disrupt insurgent activities. That left wide latitude for Mundy and his leadership team to figure out how to deploy their forces and how best to accomplish the mission. Well before they left the States, it was obvious that a robust presence in Husaybah would be critical. Accordingly, India Company would occupy Camp Gannon, securing the Port of Entry and the immediate area. Plussed up with several combat attachments, India and its supporting elements would anchor the line.

The rest of Task Force Betio would operate out of Camp Al-Qaim, located south of the river at an old Iraqi railroad depot and maintenance facility. Known as Camp AQ or just "the train station", it was a sizable base with multiple large buildings used for barracks, unit and staff offices, vehicle bays, medical facilities, supply storage, etc. While it didn't have the same amenities as Al-Asad, it boasted hot meals, makeshift showers, air-conditioned spaces, and relatively steady electrical power. It was also relatively secure from attack, miles removed from any populated area and with commanding views of the surrounding desert. From Camp AQ, Kilo Company and parts of Weapons Company could conduct far-ranging missions. In essence, Kilo and Weapons would be the battalion's maneuver forces, launching out to strike at the enemy or react to their activities.

Lima Company

As soon as they arrived in Iraq, most of 3/2's Lima Company, commanded by Captain Sean Hankard, took on security duties at Al-Asad Airbase. Initially, they manned posts and towers around the huge base and conducted patrols in the adjacent security zone. While this was an important function, it frustrated most of Lima's Marines who were eager to see action. The exception was 3rd Platoon which was slated as RCT-2's mobile reserve and saw action all across AO Denver, operating with the callsign "Beowulf".

Note: Both 3/2 and 3/25 had a Lima Company, which may cause confusion in subsequent chapters. To clarify, whenever 3/25's Lima Company is mentioned its parent battalion will be specifically referenced, such as "Lima 3/25".

FIRST MISSIONS

Whenever a newly deployed unit checked into an area, the insurgents would test them, probing to see how they would react, what their weaknesses might be. This was a longstanding pattern. The hidden enemy always seemed to know when the outgoing unit left and the new one began operating on its own. The ever-watching insurgents would strike if they perceived vulnerabilities. One way to deter them was to demonstrate competence and aggressiveness early on.

In early March 2005, 3/2 launched a flurry of missions to scout the terrain, identify danger areas, and show the locals and any hostile eyes that the battalion was a professional force. "[We] needed to get out and understand the area and get used to operating there," described Mundy. "[We] started doing some local patrolling, moving out around the area."[9] They conducted airborne surveys by helicopter and gathered intelligence information into target packages to support possible raids. A few neighborhood searches were done, so-called cordon-and-knock, or cordon-and-search missions. The cordon-and-knock technique was less intrusive, knocking on doors before searching houses and asking people for tips. The cordon-and-search was more aggressive, used when definite insurgent activity was suspected. In that case, doors were kicked, not knocked.

One of the most active elements during those early weeks was the small section of six Marines attached to 3/2 from the 4th Civil Affairs Group. Major Vincent Sumang and five enlisted men comprised the Civil Affairs section, often called the CAG team. Their main mission was to identify infrastructure and construction needs in the area, then organize civil engineering projects to address them. Elsewhere in Iraq, this usually meant repairing or building schools, medical clinics, water treatment plants, bridges, or roads. Local contractors would be hired to do the work. In less-volatile areas, CAG teams were very engaged in restoring Iraq's long-broken civilian and commercial infrastructure. There were parts of the country where coalition units saw such work as their main mission.

But in Al-Qaim in 2005, the environment did not allow much civil affairs work. It was to their credit, then, that the CAG team was so active. With their engineering and construction backgrounds, Sumang and his team were among the first to start surveying the new battlespace. "The S3 kind of joked with me during the RIP that I had been out of the wire more than some of the infantry guys," recalled Major Sumang.[10] In March and April, the CAG team left the wire nearly every day to check on a few pre-existing projects, assess possible opportunities, and engage with local businessmen and leaders.

MEETING THE MAYOR

Just outside the perimeter of Camp Al-Qaim loomed the towers and smokestacks of the super phosphate plant, the only functional industrial site in the district. Being so close to the Marine base, it was a relatively secure site and patrols would often check on activities there. On 14 March, Lieutenant Colonel Mundy, the CAG team, and members of the battalion staff went there to meet with the mayor.

Raja Nawaf Farhan al-Mahalawi was called the "mayor" of Al-Qaim, but more accurately he was Al-Qaim's district administrator. He had an office in Husaybah, but spent little time there, since he had many enemies in the city. As his surname indicates, he was a prominent member in one of the main Sunni tribes in the area, the Albu Mahal.[11] He also had a seat on the Anbar Provincial Council, so was well-connected with Sunni tribal networks and Anbari political circles. Several other local leaders were accompanying him that day.

Standard pleasantries were exchanged, tea was served, and a contract interpreter or "terp" translated the dialogue. "The overall goal...was to get a list of requests," stated Captain Jeffrey Shows, "and go over [the] projects we are going to do for them."[12] Shows was the battalion's lawyer, or staff judge advocate (JAG). Mayor Farhan said he had met with leaders in the local towns and presented a compiled list of requests. One of his main goals was to improve conditions in Husaybah, and the discussion turned to potential projects such as a new hospital, school construction, and putting in a new power line. Farhan also expressed concern that many local citizens did not understand the Marines' procedures at vehicle checkpoints. Mundy clarified those procedures, and the meeting wrapped up on a positive note.

For 3/2, this was a first step towards establishing good relations with civil authorities and would hopefully pave the way for forward progress. But there were large hurdles to overcome. "Security is a requirement for anything," Mundy later expressed..."[We] were never really sure if [civil affairs] was going to have a lasting impact on the people, because you might not be there the next week and the bad guys would be...The fact that you built them a road only lasted as long as you were around to help them drive on it."[13]

About two months later, and after many efforts to establish meaningful projects, Major Sumang also reflected some frustration. It was tough for the CAG team to get traction in

Al-Qaim, mainly because people were too afraid to cooperate with the Americans. "We haven't been able to find any contractors who will work with us," he told a USMC field historian. "We've talked to the mayor ... the teachers, we talked to the local sheikh, and they all basically say 'you are not going to find anybody ... they don't want to risk the threat that would come with it.'"[14]

As for working out the procedures at vehicle checkpoints, this was an important detail. All sides knew well that some of the most dangerous places for Iraqis and for coalition troops were the checkpoints set up to search civilian cars and trucks. Reckless driving (almost the rule on Iraq's roads), miscommunication, or a perceived threat by anxious troops all too often ended in disaster. Just a week later, in fact, tragedy would strike at one of these mobile checkpoints.

See **bastardsandbrothers.com** for notes, photos, maps, etc.

4. IMPROVISED DEATH

No other weapon is more emblematic of the Iraq War than the improvised explosive device, or IED, used by the insurgents. Most were wickedly simple, no more than an artillery shell wired to blow and buried in a shallow hole or just stuck inside a trash bag. But used in large numbers they had an undeniable strategic effect and changed the face of modern warfare. Certainly, the IED threat had a pervasive impact on 3/2. Bombs could be hidden under every street corner and road in Al-Qaim, while any approaching civilian vehicle might carry a lethal payload.

Before the war, the problem of roadside bombs was a peripheral issue for the U.S military. In fact, there were inadequate terms to categorize the first American killed by a roadside bomb in Iraq. On 26 May 2003, Private First Class Jeremiah Smith, U.S. Army, died when an IED detonated under his unarmored Humvee. Initially, his death was officially attributed to "unexploded ordnance", an oxymoron if ever there was one.[1] But soon IEDs were proliferating at staggering speed. During that first summer, monthly deaths from IEDs stayed in the single digits. In October, they entered double-digit territory with 15 troops killed. The number jumped to 35 in November and by the end of 2003, 96 coalition troops had been killed in Iraq by IEDs with ten times that number wounded.[2]

The next year, IEDs caused the majority of casualties. At least 8,400 IED incidents were recorded in 2004, killing more than 300 troops and wounding over 3,300. The toll in 2005 would be even worse.[3] Insurgents had discovered a cheap, relatively easy way to strike back against the highly mechanized U.S. military, eroding or in some cases completely neutralizing one of the coalition's main operational advantages: mobility.

The toll on troops' morale was high as well. Whenever they drove outside the wire, they knew their lives and limbs were at risk. For those performing certain missions, it was accepted they would get "blown up" at some point. The horrific injuries IEDs often inflicted added to their mental strain.

In most IED strikes the enemy was never seen, adding another insidious element. Just as Marines on Guadalcanal dreaded the sniper's shot from the shadows, and grunts in Vietnam nervously watched for booby-traps, Marines in Iraq warily eyed every trash pile, every sign of disturbed earth, for hidden bombs. They would far prefer getting caught in a small-arms ambush, where they could at least return fire, over getting hit with a mine or IED set by a hidden attacker.

TACTICS

There were two basic types of static IEDs. The first was detonated when a vehicle or individual passed over the device, triggered by an improvised pressure plate or a conventional landmine. These were called "victim-operated." The other type was known as "command-detonated", set off from a distance by a triggerman via a long wire or some kind of radio-frequency device such as a mobile phone.[4]

The ingenuity of enemy bomb makers and IED emplacers was boundless. There seemed to be no end to their creative energy, at least when it came to blowing things up. Most IEDs were concealed simply by digging a hole, dropping in the main charge, and covering it back up. But the lengths taken to disguise them could be impressive. Anything could be a bomb. IEDs were hidden in old tires, junked microwaves, fake styrofoam rocks, and piles of manure. Heavy artillery shells were bolted behind highway guardrails or strapped vertically to telephone poles. Sections of concrete curbing were poured around a bomb, then placed into an actual roadside curb. Often IEDs were hidden in the rotting carcasses of dead animals. Perhaps the most macabre case was a live donkey found wandering the streets of Ramadi with an IED inserted into its rectum.

Acquiring explosives was the least of the bombmakers' concerns. Iraq was essentially a huge ammunition dump, as coalition troops had discovered to their dismay. Large caches of artillery rounds, rockets, and mines were constantly found. Worse still, out in the desert were huge Iraqi Army ammunition supply points (ASPs) with acres of munitions in unsecured bunkers or just scattered in the sand. The vast scale of the problem was sobering:

> *On our first operation in 2005, we exploited a cache, something like 100 arty rounds. I felt jubilant. Then we found more and more. The RCT found 1,000 rounds just by walking along the river. Two weeks later, they found the same amount! Another time we passed ASP Wolf out in the desert. There were arty rounds everywhere. We stopped to blow some but were overwhelmed. There were too many.*
>
> **—Chris Ieva**[5]

To build and deploy all these weapons, the enemy used a loosely organized web of personnel. At the top were the bomb-makers, who often had impressive technical skills. Then came IED cell leaders, who orchestrated deployment of the bombs. At the bottom of the ladder were emplacers who often were paid just to dump an IED into a hole. Enabling the whole network were financiers who doled out the money.

While it could take just minutes, even seconds, for insurgents to set up a simple IED or a mine, other times it was a multi-day operation. Someone would unobtrusively dig a hole. Later, maybe days later, an emplacer might drop in an artillery shell, pre-primed and wired. Still later, someone else would connect a command-wire to the bomb. Finally, a triggerman would set up at a distance, connect a battery to the wire, then wait for a target. Typically, IEDs were concealed in natural chokepoints where military vehicles would pass. Sharp bends, a culvert under the road, the backside of a hill, or the bottom of a wadi were favorite spots.

But the most fearsome type of IED was mobile, not static. The suicide vehicle-borne IED (SVBIED) was a weapon of mass murder employed almost exclusively by Sunni jihadist groups. Primarily used to maximize civilian casualties and sow terror, they were sent against military targets as well. Packed with explosives, driven at speed by someone undeterred by death, a suicide car bomb could obliterate a hardened checkpoint or armored vehicle and the men inside. The heaviest weapons in the insurgent's arsenal were truck-mounted SVBIEDs, able to accurately deliver an explosive payload of over a ton.

Even before deploying, 3/2 had heard about the enemy's use of heavy vehicles for suicide attacks. In particular, there was much talk of a large, diesel fire engine that insurgents had stolen, armored with steel plates and packed full of explosives. Rumors and reports about it were circulating and reconnaissance assets were actively searching for it. The large, red vehicle had been spotted from the air at least once, but its location still wasn't pinned down as the battalion arrived. "Reports of the firetruck were like a ghost story," remembers Mike Hodd.[6]

LEFT, RIGHT AND CENTER

The fight against IEDs became a parallel campaign within the war, with its own organizations, equipment, and vocabulary. That vocabulary portrayed an IED attack on a timeline, with device detonation (the "boom") marked at the center. Reactive measures, such as vehicle armor, personal protective gear, first aid, and casualty evacuation were all "right-of-boom" on the timeline. But everyone realized the best way to beat IEDs was to proactively fight them "left-of-boom." Staying left-of-boom meant avoiding IEDs, discovering them early, jamming them electronically, or preventing their emplacement in the first place. It also meant aggressively hunting down the bombmakers, to capture or kill them.[7]

This counter-IED campaign was a classic case of move and countermove, with many intermeshed cycles. The EOD community and various technical intelligence cells were constantly reacting as they encountered new types of devices and triggering methods. Whenever an effective countermeasure was deployed, the bomb-makers would come up with a counter to the counter, and the cycle would continue.

Moreover, the fight in each area of operations was decidedly different, with particular types of IEDs being common in one area, but not in another. As EOD personnel and engineers encountered IEDs, they sometimes recognized the unique signatures of particular bomb-makers. Types of triggers, wiring sequences, or soldering patterns could all indicate who built the device.[8] Such clues helped to counter the bombs, or might even lead to the bomb-maker. Sometimes the appearance of a new triggering method, such as a new type of remote-control device, indicated a new IED cell was operating in the area.

But at the grunt-level, where the price in blood was paid, the most effective counter-IED tactics were simpler. If at all possible, obvious chokepoints and known IED threat areas were avoided. This might mean choosing a longer, but safer route. Often 3/2 Marines used the desert or less-travelled roads to reduce the chances of hitting IEDs or mines. Unlike units operating in Ramadi or Fallujah that were restricted to city streets, 3/2 could use open space to their advantage.

The other infantryman's countermeasure was to keep a sharp lookout for anything unusual. Recently-disturbed earth, a plastic bag that didn't blow in the wind, or rubble that hadn't been there yesterday could be signs of an IED. The ability to spot something out of place could keep them alive. John Schneekloth of Kilo Company remembers the stress of his first patrol outside the wire. "We were doing route clearance, looking for mines or IEDs," says Schneekloth. "I've never been so tired from just sitting. My eyes were honed in, totally focused, mental faculties on overdrive the whole time."[9]

ROAD WARRIORS

Several units and elements were part of the counter-IED fight in 3/2's AO. A platoon of combat engineers from the 4th Combat Engineer Battalion was attached to 3/2 and parceled out its teams to the line companies. They provided frontline expertise for engineering tasks, demolitions, and finding IEDs. Whenever a mission went out, these engineers were usually the ones who dismounted to investigate suspected IED locations. While they had handheld mine detectors that could electronically locate buried munitions, they often resorted to the old-school methods, gingerly probing the dirt with a bayonet to discover a hidden command-wire or a pressure plate. Many active-duty Marines didn't realize the engineers were reservists and found them to be highly proficient in this dangerous work:

> *Going out with them was an eye-opener. They taught us to look for variations in color on pavement. The insurgents would pour diesel fuel on asphalt to soften it, then place mines in the hole. Then they started putting plates on top, to do more damage, and later added a can of paint thinner for incendiary effect. My thought was, 'What do I know? Thank God for these guys!'*
>
> **—John Schneekloth**[10]

The second unit was an eight-man EOD section from the 8th Engineer Support Battalion, led by Gunnery Sergeant Chuck Yannizzi. When an IED was encountered, assuming time and the mission permitted, an EOD team was dispatched to disarm the device, destroy the explosives if needed, recover key components, and then examine them in detail. "We weren't just blowing IEDs in place," says Yazzinni, "We gathered info on the devices, studied the components then sent them off to an analytic cell for more exploitation."[11] This careful collection of data allowed Yazzinni and his EOD Marines to closely track the kinds of IEDs being used in different sectors.

> *On the main supply route from Al-Asad, most IEDs were employed with pressure-plates. They'd use a tuna can with a push-button, triggering a double-stack mine. But there was a section where we'd find radio-controlled devices, projectiles buried by the road next to a radio receiver.*
>
> **—Chuck Yazzinni**[12]

Another unit wasn't part of 3/2 but operated frequently in its area. The 2nd Combat Logistics Battalion, based out of Al-Asad, ran daily convoys on the main and alternate supply routes (MSRs and ASRs). Without logistics support, frontline units could hardly sustain themselves, much less conduct operations, but the IED threat made these supply runs hazardous. Each week, convoy vehicles were damaged or destroyed and casualties were suffered. While the convoys had their own embedded counter-IED teams, they were also supported by 3/2's engineers and the EOD section as needed.[13]

Two other battalion components frequently assisted the counter-IED effort by accompanying engineers or the EOD section on missions, escorting convoys, or setting up checkpoints on the main routes to deter IED emplacers and search vehicles for bomb making components. These were the Weapons Company (specifically its mobile assault platoons), and the commander's own personal security detachment. Marines in these elements spent countless dusty hours traveling the perilous roads, rolling the dice on each mission.

WARPIGS

The heavy firepower of an infantry battalion resides in its weapons company, which operates mortars, heavy machine guns, anti-tank weapons, and demolition teams. In the modern Marine Corps, weapons companies are also fully mobile, utilizing vehicles as weapons platforms and transport, providing the battalion commander a very flexible asset. Traditionally, a weapons company does not operate on its own in combat but parcels out most of its assets, such as machine-gun teams, to the rifle companies while the company commander serves as the battalion's fire support coordinator. But in 2005 a new structural model, known as the mobile assault company, was being adopted.

As they studied the lessons learned by other units in Iraq, Lieutenant Colonel Mundy and his weapons company commander, Captain Ford Phillips, decided to utilize the new concept. In late 2004, Phillips reorganized his unit along those lines, retaining the 81mm mortars and some other sections at company level while forming the rest into three platoons equipped with up-armored Humvees mounting heavy automatic weapons. The platoons were subdivided into Alpha and Bravo Sections, each with four vehicles commonly called "guntrucks." These mobile assault platoons (MAPs) would use the radio callsign WarPig. As Mundy recalls, "The decision to reorganize Weapons gave us three mobile elements that could act independently or operate as a full maneuver company."[14]

Once in-country, Phillips attached the first of his mobile assault platoons, led by First Lieutenant Brian Leahy, and a section from the 81mm mortar platoon to support India. The other two platoons and the remaining mortar section were based at Camp Al-Qaim. Often operating on their own, WarPig 2 and

WarPig 3 would be available to conduct missions across the battlespace.

First Lieutenant Gabe Diana, one of the battalion's top-rated lieutenants, commanded WarPig 3. Diana had been an enlisted reservist in 3/25 based in his home state of Ohio. He had bootstrapped his way to a college degree, secured his commission as an active-duty officer, then successfully competed to become a platoon commander. With Diana's personal connections to the Marine Reserves, WarPig 3 would be called on several times to support Lima Company, 3/25. He knew many of them personally.

WarPig 2 was commanded by Second Lieutenant Brian Stann, an intense young man raised on the tough side of Scranton, Pennsylvania. He'd gone to the Naval Academy where he played linebacker on the football team. Stann's athletic background, strong work ethic, and the fact that he was an amateur mixed martial arts fighter helped him gain acceptance and respect from the NCOs and enlisted Marines.

For the first part of the deployment, the mobile assault platoons scouted the area extensively, learning the road system and the terrain. They often escorted the CAG team on its missions, provided security for convoys, or set up vehicle checkpoints. WarPig sections also inserted scout-sniper teams then recovered them after a mission. During major operations, they were used for screening, isolating the battlefield with their long-range weapons, and providing fire support for the rifle companies.

With mobility being their primary advantage, the biggest threats to the guntruck crews were the all-too-common mines and roadside bombs. A big percentage of WarPig veterans were blown up at least once or had close encounters with IEDs.

During an early mission, one of WarPig 3's sections was sent out to Camp Gannon. While transiting the dusty desert tracks westward, one of the vehicles hit a buried mine. The explosion tore off the right front wheel and most of the engine compartment. The men inside the crew compartment were shaken, but unhurt. Up on the .50 cal, however, Lance Corporal Justin Abraham didn't escape entirely unscathed.[15]

The force of the detonation snapped his face into the gun breech, knocking out a front tooth. Dazed but quickly shaking off the blow, Abraham stayed on the gun to provide security as the crippled vehicle was rigged to tow back to base. For weeks after, he showed off his gap-toothed grin and was nicknamed "Toothless." Abraham's persistence in completing his mission, despite being blown up, and his focus on protecting fellow Marines, was typical in all the WarPig sections.

CHAOS

Another organizational innovation the Marines tried in Iraq was to establish dedicated units to protect commanders in the field. The Corps expected that after the initial fighting, a battalion commander and staff members would travel frequently to call on local officials, visit outposts, and inspect civil affairs projects, and would therefore need additional security. Accordingly, as 3/2 prepared to deploy, about 25 men were pulled from other elements to form the security platoon, which fell under the Headquarters & Support Company. Second Lieutenant Gary Hess was their commander, overseeing two sections. The platoon's callsign was Chaos.

Their original mission was to act as the personal security

detail for Mundy, protecting him and other staff sections when outside the wire. Once in-country, however, Chaos was heavily tasked, and their mission began to morph. "We hit the ground running, with a high op-tempo," says Ian Kantner, a lance corporal in the platoon. "We were running missions just a couple of days after turnover, escorting the CAG a lot. Once out by the phosphate plant I remember telling an officer we were taking machine gun fire. He thought it was just machinery noise, but I said, 'No sir, we're being shot at.'"[16]

The IED threat caused Chaos to start running many route clearance missions. Accompanied by the EOD section or combat engineers, they mounted daily patrols along the main roads searching for or clearing roadside bombs. "We started encountering IEDs and mines right off the bat," says Kantner. "At that point, it seemed like the insurgents weren't too smart. They'd use the same spots repeatedly. We'd come to a dip in the road and there would be blast and burn marks from where IEDs had gone off before."[17]

The enemy was learning, however, and almost certainly was closely observing 3/2's operational patterns. Since they were outside the wire every day, Chaos was most likely the object of frequent hostile scrutiny.

NO-NAME ROAD

On the afternoon of 21 March, Chaos had established a vehicle checkpoint (VCP) at a T-shaped intersection along ASR Silver, about six miles west of Camp AQ. Both sections were there, to perform traffic control and secure the intersection for a resupply convoy returning from Camp Gannon. Their guntrucks were set up on the approaches to the intersection. Evidently the convoy was delayed, as they had been waiting there for several hours.[18] One of the guntrucks closest to the intersection was crewed by Lance Corporal Kevin Smith as the vehicle commander (VC), along with Lance Corporals Chad Lechlinski, Brandon Overton, and A.J. Lomando. By about 1600, the convoy had still not appeared and civilian traffic had built up on the road. Smith had just switched out with Lomando, who had been up top manning the .50 cal for an extended time, when a radio call came through. It was time to return to base.

As the checkpoint was breaking down and the Humvees started to move, "a civilian vehicle left the line, and sped right at us," remembers Lomando, who was sitting in the right front seat. "We were moving about 15 mph, and it came from our rear. The other Iraqi vehicles held back. I think they had to know what was happening."[19] In the gun turret, Smith saw the danger and aimed at the speeding vehicle.

"Kevin had the gun faced backwards and probably got off a few rounds" says Lomando. But it was too late. "I heard a huge roar. I was holding a road flare at that instant and the explosion touched it off in my hand. Everything went red for a bit. When I got out of the vehicle, smoke poured out. My pistol was blown off my hip. My rifle had holes in it, was inoperative."[20]

At first, Lomando had trouble grasping what had happened. He was 19 years old, and this was his first combat experience. He thought they'd hit a mine or buried IED:

> *I could see Smith was dead. So, I grabbed his rifle, and racked in a round... I started yelling for my guys... Lechlinski was shook up. Overton saw his arm and said "my arm's done." His arm was hanging on by the bicep. Lechlinksi and I looked each other in the*

eye. He was crying. I told him to help take care of Overton, and he pulled himself together.

—A.J. Lomando[21]

Ian Kantner was about 200 meters away in another guntruck when the attack occurred, separated by a gentle rise in the ground. "Suddenly there was a big explosion over in their direction," Kantner remembers. "We couldn't see what had happened due to the terrain. We drove over there, and Sergeant Chinatomby's truck headed that way too, converging on the scene."[22]

They drove up and dismounted into a frightful situation. The blast site was scorched evidence of the explosive power that had been packed into the suicide vehicle, reportedly a flat-nosed "bongo" truck. The Humvee was thoroughly wrecked, a huge crater just behind it where the SVBIED had detonated. The bongo truck, along with its driver, had been blasted into bits which were scattered across the desert. The single exception was the engine block, largely intact after being tossed 300 meters away.

The explosion had killed Lance Corporal Smith instantly and injured the rest of the crew. Lechlinksi suffered burns and a dislocated shoulder, and Lomando had been hit with shrapnel. A large chunk of metal had punched through the rear of the guntruck, striking him in the back, just inches from the top edge of his body armor's ceramic plate. "My rear plate was pulverized," says Lomando. "If I'd been hunched down in the seat just another couple of inches, I'd be dead."[23]

The most seriously wounded was Overton, who was in mortal danger. Corpsman Dean Webster was working on him outside the wrecked Humvee. As the other Chaos Marines secured the site from further attack, Webster worked feverishly to save Overton's life and his arm. Much later, in an online memorial page, he described the intense effort:

> *Brandon's left arm was shattered and almost torn off. [He] was staggering trying to take his flak jacket off when I reached him... Chad [Lechlinski] and I grabbed Brandon before he could get his flack [off]. His arm was only attached by about two to three inches of tissue. If Chad and I didn't stop him, his arm would have fallen off when the weight of the flack hit it. I'll never forget kneeling down, with Chad on Brandon's left... as I assessed his injuries and gave him an injection of morphine to stop his pain.*
>
> —**Dean Webster**[24]

Meanwhile, a helicopter was spinning up for casualty evacuation (CASEVAC) but Webster decided Overton needed to be evacuated immediately. They loaded him into one of the guntrucks and dashed towards base. In the back, Webster worked to stabilize him in transit. "[We were] hauling ass through known minefields and IED zones," he described. "Every time I went to stick the IV in him, we'd hit bumps. I remember getting one chance when the Marines said, 'Do it now, Doc!' We had about 200 feet of smooth road, and I got [the IV in] him." [25]

Back at base, Lieutenant Colonel Mundy had heard the desperate radio calls and knew someone had been killed. "That day was a tough one," he recalls. "I normally didn't get rattled when bad things happened. On the outside I could maintain composure, focusing on how to move forward, but inside it was different. These were my Marines. I was their leader, and this felt like a kick in the gut."[26]

It had only been 12 days since the transfer of authority, and already 3/2 had suffered its first KIA and first seriously wounded men. Lachlinski and Lomando were treated and soon returned to duty. Thanks to Doc Webster's fast action, Overton's arm was saved, and he was soon on a MEDEVAC* flight back to the States for a long and painful recovery.

In the waning hours of the afternoon, Marines at Camp Al-Qaim assembled for a memorial to honor Kevin Smith. The battalion commander said a few heartfelt words, as did the chaplain, Navy Lieutenant John Anderson. Then Sergeant Clive Chinatomby spoke about the difference Smith had made. "He was a team leader and was the first one to jump up and volunteer for anything. He was always there for his Marines." Chinatomby continued, keeping his emotions in check. "We lost a friend and a good Marine. He was the quarterback on this team; my go-to guy and you truly can never replace that."[27]

The suicide attack was clearly the work of foreign-led jihadists, well-known for their cruel martyrdom operations. At this point in the war, most SVBIEDs were targeted against defenseless civilians. But here they'd employed their most lethal weapon system against a military target, most likely to test the new battalion that had arrived in the AO. It highlighted in stark terms the violence the enemy was capable of.

In reaction, 3/2 established new procedures for vehicle checkpoints. More barriers and wire would be used, and the warning line was pushed out from 300 to 500 meters. The security platoon pressed on, continuing their high-tempo operations.

---

* MEDEVAC (medical evacuation) technically refers to moving wounded or injured personnel from a forward facility to more advanced medical care in the rear. CASEVAC (casualty evacuation) refers to moving wounded personnel from the battlefield to first-level, emergency medical care.

Naturally they would be quicker on the trigger if they perceived a threat. Throughout April and May, Chaos was on the road nearly every day. During a major operation in mid-May, they fulfilled their original role by providing security to the battalion's mobile command section.

Soon after that, however, it was decided that the manpower cost of a dedicated security platoon was too much, and its men were needed elsewhere. In early June, Chaos was disbanded. Lieutenant Hess transferred to India Company to be a platoon commander and most of the unit was folded into Kilo Company.[28]

Dark Ripples

The tragic effects of the 21 March suicide attack and the loss of Kevin Smith were felt long after 3/2 left Al-Qaim. Seriously wounded in the blast, Brandon Overton began a prolonged series of operations and medical procedures. He regained use of his arm, but continued to suffer from post-traumatic stress and addictive effects of painkillers. Chad Lechlinski also recovered physically from his wounds, but struggled with post-traumatic stress afterwards. Sadly, both men eventually took their own lives, Brandon in 2011 and Chad in 2015. Like many who have returned from America's 21st century wars, some 3/2 veterans have had challenges with isolation, anger, depression and thoughts of suicide. This ongoing struggle is discussed further at the end of the book.

5. SMUGGLERS

Locals say the soil in Al-Qaim is the richest in Iraq and the many farms and orchards along the river form the traditional base of the district's economy, which supported 150,000 to 200,000 people in 2005.[1] Some industry had arrived in the 1980s, including a cement factory and a large phosphate plant to produce fertilizers. But trade is the district's primary economic engine.

While it may seem remote, Al-Qaim sits astride one of the Middle East's primary trade arteries and reaps corresponding benefits. Iraq's National Highway 12 runs along the Euphrates, following the ancient caravan routes and connecting Al-Qaim to the rest of the country, to Syria, the Mediterranean, and the greater world beyond. The city of Husaybah, in particular, boasts import-export businesses, truck stops, warehouses, vehicle repair shops, car dealerships, and bustling markets.

In 2004, however, the port-of-entry between Husaybah and Syria was shut down by U.S. forces in an attempt to stem rising insurgent activity. Barriers blocked all vehicular traffic at the border crossing and Marines occupied the facilities. This had predictable negative results on the local economy and was hugely unpopular with the residents. But barricading the official crossing point hardly meant the border was sealed.

JUST DOING BUSINESS

In many parts of the world, what the law technically calls smuggling is just doing business. This is especially true along an ill-defined border or where government authority is weak. The border between Iraq and Syria is a classic case in point. In 1921, the British drew an arbitrary line on the map to delineate the two countries.[2] The artificial line stretched invisibly across the trackless desert and made no sense geographically or culturally. It was ignored for decades. Eventually border posts and customs stations appeared, but they could be easily bypassed.

Close-knit groups of families and kinsmen were the ones who mastered the methods of moving goods across the border. These were the Sunni tribes of western Anbar who traced their roots back to nomadic Bedouins and raiding warlords on horseback. They had always been unruly, ready to take up arms against each other or the government. Even Saddam's iron-fisted regime had trouble controlling them. Early on, the dictator adopted a co-option strategy by buying off senior tribal leaders—the sheikhs. This often meant turning a blind eye to their smuggling rings, which trafficked everything from cigarettes to computers, luxury cars to factory equipment.[3]

Iraq's catastrophic defeat in the Gulf War of 1991 severely damaged Saddam's power. In response, he visibly turned to his own Sunni tribal roots and further empowered the sheikhs. Those he favored were granted authority to collect state revenue, distribute funds, and establish quasi-official security in their areas.[4] Western tribes were allowed to greatly expand their smuggling operations.

In particular, Iraq's efforts to blunt economic sanctions turned smuggling activities into government-sanctioned organized crime. The tribes were allowed to reap huge profits as long as they brought in the goods. The United Nation's massively corrupt Oil-for-Food program put this process on steroids, as illegally exported Iraqi oil generated billions in hard currency. Al-Qaim in particular became a smuggler's paradise.

TRIBES

Although tribes exist throughout Iraq, they are most powerful among the Sunnis, especially in Anbar. They are extended, multi-level patronage networks. At any of these levels, a sheikh is judged by his ability to provide economic benefits for members. He lines up jobs for his people, secures contracts or special set-asides from the government, and isn't above extorting concessions. A powerful sheikh gains influence, money, and *wasta* (clout or reputation) at the expense of rival tribes. Saddam would often play the tribes off against each other, trying to maximize his own power. This set the stage for violent internecine conflict after the regime fell in 2003.

Elks' Club with Guns

For Americans and other Westerners, it is difficult to grasp the role of tribes in Iraqi society. There is no real equivalent in U.S. culture. A rough analogy would be a cross between old-line civic groups like the Elks' Club, bare-knuckled labor unions, blood-feuding clans, and upscale gangsters like "The Sopranos". Then throw in a dash of urbane international businessmen and arm everyone with AK-47s.

The Al-Qaim District is home to several tribes with members or related clans on both sides of the border. In 2005, the three most important were the Salmonis, the Karabulis and the Albu Mahal. Each had traditional territories where members lived but there were also areas where they lived intermingled, such as in Husaybah.

The Salmoni tribe's traditional holdings were in the rich farmlands along the river, especially the Sinjar area directly north of Husaybah alongside the border. They also dominated a stretch of villages along the southern bank surrounding the town of Al-Qaim. The Salmonis had been favored under the Ba'athist patronage system and had been gaining power up until the invasion.[5]

The Karabulis were concentrated in the city of Karabilah, which bears the tribal name. Many were shepherds or involved in the traditional markets for wool and sheep.[6] Loosely allied with the Salmonis, they were also trying to maintain their position in the post-Saddam world. Karabuli and Salmoni tribesmen would usually act together in the turmoil and combat of 2005.

The chief rival to both was the Albu Mahal, whose members were known as Mahalawis. They were the most numerous tribe in the district, but their relative standing had eroded under Saddam. Their traditional areas were the town of Sadah and the farming community of Old Ubaydi. But they also controlled a key location in Husaybah. Before the Iraq War, the Border Police who ran the Port of Entry (POE) and the Customs Station were mostly Albu Mahal tribesmen. This put them in the advantageous position of controlling official cross-border trade.

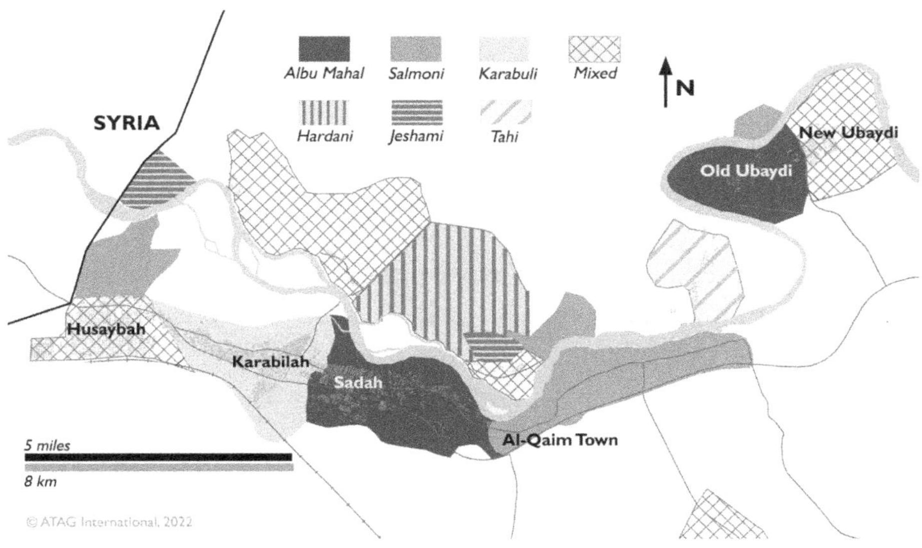

The Mahalawis were also master smugglers themselves, intimately familiar with the maze of dirt tracks that crisscrossed the desert. Having their men in the Border Police also meant they could aid the activities of fellow tribesmen, by action or inaction, while impeding those of their competitors. In the massive kleptocracy that Saddam fostered, Mahalawis were foxes guarding the henhouse.

The Albu Mahal took special pride that, during a 1920 uprising against the British, theirs was the only tribe to take up arms. In more recent years, their sheikhs had disapproved of—even resisted—government intrusions into their affairs. This had lost them Saddam's favor and put them in opposition to the rising status of the Salmoni and Karabuli. After the coalition's invasion in 2003, the Mahalawis did not initially rush to join the growing resistance. Sheikh Sabah, the tribe's senior, or paramount sheikh, was at first reluctant to side with traditional rivals on behalf of a fallen regime.[7]

But it soon became clear that the Albu Mahal would need to align with the insurgency to maintain their own interests. They could not stand by as foreign troops appeared in their streets and Mahalawi tribesmen began to actively fight the American troops that first arrived in Al-Qaim. "In any country that is invaded, a resistance will start," explained Sabah in a 2010 interview. "I don't think there's any nation that does not resist an invader."[8]

RATLINES

Over many decades, the smuggling rings of Anbar had established a deep and intricate infrastructure. Each tribal gang would use favored routes, perhaps along a well-hidden wadi or on the other side of a ridge that shielded them from prying eyes. But routes were actually of secondary importance to the interlocking system of caches or hide sites, places where goods could be stored before moving them on to a buyer. The other essential component of the smuggling infrastructure was the people themselves. For generations, residents of Al-Qaim had been involved in, or knew of, this constant flow of illicit goods through their neighborhoods and villages. Hiding things, whether stolen sheep, bootleg liquor, pirated DVDs, or mortar rounds, was second nature.

This infrastructure stretched up and down the Euphrates River Valley, intertwining families, tribes, vehicles, shops, farms, and homes. Together, they formed what the coalition called the "ratline", the clandestine supply chain that moved weapons, munitions, explosives, money, and especially enemy fighters from the border into the center of the country. Early in the war, coalition commanders realized the need to disrupt enemy lines of support, which was one of the baseline reasons for deploying Marines to Anbar. Closing ports-of-entry, launching mobile patrols far into the desert, and early efforts to build earthen berms along the border, were all attempts to cut, or at least squeeze, the ratlines.

6. MAFIA

In the Marine infantry world, the process for deciding on a unit's radio callsign is obscure, even a little mysterious. There are typical callsigns that crop up repeatedly in rifle companies. Usually they are acceptably warlike, such as "Battle" for Company B. Others are adopted to overcome a less-than-aggressive phonetic letter, such as "Dagger" instead of "Delta" for Company D. Sometimes the callsign is assigned from above, but often it is chosen formally or informally by members of the unit.

India Company went by "Evil" on the tactical nets, a play on the phrase "the evil eye." But an unofficial unit nickname was also used. It came from 2004, as the company met their new commander, Captain Frank Diorio. "We were having a unit run, and one of NCOs was getting after a Marine who was falling behind, kind of berating him. Typical stuff," remembers Rashard Minnis, one of the squad leaders. "But after the run, our new captain brought us all in and talked to us. And he set the tone. He said something like, 'Men, in this company we stick together, we help our brothers out. We're kinda like the mafia, we take care of our family'. That name and mentality stuck. We were the India 'mafia' from then on."[1]

Frank Diorio is a quiet, intense man from an Italian-American family in Danville, New Jersey. Standing only five-foot-six, with a wiry 150-pound frame, many of his Marines towered over their commander but came to respect and trust him greatly. His dedication, humility, and obvious regard for his men instilled deep loyalty among them. "He is on my short list of men who, if they ever call and ask for help, legal or not, I will be there," says Will Marconi.[2]

"The first time I met him we grabbed a beer and went on a walk," recalls Don Brazeal, the company's first sergeant. "He told me, 'This is not my company. It's our company'...And he was a man of his word," says Brazeal. "I've never seen him raise his voice. He didn't have to. Frank loved his Marines; you could just feel it."[3] The two made a great team. The slightly built captain and his gruff, six-foot-one, gunfighter first sergeant appeared to be an odd pair. But they forged a heartfelt bond that carried them and India Company through exceedingly rough times. They remain close friends to this day.

Brazeal was a rough-cut, old-school infantryman from Council Bluffs, Iowa. He'd enlisted right out of high school and by 2005 had over 22 years in the Corps. He'd been on many deployments and had seen action in Liberia and during the advance on Baghdad in 2003. He constantly worked to instill readiness and a combat mentality across the company.

A particular incident highlights Brazeal's care for his Marines and his focus on building them into warriors. One night a junior India Marine got himself hauled to jail after a bar fight downtown (a common occurrence near Marine bases). Bright and early the next morning, First Sergeant Brazeal showed up to bail him out. The offender apologized profusely and owned up to his poor judgment. But rather than dish out non-judicial punishment, Brazeal just told him, "Don't worry, Marine. We take care of each other." Then he asked the young man if he'd won the fight, receiving a quiet nod in reply. "Good!"

Brazeal exclaimed. "We need meat-eaters in this company!" Sure enough, that young Marine was soon selected to be squad leader and distinguished himself in combat.[4]

Two other key leaders in India were First Lieutenant Mike Hodd and Gunnery Sergeant Brian Hogancamp. Lieutenant Hodd, from Brooklyn, had been a rifleman in the Marine reserves then went to Officer Candidate School (OCS) to receive his commission. He'd also been part of the initial invasion and had seen action in Nasiriyah. Soft-spoken, smart, and thoughtful, Hodd ran company operations as the most experienced lieutenant and Diorio's XO. Gunnery Sergeant Brian Hogancamp, from Maryland, was another direct and blunt-spoken NCO. As the company gunny, he would handle everything from beans to bullets to building up Camp Gannon's defenses.

The company went to war with the full complement of three rifle platoons plus its weapons platoon. To bolster the camp's defenses and provide more combat power, several other elements were attached, including WarPig 1 and the 81mm mortars from Weapons Company. A scout-sniper team (SST) from H&S Company, callsign "Reaper 1", was also attached and would see much action in and around Husaybah. Four tanks from Alpha Company, 1st Tank Battalion added heavy armor and firepower, and a section of AAV "tracs" and their crews provided mobility for India's grunts.

Other attached assets included combat engineers, a Forward Air Controller (FAC), a U.S. Army psyops team, and a medical team with a U.S. Navy surgeon and about 14 Navy corpsmen running a Battalion Aid Station (BAS) and directly supporting each platoon. Counting additional communications, intelligence, maintenance and services personnel, Captain Diorio would actually command a combined-arms force of about 280 men.[5]

WELCOME TO HUSAYBAH

On the last day of February, India Company loaded up on unarmored 7-ton trucks and convoyed from Camp Al-Qaim out to Camp Gannon. "We weren't sure what to be prepared for. It was very quiet the night before," described Diorio. "You could tell the Marines were nervous. I was nervous. I wasn't sure what to expect. The ride out there itself was known to be very dangerous."[6]

To avoid mines and IEDs, they took a circuitous route out through the desert, approaching Gannon from the west. As they traveled, the convoy broke into smaller columns to avoid presenting one large target. When the first column came through the entry control point (ECP), Lieutenant Hodd and the advance party were there to meet them. "I was standing out there by post 7 when they rolled in," he remembers. "I'd been in charge of their training and as I watched everybody get off the trucks, they were squared away and professional. I knew we could handle whatever was coming. Captain Diorio got out and came over to meet me. I was so proud. The Marines were ready."[7]

The enemy showed they were ready too. As India Company unloaded, they were greeted with a salvo of mortar fire. "When 2nd Platoon got off the trucks, they took some incoming, and quickly got under cover. Then as we dismounted, I could hear machine-gun chatter from the ING compound," remembers Tyler Ogden from 3rd Platoon. "Over by the command post there was an unexploded mortar round, with the tail fins sticking out. We walked by it, and one of the Baker Marines said, 'that came in yesterday'".[8]

The mafia mentality would fit perfectly in this place. The city of Husaybah was ruled by insurgents and warring gangs, always willing to test the Marines. For seven months India and their attachments would operate essentially on their own, separated from the rest of the battalion. Their rugged, no-frills base was literally a stone's throw from the Syrian border, hemmed in by enemies all around. Under constant threat from hostile eyes and weapons, they would have to prove they were the toughest gang in a tough city.

See **bastardsandbrothers.com** for notes, photos, maps, etc.

7. COMPLACENCY KILLS

When the first Marines arrived in Husaybah in 2004, Camp Gannon did not exist. Troopers from the U.S. Army's 3rd ACR were encamped among the buildings of the Iraqi Border Police and Customs Station at the west end of the city's main avenue, known as Market Street. The cavalry troopers used the location as a temporary patrol base, which they initially dubbed Camp Husaybah.[1] As Lima Company of 3/7 took over from them, there was no running water and no definable security perimeter. The Marines quickly went to work making improvements.

Navy Seabees (construction engineers) were brought in with heavy equipment and materials to transform the patrol base. Large, foldable obstacles called HESCO barriers were filled with dirt and rocks to build the outer perimeter and sleeping quarters. These quarters, or "hooches", were long and narrow with plywood floors and lumber-reinforced roofs supporting layers of sandbags on top. Each could bunk around 20 men within their confined spaces. Fortified guard posts were set up along the perimeter.

After the prolonged street battles in April of 2004 and the heroic combat death of Lima 3/7's Company Commander, the base's name was changed to Camp Gannon in his honor. In August, Baker Company of 1/7 arrived and further hardened the defenses and improved living conditions. Baker Company also took over a cluster of buildings to the east of Gannon called the ING compound. A few Iraqi National Guard (ING) soldiers had been stationed there but had melted away. Manning that forward position put Marines right into the city.[2]

Two other key actions taken by 1/7 would shape the battlespace around Husaybah. Early in their deployment, 1/7 shut down the border crossing into Syria by placing barriers and strands of concertina wire across the road.[3] While this was unpopular with the locals, the Marines simply didn't have the resources to manage an international border crossing while also combating a growing insurgency. Additionally, Baker Company began using a dilapidated building on the north edge of the city as an observation post (OP). Located along a dirt road the Marines called Trash Road, the post naturally enough became known as Trash OP.[4]

For the Marines, building Camp Gannon was a continuous process with each successive unit making incremental improvements. The same was happening across Anbar. Up and down the Western Euphrates Valley, Marine units improved their positions, made what progress they could in their battlespace, then turned over to the next unit in the deployment cycle. Each built on what the units before them had accomplished.

INDIA'S GANNON

By the time India Company took over Camp Gannon, it was laid out in an irregular polygonal shape just over 400 meters long from east to west and 200 meters across from north to south. The northern perimeter was only yards from the Syrian border and the village of Al-Him.[5] On top of the HESCOs were fortified positions, named post 1 (P1) through post 8 (P8). Posts 1 and 2 were four-story concrete guard towers, built before the war. The rest were sturdy sandbag-and-lumber constructions with overhead cover and clear fields of fire.

Gannon's main entry control point (ECP) was situated along the south wall, providing access to the desert without having to move through Husaybah. A secondary ECP was on the northeast corner, leading to the border crossing, the ING compound, and the city beyond. Both ECPs had serpentine barriers set up outside, which forced entering vehicles to slowly wind their way through, directly under the guns of overwatching guard posts.

The men's hooches were situated in the center of the camp, surrounded by their own protective HESCO walls to shield against mortar or rocket fragments. Navy corpsmen had their Battalion Aid Station (BAS) near the hooches as well. On the eastern side of camp was a cluster of pre-existing buildings with staff offices, supply, the armory, a weight room, and an ad-hoc barber shop. The Motor Transport section's maintenance bays and more equipment storage were in a large, blue-roofed building inexplicably emblazoned with the Bridgestone company's logo.

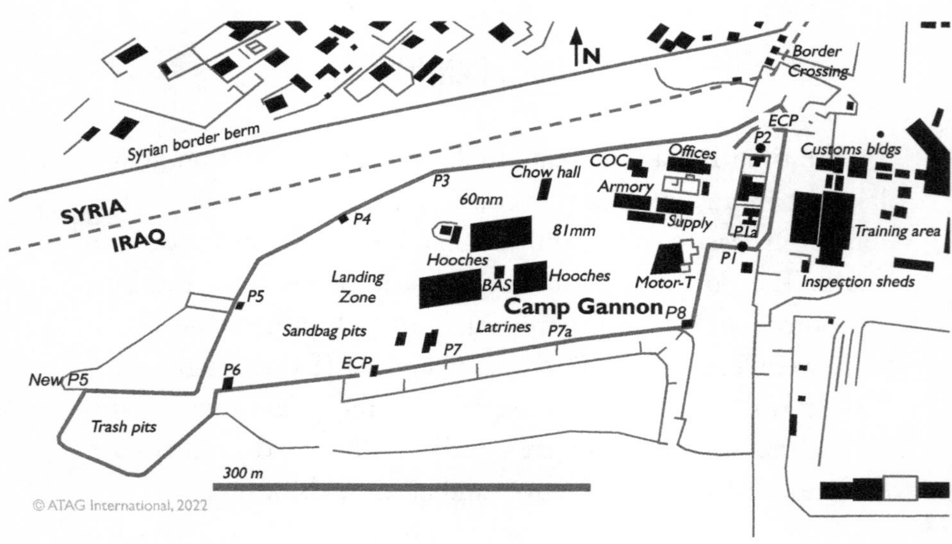

Among these buildings was the concrete-and-brick building housing India's combat operations center (COC), also called Evil CP. Inside, officers and NCOs constantly monitored the radio nets and directed all operations. On the roof was another sandbagged guard post, with the stars and stripes flying on the camp flagpole just outside.

THE NEW NORMAL

Living conditions were harsh, to say the least. Power and water were severely limited. Large diesel generators ran noisily day and night to keep lights on and to power up radios and vital computer systems in the COC. At first a rickety shower facility provided cold or lukewarm running water, depending on the time of day. But even that luxury was cut off by explosive blasts soon after India Company arrived.

For most of the deployment, the men could not shower. They cleaned themselves as best they could with bottled water and baby wipes. By standing order, they wore their helmets (typically called "kevlars") and body armor (called "flaks") anytime they were outside. Their uniforms and underwear quickly became imbued with dirt, sweat, grease, and gun oil. Everyone smelled, but soon no one noticed:

> *When we first got there, we were completely miserable. But over time, it became the new normal. Everyone was living in the same conditions, and we just accepted it... When we got a chance to wash ourselves, [it was] basically just armpits, crotch, rear end, then feet. We had to pay special attention to our feet, make sure to wash them, let them dry out... We had to wear the same stuff day*

after day. We stank. When I left Gannon and got back to Camp AQ, I finally figured out how gross I was.

—Brian Hogancamp[6]

The latrines were crude. To urinate, men stood in the open and relieved themselves into plastic PVC "piss tubes" stuck into the ground. To defecate, they used "three-holers", sweltering fly-infested boxes with simple holes in a piece of plywood. Underneath were metal burn barrels cut down from fuel drums. Of course, the most detested duty on post was the "shit detail", which entailed dragging out the barrels when full, pouring in diesel fuel, and burning the stinking mess inside (stirring was required). The stench would waft through the camp, adding to the already pungent ambience.

NO-MAN'S LAND

The camp's proximity to Syria was its other defining feature. A Marine in one of Gannon's northern posts looked directly over some ragged barbed wire barriers and an earthen berm into Syria, hostile territory for all intents and purposes. And Syrian Border Guards were looking right back at them. There were numerous reports and indications that India Company was being surveilled, either by Syrian security forces or by other entities. The insurgents and foreign fighters in Husaybah operated seamlessly on both sides of the border.

At night, headlights danced in the distance as unknown vehicles crossed the border, and at times men could be seen walking into or out of Syria. More distressing, incoming came from the other side on multiple occasions. Usually, these incidents consisted of a few rounds of small arms fire, but always posed the risk of escalation.

One night in April, a heavier weapon was involved. Around midnight, from northwest of Gannon, just a few hundred meters inside Syria, a heavy machine-gun or anti-aircraft weapon cut loose. At first the impressive stream of tracer fire stabbed vertically into the sky, but then the angle depressed, and long bursts passed directly over Camp Gannon, the rounds impacting in western Husaybah. The perpetrators and their reasons were unknown.[7]

INCOMING

The enemy had greeted India's arrival with a flurry of incoming fire and didn't let up in subsequent days and weeks. The towers and sandbagged positions on the east and south perimeter were shot at daily, as was the ING compound. The men used binoculars to constantly scan for armed individuals and suspicious activity. Even so, rounds would suddenly smack into the sandbags or snap overhead. The Marines would return fire if they could spot the shooter's location. A brief firefight on 12 March was typical of these attacks, recorded by Lance Corporal Jason Ellis in his combat journal:

> *Lance Corporal Habay and I were standing in P7, and around 3pm the camp started to get incoming. He and I saw a man with an AK-47 roughly 600 meters away. Habay took the first shot. After his shot rang out, I let out two 5-round SAW* bursts... The man was dead in his tracks*
>
> **—Jason Ellis**[8]

* "SAW" stands for the M-249 Squad Automatic Weapon, a 5.56mm light machine-gun

Mysterious vehicles often lurked in the alleys, followed by shots from their vicinity. Sometimes posts received more sustained fire from a light machine-gun, or an RPG round would streak in from the edge of the city. Even more dangerous were the all-too-common attacks by mortars or, less frequently, rockets.

The constant threats fostered a certain frame-of-mind at Camp Gannon. Everyone not under cover wore full protective gear and kept their weapon ready for action.[9] The words "complacency kills" were scrawled on various surfaces throughout the camp, first put there by Marines from 3/7. India added their own scrawlings and that sage advice was penned, painted, and carved into the bones of the beleaguered camp and the very souls of the men stationed there.

POO FIGHT

As with IEDs, insurgents frequently used mortars and rockets to make indirect fire (IDF) attacks without exposing themselves to immediate return fire. It was a cheap, effective way to attack coalition bases. At the beginning of India's tour on Gannon, IDF attacks came in daily, usually right around midday and again right around chow time. Most of the IDF came from Russian-designed 82mm mortars, firing a 10-pound shell that scattered fragments upon detonation. Anyone within 30 feet of the shell's impact was likely to be seriously wounded or killed.

Within a minute, insurgents could set up a mortar tube, fire a round or two, then withdraw either with or without the weapon. A common tactic was to fire a mortar from the bed of a pickup truck, then just drive away. Such an attack might take only seconds. Accuracy, however, required an observer who could see where the rounds fell and give adjustments to the mortar team to fire more rounds. Insurgents in Husaybah would typically place an observer on a rooftop or in a top-floor window, who would call in adjustments over a cell phone.

The main tool available to provide counter-battery fire against enemy mortars was the 81mm mortar section, led by Corporal Marlon Garcia. Chopped over to India from Weapons Company, Garcia's nine-man section had two tubes, or guns, in sandbagged pits. "We lived in the hooches right next to the pits and were on call 24/7. We needed to be ready to respond at any time," relates Garcia. "One man was always on radio watch. If anything happened, we'd rush to the guns ... I took it very seriously, and we constantly trained."[10]

The 81s were electronically tied into a small counter-battery radar (CBR) that could detect rockets and mortar shells while they were in flight and locate their point-of-origin, otherwise known as the POO or simply "poo." When it worked properly, the CBR would identify the POO nearly instantaneously when an enemy mortar fired, sending the grid to the 81mm crews within seconds. Often, Garcia and his crews would be ready to send rounds downrange within 20 seconds. But it was always a race against the insurgent mortar team who would "shoot and scoot" to escape the Marine's counter fire. Almost invariably, they would be gone by the time the counter barrage of ten or more 81mm rounds struck.

CLOSE, AND YES, CIGARS

After enduring several weeks of this deadly serious cat-and-mouse game, it was decided to try a new counter-fire tactic. One day, in reaction to yet another mortar attack on Gannon, the 81 crews fired their standard ten-round salvo at the POO which had been pinpointed with the CBR. But this time they gave a long pause, then fired a second salvo. The intent was to catch insurgents as they came out to retrieve their mortar tube.

The mortarmen had no way of immediately knowing the results, but a few days later First Sergeant Brazeal sauntered over to their pits. As Garcia remembers, "He called me over and said, 'You mortar guys are doing a great job!' Then he pulled a couple cigars out of his pocket, and tells us, 'You hit the insurgent mortar team with that delayed salvo. You got three confirmed kills.' We were pumped about that, to know we were fulfilling our mission, protecting our guys. We decided to save those cigars for a special occasion."[11]

The indirect fire attacks subsided for several weeks after, which further verified that the 81mm section had removed an experienced enemy mortar team from the battlefield.[12] Eventually, though, IDF attacks began hitting Camp Gannon again. The deadly counter-battery game would continue on and off for the rest of the deployment.

PRESENCE

Even before deploying, Captain Diorio had considered what to do about the turbulent city of Husaybah. He had connected with Captain Nelson of Baker Company and reviewed his summaries of the situation, trying to absorb their lessons learned. During the RIP, the two had exchanged ideas. "Andy and I talked many nights of what he would do if he was staying," related Diorio. "I had to get my hands wrapped around this presence idea…And Andy was struggling with it…in a town of 100,000 people [and] thousands of blocks."[13]

Both 3/7 and 1/7 had lost Marines while conducting so-called "presence patrols." Such patrols, which might be mounted or dismounted, were part of the Stability and Support Operations (SASO) concept being used elsewhere in support of local Iraqi governments. But there was no local government to speak of in Husaybah. Conducting presence patrols in the city would be sending Marines into risky urban firefights for little or no gain.

Early on, then, Diorio decided not to conduct highly vulnerable daytime patrols in Husaybah. Instead, India Company would work to gain positional advantages, using observation and firepower if necessary to control key parts of the city. Snipers would play a key role. Immediately after arriving on Gannon, the Reaper 1 scout-sniper team (SST) began setting up where they could use their long-range optics and precision engagement capabilities to maximum effect.[14]

The other key part of his plan was to exercise patience, consciously looking for opportunities to begin constructive engagement with the population. While the company would maintain a very proactive defense against attacks, India Marines would also work to figure out who was who in the city, watching and waiting for local leaders to emerge.

HOTLINE

An important contributor to the engagement part of the plan was a Marine NCO and an Iraqi-American who worked as the company commander's interpreter. Sergeant "Jimmy" (not his real name) was born in Iraq to an Assyrian Christian family, then immigrated to the U.S. He wasn't a school-trained interpreter and had to learn the Arabic dialect spoken along the border.[15] But by all accounts, he had an engaging personality and an excellent ability to relate to the locals. The sergeant had been deployed with 1/7 and voluntarily stayed on once 3/2 arrived, so already knew the area, and had contacts. As Captain Diorio later described, it was great to have "an interpreter who thought like a Marine...could talk like a Marine. He also appreciated information that was valuable."[16]

As Baker Company left, they turned over their local contacts to India as information sources.[17] These local residents could use a pre-existing phone number for the old Iraqi Customs Offices, which now rang on Gannon. They could call this line to pass on information to the Americans.[18] The phone was situated in the workspaces of the Human Intelligence Exploitation Team (HET), a pair of enlisted Marines. The HET's job was to cultivate human sources and collate, vet, and pass on the information gleaned from them. Given his language skills and cultural knowledge, Sergeant Jimmy also worked with the HET, frequently answering the hotline when locals called in.[19]

One of these contacts was a woman living in Husaybah. Insurgents had killed her husband, a member of the Border Police, and she despised them for it. During Baker Company's tenure, she had occasionally called in to describe what was going on in the city and continued to do so with India. "She was just someone who would call in from time to time," recalled Diorio, mostly to provide information on threats to the Marines. According to Diorio, it was "very little to build on."[20]

But through numerous conversations with Sergeant Jimmy, the value of her information would become more important over time. The Marines called her the "East End Lady" and eventually her reporting became known all the way up the chain of command. "I don't know if she's alive today," said Colonel Davis in a post-war interview. "If she is, she deserves a huge medal."[21]

NIGHT WOLVES

The offensive side of India's approach would be carried out through nighttime raids, to keep the enemy off balance and nab key insurgents. One of India's rifle platoons was always on mission status, ready to conduct operations. Early on, an additional unit was available for raids. During March and April, elements of the 1st Force Recon Company were operating in far west Anbar. The highly trained Recon Marines were essentially RCT-2's own direct action* force and in those months they conducted a series of capture/kill missions in and around Husaybah. Some were executed independently, some with support from India Company. After April, however, the Force Recon Company shifted its focus elsewhere.

The biggest, most notable, of India's raids into Husaybah was launched on 2 April 2005. There was no catchy name for

* "Direct action" or DA refers to short-duration strikes, raids and offensive actions to seize, destroy or capture designated targets. DA is a primary mission of special operations forces

the operation, which became known merely as the East End Raid. Lieutenant Mike Hodd had been planning it for some time based on handed-down intelligence which located an insurgent presence in the southeast corner of the city.

Just a few months before, on Christmas night, a section of up-armored Humvees from 1/7's Weapons Company had been attacked in that area by dozens of fanatical fighters at extremely close range. "They were trying to open our doors, trying to capture us," recalls Jack Sutherland, the section leader that night. "My gunner was using his 9mm [pistol] because they were so close. My driver ran down at least three guys."[22]

This time, India Company would go in heavy with the 2nd Platoon and attachments, mounted in four AAVs. Their aim was to capture or kill leaders of a cell known to be planting IEDs and firing mortars at Gannon. The cell called themselves the "Night Wolves" and were just one strand in the interlinked web of insurgent groups operating in Al-Qaim District.

The plan was to drive swiftly through the city at zero-dark-thirty, avoiding any effective opposition, then raid four target houses while the residents were still fast asleep. The column would consist of four massive AAVs, each with three crewmen from the 4th Amphibious Assault Battalion. At the trail end of the column that night, Corporal Chris Nothstine was the crew chief and .50 cal gunner in trac number four.

As with any plan, however, reality shifted rapidly after first contact with the enemy. In his hand-written journal, Nothstine describes the unexpected opposition encountered that night and the intensity of the action:

> *At the stroke of 0200 we rolled into the city... We went to Canal Street, then south on Colt 45 where the D-9 [bulldozer] had*

cleared the obstacles. Once we got on Market, we took fire two blocks in ... I was amazed when they first opened up ... Constant fire all the way down Market. The fire was from the rooftops ... They were firing straight tracers.

—Chris Nothstine[23]

The insurgents were awake and ready. As the AAVs raced east along Market Street, their gunners returned fire as did the squads in the back. In the troop compartment of Nothstine's trac were nine Marines from 1st Squad, 2nd Platoon, including SAW gunner Lance Corporal Joe Rivera. He remembers that night like it was yesterday. "I went to fire back and after two rounds my SAW jammed," says Rivera. "Somehow, I cleared the jam, put rounds back on the feed tray, slammed the cover closed, racked the bolt, and started throwing rounds down range ... I went through three drums of 5.56 on that raid."[24]

Amid all the incoming fire, the deafening roar of the guns and with the AAV drivers' hearts pounding, trac three and four made a wrong turn and ended up in the narrow, dangerous backstreets of eastern Husaybah. As Nothstine makes clear, they were hemmed in and highly vulnerable to close-range attack:

Two-story buildings were on both sides. We took accurate AK fire. I opened up with the .50 cal to suppress as Rivera did the same. Then we took a left on a dead end. Massa (my driver) reported an RPG ten meters in front. We turned around, and ran over two fences, a garden, and a car. On the way back no one fired [at us], thanks to the .50 cal and the grunts laying down suppressing fire.

—Chris Nothstine[25]

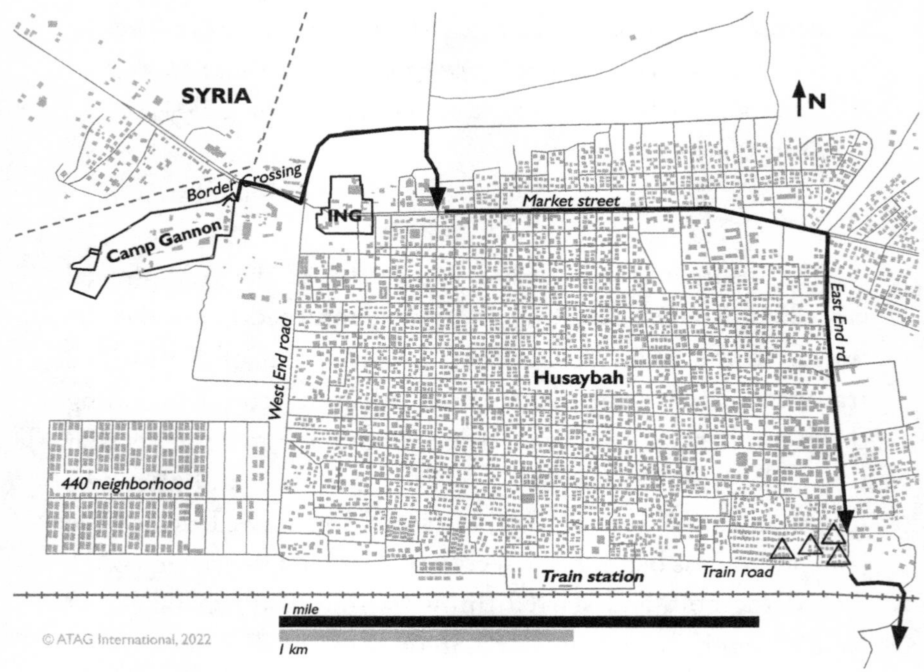

After several gut-wrenching moments, the two crews found their objectives and their tracs lurched to a halt. The grunts flowed out the back and hit their target houses, taking sporadic enemy fire. Suddenly an insurgent with an RPG popped out from the shadows just 25 meters from a still-loaded AAV. Fortunately, a guardian angel intervened. From a well-selected overwatch position south of the city, a scout-sniper engaged from about 250 meters out, killing the RPG gunner just as he was sighting in.

There was no time to think about the near disaster. They needed to finish the raid before the enemy could coalesce. A few IED materials and a few weapons were found, according to Nothstine, then blown in place. The HVIs and other military-aged males were detained, flexi-cuffed, blindfolded, and loaded into AAVs. Then the column pulled out under a few last bursts of AK fire, crossing the train tracks to the south to head back to Gannon. Sometime later, after the adrenaline started to wear off and he had a moment to reflect, Chris Nothstine recorded some post-mission details and intense feelings:

> *We're all back... [and] we did awesome. Thank God... My crew did great... Our grunts were constantly laying down fire... [We hit] four target houses. 15 confirmed kills. No WIA, no KIA... When the first rounds went off over my head and tracers were everywhere, I thought of Lisa, and then that was it. The rest of the time we were under fire and in the zone... [There are] many bullet holes in the track, and the 3rd shock on the starboard side was sheared off.*
>
> —**Chris Nothstine**[26]

While the East End Raid accomplished its tactical objectives, it was also a wake-up call. The heavy enemy fire and the number of insurgents encountered showed how dangerous the city was. There'd been no friendly casualties, but they'd had several close calls. And while leaders of the so-called Night Wolves had been snared, there were no illusions that the wider insurgent network in Husaybah had been significantly dampened. In a post-mission summary, Lieutenant Hodd made the following remarks and recommendations:

> *Unit engaged at multiple locations during movement indicating a large presence of insurgent activity in Husaybah... If traveling in vehicles, rehearse dismount under fire, dismounting with casualties, actions with disabled vehicles under fire, etc... The*

EMDCOA [enemy's most dangerous course of action] is a layered ambush within the city and this can happen anywhere at any time. Have immediate action drills down.[27]

After the East End Raid, India Company would focus on smaller, dismounted raids and building a new position north of the city to draw out the enemy and change the dynamic.

See **bastardsandbrothers.com** for notes, photos, maps, etc.

8. FURY

With Lima Company guarding Al-Asad and India Company ensconced on Camp Gannon, the core of 3/2's available combat power resided in Kilo Company. For the majority of the deployment, Lieutenant Colonel Mundy and Major Day relied on the 180 Marines of Company K to patrol across the entire battalion AO, secure Camp Al-Qaim and other key terrain, and execute larger combat operations. In essence, Kilo Company was the battalion's strike force that could be brought to bear when and where necessary.

Additionally, from RCT-2's perspective, Kilo Company was the only active-duty rifle company available to conduct operations throughout AO Denver. As such, Colonel Davis would frequently call for Kilo Company to bolster 3/25 during operations in the Haditha-Hit corridor. The regimental commander had high confidence in the unit's abilities and more than once referred to Kilo Company as the "fire brigade" he could move quickly to quench the hotspots.

Captain Chris Ieva (pronounced "eye-ee-vah") was a highly motivated officer who had been in the battalion since 2003. Coming from New Brunswick, NJ and a strong Italian-American family, he had a lifelong ambition to become a Marine officer and worked to secure a nomination to the U.S. Naval Academy in Annapolis. There he chose the Marine Corps option and was commissioned as a second lieutenant in 1996. After leading a rifle platoon for another battalion and then commanding 3/2's Headquarters Company in late 2003, he became Kilo's commander in the summer of 2004.

At 31 years old, he had nine years in the Corps and had earned a reputation as an intense, tactically-oriented leader who pushed for maximum performance from himself and his men. By the end of 2004, Ieva had put the stamp of his personality on Kilo and was driving hard to prepare the unit for Iraq. This would be his second overseas deployment. Anticipating the dangers ahead, he worked relentlessly to fill Kilo's training schedule with events to get them ready for the fight.

This put high expectations, and pressure, on his lieutenants. "He was always switched on," remembers Nate Smith. "He pushed us really hard."[1] Marc Bullock expressed similar feelings. "At the time, I hated his guts, but he understood the threat we were facing and prepared us for that. Now I greatly appreciate his leadership...His ruthlessness in training us and his aggressiveness in combat saved lives."[2]

The other half of the company's senior leadership came to Kilo right before deployment. First Sergeant Sean Gregory arrived in December, just in time for the battalion's training in California. Normally, plugging in a first sergeant that close to deployment wouldn't be ideal, but in this case, it worked out well. Gregory had already been in a position at 2nd Regiment for several months so knew many of 3/2's key players. He proved to be an exceptional choice.

Raised on a North Carolina farm, Gregory enlisted in the Marines right out of high school. By the time he joined 3/2, he had 18 years of service under his belt, including a Drill Instructor tour at Quantico, and had combat experience in Panama and Liberia. He and First Sergeant Donnie Brazeal of India Company had seen action together in the chaotic streets of Monrovia during the evacuation of U.S. citizens from Liberia in 1996, so the two senior NCOs had a strong connection.

Upon arrival in Kilo, Gregory quickly made an impact. "My emphasis was to keep our Marines busy and focused," he says. "I've always believed if you take care of the little things, big things will take care of themselves."[3] He and Captain Ieva pried every useful hour out of the training schedule, working on land navigation, house clearing, fire and maneuver, calls for fire, and coordination with other units. "We'd run drills in a barracks courtyard or anyplace we could," he recalls. "Sean Gregory was rock solid," remembers Ieva. "He was a professional. I always got his unvarnished opinion, which I needed and appreciated... But I knew once an order was given, he would execute it as if it were his own."[4]

Rounding out Kilo's headquarters section were the XO and the company Gunny. First Lieutenant John Hayes was a highly-skilled young officer and the company's second-in-command. "Hayes was brilliant," says Ieva. As XO, Hayes made sure the company's weapons, training, and organization were harmonized, and at several crucial junctures during combat he would step into the action. Gunnery Sergeant Tracy Linch was another vital component. Like First Sergeant Gregory, he was brand new to Kilo. He'd barely had time to unpack before he was on his way to Iraq as part of the advance team, but he quickly made his mark. "Gunny Linch was always positive and a huge motivator. The Marines loved him." says Gregory. "He ensured the platoons were kept supplied with ammo, chow, water, whatever they needed for the mission. He was the backbone of the company."[5]

As standard, Kilo was made up of a weapons platoon and three rifle platoons. First Lieutenant Clint Cummings capably led the fire support team and managed the effective employment of mortars, machine guns, and assault teams in the weapons platoon. Cummings also ran the newly-formed company intelligence cell, a unique innovation at the time. Later on, the Marine Corps formally adopted the formation of such teams, but in 2005, Kilo Company was blazing new trails with its organically-formed intel cell. The information it generated was pivotal to success in several operations.

Second Lieutenants Marc Bullock and Nate Smith led 1st and 2nd Platoons, and each would be promoted to First Lieutenant during the deployment. Kilo's most experienced platoon commander, First Lieutenant Joe Clemmey, led 3rd Platoon. Naturally taciturn, with a strong Massachusetts brogue, Clemmey had been an enlisted Marine just a few years before and brooked no bullshit. "He was a quick learner and a gifted combat leader," recalls Ieva.[6]

TIE GOES TO THE MARINES

A primary feature of Kilo's commander, and hence the company as a whole, was technical and tactical competence. Earlier in his career, Ieva had led a mortar platoon and was well-versed in weapons capabilities, how to employ them most effectively, and using what infantry professionals call "geometry of fires" to maximum advantage. "He was by far the best tactician I had the pleasure to serve with," recalls Gregory. "Watching him fight Kilo Company was like watching a work of art."[7]

This focus on technical excellence, backed up by strong leaders at every level, permeated the company. Kilo had studied and adopted the hard-won lessons from other units' after-action reports. One was to win the "four-second firefight," gaining fire superiority at the outset of any clash. Marksmanship was key, as was using all weapons in a combined-arms approach. The enemy needed to be isolated, cutting them off from retreating. These tenets were stressed at company level all the way down to the fire teams.

The company's other defining characteristic was the unsparing use of firepower when Marine lives were on the line. "His approach was always to avoid casualties by being smart and using firepower as needed," recalls Bullock.[8] While the Rules of Engagement (ROE) were scrupulously followed, once those conditions were met, Captain Ieva was willing to unleash whatever weapons were available to kill the enemy. "This wasn't a game, and we didn't fight at parity," he reflects. "We focused on winning...I always felt my knowledge and tactical education should help Marines survive and win. So, in a firefight I didn't want to be proportional."[9] His shorthand phrase for this uncompromising approach towards any armed adversary was, "Tie goes to the Marines."

Underpinning everything was the drive to get the fundamentals right. "We had thorough and mature pre-combat routines, and we simplified our procedures for CASEVAC," stresses Ieva.[10] Another subtle, but important, technique was the use of platoon recognition symbols for quick visual ID. On the back of each Kilo Marine's helmet was stitched a small, colored patch. Red was for 1st Platoon, white for 2nd, blue for 3rd and green for Weapons. In close urban combat, leaders could quickly see where their men were and locate the seams between units. These were the little things that proved time and again to be lifesavers when the bullets began to fly.

Back home, the company's callsign had been "Voodoo," but soon after arriving in Al-Qaim it was discovered that a Marine air unit was already using that name. To avoid potential for confusion over the radios and other channels, Captain Ieva would need to pick a new callsign. With no time to get ideas from within the company, he came up with a name that had a personal meaning. "I picked something that reminded me of my son, Fiorello, nicknamed 'Fiori'. It reminded me that I was entrusted with other folks' sons." says Ieva.[11] Kilo Company would use the tactical callsign "Fury" for the duration of the 2005 deployment and as its commander, Ieva would go by "Fury 6."

---

9. OUTPOSTS

We were a squad plus, up on a hill with a 60-foot antenna sticking up. The enemy could see everything we did and hit us constantly. We could pretty much guarantee that after changeover we were going to get hit… It sucked! The all-MRE diet, sleeping in bunkers, and the godawful heat. But there were good times too. We dropped hundreds of mortar rounds, ran illum [illumination] missions for snipers, and had some serious Spades tournaments. And I saw the most beautiful sunsets and stars I've ever seen.

—**David Pape**[1]

RETRANS

About five miles north of Camp Al-Qaim, on a barren rise in the landscape, a cluster of sandbagged bunkers had been hacked out of hard-baked earth. The bunkers fortified an austere outpost set up by previous battalions as a radio relay, or retransmission site, with a tall antenna mast and equipment that received and boosted radio signals. In place for at least a year before 3/2's arrival, its purpose was to extend communications coverage into the low ground along the river.

It was configured in a rough triangle with weapons bunkers

at each corner. At the western corner was the big .50 cal machine gun, the "Ma-Deuce," covering a bridge across a dry wadi and a long stretch of highway. From the northern bunker, the Mark-19 could lob 40mm grenades out to an extreme range of over 2,000 meters, across a wide stretch of the highway and surrounding terrain. Behind them to the southeast, a third low-slung bunker housed the M240 medium machine-gun, with a wide arc of fire covering the open desert from the southwest to northeast. In the center were the communications and command post (CP) bunkers.

Responsibility for protecting the retransmission site fell to Kilo Company, adding to the company's burden of manning static defensive positions at Camp Al-Qaim. Any Marines manning towers and bunkers were not available for offensive operations. Consequently, Kilo Company took several steps early on to improve the position's defenses and sustainability. Manning was standardized at a squad plus the heavy weapons crews and the rotation was set at a week, although the pace of battalion operations meant some men would get stranded at Retrans for considerably longer.

Captain Ieva christened the humble post "Battle Position Khe Sahn," to instill a sense of purpose. The name harkened back to the embattled forward base in the highlands of South Vietnam and the Marines' historic fight in 1969 to keep it from being overrun. Among themselves, though, the grunts of 3/2 mostly called the place "Retrans."

SQUAD LEADERS REALM

Conditions were incredibly primitive, with the men literally living in holes in the ground, under cover of plywood, two-by-fours, and sandbags. The summer heat was crippling, easily topping 120 degrees in the open, even worse in the sweltering bunkers. Without refrigeration, bottled water matched the ambient temperature. The contents tasted like brewed, plastic-tasting tea. Meals were MREs, augmented by junk food sent from home. Bodily waste was disposed of in the time-honored ways, including regularly burning it in foul-smelling shitcans, hopefully downwind of the bunkers.

Officers and senior NCOs mostly stayed away from Retrans. There was a conscious decision by Kilo's leadership to let the squad leaders have free reign there, keeping PFCs and lance corporals on task and on mission in the way they saw fit. This translated into a degree of freedom from the rules enforced on Camp AQ, particularly the Sergeant Major's uniform standards. As long as a Marine was ready to man a weapon, no one cared much if his boots were tied, his pants bloused, or even if they were on.

Retrans took frequent enemy fire, though, which could make the relaxed dress standards risky. Corporal Jimmy Rooks narrowly escaped disaster during an early attack. "On our very first day there, we got hit." he says. "It was so hot, and I'd gone outside the Mk19 bunker without my flak or kevlar to take a piss. Just as I got by the wire, a rocket sailed overhead and a mortar round hit about twenty yards in front of me, spraying me with rocks. I ran back and dove through the bunker window."[2]

The gunners defending Retrans prided themselves on their speed and accuracy in responding. The crew of the 81mm mortar was especially busy. "Our mortar guys were really good," recalls Steve Gray, a machine gunner with Kilo's weapons platoon. "They could return fire so quickly, getting rounds out of the tubes, putting them downrange really accurately."

The indirect fire attacks were rarely accurate enough to cause damage, but sometimes they managed to get everyone's attention. "Because of the terrain and elevation, rounds would usually fall short, or go long over us. They couldn't zero in on our little hilltop," Gray says. "But one time a rocket came in and hit just below the Mark19 bunker. It came in on a very flat trajectory and impacted only about 40 meters short of us. Fortunately, it didn't go off, and we went out later and looked at it. It was a Chinese-made rocket, about six feet long."[3]

Between attacks, fighting off boredom was the primary challenge. Marines on watch had to be alert at their posts, but that left their buddies to come up with innovative ways to entertain themselves. Death matches were staged between scorpions and vicious-looking camel spiders placed in an empty ammo can or MRE box. Less-than-lethal, but equally raucous MMA matches between Marines were also common. For musical entertainment, a CD player was wired into an old military radio set. There were also legendary Poker or Spades tournaments and marathon Monopoly games. The anti-boredom activities, however, could always be rudely interrupted:

> *After we'd been there awhile, the attacks got routine for us. Late in the deployment, one of the comms guys came out from AQ to pull a tour at Retrans. He hadn't seen any combat. He was playing Monopoly in one of the bunkers with us. Suddenly we hear the "ka-chunk, ka-chunk" of enemy mortars going off. By then, we knew exactly how much time rounds would take to hit, so our first*

priority was to tidy up the game board, straighten up the little houses and such. Then we scrambled to take cover. While we did that, the comms guy kind of froze up. Freaked out. The rounds hit a ways away, no big deal, and we came right back to the game, like nothing had happened. We were just saying, "So whose turn is it?" but this guy's still traumatized. He thought we were being overrun or something.

—Steve Gray[4]

In truth, though, there was a real chance that the enemy might mount a determined attack against Retrans. One particular incident highlighted that possibility. On 19 April, multiple insurgents used the cover of a heavy sandstorm to engage Retrans with more than harassment fire. Just after noon, apparently thinking the blowing sand would keep the Marines from responding, about 15 to 20 men started firing machine guns and rockets at Retrans from down by the highway bridge and a nearby building. John Parina, another gunner in Kilo Company, describes the action:

We were playing spades in the CP when we started taking small arms fire... The insurgents tried to make their move when we couldn't see. But unfortunately for them, we could see their muzzle flashes. We all ran to our respective bunkers and started firing back... The .50 and Mk19 were in the front where we were taking fire. We also dismounted the 240 and ran it up to the .50 cal bunker and [used it] to return fire. I was on the Mk19, and took the traverse and elevation off the gun, so I could track targets faster. We returned a lot of rounds before it quieted down.

—John Parina[5]

The Marines had put down heavy fire in spite of the sandstorm, including four hundred .50 cal rounds and some thirty 40mm grenades, quashing any plans the enemy may have had. But there was cause for concern. "That incident was somewhat prolonged, a clear probe," Chris Ieva recalls. "It alarmed me a bit because it underlined the risk...But it also gave me confidence that the squad leaders out there were capable of handling things."[6]

As the deployment progressed, Retrans was increasingly used as a staging point for raids and other operations. The scout-sniper platoon utilized it as a start-point for missions into the river towns while WarPig mobile assault platoons would sometimes launch raids from the windblown hilltop.

SHEEP ON THE BARBIE

As Kilo Marines rotated through, they gradually improved their defenses and living conditions at the outpost. Mortar crews probably spent the most time there, spearheading many of these improvements. One of them, Lance Corporal David Pape, came up with a new way to relieve the culinary monotony of MREs, at least for a day:

> *The week of July 4th I told everybody to watch for the sheepherders and if they came let me know. On the 3rd, two kids had a herd down by the bridge. So, six or eight of us kicked out a little patrol... We get down there and traded 20 American dollars and a case of MREs for a sheep. We put it in the M240 bunker overnight. Next day we killed it and gutted it. Hung it on the front of a 7-ton, skinned it out and quartered it. They had a pan and a grate*

in the .50 cal bunker, and some Tony Cajun's seasoning. So, me and Wheatley, a kid from the 81s, cooked it up and we all gathered around the fire and ate our fill. It came out pretty good. It was fresh meat, hoof-to-table... It felt symbolic. We were Marines at war on Independence Day, and it was rugged and manly. We were all thinking what other guys our age were doing back home, or what we would have been doing. And that what we were actually doing was way more badass!!

— **David Pape**[7]

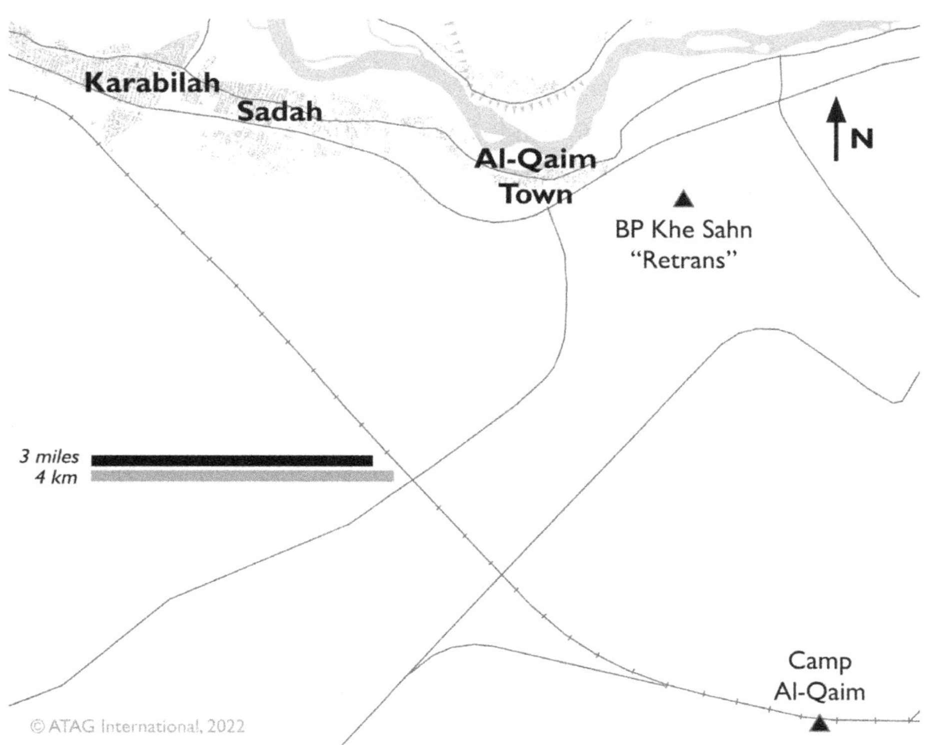

TRASH OP

On a warm June night, Corporal Will Marconi and the men of 3rd Squad, 1st Platoon, India Company were fully alert at their observation post (OP) overlooking Husaybah. There had been a lot of action that day, as insurgents engaged them from various buildings in the city. The firefights intensified that night, involving three different elements; Marconi's squad in their heavily sandbagged position, the men of 2nd Platoon posted at the ING compound, and a scout-sniper team operating from within the city.[8] For some reason, the insurgents had decided to test the Marine positions with more than their usual pop shots. Gunfire echoed from multiple engagements, while tracers crisscrossed over the northern neighborhoods.

An RPG round suddenly streaked towards the OP, exploding short of 3rd Squad's position. Then another exploded behind them. "I was getting concerned for our safety," says Marconi. "We kept two AT-4 rockets out there, to counter possible VBIED attacks, but I decided we needed to use one to respond."[9] He told Lance Corporal Hartsock to prep an AT-4, while tossing Lance Corporal Ron Jackson a mag full of 5.56mm tracer rounds. Jackson had spotted the exact location of the RPG launches and used the tracers to mark the target.

After positively ID'ing the building, then literally hanging off the side of the OP with his squad mates grabbing his belt, Hartsock launched the AT-4 and it flew straight and true for some 400 meters. It was a phenomenal shot. The unguided 84mm rocket struck the exact spot Jackson had marked. The results were dramatic. The building immediately exploded and burst into flames, with raging columns of fire reaching a hundred feet into the air. By the light of the conflagration, enemy fighters could be seen, some fleeing, others advancing to fire at the OP. Some were caught in the open and engaged by the scout-snipers:

> *It was pretty wild. Something in that house exploded, and there were flames everywhere. It seemed like the whole street caught on fire. At the time, we thought we'd hit an arms cache or something, the way it went up like that... Later, we found out it was a bakery and the locals complained because it was destroyed... But we knew the RPGs had come from there. No doubt. And us shooting that AT-4 pretty much ended the fight that night.*
>
> **—Will Marconi**[10]

CHANGING THE GAME

The observation post Marconi, Jackson, and Hartsock were manning that night was officially named "Battle Position Harman", after a popular lieutenant who had died back in North Carolina. But India Marines mostly called it "Trash OP." It was a two-story fortification made of sandbags, lumber, and HESCO barriers, situated in the open fields just north of Husaybah.

Before 3/2's arrival, Baker Company 1/7 had used an abandoned house along "Trash Road" as an observation post. But insurgents had eventually attacked that position with a suicide car bomb, injuring several Marines. The house was subsequently demolished before 3/2 arrived. That left key parts of northern Husaybah, especially Market Street, unobserved. Gunny Hogancamp took on the task of building an entirely new OP, impregnable to any conceivable attack. There were limited resources to build it, so Hogancamp relied on those he did have; men, sand and innovation.

Everyone who was at Camp Gannon in March of 2005 remembers the "sandbag rule." Before anyone could eat a hot meal, they had to fill ten sandbags, regardless of rank or position. With some 280 personnel and two hot meals a day, the sandbags piled up quickly. Meanwhile, construction plans were drawn up and resources gathered. "Our intent was to accelerate operations and make certain changes to our position," explains Mike Hodd. "Trash OP was part of Frank Diorio's vision. It was a first step to gaining greater maneuverability around the northern side of the city, and the ability to more surgically insert forces where and when we needed to."[11]

Another part of the vision was to build the OP rapidly, to achieve a certain level of shock on the enemy. For months, insurgents had enjoyed free reign in the northeast quadrant of the city and along Market Street. Building the new outpost would change that:

> *Trash OP would free us up to maneuver into the city from the north, and to observe enemy activities along north/south streets into the city. We wanted to build a structure overnight, so when the residents and insurgents woke up, they'd see it and realize we had an unassailable position, we'd changed the game up.*
>
> **—Brian Hogancamp**[12]

By early April, thousands of sandbags had been filled and other construction materials were in place. The intense and unexpected resistance encountered by the East End raid on April 2nd drove home the necessity for the new battle position. It was time to execute the plan.

Just after dark on 6 April, a convoy of Humvees, AAVs, two tanks, a front-loader, and a massive D-9 bulldozer rolled out the eastern gate of Camp Gannon, cut north of the ING compound then out into the farm fields. In darkness, infantrymen disgorged from the tracs to set up security, while the engineers started unloading gear. Because of the threat, all the work would be done lights-out, using night vision goggles (NVGs).

It was a race against daylight. The first task was to set up and fill the HESCO barriers, to protect against incoming. Next came the center structure, built with thousands of sandbags. This created a two-story "castle" with walls several feet thick, reinforced with lumber. Without proper building materials, creative solutions were employed to get the job done. "We used aircraft cargo pallets as the floor of the second story," recalls Hogancamp.[13]

By dawn, as insurgents in Husaybah began stirring, they were met with an unfamiliar sight. There, in plain view, loomed a new and imposing structure. While they'd heard the heavy equipment operating that night, they had no idea the Marines had built a heavily fortified position in their backyard. Quickly, they started to realize its significance.

From that point forward, the battle position was constantly manned on a rotating basis by a full-up rifle squad, along with a guntruck crew from WarPig 1, a forward observer (FO) to coordinate mortar fire from Camp Gannon, a corpsman, and sometimes a scout-sniper team. The post's machine-gun positions provided interlocking fire in all directions, and mutually supported the ING compound. More importantly, Marines could now scan down the north-south length of key streets for several blocks into the commercial center of the city.

Over the next few weeks, the position was improved and further hardened. More HESCO barriers were set up on all four sides. A fortified position was built to fit one of WarPig's guntrucks, which added another heavy weapon. With HESCOs walling off the perimeter and open fields beyond them, there was virtually no chance an enemy could approach without being decisively engaged.

Insurgents would attack from longer range, however, firing from cover along the north edge of the city. Usually, they fired just a few desultory shots, but sometimes they would open up with more numbers and heavier weapons. Almost every day there was at least one firefight involving Trash OP. This was by design. "We put it 350 meters from the edge of the city on purpose," Diorio later explained. "It was not quite max-effective range of their weapons systems, but close enough that they would probably try to expose themselves to try to hit it."[14]

As the point man for constructing the BP Harman, Gunny Hogancamp pulled off a feat that usually requires a battalion of Navy Seabees. Thousands of sandbags were filled, some 300 HESCO barriers were set up, and 70 tons of dirt, sand, and gravel were moved, all under fire or the threat of attack. In the months ahead, the position would play a key part in India Company's fight. It provided mutual support for the ING compound (a fact many insurgents learned the hard way), a secure base to launch raids into the city or the farm country to the north, and excellent early warning of insurgent activity.

But essentially, Trash OP was built as "insurgent bait." This made it popular with the grunts as they knew they would probably get into a fight whenever they pulled a rotation there. A Marine posted at Trash OP was literally on the very edge, his squad standing watch between the Syrian border and a hostile city, living on MREs, sleeping on a cot in the bowels of a sandbag fortress, and hoping for another firefight. It was exactly what they'd signed up for.

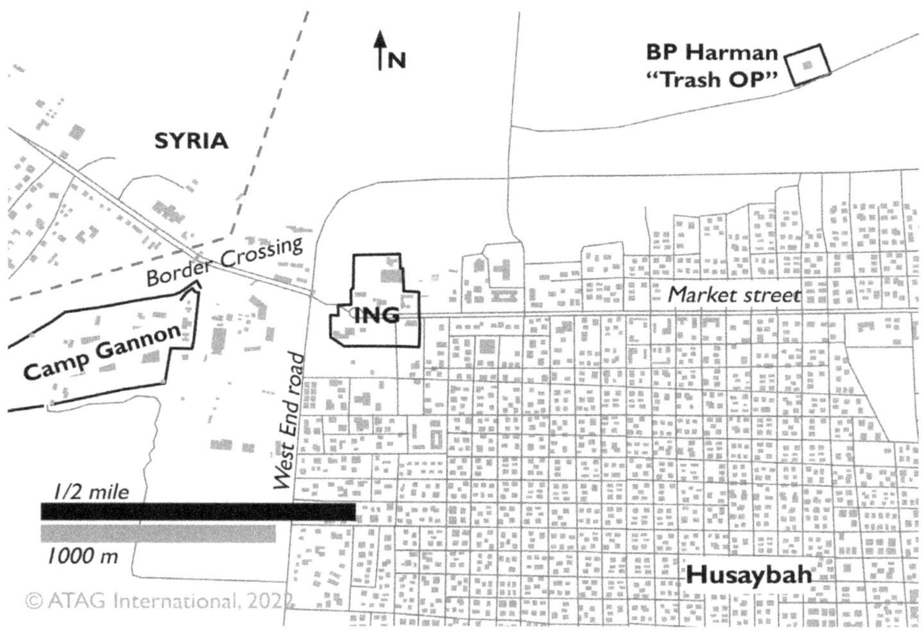

See **bastardsandbrothers.com** for notes, photos, maps, etc.

10. ENEMIES

One day early in the deployment, Kilo's 2nd Platoon was given a pop-up mission and loaded into AAVs to check out a report of dead bodies at an intersection. "It was the middle of the day when we got out there," remembers Jimmy Rooks, one of the squad leaders. "Even before we could see them, we could smell the blood and the bodies."[1] Lance Corporal Brandon Puhlman also witnessed the macabre scene:

> *There were eight bodies. Apparently, it was a family. They all had their heads cut off and placed on their stomachs, hands under their chin. There were men, women, and a little boy eight or nine years old. A little girl too. We heard later they'd been killed for helping out the U.S.*
>
> —**Brandon Puhlman**[2]

It was a jarring reminder that they had crossed into a dark-hearted realm where life was cheap, and the enemy's brutality knew no bounds. "I wanted to wage death on whoever had done this, but we didn't know who it was. It left me with a festering anger," says Puhlman. "I can still see that sight so vividly. The little girl had on a blue floral dress."

THE I-WORD

Many 3/2 Marines have haunting memories of the savagery they witnessed in Al-Qaim, almost always carried out by unseen, unknown perpetrators. Their experience highlights one of the war's most perplexing questions; Who exactly was the enemy?

Early on, Bush administration officials described anyone fighting against the coalition as "dead-enders" and "evil-doers." Secretary of Defense Donald Rumsfeld stubbornly refused to call them insurgents. To acknowledge there was an insurgency would be a tacit admission that the war would be long and costly.

Eventually, the semantic charade became too painful, and the dreaded I-word crept back into the military's lexicon, but a conceptual problem still caused muddled thinking up and down the command chain. It took too long for the coalition to grasp that rather than facing a single enemy in Iraq, they were fighting a multi-headed hydra. The insurgency had no central leadership or organized hierarchy. It was a viral, amorphous, and highly-adaptable network of networks.

As 2004 turned into 2005, coalition leaders and spokesmen were still using made-up, catchall terms such as "Anti-Iraqi-Forces" (AIF), "Anti-Iraqi Elements" (AIE) or "Anti Coalition Forces" (ACF), lumping together a baffling array of extremist groups. The most obvious problem with such crude labels was the lack of distinction between insurgent organizations. For example, Sunni- and Shiite-based groups operated (with rare exceptions) in different areas and as wholly separate insurgencies with very different motivations. Lumping them all into the same category was a gross oversimplification.

For the Marines in Anbar, fighting exclusively against Sunni groups, categorizing the enemy was only slightly less daunting. By 2005, Marine intelligence assessments broke the insurgency in Anbar into four main strains or branches, according to now-declassified documents:*

Former Regime Elements (FRE) were loosely defined as groups with a nationalistic bent, focused on ejecting foreign troops from Iraq.[3] Many had connections with the Ba'athist party and Saddam's military or security apparatus. Typically, they were less motivated by religion and the jihadist ideology, although some FREs used Islamic labels and leveraged religion for their own purposes. The nationalist-leaning 1920 Revolution Brigade was initially categorized as an FRE group. It had a strong presence in Ramadi and the Hit-Haditha corridor and many fighters with military training.

Sunni Arab Rejectionists (SAR), was a new category coined as individuals and groups emerged that were willing to engage in the political process, while still fighting against foreign troops. Basically, they co-opted the motivations of nationalist FRE groups and tribal coalitions while rejecting the extreme ideology and tactics of the jihadists. As an example of this shift, by late 2005 Marine intel analysts had moved the 1920 Brigade from the FRE category into the SAR column.[4]

Criminal elements was a catchall term reflecting the hybridization of the insurgency. It encompassed smuggling gangs,

---

* A primary source for this chapter is the Marine Corps document, Study of the Insurgency in Anbar Province, Iraq, from 13 June 2007, which was declassified in 2015. This remarkable, multi-chapter study was compiled from hundreds of contemporaneous intelligence reports and summaries. See https://ahec.armywarcollege.edu/CENTCOM-IRAQ-papers/

mercenary IED cells, and guns-for-hire as well as tribal militias. As one intel assessment stated, "this dynamic of criminal elements allying with insurgents—or insurgents acting as profit-driven criminals—became a constant problem."[5] At the start of 2005, while the Marines were still figuring out how to relate to the Sunni tribes, most tribal forces were simply labeled as criminals.

Sunni Religious Extremist (SRE) groups, or jihadists, rose in power through 2004 to become the most dangerous component of the insurgency. Their main objective was to impose an Islamic caliphate in Iraq by any means necessary. These were the groups bringing mujahideen from across the Islamic world to fight in Iraq. Although they included Iraqis, they were usually led and dominated by foreign-born jihadists, leading many analysts to tag them as foreign fighter (FF) groups. The most prominent of these were Ansar al-Sunna, (Protectors of the Sunni or AS), and the extremely violent, fast-growing network calling itself Unity and Jihad (JTJ).

While the number of insurgents in Anbar was extremely hard to judge, Marine intelligence estimated 10,000 active fighters, with 45% in nationalist groups (FRE and SAR), 25% in criminal elements, and 30% as religious extremists.6 But the mix was anything but static. The insurgency was an ever-shifting kaleidoscope with hundreds of groups and cells combining, recombining, and often taking new names. Some groups were blatantly mercenary, hiring out to the highest bidder. As the same estimate notes, the insurgency showed "a remarkable fluidity of alliances, motivations and ideologies."

WOLF AT THE DOOR

A perfect example of this fluidity was seen in Al-Qaim. As the war began, the main militant group in the district was a hybrid of criminals, former regime members and Islamic extremists known as *Al-Theeb*, meaning "The Wolf." Based in Husaybah, the group had been a smuggling gang even before the war. Reportedly started in 1997 by a former Iraqi soldier, in 2003 foreign and Iraqi jihadists joined Al-Theeb, transforming it into what intel analysts described as a criminal insurgency.[7]

The enemy in Al-Qaim had morphed still further by the time 3/2 arrived. Intelligence reporting at the time listed four identifiable groups in the area, including two jihadist splinter groups and one categorized as FRE. The fourth, and still the largest, was the Al-Theeb criminal organization, although it had also merged with jihadists and foreign fighters. It is quite likely, then, that the "Night Wolves" targeted by India Company during the East End Raid were part of, or an offshoot from, Al-Theeb.

For most Marines, it hardly mattered which group was which or what they called themselves. If someone shot at them, he was an enemy and deserved whatever return fire could be sent his way. The esoteric art of tracking and describing the ever-shifting insurgency was the realm of the intel types, not the grunts. But well out of a rifleman's line-of-sight, beyond the range of their sensors and standoff weapons, their enemy was shape-shifting again.

SHEIKH OF THE SLAUGHTERERS

Five black-clad men stand solemnly in a featureless room, their faces shrouded. The man in the middle, stockier than the others, reads a rambling statement in Arabic. Sitting before them sits a young, Caucasian man, shackled, and dressed in an orange jumpsuit. As the statement ends, the hooded reader declares, "We tell you that the dignity of the Muslims is not redeemed except by blood and souls ... You will receive nothing from us but coffin after coffin slaughtered in this way." He draws a knife from under his clothing, and the others begin chanting "Alla-hu akhbar!" The knife is a common butcher's blade, used for slaughtering goats and sheep. And then the screaming begins.

The horrific video of 11 May 2004, showing the beheading of the American contractor, Nick Berg, was the world's gruesome introduction to the man known as Abu-Musab al-Zarqawi. In subsequent months, more macabre videos were released by Zarqawi's agile and adept media arm, catapulting him to the forefront of the global jihadist movement.

Ahmad Fadhil Nazzal al-Khalaylah, born in 1966, was raised in the hard-scrabble industrial city of Zarqa, Jordan. By the time he was a teenager, he was a street-level thug with a history of violence. At age 19, he fled arrest in Jordan to fight in Afghanistan. He returned to Jordan in 1993 and was quickly arrested for extremist activities. When he left prison five years later, he had the status of an "emir", with followers and connections across the region. He had also taken on his nom-de-guerre Abu-Musab al-Zarqawi, which roughly translates to "our strong brother from Zarqa."

Zarqawi returned to Afghanistan in 1999 as a jihadist leader in his own right. He met Osama Bin Laden there but did not offer bayat or formal allegiance. While al-Qaeda helped finance his training camp, Zarqawi ran his own organization, called Jama'at al-Tawhid wal-Jihad (Unity and Jihad, or Monotheism and Jihad), often abbreviated as JTJ. Reportedly he thought neither al-Qaeda nor the Taliban were sufficiently serious about waging holy war. For his part, Bin Laden thought Zarqawi was "aggressively ambitious, abrasive, and overbearing."[8]

After 9/11 and the resulting American onslaught, Zarqawi fled Afghanistan, first to Iran, and then Iraq. Soon after the 2003 invasion, Zarqawi and JTJ began carving a violent path of terror. He was behind the suicide bombing of the UN headquarters in August and a similar attack on the Red Cross in October, driving both organizations out of the country and setting a pattern that would only worsen. Through further barbaric spectacles like the Berg killing and more suicide bombings, he rapidly gained funding and followers, who called him the "Sheikh of the Slaughterers."

UNHOLY ALLIANCE

In mid-2004, the U.S. raised the bounty for Zarqawi's capture to $25 million, equaling the reward for Osama Bin Laden. In the press he was billed as the new face of jihad and by 2004 his growing terror network was arguably more important than al-Qaeda's. He was the man on the battlefield, gaining recruits, power, and influence while Bin Laden and senior al-Qaeda figures were in hiding. And it was Zarqawi who saw conflict in Iraq as an opportunity to ignite sectarian war, then build a new Islamic caliphate amidst the ashes. When al-Qaeda Central urged Zarqawi to scale back his savage attacks against Shiites, he responded defiantly, “Souls will perish, and blood will be spilled. This is exactly what we want.”[9]

Despite substantial differences over tactics and objectives, Zarqawi and al-Qaeda's leadership eventually reached some sort of accord. On 17 October, 2004, after months of long-distance negotiations, Zarqawi formally declared *bayat* to Osama Bin Laden and al-Qaeda in a statement issued via the web:

> *Let it be known that al-Tawhid wal-Jihad pledges both its leaders and its soldiers to the mujahid commander, Sheikh Osama bin Laden, in word and in deed, and to jihad for the sake of God... Let us cleanse all Muslim lands of every infidel and wicked apostate.*[10]

Soon after the declaration, JTJ also announced its new name to be *Tanzim Qaedat al-Jihad fi Bilad al-Rafidayn* (abbreviated as TQJBR or QJBR). This literally translates into the grandiose The Al-Qaeda Organization for Jihad in the Land of the Two Rivers, or more roughly, Al-Qaeda in Iraq. Then in late December, al-Qaeda Central issued its own statement publicly accepting and endorsing Zarqawi:

> *We in the al-Qaeda organization warmly welcome [Zarqawi and his group's] union with us... Abu Musab al-Zarqawi is the emir of the al-Qaeda organization in Iraq. Brothers in the group there should heed his orders and obey him.*[11]

Zarqawi's emergence as the acknowledged head of al-Qaeda in Iraq (AQI)* helped his network grow in numbers of fighters, resources, funding, and influence among other Sunni-based insurgent groups. As 2004 ended, AQI was gearing up to unleash a murderous bombing campaign across the country.

MURDER AND INTIMIDATION

After the fight for Fallujah, Zarqawi had dispersed his network to other areas, primarily further west. In particular, the border district of Al-Qaim, and the Sinjar-Tal-Afar corridor 130 miles to the north, were key terrain for them. These were the entries to the main ratlines, the first leading into Baghdad and the second into Mosul.

Accordingly, AQI was busy rooting itself into the towns and villages of Al-Qaim. This was a conscious part of their plan to unhinge the society and push the country into civil war and chaos. Zarqawi and his allies were setting up a pipeline, with safe houses, arms caches, IED workshops, and even in-processing centers, to handle the influx of foreign fighters. Men, money, and materiel would flow through this pipeline into staging areas outside the capital. Later in 2006 and 2007, coalition operations against AQI would be centered on these staging areas, the suburban and quasi-rural and "belts" around Baghdad. But in 2005, AQI's bid to control the start point of the Euphrates

* A range of acronyms were used to describe Zarqawi's organization. In late 2004 and much of 2005, JTJ was still common. After Zarqawi's pledge of allegiance to Bin Laden, TQJBR or QJBR were often used, as were AMZ or AQIZ. But by late 2005, AQI was accepted by most as the standard term.

ratline kicked off a bitter fight for Al-Qaim, the mouth of Zarqawi's funnel of violence.

From their perspective, AQI's objective in the district was to impose themselves as the de-facto power structure. One step towards that objective was to dominate the local insurgency, which appears to have been mostly accomplished by 2005. The Al-Theeb insurgent/criminal gang was probably co-opted or taken over by AQI's foreign fighters. The profile of other groups also faded, indicating a merger with Zarqawi's group. Another step was to systematically dismantle the local government. While most officials and security forces had already been run off or neutralized, AQI attacked any vestiges of government authority in the district. Assassinations of police, government personnel, or their family members, often by beheading, accelerated.

To cow any opposition, AQI engaged in what U.S. troops called murder and intimidation (M&I) activities. These included truly savage methods of torture, rape, and execution. Kidnappings were a favorite tactic. Anyone who had sons or daughters fall into the hands of these vicious killers were normally very compliant thereafter. Often these episodes ended tragically, with the hostages meeting horrible ends. The bodies found by Rooks and Puhlman were likely victims of such an incident.

Another of Zarqawi's major objectives was to co-opt tribal networks, and his emirs throughout Anbar worked to set up tacit alliances with certain tribes, drafting local manpower into their holy war. In Al-Qaim, the Karabuli and Salmoni tribes were recognized AQI allies and 3/2 understood their traditional areas to be insurgent strongholds.

AQI's methods to convince or coerce the tribes varied. They might place a radicalized imam in a mosque or establish a cell of fighters in the tribe's area to recruit and pay youths to employ

IEDs. Perhaps a foreign fighter would marry into the tribe, taking one of the sheikh's daughters as a wife. This could happen either with the sheikh's cooperation or through intimidation, subtle or otherwise.

But if a tribe was uncooperative AQI turned up the heat. Such was the case with the Albu Mahal, which had previously cooperated with the jihadists, fighting with them against the Marines of 1/7. But by late 2004, the Albu Mahal had begun to turn against Zarqawi's designs and were mobilizing their own tribal militia to fend off AQI attacks, assassination attempts, and kidnappings. The foreign fighters, however, were not about to let defiant tribesmen stand in their way. Al-Qaim was too important to their plans.

As 3/2 arrived on the scene, the tension between the Albu Mahal and AQI had reached a breaking point. Both sides were gearing up for a fight, but to the newly-deployed battalion the simmering animosity between local tribesmen and foreign fighters was all but invisible. The Marines had only cursory knowledge of local history, limited sources of information, and were still building awareness of what was happening outside their perimeter.

It was painfully obvious, though, that shadowy insurgents were actively seeking their destruction. The frequent encounters with IEDs, the daily attacks against Camp Gannon, and the death of Lance Corporal Smith in a suicide attack were the work of deadly foes. And there were unsettling indications that the enemy, whether unified or fragmented, was increasing in strength and lethal capability. An ominous storm was gathering on the horizon.

Blood in the Streets

During January and February of 2005, just before 3/2 arrived in-country, AQI conducted a string of suicide attacks across Iraq, demonstrating in ruthless fashion their intent to ignite a sectarian civil war:

4 Jan 05 — Governor of Baghdad assassinated by gunmen. Suicide truck bomb hits Iraqi Police Special Commando unit, killing 10.

11 Jan 05 — Suicide car bomb near police station in Tikrit, 7 policemen killed

19 Jan 05 — Four suicide car bomb attacks in Baghdad, and a fifth in Hillah, a mostly-Shiite city south of Baghdad. 26 Iraqis killed.

25 Jan 05 — Suicide bomber detonates fuel-tanker truck near Kurdish Democratic Party offices in Sinjar, 15 killed.

27 Jan 05 — Suicide carbomb outside the Governor's office in Diyalah, kills 5. Governor (not injured) was coming to a "Peace Day" meeting.

8 Feb 05 — Suicide bomber detonates among crowd of Iraqi Army recruits in Baghdad, 21 killed.

19 Feb 05 — Multiple suicide bombers hit Baghdad during the Shiite festival of Ashura. Several of the attacks are claimed by AQI. Over 40 killed.

28 Feb 05 — Suicide car bomb detonates outside medical center in Hillah. 127 Iraqis killed, making it the deadliest single bombing in Iraq's history. The bomber was from Jordan, acting in the name of AQI.

See **bastardsandbrothers.com** for notes, photos, maps, etc.

11. SHOCKWAVES

That storm broke violently over India Company just after changeover on April 11, 2005. Out in the towers along Camp Gannon's perimeter and on the fortified rooftops of the nearby ING compound, Marines stood watch over a waking city. Some had just come off post and were hitting their racks. Others were already asleep after returning from a night mission.

The first mortar rounds exploded in quick succession at about 0815. Lance Corporal Roy Mitros noticed how closely they were grouped. "This was definitely out of the norm," Mitros later recalled. The impacts were "within five or ten meters of each other."[1] Then, as if on cue, the guard posts were hit with a wave of incoming small arms fire and RPGs from the south and east. This was no hit-and-run attack.

As that opening salvo hit, no one on Gannon realized their dusty little base was the target of a preplanned, well-coordinated attack by al-Qaeda in Iraq. Recently, AQI had begun using so-called complex attacks against coalition forces. Just a few days before, on April 2nd, over a hundred insurgents in multiple teams used automatic weapons, RPGs, mortars, rockets, and suicide vehicle bombs to attack Abu-Ghraib prison. Nine days later, AQI was aiming for a big symbolic victory against Camp

Gannon, complete with fiery explosions and rows of dead Marines for TV screens around the world. At least one insurgent video team was in place as the attack unfolded, ready to capture the carnage.

FIRST STRIKE

Following the opening salvo, a large suburban utility vehicle sped into view traveling north on West End Road. Instead of pressing directly towards the east side of Camp Gannon, it turned right into the neighborhood just south of the ING compound. The driver made one more turn north then accelerated along a narrow dirt street, with only a coil of concertina wire in his way. Lance Corporal David Pinkham was at the ING that day, along with 3rd Platoon. He had just come off post after shift change, and was inside trying to get some sleep:

> *I heard or felt mortar rounds land close to our building but started to drift off again. Then, BOOOM! I was thrown from my cot into the wall…A VBIED had exploded right outside… One of my squad mates screamed, "We're hit!!" All I could see was dust and my ears were ringing. I grabbed boots, flak, helmet, and rifle and started running to the roof. My ears started to pick up lots of gunfire.*
>
> **—David Pinkham**[2]

For whatever reason, the driver had touched off his lethal payload prematurely in a trash-strewn lot just south of Pinkham's position. He may have become disoriented, or the concertina wire entangled the vehicle, but fortunately he had not come close enough to cause casualties or major damage. In retrospect, the SUV's attack run was probably a diversion to draw the Marine's attention away from the main event. The primary attack was just getting started.

GANNON GETS ROCKED

Moments after the first suicide bomber hit, Marines standing post along Camp Gannon's perimeter sighted a white dump truck barreling up West End Road. Instead of veering into the neighborhood, though, this vehicle pressed all the way north towards an arched gateway structure that led into the training area outside Gannon.

Access to the training area was impeded by several wrecked vehicles arrayed across the road. Marines from 3rd Platoon could see that approach from rooftop positions within the ING compound. As the truck came within their view, they engaged it with two 40mm grenades but to no effect. The hulking dump truck easily brushed the wrecked vehicles aside and the driver turned left into the training area. Then he accelerated towards the Entry Control Point (ECP) at the northeast corner of Gannon.

In front of the ECP were HESCO barriers arranged in the typical serpentine pattern to slow down and confuse an attacker. Overlooking the ECP and the barriers was the four-story P2 guard tower, manned that morning by 21-year-old Lance Corporal Josh Butler.

The story of how Butler ended up in that tower will probably never be fully told. It involves headstrong personalities and traditional but now disfavored disciplinary methods. Suffice it to say that Butler had been deep in the proverbial doghouse with his squad leader and other NCOs. For weeks before the attack, he'd been the focus of intense "remedial counseling." Butler hardly describes himself as a model Marine. "I was never a guy you'd put on a recruiting poster. I was a combat Marine, that's all."[3] That morning he proved it.

As the dump truck accelerated straight at his position, Butler stood in the open-air parapet of the concrete tower. He braced the stock of his Squad Automatic Weapon (SAW) against his shoulder and began firing:

> *It wasn't my weapon, and wouldn't ya know, the damn thing jams right off. I go into my immediate action to clear it, and I can hear the diesel whining as it gets closer. But I got the weapon cleared and started lighting him up. I probably used about a quarter of my ammo in three bursts. I knew I had to conserve, since I just had that one can. It was just like we did in dryfire drills, "butter-butter-jam, butter-butter-jam, butter-butter-butter-jam." I was aiming right at the windshield, and it was pretty well spidered. I'm pretty sure I killed him in the seat.*
>
> **—Josh Butler**[4]

His rounds started impacting the dump-truck when it was about 100 meters from the tower. As they pierced the windshield, the driver was either killed outright, wounded, or disoriented and the truck veered left instead of continuing straight towards P2. Then it exploded in a massive fireball. In an instant, the shockwave radiated from the blast, mangling metal and masonry, filling the air with deadly shards. It also slammed Butler violently against the back wall of the concrete tower, knocking him unconscious.

About 200 meters away inside the ops center, Captain Diorio also felt the blast. "The next thing I know the roof lifts up...It was a cement-poured roof," he later described. "It lifts up and you can see daylight between the roof and the top of the walls. The doors get blown off and everyone gets knocked off their feet."[5]

During the night, insurgents had moved into buildings with good fields of fire. They had pushed families out of their homes, threatening them to keep quiet. Now small teams of fighters were firing from windows and rooftops along West End Road and from the apartment blocks of the 440 sector, trying to force the defenders' heads down so they couldn't respond effectively.

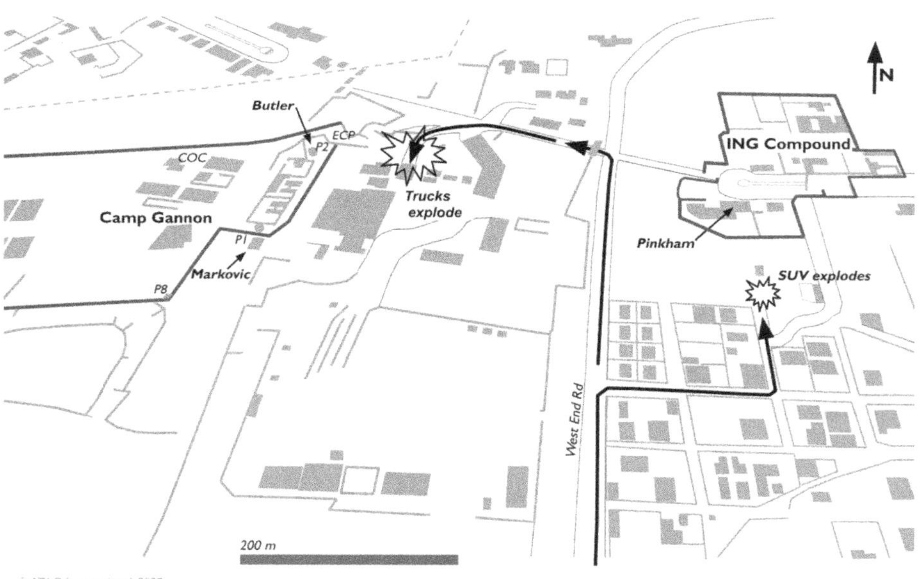

But as soon as the first rounds hit, Marines were grabbing gear, ammo, and weapons and rushing to reinforce. Many of them credit their training, their leaders, and a well-prepared defense plan for their ability to react so quickly and effectively. "It was scary, but then your training takes over," says Ron Jackson of 1st Platoon. "I got blown out of my rack when the attack started. Mortars landed on top of us. I had that moment of intense fear before running out, but you have a bigger fear of letting your brothers down." Jackson sprinted out to P7, joining two other Marines already there and bringing extra ammo to the post. "I could see muzzle flashes and men on the rooftops. We started engaging them and reporting what we saw. We were aggressive but professional."[6]

BUTLER'S LAST STAND

Butler came to on the floor of P2 tower, the air around him filled with dust from the dump truck blast. Over the handheld radio clipped to his gear, a garble of urgent transmissions were stepping on each other. Then, through the radio chatter and the ringing in his ears, he heard another diesel engine whining. Instantly he knew what it was:

> *I was knocked out for a second, but it was like everything just clicked right back on. When I heard it, I knew right away it was that damn fire truck and was like, "You gotta be shitting me! Again?" I jumped up, and it was coming right through the smoke. Just like a scene from "Lethal Weapon" or something. Smoke was swirling around it as it came through.*
>
> **—Josh Butler**[7]

The cyclic rate-of-fire for the M249 is between 650 and 800 rounds per minute. Which means if you hold the trigger down without letting up, it will fire about 13 bullets every second and chew through a 200-round belt in under 20 seconds. Firing cyclic, however, will quickly overheat the barrel and jam the weapon. A good SAW gunner fires in short, disciplined bursts of six to ten rounds.

Butler was a good gunner that morning. Knocked down by the first explosion and now back up and watching the fearsome fire truck accelerate towards him, he showed poise and fire discipline. Again, he aimed to kill or disable the driver, firing in controlled bursts at the windshield:

> *I could see into the cab, and there were two guys with black ski masks. They were wearing helmets and old-style flak vests. I aimed bursts right at the windshield, and saw my rounds impact, kind of fogging the glass. Later we found out they had a bullet-proof windshield installed. I don't know if I penetrated it, but I don't think they could see much after that. The driver just basically followed where the first truck went.*
>
> **—Josh Butler**[8]

Just like the dump truck, the fire truck veered left under Butler's onslaught and detonated in almost the exact same spot as the previous blast, about 80 meters from P2 and 40 meters from the serpentine barriers. This explosion was even larger, again knocking many Marines down, tearing off plywood doors throughout the camp, demolishing several buildings in the training area, and filling the air with chunks of metal, engine parts, and splinters. The massive explosion was clearly heard and felt thirteen miles away at Camp Al-Qaim and a dark, ominous mushroom cloud rose several hundred feet over Husaybah.

The concrete structure of P2 tower was cracked and chunks had been taken out, but it was still standing. As was Butler. He was battered and bruised with multiple pieces of metal embedded in his Kevlar body armor, but still had ammo for his SAW and was ready to take on whatever came next. A large bit of shrapnel had struck the aluminum NVG mount bolted to the front of his helmet. Just an inch lower and it would have pierced his face.

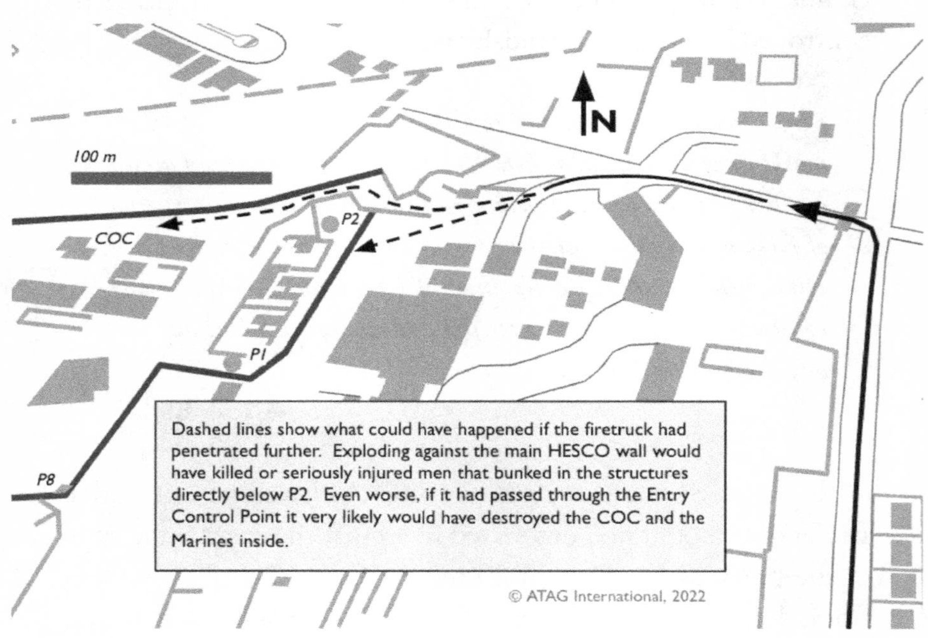

FIRE SUPERIORITY

Rocked by the explosions, Diorio and others in the COC struggled to figure out what was happening and get a handle on the situation:

> *I didn't know whether my Marines on the perimeter were alive. We can't see anything because it's just dust everywhere. You can't see in front of your face... We got RPGs and small arms fire coming in... Can't hear anything because Marines are firing back... I thought part of the base had been taken over. As the smoke clears, I can see where the fire truck hit, and my heart sank.*
>
> **—Frank Diorio**[9]

Meanwhile, the firefight along the perimeters of Gannon and the ING compound continued to rage. Post number 8, a sandbagged position on the southeast corner of Gannon, was at the center of the action. With its M240 machine-gun and a dominant field of fire, it was critical to the base's defense, and both the Marines and the AQI fighters knew it.

At the very beginning of the attack, an RPG round had hit the post. The impact blew apart the outer layer of sandbags and threw Corporal Anthony Fink, and Lance Corporals Lampe and Leyton to the floor. They quickly recovered and returned fire, but the incoming was getting more intense. Heavy and accurate enemy fire was coming from the houses across West End Road.

Recognizing that P8 needed immediate support, First Sergeant Brazeal rushed from the COC across an exposed area to the point of danger. "Fink told me it was coming from beyond a wall 300 meters from the post, so we reset the gun to suppress that."[10] Brazeal and Fink each grabbed an AT-4 rocket and stood outside the protection of the sandbagged fighting position to aim in and fire. Both rockets hit the wall, killing several attackers.

Over at the ING, 3rd Platoon was engaging insurgents at even closer range, 100 to 150 meters away. David Pinkham had scrambled onto a rooftop, rifle in hand. "The houses closest to us had been taken by attackers. As best I could assess there were fifteen to twenty enemy there," recalls Pinkham. "We took to the wall of the rooftop for cover and began to gain fire superiority. I remember concrete chips from bullet impacts hitting us. In that split second, time morphed into an eternity."[11]

India's leadership worked the radios feverishly to get headcounts, ammo status, and casualty reports. Calls for air support and CASEVAC went out and rotors started turning at Camp Al-Qaim. After such massive blasts, Diorio assumed multiple Marines were dead or wounded. "We weren't sure what we were dealing with," he recalled. "I thought I had lost about 150 Marines."[12]

Ammo distribution became a priority as the posts were still dealing with heavy incoming. The Marines were pouring out suppressive fire, dealing with multiple clusters of attackers. Several posts were low on ammunition. Squad leaders and other NCOs exposed themselves to enemy fire to run ammo cans out to the towers and sandbagged positions.

Having failed to breach the perimeter with the SVBIEDs, the insurgents were now getting outgunned. Gannon's mortar crews were engaging. Soon attack helicopters from Camp AQ were overhead, searching for targets. The heaviest part of the fight had lasted for about 45 minutes, but started to slack off as insurgents were suppressed, killed, or withdrew back into the city.

At one point, Marines in P1 tower used binoculars to spot a camera team on a rooftop 800 meters southeast of Gannon. "We considered them hostile due to their activity and the fact that we were receiving fire from that direction," remembers Dali Markovic, from India's 2nd Platoon. "We called for mortar fire on the location, but it was declined due to the helicopter being too close."[13] Even while AQI's media team was shooting their propaganda video, then, India Marines had their position dialed in and were trying to kill them.

One by one each platoon commander checked in, reporting "all accounted for," to their company commander's immense relief. Three Marines had received blast-related injuries but weren't seriously hurt. Just outside Camp Gannon's perimeter lay a mass of smoldering debris and wreckage where the two truck bombs had detonated. But inside everyone was safe.

AFTERMATH

One of the main after-effects of the triple suicide bombing was a fight to control the narrative. Well before the first explosion, Zarqawi's sophisticated media arm had prepped the information battleground. The camera team was ready to video the attack as it unfolded and, based on how fast their post-attack propaganda appeared, AQI had video editors standing by and jihadist websites ready to upload. The speed of their information operations (IO) was impressive. "Their stringers in Husaybah were already primed," said Colonel Davis later. "When that second [truck bomb] went off, they had a report out there about the insurgent attack on Gannon. That's how well connected they were."[14]

According to Davis, even as the firetruck was barreling towards the ECP, a story popped up on a major U.S. newspaper's web feed reporting a massive suicide bombing in Husaybah. Just a short time later, the edited attack video appeared on extremist websites, with narration claiming that many Americans were killed and declaring a great victory against the infidels.*

But in this instance, AQI's attempt to drive the media narrative unraveled. As India Company reported up the chain that their perimeter was secure and they'd suffered only minor injuries, coalition press officers released that information to reporters. Instead of generating headlines about dead Marines and horrible losses, the press stories written after the attack were of heroism and incredible bravery under fire. For the coalition, it was a rare win in the realm of information operations.

The other main impact was operational. While India Company had come through the attack unscathed, April 11, 2005 was a violent reminder that they faced a resourceful, fanatical foe that would kill them if ever given the chance. It also underlined that reinforcements, even air assets, could not arrive in time if a determined assault penetrated their perimeter. They needed to rely on their own weapons, resources, and competence. From that point forward, India and its attachments would concentrate on defending Camp Gannon and the ING compound while making limited forays into the city.

There was a long-term, strategic effect as well. The complex attack prompted India Company to take an innovative, non-traditional approach towards engaging the population of

* The video can still be found online, but it gives a misleading picture of what occurred.

Husaybah. Soon after the attack, Captain Diorio and his leadership team noticed a growing divide between locals and AQI. "Foreign fighters started heavy-handing the locals," he related. "I learned this through multiple intelligence sources. I would say about a month after [April 11th] locals started to call on us with information."[15]

Over time, this engagement with the population became more important than the dramatic attack itself. AQI's premature announcement of a great victory turned out to work against them as the truth became known. The glaring gap between the foreign fighters' propaganda and their obvious failure accelerated a growing split between AQI and the locals, including key tribal leaders. Over the next several weeks, red-on-red firefights occurred in the streets and back alleys of Husaybah. Through local contacts and delicate negotiations, India Company started taking steps to exploit that split, steps which would have big implications down the road.

CALM AGAINST THE STORM

As the dust settled on April 11th, the Marines' focus was on how narrow the margin had been between survival and disaster. The enemy had clearly planned to penetrate Gannon's perimeter, with the dump truck blasting aside the HESCO barriers, the fire truck punching through to cause mass casualties, followed by insurgents assaulting on foot. They had come very close to succeeding. Had the dump truck pressed straight ahead a little further, had Butler been killed or incapacitated, or had the fire truck crashed through the ECP and detonated near the ops center, many Marines would have died.

While some men's actions stood out that day, based on being at key locations at crucial times, in truth it was their concerted action that was remarkable. When India Company veterans recall that incredible experience, they speak with pride about their brothers reacting calmly under fire, engaging the enemy as a team. As First Sergeant Brazeal told a reporter a few days after the fight: "This whole company is full of Marines who do the right thing at the right time in the right way, and [April 11th] is proof of that."[16] Their company commander expressed similar feelings:

> *The Marines did what Marines do. They knew their fields of fire. They reinforced, they resupplied, they went into harm's way… Proud doesn't really say it… I truly am humbled to be amongst them… It was inspiring. They were calm against a raging storm.*
>
> —**Frank Diorio**[17]

See **bastardsandbrothers.com** for notes, photos, maps, etc.

12. REAPER

The art of engaging individual targets with precision rifle fire is embedded in Marine Corps history and culture. The first U.S. Marines climbed high into the rigging of sailing ships, firing muskets to pick off the enemy officers on the deck of the opposing vessel. Unique among America's armed services, the Marines have built a tradition where long-range shooting is a core competency. Today, the essence of that tradition lies in the scout-sniper platoons (SSP), which are integrated into Marine infantry battalions as part of the Headquarters and Support Company.

The designation of scout-sniper is significant, as it explicitly recognizes and elevates the platoon's reconnaissance role. The SSP is considered an Intelligence, Surveillance and Reconnaissance (ISR) asset, albeit a lethal one. As such, scout-snipers officially report to the S2 (intelligence) section and are known as the eyes, ears, and trigger fingers of the battalion.

About half the size of a line infantry platoon, the SSP operates in small teams, usually four to six men. The basic component is the two-man shooter/spotter pair, supported by a SAW gunner or rifleman for security and another to man the radio and call in heavier firepower. As 3/2 went through its pre-deployment training, the SSP consisted of 26 men organized into four teams and the command section, all operating under the callsign "Reaper."

To become a scout-sniper, a Marine must first be an infantryman and meet high standards of performance to try out for the scout-sniper platoon. He must then pass numerous additional physical training and weapons qualifications to become a "professionally instructed gunman" or PIG. After further proving himself, he can be selected to attend the rigorous and legendary Marine scout-sniper course. The standards are high and typically less than half of any class completes the course. Those who do earn the right to be called a HOG, a "hunter of gunmen."

First Lieutenant Paul Habenicht had taken command of 3/2's SSP in 2004 and was on his second combat deployment. The commander of an SSP is typically an intelligence officer, not an infantryman. While they also attend the infantry officers' course, they have to pull off a tough balancing act when they reach their platoon. The scout-snipers they will lead are usually considerably more experienced in their lethal art than their commander. The young officer must exhibit competence and exercise authority when needed, while also being humble and teachable. By all accounts, Paul Habenicht handled this difficult balance well.

"Our Lieutenant was excellent," says Anthony Cunha, a member of Reaper 1. "He recognized the difficulty of what we were doing and respected us. Back in the States, he did wonders to get us good training. Once we were in-theater, he made sure we had what we needed then stood back and let us do our job. He respected us, and we respected him."[1]

While he did go into the field on larger operations, during most SSP missions Habenicht's role was to manage missions from the COC. The key to safe, successful scout-sniper missions was to keep information flowing and ensure everyone was aware of what was happening. "Lieutenant Habenicht was great at facilitating and coordinating up and down the chain," remembers Aaron Smith, an assistant team leader. Platoon members also appreciated the unforced way the lieutenant related to his men. "After an op, he'd kick back and smoke a cigar with us. He fit in very naturally," recalls Smith.[2]

Reaper's Platoon Sergeant had just returned to the battalion to take his position a few weeks before deployment. Staff Sergeant Jason Gallant was an experienced scout-sniper with wartime deployments under his belt. He had previously served with 3/2 in 2002. Now the senior HOG, Gallant quickly gained respect from the teams and forged an effective partnership with Lieutenant Habenicht. Throughout the deployment, he frequently went out on missions, but always let the team leaders run the show.

Sergeant C.J. Quinlan was the chief scout, essentially the ops NCO for the platoon. Beyond his experience as a Marine scout-sniper, Sergeant Quinlan had also been in the U.S. Army before joining the Marines, so had a wealth of tactical experience which he worked hard to instill with the rest of Reaper. Quinlan had been the driving force behind the SSP's stateside training program and was eager for the platoon to put those hard-won skills into action.

Upon arrival in Iraq, the command section set up at Camp Al-Qaim while Reaper 2 and Reaper 7 were assigned to support Kilo and WarPig, respectively. Reaper 4 was assigned as battalion support. These three teams initially were billeted at Camp AQ, while Reaper 1 was sent to Camp Gannon to support India Company.

This structure was loose and situationally dependent, however. Flexibility was inherent to Reaper's operational method. Team members would often be cross-attached to other teams, or teams could be mixed and matched in various ways to support the line companies or conduct independent missions. For example, soon after the deployment began, Sergeant Quinlan set up an additional team, provisionally dubbed Reaper 6, which absorbed anyone waiting for a mission or not assigned to the other teams.

Another key figure wasn't part of the leadership, nor was he a school-trained HOG. Corporal Eddie Ryan, from Ellenville, New York, was already a combat veteran from the 2003 invasion and the Battle of Nasiriyah. After that first deployment, he'd tried out for scout snipers and earned a slot as a PIG. With his thick New York accent, quick wit, and boundless enthusiasm, he made friends easily.

As a kind of trademark, Ryan would carry a machete across his back as part of his field gear. Once at a small-arms range, he engaged a paper target with his rifle, transitioned to his pistol, then rushed forward. Drawing his machete mid-stride, he hacked the wooden-framed target into submission, accompanied by raucous shouts and laughter from the rest of the platoon. Everyone remembers his cheesy Italian accent and his famous "crazy legs dance." In many ways, Eddie Ryan was Reaper's heart and soul.

Quickly after settling into Camp Al-Qaim and Gannon, the Reaper teams started pushing outside the wire on nighttime missions, finding hide sites with good fields of fire, setting up their comms and feeding detailed observations and information into the COC. When employed correctly, the scout-sniper teams provide an unmatched source of highly accurate, immediate, and often actionable information. As Jeff Weaver from Reaper 7 expressed, "Our perspective as scout-snipers is different than in other units. We watch the enemy in their natural setting, we see how they act, who they talk to, what they do, when they think no one can see them. That gives us an understanding of the enemy no one else gets."[3]

See **bastardsandbrothers.com** for notes, photos, maps, etc.

13. DEVIL DOCS

Battlefield medicine has undergone a revolution in recent decades, with the most significant changes coming since 2001. New techniques and technologies are focused on treating battlefield casualties in the "golden hour" after injury. If a casualty can get to a well-equipped, well-trained medical team in that hour, the odds of survival increase dramatically. This means pushing medical capabilities far forward, performing care under fire if necessary, and rapidly evacuating casualties. Results have been dramatic. The percentage of combat casualties that expire from wounds is now below ten percent, a steep decline since Vietnam. Thousands of lives have been saved.

A mix of units and teams provided medical support for 3/2. A small Navy shock-trauma team was set up at Camp Al-Qaim, representing the first echelon of advanced care to handle life-threatening or limb-threatening injuries. An air ambulance detachment was also there, from the Army's 571st Medical Company. With specially-equipped Blackhawk helicopters and skilled medics, they answered most CASEVAC calls. On multiple occasions, their speedy response was the difference between a Marine living or dying.

CORPSMAN UP!

But it was 3/2's contingent of Navy corpsmen, directly assigned to the battalion, that provided the Marines day-to-day care and went with them into combat. The relationship between Marines and Navy corpsmen is unique in the U.S. military. Since 1898, when Congress established the Navy Hospital Corps, enlisted sailors have accompanied the Marines into every conflict, receiving 22 Medals of Honor in the process. While there are several grades or rates of corpsman*, Marines usually call them "Doc". Fleet Marine Force (FMF) corpsmen assigned to Marine combat units are called "Devil Docs."

Right before deployment, 3/2 had brought additional corpsmen onboard to man two battalion aid stations (BAS) and provide more support on the battlefield. The main BAS was established at Camp AQ and the other on Gannon. Both were led by a Navy doctor overseeing teams of corpsmen attached out to companies and platoons. Routinely, they delivered preventive and primary care, even emergency dental care, to their Marines. "One minute you're tending to sniffles, plucking out splinters, or treating a spider bite. The next you're treating heat stroke or a fracture," describes Jesse Bedia, the senior corpsman at Gannon's BAS.[1]

On the battlefield, though, a corpsman is an armed combatant, trained on weapons and ready to engage the enemy if necessary. When giving care under fire, their very first priority is to shoot back. Once the casualty is protected—which may involve the corpsman placing his own body in the line of

* A Hospital Corpsman Third Class (HM3) is equivalent in rank to a Marine Corporal. An HM2 equates to a Sergeant, an HM1 to a Staff Sergeant, and an HMC (Chief Hospital Corpsman) equates to a Gunnery Sergeant.

fire—emergency medical priorities are aggressively addressed. Tourniquets and clotting agents are applied early and often to prevent bleeding out, the leading cause of battlefield deaths. Then the airway is checked and cleared. A breathing tube may be needed to assure respiration, or a thoracic needle required to decompress the chest cavity. If at all possible, an IV is established to ensure blood circulation and deliver fluids or medication. This helps address shock, the other great battlefield killer.

Performing all this in combat conditions, far removed from even rudimentary facilities, entails challenges that are difficult to adequately describe. Controlling hemorrhage often means being literally awash in a wounded man's blood. Clearing the airway when someone's throat is mangled is not a clean, straightforward medical procedure. And keeping a stricken Marine warm in a sodden, waste-laden ditch as his blood pressure drops and rounds snap overhead will test any corpsman's mettle.

This is what sets corpsmen apart. Marines know if they are hurt on the battlefield, regardless of pitfall or peril, a corpsman will come to their aid. If the air is filled with the crack and hum of incoming, he will come. If mortar rounds are slamming in, he will come. If he faces the sacrifice of his own life, still he will come. This bond is a strong and sacred one. It gives the anguished cry of "corpsman up!" a deep, even mystical significance:

> *The title of Doc, and being entrusted with the lives of Marines is not only humbling but a distinguished station to hold... I would describe the relationship as a brotherhood of warriors... We were family. When you boil it all down, it's love that makes us do what*

we do. A love for our country, for freedom, our families and most of all for my brothers standing next to me in battle. For them, I will violently go through the gates of hell."

—Jesse Bedia[2]

SAVING EDDIE

Of all the nightmares combat can bring, the most terrible is the heartbreak of friendly fire. When a warrior is struck down, not by an enemy, but by inadvertent action from his own side, the resulting pain and remorse can be overwhelming. Paradoxically, the precision of modern weapons increases the potential for such tragedies. The American military has invested billions of dollars, established countless procedures, and trains relentlessly to avoid such incidents. One of the cornerstones of modern tactics is to safely control fires and correctly separate friend from foe so friendly fire cannot happen.

And yet it does.

Late at night on 12 April, a scout-sniper team left Camp Gannon and carefully infiltrated into Husaybah. Their mission, planned in the wake of the suicide attacks the day before, was to set up in a hide site inside the city where they could observe and perhaps eliminate key insurgents. As the scout-sniper platoon's Chief Scout, Sergeant C.J. Quinlan led the team, which included Sergeant Carl Schaeffer and his team members in Reaper 1 along with Corporal Eddie Ryan who had accompanied Quinlan from Camp AQ. Other elements were ready to support them. These included Marines at the newly-built Trash

OP, tanks positioned in the fields north of the city, and WarPig guntrucks on Gannon ready to roll.

At daybreak on the 13th, the snipers were in position atop a three-story building, peeking up over the low wall around the rooftop. Suddenly, they came under intense and accurate machine-gun fire. Immediately, Eddie Ryan was hit in the head and fell to the hard concrete.

The next moments were chaotic and traumatic in the extreme. The scout-snipers rushed to care for their fallen man while trying to identify the source of fire and protect themselves from further attack. Sergeant Schaeffer and Corporal Andrew Senor crawled to Ryan, covering him with their own bodies while even more rounds slammed into the wall and screamed over their heads. They began administering first aid, trying to stop his copious bleeding.

At first, the source of the incoming was unclear. The team popped colored smoke to identify their position to friendlies while making urgent calls for immediate CASEVAC and QRF support from Gannon. The initial firing stopped, and the race to save Eddie Ryan began. With their location compromised and expecting an enemy attack at any moment, the sniper team worked under unimaginable pressure. The gravity of Ryan's wounds was obvious to all. He was hanging onto life by a thin thread.

Within minutes that stretched to eternity, the QRF from Gannon arrived with several up-armored Humvees and an armored ambulance. A team of three corpsmen crewed the ambulance, HM3 Ralf Lange, HM3 Rawley Dilley and HM2 Jesse Bedia. In Husaybah's urban maze the column initially had trouble locating the correct building. Private First Class Evan John was in the tail-end guntruck and relates the moment when they made contact. "I looked over and saw one of the snipers come out of a building. He yelled over at me. 'We need help!' I ran over to him, and he was covered in blood."[3]

PFC John dashed into the building and corpsmen Bedia and Dilley followed moments later. They pounded up the stairs while the QRF set up security outside. "When I got out on the roof, one of the snipers grabbed my kevlar to keep me down below the parapet," says John. "I remember Ryan was moaning and choking."[4]

Keeping their heads below the wall, Bedia and Dilley crawled over to Ryan. As the senior corpsman, Bedia had to make critical decisions. "I could see how severe and life-threatening his wounds were," says Bedia. I knew we'd need to put him on a bird ASAP. We didn't have advanced life support at Gannon. There was no time to take him there."[5]

Ryan was then strapped to a stretcher and taken gingerly down three steep flights of stairs. "We had to hold fast at the exit, to try and figure out where the incoming had come from," remembers Bedia. "But I just thought, 'it's now or never' and we took him out, carrying him so our bodies stayed between him and any incoming, and loaded him into the ambulance." The column pulled out, headed to a landing zone (LZ) just outside Gannon. Inside the armored ambulance, the corpsmen knew they had to make the most of each golden minute:

> *We worked on him the whole time, started IVs, kept the airway viable, checked and rechecked all his vitals. That was one of the hardest cases in my career. I put everything I had into saving Eddie Ryan. All my training, all my knowledge gained from cases and those who taught me. The whole time, I was talking to him, telling him to hang on. He couldn't speak but was conscious. I could see the*

fear... I just kept telling him, 'Don't give up! I'm not leaving your side until we get you to the helo, no matter what. It's you and me. I'm not leaving'... And inside, I was talking to God. I said 'Not today, God. You're not taking my Marine!'

—Jesse Bedia[6]

As they bumped through the streets, Bedia dictated a running commentary on Ryan's condition, which Dilley relayed over the radio through Doc Wichman on Gannon and onward to the Army medics as they were enroute. A dustoff helicopter had been scrambled only minutes after the event was reported. Incredibly, the bird was already there waiting, rotors turning, as the ambulance rolled up. But danger was still present:

When we got to the LZ, we realized the Blackhawk had landed in a suspected minefield, right up by the border. Myself, Dilley, and two other Marines grabbed the stretcher and ran out through the minefield... I didn't care. I was going to do whatever it took to get him on that bird. I met the Army medic right under the rotor wash. I had to cup my hands and yell into his ear to give him the patient update.

—Jesse Bedia[7]

After the helicopter lifted off, the convoy drove back onto Gannon. "We parked right outside the COC," Bedia recalls. "There was a group gathered outside waiting for us. When we opened the ambulance doors, blood poured out of it. First Sergeant Brazeal met me there, and asked, 'What do you think, Doc?' I just kind of shook my head... I was totally spent. Exhausted."[8]

The Blackhawk raced to Camp Al-Qaim where the Navy

shock trauma team was ready to receive Ryan. In an amazingly short time, he had been whisked from the front line into the hands of a surgical team. Considering the seriousness of his wounds and that the incident occurred inside a hostile area, this was a miracle in itself. At each step, Ryan's fellow Marines, Navy corpsmen, and Army medics made herculean efforts to save him.

Those efforts continued as he passed up through multiple levels of advanced care. From Camp AQ, Eddie was flown to Balad Airbase, Iraq, into the care of a neurosurgical team. Subsequently, he was flown to the world-class U.S. medical facilities at Landstuhl, Germany. His condition remained extremely critical, and he was nearly lost on several occasions.

The Marines of 3/2 struggled to deal with the aftermath. An official investigation found that Corporal Ryan had been hit by 7.62mm rounds from a coax machine-gun on one of the tanks. The snipers had been erroneously identified as hostile targets. Clearly, there had been serious miscommunication.

For Reaper, this knowledge was emotionally devastating. On top of the trauma from the actual incident and losing one of their own, finding out that it resulted from friendly fire was an additional blow to morale that rippled through everyone at Camp Gannon and the rest of the battalion. "I was a boot on my first deployment," recalls Evan John. "I hadn't seen anyone hit before. It was humbling to see a fellow Marine wounded like that, especially one of the snipers. For a long time after, I would have dreams where I'd see Ryan on that rooftop."[9]

Heroes All

It is not the author's purpose to second-guess individuals or decisions involved in this tragic incident. Horrible things happen in war. Often they can never be adequately explained. The sole intent is to highlight the heroism and professionalism of the Marines, corpsmen and medical personnel who saved Eddie Ryan's life.

14. RAMANA

When viewed from a helicopter or other aircraft, the richness of the land along Iraq's rivers is striking. Flying for mile after mile over lush vegetation, orderly palm groves, and cultivated green fields turns the abstract phrase "fertile crescent" into verdant reality. The irrigated fields along the Tigris and Euphrates have been under cultivation for thousands of years. On close examination, the ingrained history of Iraq emerges from them.

One pattern that stands out is the orientation of so many Iraqi farm fields in long, narrow strips. This results from a timeless practice known as ribbon farming that maximizes the number of farms with direct access to the water. The farms' boundaries dictate where roads, canals, and communities are established. Deeper still, they also define inherited wealth and status, settlement patterns, and relative power among families and tribes. Whether U.S. troops realized it or not, the population, economy, smuggling routes, bitter tribal rivalries—and the war itself—were all superimposed on this interlaced grid.

Within Al-Qaim District, the area just north of the Euphrates contained 40 square miles of rich agricultural terrain. Jammed between the river and the desert plateau, this patchwork of roadside villages, canals, and ribbon farms was known as *Ramana*, or *Rummanah*, the Arabic word for pomegranate. It extended roughly from New Ubaydi west to the Syrian border and was isolated from the rest of the district by very limited road access.

In 2005, only one bridge could support vehicles crossing from south of the river into the farmlands along the north bank. This was a low-slung steel latticework, supported by multiple large pontoons. It was located on the road heading northeast out of Karabilah and was named the Ramana Bridge on most maps. It was hardly an engineering marvel, but with their typical sense of irony, the Marines had dubbed it Golden Gate Bridge.

Coalition forces of any stripe had rarely set foot in Ramana and even before 3/2 arrived, the area was known as a safe haven for insurgents. Through March and April 2005, more frequent and detailed reporting indicated that foreign fighters in Ramana were intimidating the population, seizing all weapons from the locals, and taking away their cell phones. Moreover, high-level SOF units were keenly interested in the area and had found actionable targets there:

> *A couple weeks before the attack on Camp Gannon, a raid was conducted north of the river by [national SOF], which resulted in significant enemy KIA. That there was that kind of [enemy] strength up there and nobody had any inkling of it was disconcerting.*
>
> **—Stephen Davis**[1]

The apparent presence of an AQI-controlled safe haven just across the river, and its very feasible link to the nearly-catastrophic April 11th suicide operation in Husaybah, motivated the leadership in both RCT-2 and 3/2 as they considered their next moves:

> *The realization that we were giving them free run north of the river, that they were moving back and forth, led to what became Operation Matador... [And the attack on] Gannon made it a lot easier to sell back up the chain... We needed to get out there.*
>
> **—Tim Mundy**[2]

SCHISM

In the last part of April and early May, another trend was accelerating. Captain Diorio and the Marines of India were seeing more evidence of a growing split inside Husaybah. The residents' response to the April 11th attack and the propaganda put out by the jihadists had been revealing. Immediately after the suicide runs against Gannon, AQI disseminated their notorious post-attack video showing the dramatic explosions. The jihadist voice-over boasted that they had killed and wounded many Marines, and that "the mujahideen withdrew without any injuries."

Martyrs, Lies and Videotape

As-salāmu 'alaykum [Peace be unto you]. From Mesopotamia we launch attack after attack, from the east of the country to the west, and from the north to the south, against the cross-bearers and the unbelievers, against the Americans and their allies, against the apostates [Shiites]. In this blessed attack, our brother the Lebanese martyr, struck the Americans in the Customs Area in Al-Qaim, in the west of the country.

It was a unique tactical operation the enemy has not seen before, with a specially-developed weapon, car bombs and attacks by rockets, which led to the bombing of their headquarters and the special fortified buildings for their engineers and experts inside the Customs Area. This resulted in great terror among the enemy and the killing of a large number of them. Ambulances were seen carrying their dead and wounded. And the mujahideen withdrew without any injuries, thanks to God.

We send this message to the American media and the Arabic media, and to the children of the Zionists [Israel]: We pledge to Allah almighty, to the Muslims — who are downtrodden everywhere — and to our brothers captured by the enemy, that we will continue on this path and take one of the two pillars, either victory or martyrdom.

(Translation of the audio on AQI's April 11th post-attack video)

But word had traveled fast among the locals that the attack had not penetrated Gannon, and the attackers had paid a heavy price in the ensuing gunfight. Some had seen their bodies in the street. Moreover, in subsequent days, a flood of western media accounts reported that not a single American had died. Rather than garnering respect, the failed attack and jihadist lies about it fostered ridicule among the populace. "The locals actually started making fun of the people who did it," recalled Frank Diorio. "I started hearing [about the attackers], "You guys failed ... You don't know what you're doing."[3]

The Marines kept tabs on the city's mood by listening to and translating the sermons the imams would broadcast from the mosques' PA systems. About a week after April 11th, during one of the evening broadcasts, a new voice was heard blaring out across the rooftops. It was obvious that outsiders were using the mosques to put out their message. It was a rebuke from foreign fighters to disrespectful locals, claiming that "Americans didn't die because you're bad Muslims ... God wasn't honored because Americans didn't die."

Just a few days later, a violent altercation emphasized the growing tension on the streets. From their overwatch positions, Marines heard shooting on Market Street, but no rounds came towards them. To find out what was happening, a call was made to their primary local contact, the East End Lady, who reported there had been an argument between foreign fighters and a local. She told the Marines, "The local made fun of them for not killing any of you guys and the foreign fighters shot and killed him."[4]

The incident fit an emerging pattern. Other information was confirming that the foreign-led jihadists were strong-arming residents. Up to that point, India Company's fight had been totally kinetic. There were mortar attacks and direct fire against the posts every day. They'd been hit by a nearly catastrophic suicide attack. Their focus had been on fortifying positions, building Trash OP, conducting night raids, and improving fields of fire.

But the incident on Market Street opened up the possibility that events might be steered in a different way. The Marines at Gannon sensed a growing rift between local Iraqis and the fanatical outsiders. In an interview with a reporter, Lieutenant Ronnie Choe described other aspects of what was unfolding. "Tensions in Husaybah arose from foreign fighters coming here and staying," said Choe. He related that a local imam had been kidnapped and foreigners had apparently taken over the Friday afternoon sermons. "You'll hear one voice giving the sermon, and then someone else will get on."[5]

RED-ON-RED

While it was unclear to the Marines at the time, those weeks in April were a critical juncture as leaders of the Albu Mahal tribe were flexing their muscle against the foreign fighters of AQI. They were pressing to use their tribal militia, that they called *Khatahb al-Hamza* (Hamza battalion), to control Husaybah and other parts of the district.

In a series of remarkable interviews conducted in 2010 by Dr. Bill Knarr and associates, the Mahalawi sheikhs talked about the genesis of their fight with AQI. Sheikh Kurdi Rafee Farhan spoke of a meeting in February or March 2005, where they tried parlaying with AQI. The tribes wanted armed control over their own areas, what they called "local authority." In response, the foreign fighters angrily declared, "We are responsible here for security, you are not!"[6] In the ensuing weeks, however, the Mahalawis defied AQI and went ahead with their plans:

> *The Albu Mahal tribe then established that authority. It secured the position of the mayor and began forming the police [i.e., militia] from within the ranks of the Albu Mahal tribe... Al-Qaeda completely rejected this and that was the beginning of the Albu Mahal tribe separating from al-Qaeda.*
>
> **—Sheikh Kurdi**[7]

This was an open challenge and AQI responded forcefully by sending fighters into Husaybah, probably from Ramana, to enforce their iron-fisted rule. "Al-Qaim's strategic location was very significant to al-Qaeda," described Sheikh Sabah. "They were foreigners who entered from Yemen, Saudi Arabia, Syria, and they called themselves emirs. They wanted to have their word and their opinion over us... Al-Qaeda tried to isolate and to humiliate the tribals."[8]

BLOODY MONDAY

On May 2, 2005, the growing tensions boiled over. That Monday in Husaybah, Ahmed Adiya Asaf walked openly among the shoppers and merchant stalls along Market Street. He had recently been installed as the new chief of police, with the rank of major. He was a well-connected Mahawali and a relative of Sheikh Sabah. By placing him in the position, the tribe was establishing security on their own terms, not as puppets of foreign-born radicals.

Suddenly, seven men emerged from the crowd and shot Major Ahmed dead, then publicly beheaded him on the street. News of the gruesome murder pulsed through the population, a blood-spattered announcement of the costs of resisting AQI. Yet there were those ready to resist, meeting violence with violence:

> *We started to understand their mission was to destroy our tribe. They assassinated the chief of police, who was a member of our tribe. And then I said, "That's it. Now the time has come." And we started fighting them.*
>
> **—Sheikh Sabah**[9]

From their posts, India Company had limited awareness of what was happening in the streets that day but received reports of red-on-red fighting. A large group of armed men was spotted, and a Cobra/Huey team was dispatched. Upon arrival over the city, the helo crews observed a firefight between two armed Iraqi groups. At one point, the helicopters themselves took ground fire and the Huey was damaged seriously enough to make an emergency landing.[10]

Marines at Trash OP also came under attack and responded, kicking off a sustained firefight that lasted through the afternoon. Jason Ellis was on duty there with his trusty M249 SAW, nicknamed "Boondocks:"

> *Roughly at noon we took full contact to our post. Corporal [Luis] Maxwell had us get online and fire into the house we were getting contact from. We opened up with a 30-round burst… Then we were in a full firefight… You could hear the enemy's rounds whizzing over our heads… At times, I was firing 100-round bursts at the enemy. It got so bad that we were running out of ammo. I alone fired 2,000 rounds.*
>
> **—Jason Ellis**[11]

Looking back, the firing against Trash OP and the helicopters appear to be peripheral events. The Marines were not the main targets that day. The assassination of Major Ahmed had kicked off a battle between the Mahalawis and the foreign fighters. "This sparked the first fight between the Albu Mahal tribe and al-Qaeda," recalled Sheikh Kurdi. "This big fight began on the 2nd of May 2005."[12]

More clashes erupted across the district over the next several days, as 3/2 and RCT-2 prepared for Operation Matador. The mounting red-on-red violence was widespread enough that it was being monitored at the regimental level. Colonel Davis was well aware of it, as he described:

> *All of a sudden, a whole bunch of red-on-red intramural fighting starts... We've got fights going on from Husaybah east into Karabilah... From Sadah into Ushsh... Between New Ubaydi and Old Ubaydi, and we don't understand why. We think its tribal. [There was talk] about AMZ [Abu Musab al-Zarqawi] with foreign fighters... They are very disappointed that the Iraqis are not more pure, religiously. The [locals] are not willing to fight for the jihad... That's where this big schism comes in.*
>
> —**Stephen Davis**[13]

The open combat in May between AQI and the Albu Mahal would have far-reaching implications for subsequent operations by 3/2 and for further development of relations with tribal leaders.

FROM THE SHADOWS

The lead-up to Operation Matador also reveals the accelerating pace of elite special operations forces (SOF) actions in the Al-Qaim area. The U.S. military's organization charged with hunting Zarqawi and dismantling AQI was known as Task Force 714, or just the "Task Force", under command of Army Major General Stanley McChrystal.[14] The record of the Task Force's operations in early 2005 remains mostly shrouded to this day, but some reports did come to light at the time and are part of the public record.

According to Department of Defense press releases and contemporary press stories, on May 2nd, unspecified coalition forces were operating near the Syrian border. They identified a truck carrying fighters and materiel from an isolated, Zarqawi-linked camp into the Al-Qaim area. A heliborne raid force was launched and an intense fight ensued as they intercepted the truck. Twelve militants were subsequently killed, and six coalition personnel were wounded, along with a six-year-old Iraqi girl.[15] This incident may have been related to the internecine fighting in Husaybah that day, with AQI attempting to bolster its forces there, but the connection is unclear.

The Task Force was finding AQI-associated targets in the Al-Qaim area, and was shifting its focus to address them, according to McChrystal's own memoir.[16] Many 3/2 veterans remember being briefed or told informally that Zarqawi or some of his top leaders were in the vicinity of Ramana and that other coalition forces were hot on their trail.

THE PLAN COMES TOGETHER

After several iterations, the finalized plan for Operation Matador was a classic hammer and anvil approach. Blocking positions would be put in place on the northern side of the river along the Syrian border and at the Golden Gate bridge to keep insurgents from escaping. The main maneuver elements would cross the Euphrates near the town of New Ubaydi and clear Ramana from east to west up to the border. The desert plateau to the north would be screened by Light Armored Vehicles (LAVs) or helicopters.

This would be a battalion-sized effort, the first for 3/2, but would also involve other units cross-attached to bolster the operation. Lieutenant Colonel Mundy would command the force. Kilo Company from 3/2 and Lima Company from 3/25 would provide the infantry for clearing operations, with mobile fire support from WarPig. A company of LAVs from 2nd LAR would be the screening force, and a section of tanks would provide direct support when needed.[17]

Another temporarily attached asset literally held the linchpin of the entire operation. The U.S. Army's 814th Mobile Bridging Company would be brought in to assemble a floating ribbon bridge. This would enable the main force, including tanks, to rapidly cross the Euphrates into the eastern edge of Ramana, hopefully surprising the enemy in their rural sanctuary. The conservative estimate was that emplacing the bridge would take 12 hours. Mundy's aim was to have mobile forces across the river and rolling through the villages on the northern bank on the first day.

Colonel Davis and members of the RCT-2 staff would deploy out to Al-Qaim in their mobile command post, known as the "jump" From the regimental perspective, Operation Matador fit into the colonel's overall campaign plan of projecting power all along the Euphrates at unpredictable intervals and locations, "to be everywhere but nowhere."

CLOSE AIR

Additional aviation assets were also allocated to support the operation, including several types of helicopters (rotary-wing aircraft), jet fighter-bombers (fixed-wing aircraft) and unmanned drones. In fact, the use of aircraft during Matador would illustrate another defining characteristic of the modern Marine Corps, the tight linkage between air assets and ground forces.

Operationally, Marine aviation forms one side of an integrated air-ground team, or what the Corps calls the Marine Air Ground Task Force (MAGTF, pronounced "mag-taf"). In 2005, the aviation side of the MAGTF was the 2nd Marine Air Wing (2nd MAW), headquartered at Al-Asad airbase. The wing had a full range of capabilities, but at its core were attack squadrons flying close air support (CAS) missions.

In Anbar, most calls for air support would be handled by attack helicopters in the HMLA (Helicopter Marine Light Attack) squadrons. These composite units flew modernized versions of the venerable UH-1 Huey and the AH-1 Cobra. For most of the deployment, 3/2's first option for air support was HMLA 269, known as the Gunrunners. The squadron sent a detachment or "det" out to Camp Al-Qaim, with four to six aircraft. Having attack helicopters co-located was a big advantage for 3/2 and they were integrated into all battalion operations.

When HMLA 269 redeployed in late summer, another squadron, the Coyotes of HMLA 775, replaced them:

> *Having the det right there worked fantastic... I wasn't their commander, but we operated almost like a MEU [Marine Expeditionary Unit], as a cohesive Marine air-ground task force... It was important to me that they felt they were as much a part of our team as my own Marines.*
>
> **—Tim Mundy**[18]

In combat, the Hueys and Cobras usually operated in complementary pairs. The UH-1N "November" model Hueys used door-mounted 7.62mm miniguns and .50 cal machine-guns to deliver heavy suppressive fire. Their three radios allowed the crew to coordinate directly with other aircraft, ground units, and higher command. The Hueys could also carry extra personnel and gear, an extremely useful capability. The AH-1W Super Cobras were faster than the Hueys and their 20mm gatling gun and up to four rocket pods gave them heavier firepower. The "Whiskeys" could also deliver guided Hellfire and TOW missiles which could hit the window of a house or a moving vehicle from long range.

If targets required heavier ordnance, or could not be easily reached by helicopters, fast-moving fighter/attack jets would respond. Two squadrons of Marine attack jets were part of 2nd MAW; the Flying Bengals of VMFA-224 in sleek F/A-18 Hornets and VMA-311 flying AV-8B Harrier "jump jets." Both were typically loaded with laser-guided or satellite-guided bombs that could strike within just a few feet of a target.

High-tech aircraft and weapons are all but useless, however, without detailed knowledge of how and where to employ them. This makes the Forward Air Controller (FAC) one of the most important figures on the battlefield and the glue holding the air-ground team together. There were three FACs in 3/2's Air Team, each a rated Marine pilot with hundreds of missions in the cockpit and qualified as a Joint Terminal Attack Controller (JTAC).[19]

The senior air officer for 3/2 was Captain Scott "Special" Edwards, an experienced F/A-18 pilot. As the battalion commander's primary link to the air support system, he usually worked in the COC. Captain Nathaniel "Pest" Stusse was a Harrier pilot assigned to support India Company. Captain Joey "Flatz" Martin came from the heavy-lift world where he'd flown CH-53s. Martin would often support Kilo or WarPig missions.[20]

Another FAC closely involved with 3/2 was Mark "Rock" Lister. Lister was the air officer for RCT-2 and a key part of Colonel Davis' staff. He was another seasoned Hornet pilot, coming out of VMFA-224, the same squadron then deployed to Al-Asad. Together these ground-pounding pilots formed a tight, flexible network that could adapt quickly to get the right aircraft with the right weapons to the right targets.

Controlling airstrikes in proximity to friendly troops requires a high degree of technical skill, excellent situational awareness, and quick thinking. Getting something wrong can be disastrous. If a FAC or JTAC miscommunicates with the pilot, releases inappropriate ordnance, or passes the wrong coordinates, the results can be catastrophic. There have been tragic instances where bombs have been erroneously called in on friendly troops, civilians, or the FAC's own position.

To prevent this, FACs take great care to precisely know and communicate the position and nature of the target, and especially friendly locations. Everything gets more complex in bad weather, hazy conditions, blowing sand, or at night. In such conditions, the factors involved are compounded and scenarios multiply towards infinity. Terminal control of CAS missions can be described as four-dimensional chess with explosive effects.

NEW-MODEL CAS

Technologies and operational procedures were also fundamentally changing the way CAS was conducted, and the FACs of 3/2 and RCT-2 were working right at the cusp of this change. For one, joint regulations had recently been updated to allow the use of downlinked video from an aircraft, drone, or other platform to "see" and strike targets. This opened up a wide range of tactics the FACs could use for so-called Type-2 and Type-3 attacks*, leveraging real-time targeting data from UAVs, SOF teams, or other assets. "This stuff had been around since 2003," recalls Nathaniel Stusse, "But as we got to Iraq, the wider CAS world was just starting to figure out how to use them."[21]

Two other developments were unobtrusive, practically invisible, but would have big effects. The first was a new communications and video system called Rover-III. Loaded on a

* Joint Publication 3-09.3, Joint Fire Support, Chapter V, clarifies that; "In Type 2 or 3 control, JTACs may be required to coordinate CAS attacks using targeting information from an observer. An observer may be a scout... UAV, SOF, or other asset with real time targeting information."

ruggedized laptop, Rover linked to the video feed from a remote platform, such as a Predator or a targeting pod strapped under the wing of a fighter jet:

> *They gave us four Rover-III sets and said, "go ahead and start learning how these work." I took one out to the flightline and figured out how to downlink from a Lightning pod mounted on a Hornet. I realized we had a pretty cool capability. Once Rover was synced up, I could see whatever the pilot saw through the pod.*
>
> —**Mark Lister**[22]

For the FACs, viewing a target on Rover was better in many ways than seeing it from ground level through binoculars or their own eyes. Major Lister sent a couple of the sets to 3/2, another went to 2nd LAR, and he kept one for himself. "We were one of the first Marine battalions to get Rovers," recalls Edwards. "We had to figure it out on-the-fly. But we did, and I started taking that thing everywhere."

The second key development was the use of detailed maps, known as Ground Reference Graphics or GRGs. The battalion's mapping section produced them from current satellite imagery and added graphic overlays. Roads and terrain features were named, each town divided into designated sectors and individual buildings were numbered. The GRGs became a vital tool to speed coordination between ground units and supporting aircraft. "Before we got to Iraq, use of GRGs wasn't so prevalent," recalls Martin. "[But] when we really learned how to use them, it helped quickly ID friendlies, target locations, and fire trajectories."

This combination of technology and techniques pushed the emergence of close air support that was more responsive, flexible, and precise. "We didn't know it at the time, but we were at the forefront of all this," says Lister. "Learning how to do CAS in a non-linear battlefield, a counter-insurgency environment, and very amorphous tactical situations. We were controlling rapid, reactive, surgical strikes. Lots of those lessons we learned are still being used today."

The first real test for 3/2's Air Team had come during the big assault on Camp Gannon. Within minutes of the suicide attacks, HMLA 269 launched a mission in response. "I was in the battalion COC, and could hear Stusse coordinating," says Martin. "It was like listening to a master class in CAS. It was impressive." It also impressed 3/2's leadership. "11 April was a game changer. The battalion gained confidence in using air as an equalizer for the grunts," Martin recalls.[23]

By May, the Air Team's capabilities had been further honed. "The cooperation we had with 3/2 was great," Edwards described. "Lieutenant Colonel Mundy and Major Day loved aviation . . . I think 3/2 was using more air than any other battalion at that time."[24] Operation Matador would showcase new-model CAS techniques and demonstrate how innovative the FACs could be.

15. HAMMER & ANVIL

The combined force assembled on Camp Al-Qaim just before the operation, with parts of the regimental combat team reinforcing 3/2. Only days before, both Lima Company 3/25 and most of 3/2's Kilo Company were conducting Operation Outer Banks in Haditha, searching for weapons caches. This showed RCT-2's aggressive tempo and the ability to focus its scarce combat power. As that mission wrapped up, both units moved by night up to Camp AQ on May 3, 2005.[1]

By the 7th, the base was crowded with extra vehicles and personnel and pulsed with excitement. Lieutenant Nate Smith, Commander of Kilo's 2nd Platoon, could sense the anticipation. "In my experience, the guys look forward to combat," he recalls. "It's not like in movies where guys are nervous and fearful. Not at all like that. With the all-volunteer Marine infantry, they're always eager for action. Morale was always highest right before a major operation."[2]

Some Marines also took the opportunity to prepare spiritually. The night before the operation, Chaplain John Anderson held a service in the "Soul Train," an old railroad passenger car converted into a small chapel. Two key NCOs attended and had a brief, but weighty, exchange after the service. First Sergeant Sean Gregory, of Kilo, met there with his old friend Anthony Goodwin. They'd worked together back in Lejeune and now

Goodwin was assigned to Lima 3/25, chopped over from regimental staff to bolster the unit's experience level. As the two seasoned NCOs shook hands, Gregory said "Take care, brother, we'll see you on the other side."[3]

The first vehicles started moving out after midnight on Sunday, May 8th, which happened to be Mother's Day. A stream of Humvees, AAVs and 7-ton trucks wound their way through the entry control point, then out into the desert. They were joined by the nimble LAVs of Bravo Company, and the menacing, angular shapes of four Abrams tanks. The Army bridging company followed in a long train of over forty huge eight-wheeled trucks hauling bulky pontoon sections, engineering equipment, and even small tugboats.[4]

The bridge they carried would allow Lieutenant Colonel Mundy to push his main force, the "hammer", across the river. Meanwhile, a smaller column was pushing out from Camp Gannon. WarPig 1 had orders to establish a blocking position at the Golden Gate bridge, a crucial part of the "anvil" to prevent enemy movements.[5] Almost as soon as the operation started, however, the sands of friction sifted in to clog the gears. As the main force snaked its way towards the bridging site, one of the AAVs carrying Kilo Company hit a mine. Sitting towards the front of the vehicle, Lance Corporal Matt Greene was just over the mine when it went off. "It was so violent it threw me and a couple other Marines into the air," recalls Greene. "I was shook up, but OK. A corpsman hurt his back though, and the mine blew the rollers off of one side…It took us a while to get a replacement trac."[6]

The Army bridging company was running into even bigger problems. The soldiers operating their heavy equipment transports had little experience driving at night, which slowed their progress. Some turned on their headlights which made them vulnerable to attack, but still didn't speed things up. One of the massive trucks hit a soft shoulder and tipped over in the dark, while two other vehicles collided.[7] Sorting out the snags soaked up more precious time and the bridging equipment barely made it to the crossing site before dawn.

CONTACT

As the sun rose behind them that morning, the Marines in the main force were looking west over the placid waters of the Euphrates. In that location, the river turned back on itself and flowed west to east for a stretch. Across it they could see green fields and a village beyond. The river was only 200 meters wide at that point, but it would be hours before they could cross. The engineers had discovered the bank was too muddy and steep, and the current too strong, to allow easy deployment of the bridge sections. They were working feverishly on a solution. While bulldozers began to excavate a better approach to the water, Mundy and his staff could only watch and wait, with units spread out in the bare terrain around them. About a mile to the northeast, basically to their rear, lay the sizable town of New Ubaydi. Constructed in the 1970s, its modern homes and public buildings were arrayed in orderly city blocks. Just to the west of it was Old Ubaydi, tucked into a bend in the river.

About an hour after sunrise, gunfire was heard in New Ubaydi and some units reported incoming. At first, only a few desultory shots were thrown their way, posing little danger, but the firing intensified as the morning dragged on. This was another unexpected development.

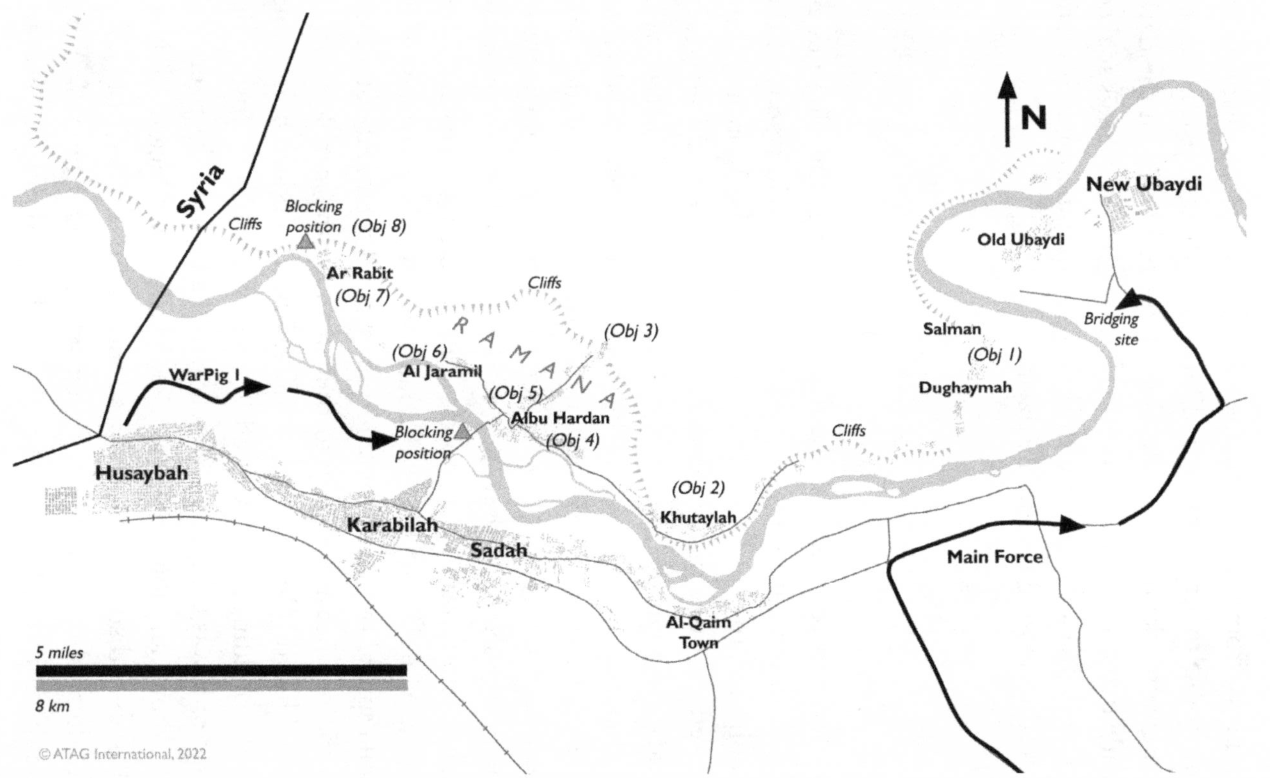
N
Syria
Cliffs
Blocking position
(Obj 8)
Ar Rabit
(Obj 7)
Cliffs
R A M A N A
(Obj 3)
(Obj 6)
Al Jaramil
(Obj 5)
Albu Hardan
(Obj 4)
WarPig I
Blocking position
Husaybah
Karabilah
Sadah
(Obj 2)
Khutaylah
Cliffs
Al-Qaim Town
New Ubaydi
Old Ubaydi
Salman
(Obj 1)
Dughaymah
Bridging site
Main Force
5 miles
8 km
© ATAG International, 2022

Three weeks before, on April 12th, the civil affairs detachment had visited New Ubaydi and met with some of the town's leaders.[8] On that day, the locals were cordial and the discussions were amiable. But something had apparently changed since then.

While this threat emerged from New Ubaydi, Mundy was also monitoring an extended firefight that had broken out at the Golden Gate bridge a few miles to his west. The radio nets were crackling with reports of WarPig's guntrucks engaging insurgents. Tension was rising across the battlespace. Then things got worse.

The distinctive thunk of mortar fire came from New Ubaydi. That got everyone's attention. "The insurgents over there had some pretty remarkable mortarmen," related Mundy. "They were able to basically dial us in." Now the costs of waiting by the riverbank were evident. "I had a couple land really close to where I was," he continued, "They basically had the range, knew where we were, and were able to figure it out pretty quick."[9]

Other Marines with the command section also had close calls. "We had impacts just 25 or 50 meters from us," describes Chris Ieva. "I can remember the pressure wave and the sound of the shrapnel in the air, like invisible whiffle-balls going by your head."[10] Lance Corporal Tonie Sims, in the security platoon, had an even closer brush. "The first rounds were way off, maybe 200 meters out and no real direction. We kinda laughed at it," Sims recalls. "But then the second volley hit smack in the middle of our perimeter. One landed beside the truck where I was...I was knocked unconscious, and had some cuts and burns, but nothing serious."[11]

HASTY ATTACK

It was now obvious New Ubaydi would have to be dealt with. Pop-shots from small arms were one thing. Accurate mortar fire was quite another. Mundy called on his unit commanders to formulate a plan and they began to coordinate air and other assets for a hasty attack. With a flurry of unfolding maps, radio calls, and digital messages, Major Day coordinated with company commanders and quickly put together a bold, simple plan.

Kilo Company would push directly north and assault the southwest corner of the town, clearing west to east. Lima 3/25 would take a more circuitous route near Old Ubaydi, approach from the west and enter the northwest sector. Guntrucks of WarPig 3 and Bravo Company's LAVs would take support-by-fire positions in the open areas, screening off the town. Tanks would provide long-range fires and move in to provide direct support as required.

While the attack was planned on-the-fly, unit leaders quickly absorbed it and prepared to execute. But there was no time to brief it thoroughly down through the ranks. Sergeant Andrew Taylor, a squad leader in Lima Company 3/25, remembers the abbreviated mission briefing he received:

> *We sat there for what seemed like forever as the rounds kept coming in. I told the guys to keep their heads down till we were told what to do. Finally, squad leaders were rounded up and a couple of tiny maps were shown to us. The objective was New Ubaydi. The tracs would take us around to the west side, to throw the insurgents off and make them react to us. Then 3/2 would come in on our right*

flank... We were to gain a foothold and wait for further word. The brief took only five minutes.

—**Andrew Taylor**[12]

Further down the food chain, the grunts had even less understanding of the situation. Enclosed in the noisy, smelly, vibrating innards of the AAVs, they were about to go through a jarring experience.

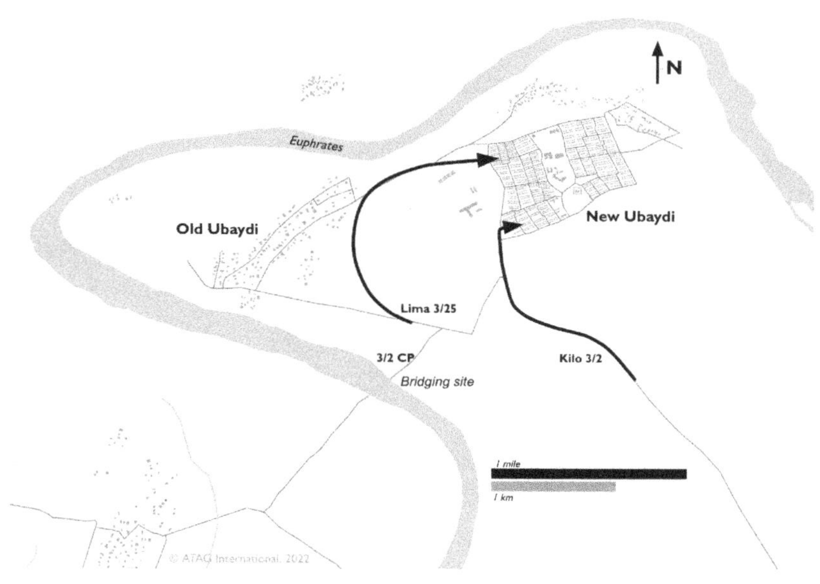

INTO THE FIRE

The assault was launched at 1130. Tracs carrying Kilo's 2nd and 3rd Platoons rolled north up the hardball road parallel to the town, while 1st Platoon and Kilo's command section took positions in the open ground to the south. In 2nd Platoon's lead trac, Lieutenant Smith was perplexed as his vehicle's gunner cut loose with the .50 cal. Then he noticed multiple sparkles in the darkened windows of the town. He didn't immediately recognize them as the muzzle flashes of incoming fire.[13]

The AAVs pivoted abruptly to their right, about 25 meters apart, their blunt noses facing east. The crews were executing a textbook mobile assault, positioned as close to the objective as practical without putting their vehicles at excessive risk. To the men cramped inside, though, the maneuver was a sudden, lurching stop followed immediately by sheer madness. The ramps dropped about fifty meters from the edge of town and Marines poured out, peeling left and right. Heavy fire came from their front and from more distant buildings off to their left. Soon the enemy also opened up from some low warehouses behind them. Tracers laced the air and RPGs shrieked by, some exploding among them. One struck a trac, fortunately causing only minor damage. The AAV gunners fired back with a deafening roar.

This was the first real combat experience for most Kilo Marines, and it was a rude awakening, particularly for Private First Class Emmanuel Nelson. "I had actually nodded off in the trac, and I woke up with rounds pinging off the sides," he remembers. "We dismounted and went into a shallow, filthy ditch. There were feces in that ditch. There was lots of gunfire. I'd never seen anything like it. Everything seemed so fast."[14]

Lance Corporal Derek Buskey dove into the same ditch alongside Nelson. "It was nasty," he remembers. "Nelson was to my right...An RPG flew over my head, I heard it swoosh by, about a foot above me. It passed basically parallel to the ditch, right over everyone."[15] For several life-long moments they ignored the trash and filth, returning fire, and scanning for targets. Off to their right, 3rd platoon pushed into the streets and started clearing while the 2nd platoon covered them. Then Lieutenant Smith yelled above the fray and his platoon rushed forward.

HOUSE TO HOUSE

Corporal Kris Borch, a veteran of Nasiriyah, led 1st Squad into one of the streets. He was overseeing two fire teams, augmented by machine gunners and assaulters from the weapons platoon, as well as two corpsmen. Corporal Eric Rainey and his team took the right side of the street. Lance Corporal Larry Philippon, Privates First Class Travis Kern and Emmanuel Nelson, and corpsman Ramon Alfaro took the left side. The houses were surrounded by a nine-foot-high cinder block wall. At the front were large, double gates for vehicle access and a smaller pedestrian gate.

Each fire team carried custom-made breaching charges with them, but a firm kick would usually break open the pedestrian gates. The Marines would then cross the inner courtyard and stack next to the front door. On signal, the point man kicked in or breached the front door and the team flowed into the house, searching each room. This took only a minute if things were simple. But there were often complications, sometimes intentional ones.

They began encountering obstacles the enemy had placed within the houses. Brandon Puhlman, a block south with 2nd Squad, received a severe jolt as he touched a metal door. "It threw me back several feet," he describes. "I thought my arm was gone and started yelling." Right behind him, his squad leader, Jimmy Rooks, had seen him recoil suddenly and calmed him down. "You're OK, your arm's still there," Rooks told him. Upon entering, they discovered a car battery wired to the door, to shock whoever tried to open it. "There were also warm shell casings in there," remembers Puhlman. "They'd just been fired. The enemy was close."[16]

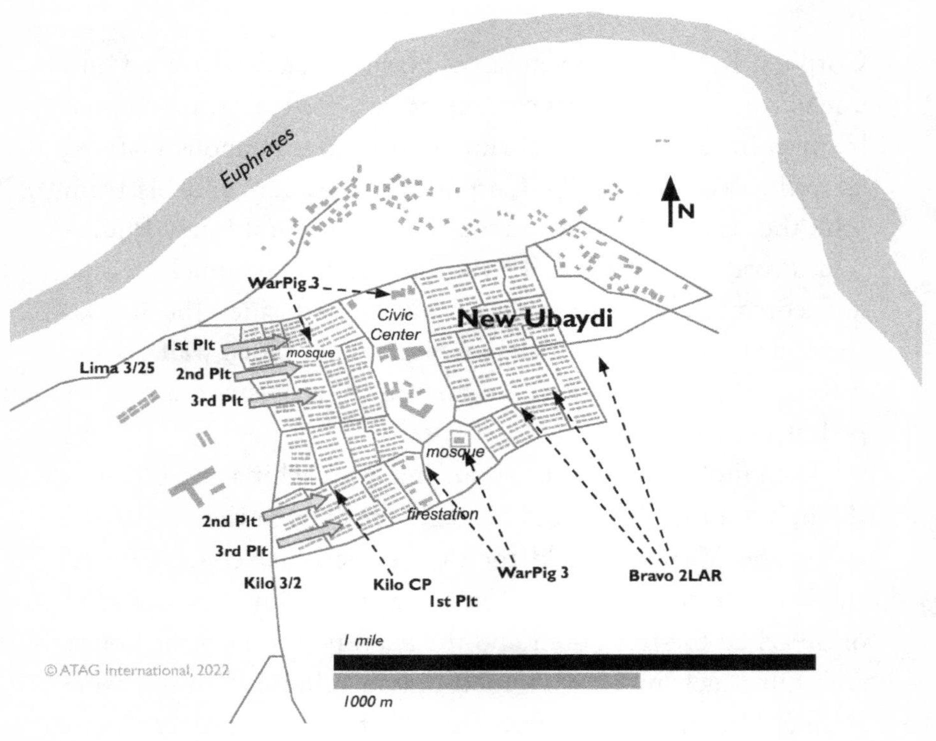

Back with 1st Squad, Corporal Borch stayed in the street directing his men. Assaulters and combat engineers were nearby with heavier explosives if needed, and an M240 gun team was sent to the end of the street for security. At one point, Borch decided to augment that security and called for Lance Corporal Matt Gundlach, a SAW gunner in Rainey's team. "He tells me to run up the street to the corner, to be with the other gun. We like to work the MGs in pairs," says Gundlach. "Just after I got to the corner, a firefight broke out in a house behind me, on the left side of the street."[17]

IN AN INSTANT

A few moments before, Lance Corporal Larry Philippon's team had broken into the courtyard of a house. Travis Kern figured it was his turn to kick a door and offered to take point. But Philippon answered, "It's OK, I got it," then stacked to the left of the entryway with Nelson and Alfaro behind.[18] Kern took position behind a car parked in the courtyard to cover the front windows. Philippon kicked the door once, then harder a second time and it gave way. The moment he entered the house, a burst of automatic fire slammed into him, and he dropped. In an instant, everything changed. The same burst caught Nelson, shattering his forearm, and bullet fragments hit Alfaro in the leg.

Kern remembers that instant in agonizing detail. "The door was kind of in an alcove, and just as Philippon kicked it, an MG opened up almost simultaneously. He went down hard, and Nelson and Alfaro were hit at the same time."[19] Alfaro also recalls that fateful moment vividly. "I just knew we had to get out of that doorway. I grabbed Nelson and pulled him back and called for help."[20] Then a second burst of fire came at Kern, bullets punching through the car's thin metal body. At least one round hit his lower leg, fracturing it. He crumpled behind the car, and looked down to see bone sticking through his skin above the ankle:

> *Next thing I know, Borch charges in, grabs me and pulls me behind the wall and out into the street. He asked me where Phillipon was, and I said, "I think Larry's dead." Matt Gundlach came over and put a tourniquet on my leg. Nelson was out there already, and Doc Alfaro was working on him. Nelly was cussing Doc because he was more worried about me and Philippon.*
>
> —**Travis Kern**[21]

BONDS

Nelson remembers Alfaro and others trying to get him to lay down, which bothered him because he knew others needed help. "I felt like my wound was minor and I was getting too much attention," Nelson recalls. "I was just concerned about Philippon and Kern. I don't remember going into shock, but I had no control of my arm, and my thumb was pulsating up and down."[22] A block to the south, Lieutenant Smith had heard the gunfire erupt, but didn't immediately equate it with hostile action:

> *Then I saw Puhlman come around the corner, alone, which is odd in a close-quarters urban fight. He walked towards me and had this look on his face. He said, 'Sir, we've got some KIAs', and I said, 'Ours or theirs'? It hadn't really sunk in with me yet that my guys could get killed.*
>
> —**Nate Smith**[23]

At this point, the unshakeable bonds between brother warriors, and between the corpsmen and their Marines, came into sharp focus. With Philippon down inside the front door, Corporal Borsh rallied several Marines to rush the house, knowing full well they might be charging into the same deadly fire. By this time, men from 2nd Squad had joined them. Borch led the way as they dashed across the courtyard, took up firing positions by the door and windows, and suppressed the interior.

When no enemy fire came in response, Corporal Rooks pushed into the entryway, firing down the hallway, grabbed Philippon and pulled him out of the house. Outside, they wrapped their friend's lifeless body in a poncho. Others joined them while they bore him up gingerly and carried him out of the courtyard.

Meanwhile, amid the dust and fear and blood in the street, Alfaro ignored his own wounds to tend to Nelson's arm. Another corpsman rushed over to render aid to Kern, forming an impromptu casualty collection point (CCP) as other Marines rushed to the scene:

> *Nelson was hit bad in the forearm and the bicep. He was going into shock... It was very intense as I worked on him. But I also kept asking about Philippon, until Staff Sergeant Hanson told me, "There's nothing else you can do for Philippon." That's when it really hit me. It felt like I had failed him. It was horrible.*
>
> —**Ramon Alfaro**[24]

More Marines had converged by that time, focused on neutralizing any threat that remained inside the house. Smith ordered a pair of assaulters to blast it with the SMAW rocket system. "I lined up the shot and punched an HE rocket through the side of the house," recalls Stephen Carouthers. "Then Buskey loads me up a second round, and I fire that in there too. Finally, combat engineers prepped 20-pound satchel charges and threw those in, which totally leveled the house."[25]

EXHAUSTION

Meanwhile, it fell to the platoon commander to call in the casualties. For a moment, Smith hesitated to key the mic, reluctant to acknowledge the bitter loss. "I thought Captain Ieva would chew my ass," remembers Smith. "But when I made the call, it was like he took his bars off for a second. He tempered his voice, and said, 'OK, buddy, we'll take care of the CASEVAC. What do you need?' He knew what I was feeling. I'll always be grateful for that."[26]

The emotional blow of Philippon's loss unfolded in different ways for each man. For the wounded, the exigencies of combat forced a traumatic reality upon them. "They put us in an AAV to get us over to the dustoff LZ outside the city," describes Kern. "Nelson, Alfaro, myself, and another guy with a concussion were all in there. Then they brought Philippon's body in. Normally that's not supposed to happen... That's our friend laying there. We were kinda freaked out by that."[27]

For others, consumed in the intensity of the moment and immersed in the violent cacophony of shouts, gunfire, and explosions, it was hard to immediately absorb what had happened. But as the adrenaline wore off, the effects took their toll. Larry Philippon was a friend to many, a good leader, and a positive influence in the platoon. Suddenly he was gone. "It was unbelievable how emotionally draining it was," says Smith. "There was this sense of failure, deflation. We'd failed. I'd failed. Then trying to pick back up, to get amped back up for whatever came next was a huge challenge."[28] Matt Gundlach relates his delayed reaction. "When we went back to the tracs I was exhausted. I looked over at Corporal Uridya and said, 'They got Philippon', and just burst into tears. Then I fell asleep."[29]

TRADING SHOTS

With Kilo's platoons clearing from the west, another fight developed along the southern edge of town. In the opening moments of the assault, Ieva had the company's command section with two AAVs, and 1st Platoon in high-backed Humvees, race to take up support-by-fire positions some 500 meters out in the flat. They were joined by a section of WarPig 3 and on their right the LAVs of Bravo Company. "It started as a feint, diverting enemy attention and drawing their fire," Ieva recalls. "We headed over there at full speed. It felt like a cavalry charge."[30]

The captain positioned his trac with a clear field of fire up one of the north-south streets. The other vehicles did the same, and their gunners picked off any insurgents who exposed themselves. The LAVs were situated further out on higher ground to take full advantage of their weapons systems. "With our optics, we could sit back there and see all the way into the city," recalls Sam McAmis, a platoon commander in Bravo Company. "Even from way out there we can zoom right in to see individuals, and that 25mm gun is super accurate."[31]

New Ubaydi's grid-like layout and straight streets turned large swathes of the town into kill-zones. As enemy fighters withdrew from the advancing infantry, they became targets.

"We were operating kind of like a broom, pushing them into a dustpan," relates Smith.[32] The tactic worked as intended, and numbers of insurgents were cut down by long-range fires.

But some enemy gunners traded shots with the vehicles. In particular, several of them were shooting from a fire station with a multi-story tower. It seemed to be an enemy strongpoint, with insurgents entering and leaving. In one of the WarPig guntrucks, 21-year-old Corporal Jonathan Penland was behind a Mk19 grenade launcher. He started trading fire with the enemy near the fire station:

> *Every time I'd reach my arm out to reload, more rounds would hit. Garcia started yelling, "Penny get down!!"and yanked me by the belt. Almost pulled my pants down. Just as he did, there was a huge 'clang!' A round had hit right where I'd been, and the fragments stung my face. It left a huge mark on the metal. Then Staff Sergeant Vargas comes over the radio. "Vehicle 5, shoot the middle window of the tower!" I fired about six rounds, and they arced out and splashed directly on the middle window. I pegged it again and the incoming stopped. When the day was over, our truck was a mess. Dents and gouges all over it. I owe my life to Daniel Garcia. If he hadn't pulled me down, I don't know what that slug would have done. That's how I got my nickname. After that everybody started calling me "Penny."*
>
> **—Jonathan Penland**[33]

FLEETING TARGETS

The attack helicopters and jets were finding other targets, directed by the FACs. Just prior to Matador, "Rock" Lister had moved into 3/2's COC. He set up his maps, radios, and the Rover system in the operations office and was working there as the operation kicked off.

The office had a small window, which proved important. To hook up the Rover, a cable was run out the window to an antenna outside. The setup was a little rickety and there were problems positioning the antenna to ensure good video downlink. But Lister was eventually able to watch the feed from fighter aircraft through their targeting pods and from an orbiting Predator.

At a crucial point during the fighting, however, a technical glitch popped up. The Rover system overheated, and the video link was lost. Just then, Lieutenant Colonel Starling, the regimental ops officer, received an urgent radio call. It was from another officer watching the live Predator feed at Al-Asad. He was observing 30 to 40 enemy fighters leaving the city with weapons, executing an organized withdrawal across the river. "I was standing there with a map ... with [radio contact] to some aircraft and I had targets," related Lister. "Technically, it was Type-2 since I did have an observer, being the Predator."[34]

Lister and the others quickly put together a lashed-up control. With the drone's camera zoomed in on the insurgents, the RCT officer at Al-Asad watched the video feed. Over the radio, he described the target to Starling who stood outside the COC to get good reception. Then another officer ran to the open window to verbally relay the information to Lister.

> *[He was] telling me what the Predator was seeing, and I was looking at the map, giving the grid to the pilots, asking them what they saw ... If it didn't match up, then I certainly wasn't going to let [them] drop ordnance. But lo and behold ... the picture was very*

clear. Enemy crossing the river… [We] ended up delivering four GBU-12s, which are 500-pound laser guided bombs… We sank three boats, probably killed between 25–30 of the enemy.

—Mark Lister[35]

Despite the glitches and working from locations miles away from the action, they had exploited live video from a drone, the greater latitude of Type-2 control, and an ad-hoc comms setup to eliminate a platoon-sized enemy force.

HORNETS' NEST

Meanwhile, the platoons of Lima 3/25 pushed east through the northwest quadrant. A section from WarPig 3 provided fire support on the northern edge of the town. The enemy was more concentrated in this sector of New Ubaydi, judging from several eye-witness accounts.

As Sergeant Andrew Taylor led his squad from house to house, they were frequently engaged from the rooftops. "The guys who shot at us would run from building to building. The roofs were adjoining and had high parapets, so they could slip away," Taylor remembers.[36] It was hard, dangerous work. The 1st Platoon anchored the left of the line, clearing the blocks on the far north, while 3rd Platoon worked in the center and 2nd Platoon took the right flank. Soon they started discovering the insurgents' extensive preparations:

They had staged weapons and ammo in the houses, ready to go… [In one] house was the biggest cache I had ever seen. There were a half dozen machine-guns and RPGs, rockets, artillery

> *shells. There was ammo in bins and boxes, hand grenades of assorted shapes and sizes. There were enough weapons in this living room for a small army.*
>
> **—Andrew Taylor**[37]

While some of the caches were blown in place, others had to be left behind. There simply wasn't time to destroy them while the enemy still needed to be rooted out. In the center of that sector, fighters were using a mosque as a strongpoint. "The loudspeakers began blaring in Arabic," recalls Taylor. "The muj were using the mosque's speakers to tell where we were and shout commands. Others sat in the windows of the mosque and used it as a last stand."[38]

Corporal Henry Sowell, a vehicle commander with WarPig 3, was at the north edge of town. Across the radio, he heard that Lima Company's command group was pinned down on the street near the mosque, one Marine bleeding severely from a gunshot to the leg. Sowell's crew spotted men firing from the balcony of the mosque's slender minaret and asked for permission to engage. There were strict rules for firing at a mosque, but in this instance approval came quickly.[39]

Heavy .50 caliber rounds started taking chunks out of the minaret, but the steep angle of fire kept them from hitting the insurgents. Sowell then exited the safety of the vehicle for a shot with his M203 grenade launcher. From approximately 200 meters out, he dropped his first grenade directly on top of the fighters in the minaret. Hostile fire immediately slackened, letting Lima 3/25's command group pull back to safety.

LAST HOUSE ON THE BLOCK

Frustration was mounting at the command level as problems multiplied. Both Kilo 3/2 and Lima 3/25 had suffered casualties. WarPig was heavily engaged at the Golden Gate bridge. Moreover, the Army's ribbon bridge was still not assembled. A small forward element had been sent over for far-side security, but the main force still could not cross.

While the fighting in Kilo Company's sector had ended, Lima 3/25 was still in sporadic contact. As their 1st Platoon cleared the last block of houses, Corporal Dustin Derga, a volunteer firefighter back in Ohio, led his fire team as they breached a door. They were met with an instant fusillade of gunfire and Derga went down, mortally wounded. Several others were hit too. Sergeant Dennis Woullard, a deputy sheriff back home, narrowly escaped when a slug glanced off his helmet, shredding the kevlar, and knocking him out momentarily. When he came to, he dragged the stricken Derga out of the doorway.

Staff Sergeant Goodwin, who had shaken hands with his old friend Sean Gregory outside the "Soul Train" hours before, quickly gathered several Marines and pushed back in. They killed two insurgents who tried to escape out the back. They were still clearing rooms when a burst of full-auto fire suddenly exploded from within the house, sending them scrambling out. But once outside they realized Goodwin had been cut down and was still inside.

It was a horrible, confused situation. They patched up several wounded Marines and cared for Derga as best they could in his final moments. Their platoon sergeant was still inside, assumed dead, but nobody knew where the fire had come from. A series of desperate actions followed, including throwing in multiple grenades, and calling up a tank to blast the house with its main gun. But ultimately, they realized they'd have to go back in to recover Goodwin.

OUT OF NOWHERE

The late afternoon shadows were lengthening as Taylor stacked another team outside the shattered house, then entered, nerves on edge:

> *We were almost at the end of the hall... I could see Goodwin's feet and ankles. He was not moving. Suddenly bullets came out of nowhere. There was no source, just the blasting of the machine-gun and the walls shredding all around us. The noise was deafening... tracer rounds passed by us, narrowly missing. Everyone dove into the kitchen. I jumped through the door and fell hard on my side. The room flashed as the tracers flew over our bodies. I could see and feel the rounds as they sliced an inch above me. I tried to squish into the floor and roll over, but I couldn't move... I lifted my rifle and began shooting the wall. Thomas did the same... Then as suddenly as the shooting started it stopped. Everyone sprang to their feet and ran for the door and dove outside.*
>
> —**Andrew Taylor**[40]

Just minutes later, they formed up and tried again, the fourth time. By then it was completely dark inside the house. This time Corporal Scott Bunker led the way since he was the only one with a flashlight on his weapon. A few months before, he'd been a fulltime student at the University of Ohio:

We went in with rifles shouldered. We knew brutal close combat was imminent. My eyes strained to see down the long dark hallway. The sight was straight out of a horror film. The hallway was littered with empty shell casings and a long trail of blood ascended the stairs to the roof. One of the tank rounds had struck a propane tank and caused the building to ignite. Shadows from the flickering flames danced eerily. Further down the blood-soaked hall, my heart sank as I saw the boots and camouflaged utility pants of a United States Marine.

—Scott Bunker[41]

Bunker and another Marine found Goodwin's body lying next to a small closet door tucked underneath the stairway. They carefully approached the door and on a silent count, opened it. Immediately, white-hot muzzle blasts stabbed out of the pitch-dark space. Bunker was hit in the arm, upper body, and right eye. Amid the deadly hail, somehow his buddies managed to drag him away from the line of fire. When the machine-gun opened up again, Andrew Taylor was at the front door and dove headlong into the courtyard to escape its fire. Moments later he watched as Bunker was brought out.

He was covered in blood and unrecognizable. I grabbed his shoulder. Others grabbed the rest of him, and we picked him up and heaved him out the doorway. His body went limp. I thought he'd died. Bunker was a close friend and brother. When he went limp, I let go and fell over. I just sat there in shock. I watched as Marines dragged him through the yard and into the street.

—Andrew Taylor[42]

The threat had finally been identified after four attempts

to clear the house, two KIA and multiple wounded (including Bunker, who survived his injuries). Insurgents had dug through the floor of the small closet under the stairs and at least two were entrenched below floor level. There they manned a belt-fed machine-gun, firing 7.62mm armor-piercing (AP) rounds that could slice through concrete and brick. Their position was immune from anything but a direct hit, and in that darkened hole they had survived grenade blasts and several 120mm tank rounds. They were almost certainly deafened, concussed, and likely had serious internal injuries. But they could still unleash devastating streams of heavy AP rounds.

No one wanted to leave Goodwin inside, but finally the decision was made to pull back and call in an airstrike to level the building. From the darkened sky, an F/A-18 dropped a pair of precision weapons on what had become known as the "death house." Finally, after all opposition was silenced, Anthony Goodwin's body was recovered from the rubble.

FIRE FROM THE SKY

As night closed in on Day 1, the situation was less than ideal. On the positive side, the hasty attack had been rapidly planned and well-executed, unleashing firepower with great effect. Multiple enemy fighters had been killed by long-range fire as they tried to withdraw. The most lethal element that day was the Air Team. Cobra and Huey gunships had cut down multiple insurgents while others were destroyed by fighter jets. In and around New Ubaydi and at the Golden Gate bridge, an estimated 75 enemy fighters had been killed.[43]

But there was plenty of downside. Any hope of sweeping

rapidly into Ramana and achieving surprise was gone. The Army engineers were still struggling to get the floating bridge sections together in a current that was swifter than expected. Word of the Americans gathered by the river had spread quickly. Worst of all, three Marines had been killed entering fortified houses. For the families of the fallen, Mother's Day 2005 would forever be wrapped in a shroud of loss and sadness.

Late in the day, Kilo Company pulled back to recover and prepare for a river crossing. They set up on the backside of the high ground to the south of town where they couldn't be seen by searching eyes. As night fell, tanks and LAVs used thermal sights to ID enemy positions and airborne sensors were still finding valid targets.

"We pulled back behind the rise south of town," recalls Matt Greene. "I got up there and watched the gun runs. Multiple streams of tracers were coming in from the helos. It was like some kind of bizarre light show or something out of 'Star Wars'. Like fire from the sky."[44]

See **bastardsandbrothers.com** for notes, photos, maps, etc.

16. GOLDEN GATE

Early in the deployment, Lieutenant Colonel Mundy and Major Day had advocated demolishing the Golden Gate bridge, since it provided an easy route for infiltrating foreign fighters. Other bridges along the Euphrates and Tigris had been dropped by the coalition to force traffic through military-controlled roads and checkpoints and constrict insurgent movement. But in this case, the request was denied. Higher-ups still saw the bridge as too important to the regional economy.

It was certainly important to the enemy. They had demonstrated their intent to control it, or at least keep the Americans away. On September 3, 2004, during the changeover between 3/7 and 1/7, four Marines were killed by an IED emplaced at the bridge. Since then, it was assumed to be rigged with multiple explosive devices. No Marine had crossed it for months.

ENROUTE

Late on the night of May 7th, Lieutenant Bryan Leahy and Gunny John Harman gathered both sections of WarPig 1 together on Gannon. "About 2130 the lieutenant came in to brief us," recalls Ryan Masterson. "We were going to secure the critical bridge outside Karabilah. We went over the route, and he told us to battle-zero the .50s. Contact was imminent."[1]

Their mission was to establish a blocking position on the south bank of the river, to prevent the enemy from escaping south across the bridge or sending reinforcements across it. This was a crucial part of the "anvil". The force consisted of Alpha and Bravo Sections with four guntrucks each, a high-back Humvee carrying supplies and two more Humvees carrying a section of FACs and comms gear. This was an ANGLICO* Team, attached to Leahy from echelons above.

They would use the cover of night to drive to the bridge, just five miles to their east, to be in place before the sun came up at 0615. In normal circumstances, the trip would take 30 to 45 minutes. It would take longer in darkness with bad roads, lurking insurgents, and the threat of IEDs, but they still expected to get there and set up in plenty of time.

To minimize the risk, they'd chosen a route through the farm fields northeast of Husaybah, specifically to avoid command-detonated IEDs. Blacked-out vehicles moving along back roads in the dead of night would attract little, if any, attention. And potential IED trigger-men would hopefully be asleep or inattentive.

Exactly one minute after midnight,[2] WarPig 1 rolled out of Camp Gannon and began winding their way towards the objective. Everything went smoothly at first. Then suddenly a vehicle loomed out of the darkness. Masterson, gunner in the lead

---

* ANGLICO stands for Air Naval Gunfire Liaison Company. These specialized units are unique to the Marine Corps, fielding small teams of specialists to coordinate airstrikes and long-range artillery fire. In Matador, these teams came from 2nd ANGLICO Company, an RCT-2 asset based out of Al-Asad.

Humvee, reacted instinctively. "He was lights out in the dark, heading right towards us," says Masterson. "I opened up with my Mk19, but it was only about 40 meters away. The rounds didn't even have time to arm, they just skipped off the road. The SUV veered off into a tree line and I opened up on him there. We didn't stop to see effects. We just kept going."[3]

The terrain itself soon posed a new threat. As they got nearer to the river, the ground beneath turned sodden and soft. "We got to a particular T-intersection and turned north," recalls Leahy. "That spot had been reconned before, but drone footage can't tell you everything. As soon as we turned down that trail, we had eight out of ten vehicles stuck in the Euphrates mud."[4]

The next four and a half hours would be an exercise in frustration as WarPig 1 struggled to free their vehicles from the morass and get back on the mission timeline. "We'd pull one truck out, and another would get stuck," recalls Masterson. "Some were sinking up to the axles. It was a mess."[5]

Their progress was monitored with growing concern at Mundy's forward CP and in the battalion COC. By 0530 it was obvious WarPig 1 would not make it to the bridge in time and the decision was made to commit the designated Quick Reaction Force (QRF). Second Lieutenant Brian Stann, commander of WarPig 2, quickly rallied his Bravo section with four guntrucks and two tanks attached.*

* Brian Stann published his autobiography, Heart for the Fight, in 2010. The book covers his life before and after the Marine Corps, including Stann's career as a professional Mixed Martial Arts fighter. It also features his extensive first-person telling of engagements he was in during Operation Matador. Stann's riveting account, along with other publicly available interviews he has given, were key sources for this chapter. This chapter complements and extends Stann's story, based on interviews conducted with several other Marines who were there.

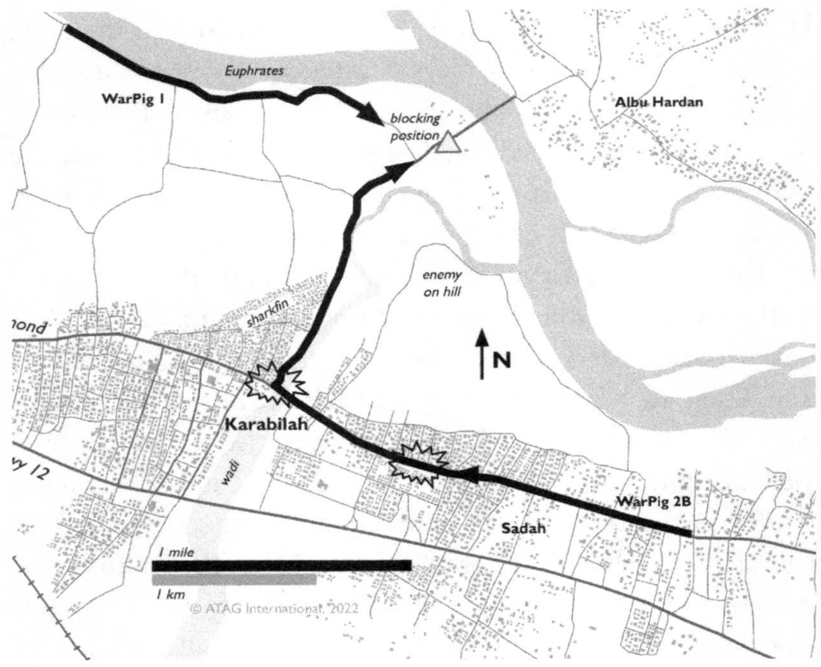

They pushed hard and fast up to Route Diamond then turned west, dashing through several small communities. No one in 3/2 had yet ventured along this stretch of road. As the column sped through the darkened town of Sadah, tracers and RPGs lanced out at them. Returning fire at fleeting targets, they barreled towards the intersection with Route Emerald.[6]

They took more fire as they approached the right turn onto Emerald. A sedan came at them, insurgents firing out its rolled-down windows. But it was an uneven fight. Corporal Rene Delatorre, gunner in the lead Humvee, swung his muzzle towards the car and let fly. The heavy .50 cal rounds chopped through the car and the men inside. With its engine destroyed and smoking, the shattered vehicle rolled to a stop, driver slumped lifelessly, half-in and half-out of the car. Moments later, Stann's column reached a crossroads just south of the bridge and deployed in the open. The sun was just rising.

Almost immediately, they began receiving incoming from across the river. The fire was sporadic at first but escalated quickly. "They started in on us almost as soon as we rolled up," says Pete Culver, the gunner in Stann's Humvee. "We were on the raised hardball road, so it was easy to spot us."[7]

Then rounds started zipping overhead from a new direction. Insurgents were engaging from the southwest, from a neighborhood in Karabilah the Marines called "the sharkfin." Now Stann and his men were caught in a crossfire. Inside the armored Humvees, they were relatively safe from small arms fire. But up top, the gunners were only partially protected. And as the morning progressed the enemy brought heavier firepower to bear:

> *I remember a house on the north bank, and there was a machine gun firing from inside, set way back inside a room. I was targeting it specifically with my .50 and could see the muzzle flashes. It was something big. Some kind of heavy weapon, like a 12.7mm, I'm sure.*
>
> —**Pete Culver**[8]

At first, Stann was reluctant to have the tanks unleash their 120mm cannons because of collateral damage concerns. But after the enemy fire escalated from AKs to heavy machine guns, then RPGs and mortars, Stann took the gloves off. One tank destroyed a vehicle on the north bank that was resupplying enemy gunners. Another swiveled its gun to the south and destroyed a dump-truck insurgents were using as cover.

Still, the volume of enemy fire increased. Even with the tanks, WarPig 2 was having trouble gaining fire superiority. Feeling the pressure mounting, Stann called for air support and soon attack helicopters swooped overhead and engaged with rockets and guns.

BULLET MAGNETS

Finally freed from the bog, WarPig 1 arrived at the blocking position around 1000[9] in the midst of the ongoing firefight. By that time insurgents had moved into the large wadi to the southeast and were popping up to fire RPGs. Leahy's column approached from the west along a narrow dirt road, just wide enough for their Humvees.

Once he located WarPig 2, Leahy contacted Stann over the radio and worked out a battle handoff under fire. As the senior lieutenant, Leahy assumed overall command of the position at that point. The WarPig 1 guntrucks began pulling into WarPig 2's positions, acquiring their targets and letting them pull back and regroup.

As vehicles repositioned, there was a loud *crump!* and a geyser of dust abruptly clouded one of the tanks. Leahy happened to be looking that way. "There was a large, muffled explosion," he remembers. "I watched a 70-ton tank physically lifted up off the ground. It had hit a triple-stacked IED. We could tell it was bad."[10]

Inside the stricken M1, three of its four crewmen were seriously injured. They were from Charlie Company of 4th Tank Battalion, a Marine Reserve unit out of Boise, Idaho. Staff Sergeant Chad Brumpton and Lance Corporal Joe Lowe needed immediate surgical care. Lance Corporal Mitch Ehlke was also seriously hurt and bleeding. The call went out for an immediate CASEVAC, but the dedicated Army Blackhawks were already busy evacuating casualties from New Ubaydi.

In this moment of extreme stress, Major Greg Hanville, Huey gunship pilot and ops officer for HMLA 269, happened to be overhead. When the IED detonated, he had also been looking right at the tank and saw a cloud of smoke and dirt suddenly blossom from underneath its armored hull:

> *I was flying straight towards it, and once I got directly above, 50-100 feet overhead, one of the tankers popped out of a hatch. He looked up and we made eye contact. He looked me right in the eye and made a waving-down motion with his hand. They needed help. I called over to our section lead, "There's wounded down there, I'm going in."*
>
> —**Greg Hanville**[11]

The Cobra/Huey section's mission was to provide close air support, not casualty evacuation, but Hanville flared and put his bird down between the two tanks, completely exposed to enemy fire. "Man, he showed some guts," recalled Stann. "He knew there was a Marine there that needed to get out and needed to get out now."[12] The Huey crew jumped out to help recover the injured men, while Hanville kept the rotors turning.

But now the crippled tank and the stationary Huey became bullet magnets, the focus of every insurgent in range. Hanville watched as little puffs of dirt appeared out in front of the cockpit. "I realized these were enemy rounds," he recalls. "They kept getting closer until they were hitting just under my feet. Looking down through the chin bubble, I could see the impacts."[13]

For several minutes, the Huey crewmen braved increasing enemy fire to help get Brumpton and Ehlke out of the tank and onto the helicopter. As soon as they were aboard, Hanville lifted off for Camp Al-Qaim. Crew chief and door gunner, Corporal Jeremy Anderson, held tightly to one of the casualties in the back as the bird pitched forward and accelerated. "We were in such a hurry we hadn't strapped him in," says Anderson. "I was holding his hand and my other was on the gun, firing at the enemy."[14]

A third tanker, however, still needed to be recovered. Paralyzed by the blast, Joe Lowe was still pinned in his loader's position deep in the tank's belly. Sergeant Luke Miller, commander of the other tank, was now inside working to free him. Outside they could hear the battle raging and bullets striking the armor. "We knew we were skylined targets as soon as we climbed out the top hatch," says Miller.[15]

At this crucial juncture, Lieutenant Stann, Staff Sergeant Robertson, and Lance Corporal Richard Mcelhinny from WarPig 2 dashed through the heavy incoming to help recover Lowe. While Peterson and Mcelhinny laid down suppressive fire, Stann climbed up onto the tank's turret, brazenly highlighting himself to enemy gunners. He reached down into the turret and, with Miller's help, finally managed to pull Lowe out of the tank. Miraculously, no one was hit in the process.

Meanwhile, a second Huey pilot, Captain Dale Finke, had made another daring landing near the tanks. As several Marines carried Lowe over and bundled him onto the bird, Finke observed muzzle flashes from over a dozen enemy weapons and calmly talked attack helos onto those targets. Moments later, Lowe was on his way to the trauma team at Camp AQ.

The impromptu rescue of the tankers from a hot LZ

dramatically illustrates the relationship between Marine aviators with their ground-based brothers. Roles and doctrine took a backseat when fellow Marines were hurt on the battlefield. After unloading the casualties at Camp AQ, both Hueys were rearmed, had bullet holes quickly taped over, and in minutes were pitching back into the fight.

RUNNING THE GAUNTLET

WarPig 2's Bravo Section readied their guntrucks for the return trip to Camp AQ. They would be driving right back through the same streets where they'd been ambushed hours before. Stann expected the enemy would be waiting and briefed his men to get ready for a fight. Heading south on Emerald into Karabilah, they encountered an impromptu roadblock ahead forcing them to turn left onto Diamond. It was obvious they were being channeled into an ambush. Sure enough, just after making the turn they came under fire.

Rounds slammed into the doors and thickened glass and RPGs sizzled by from several directions. But something was different and more sinister about these insurgents. "They were wearing black body armor, almost like police-issued gear, black face masks," said Stann. They clearly had training and discipline. "We'd never had any activity from the locals like this before."[16]

Amazingly, the black-clad fighters swarmed close to the guntrucks as they tore past, firing at point-blank range. "We were taking heavy fire from both sides," says Pete Culver. "More and more of these guys kept coming out, dressed in black with bulky vests. They got in real close. I actually saw our lead vehicle clip a guy with its mirror as they went past."[17]

Again, they encountered fighters in speeding vehicles. Culver saw two large black sedans pull out from a side street in front of the lead Humvee, Bravo 1, racing about 75 meters ahead of the column. Suddenly they were in a Hollywood-style tail chase, with men firing out of the sedans' rear window. Culver fired a burst or two but couldn't get a clean shot past Bravo 1. The sedans accelerated and disappeared.

The convoy cleared the ambush and left the black-clad fighters in their dust. They jogged right, then left to get onto Route Jade, but a new threat emerged. Another sedan followed them, closing aggressively. Now there was civilian traffic on the road, but the driver bored through, ignoring warning shots. It showed all the signs of a suicide vehicle, and finally one of the WarPig gunners gave it a devastating burst, shredding the sedan and killing the driver. The guntrucks pushed on.

BRUSH WITH ZARQAWI?

Back at Camp Al-Qaim, WarPig 2's Bravo Section parked their battered vehicles and got out to inspect the damage. The up-armored Humvees were covered with multiple bullet impacts and scars from RPG blasts, but they had protected their crews. No one had been hit. Moreover, the scarred vehicles held intriguing clues about the enemy they had just faced.

Embedded in the bullet-proof glass and the armored doors were small, needle-like projectiles called flechettes. These came from specialized RPG rounds designed to penetrate body armor. Such rounds are rare, exotic even, and definitely not part of a typical insurgent's ammo loadout.

Lieutenant Stann debriefed the mission in the COC, telling

of the black-uniformed fighters with body armor, masks, superior weapons handling, and aggressiveness. Intelligence personnel came out to view the evidence themselves. Seeing the flechettes buried in the ballistic glass and hearing about speeding black sedans and the probable attack run by an SVBIED got their attention. Their immediate assessment was that WarPig 2 had just encountered bodyguards of AQI's leader, Abu-Musab al-Zarqawi.

There was little time for further reflection, however. The vehicles had to be refueled, repaired where needed, and rearmed. "That morning I'd gone out with a full load of 4,000 rounds for the .50cal," recalls Culver. "When we left the bridge to head back, I only had 400 left and I shot some of that on the way back"[18]

Everyone knew they'd soon be called on to make another run. WarPig 1 was still engaged back by the bridge, and needed more fuel, ammo, and especially water. Sure enough, around 1800 orders came down for WarPig 2 to make a resupply run back through Karabilah. It was the only way to reach the blocking position. They left before midnight, this time escorting a 7-ton truck and a large fuel tanker. The trip out was uneventful, and they offloaded quickly. But on the return leg they took enemy fire once again. With daring and quick thinking, they made it back without losses early in the pre-dawn hours of May 9th.

Thus far, Lieutenant Stann and his Bravo Section had made four trips directly through an enemy-held urban area. Three out of the four times they'd been ambushed and had high-risk running gunfights with men ready to die to take an American with them. Remarkably, they'd come through it all unscathed.

HOT SEAT

As the sun rose on May 9th, WarPig 1 was prepared for another day of combat at the blocking position. Across the radio they heard the main force finally crossing the Euphrates into Ramana. That might well prompt insurgents to try slipping across the river into their fields of fire. Alternatively, the enemy in Karabilah might move to reinforce positions on the north bank.

Either way, Lieutenant Leahy and his men were ready. They had vehicles on both sides of Emerald. One section was northwest of the road. The other section was on the southeast side, along with the undamaged tank. They started receiving fire again soon after first light. Like the day before, the volume of fire increased as more insurgents joined in. WarPig gunners got busy zeroing in on enemy positions and suppressing them. Bullets began to snap overhead. Then RPGs started arcing in, exploding in midair. They were being launched at max range, detonating as they timed out. In their turrets, gunners strained to spot where fire was coming from, then dialed in their traverse and elevation mechanisms for maximum accuracy. Precision was the key to achieving fire superiority in this kind of long-range punching match.

Leahy also had another asset at hand. Before deploying, Corporal Cody Ellison and Lance Corporal Stephen Person had attended a basic Arabic class. Now they were putting their language skills to good use. Insurgents in Iraq often used commercial walkie-talkies to communicate during combat. Marines had learned to monitor such chatter using their own off-the-shelf radios. Even with their limited language skills, Ellison and Person could often tell when an attack would come and sometimes from where. This proved to be a key advantage as WarPig 1 continuously searched out enemy firing positions.

Just like the day before, insurgents attacked from multiple locations, putting the Marines in a crossfire. Small teams moved along the main wadi or crawled closer through the many shallow irrigation ditches. They would pop up to let off an RPG or full-auto burst, then shift to a new spot. Also, across the wadi to the south, fighters were using the hill rising over the fields to fire from an elevation advantage.

By far the most dangerous threat came from enemy mortar teams. They were surprisingly accurate and adept at shoot-and-scoot tactics. Mortar strikes forced the guntrucks to shift positions frequently, which could throw off their own gunners' aim. "Whenever we got mortared, it was frustrating." recalls Leahy. "You had to guess. If we stay put, will they zero in on us? But if we move will that put the truck right where they'll hit next?"[19]

In one such instance, mortar rounds exploded within a few feet of a vehicle in Alpha section. "I was in the truck right behind them," says Jonathan Maines, "We were moving, and they were bracketing us pretty accurately, very close. We tried to shift positions and they just seemed to be getting closer."[20] Fragments shredded two of the vehicle's tires and sliced through gas cans strapped to the back.

As the heat rose to 100 degrees and beyond, incoming fire started to slack off. By late morning, things were much quieter. But no one could really relax. Except for bodily functions, the crews stayed inside their vehicles which were soon sweltering. "During the day, we just cooked," describes Leahy. "It was so hot. In the Humvees, you can't get comfortable. You'd get leg cramps. I curse whoever designed that eff'ing bar on the seat that would hit you right across the shin bone."[21]

Later in the day, as the sun was sinking lower towards the horizon, Leahy experienced what he calls a classic "lieutenant moment." Sensing a lull, he got out of the vehicle to relieve himself. He found some tall grass and assumed the time-honored position:

> *After I did my business, I stood up and closed my flak jacket. Just then a machine gun opened up on me. I could feel bullets going past my head. I ran to my truck and the MG rounds chased after me. I dove behind a rear tire as they kept whipping past us. I reached up, opened the door, and climbed in.*
>
> **—Bryan Leahy**[22]

Breathless but safe, Leahy had a flash of insight. The insurgent gunner had singled him out because the reddening sky behind had made him an easy target. He also realized something more significant. During midday hours, the accumulation of haze, dust and heat waves made target acquisition more difficult. This explained why enemy fighters were engaging in the morning until about 1000, then again in late afternoon or evening. This pattern would hold as WarPig doggedly held the position for the next four days.

INTO THE DARK

Back at Camp AQ, on the afternoon of May 9th, WarPig 2 was tasked with yet another mission to return to Golden Gate bridge. This time they'd be escorting a heavy armored recovery vehicle, an M88 Hercules, to recover the damaged tank. Two more tanks from Tiger Section at Camp Gannon would join them on the way.

Just before midnight, Lieutenant Stann sent his Bravo section ahead to an overwatch position south of Karabilah. Then he took Alpha section and the M88 through the desert to meet up with the tanks. At the rally point he told the men to get ready. In ten minutes they'd be in a firefight. This was Alpha section's first run through the gauntlet. It would be Stann's fifth.

But this trip would resemble a painfully slow jog. The massive M88 was notoriously slow, especially on paved roads. As they entered the southern edge of Karabilah and drove north on Emerald, the M88 and its escorts slowed to about ten miles-per-hour. The lead vehicle was Alpha 1, with Staff Sergeant John Francis, the section leader, in the right front seat. Lance Corporal Jeff Lamson was driving, with Lance Corporals Scott Hauslyak and Jason Goldsmith in the rear seats. Up in the turret, Corporal Robert Gass was behind the .50 cal.

They passed through a zig-zag portion on Emerald, with houses on both sides, and as they came out of a turn Hauslyak remembers seeing a car on the side of the road. "It flashed its headlights, and suddenly all the streetlights went off. Something was about to go down. It was eerie," he recalls. "Goldsmith and I looked at each other and I told him to unhook the strap over the ammo cans."[22]

Excruciating seconds followed on the darkened street, then Gass yelled from the turret, "RPG!!" and started rocking on the .50 cal. It was madness from then on. Looking out through the ballistic glass, Francis saw a flash in the blackness. "There was a star-shaped flame on our right," he recalls. "It was the backblast of an RPG. We were going so slow; I don't see how he missed."[23]

Lamson had to control a nearly-overpowering urge to accelerate. He knew they had to stay with the M88 and the other vehicles but pushed forward as fast as he dared. Rounds slammed the vehicle from every angle and more RPGs screamed in. Alpha's gunners responded, lighting up anything they saw as a threat. The tanks blasted buildings, filling the street with dust and debris. It was a slow-motion ambush unfolding in deafening sound and fury. "Robbie was pounding away. Below him we just kept hooking new ammo belts together as a continuous feed up to his gun," says Hauslyak. "The smoke was so thick; it was like fog. Thick, dark smoke everywhere around us."[24]

As the lead driver, Lamson's one overriding instinct was to push through the ambush as he'd been trained. Stalling in a kill zone was the kiss of death. But enveloped in smoke and debris and chaos, he missed the crucial right turn to proceed north on Emerald.

Stann now faced a tough command decision and he made it without hesitation. He ordered the rest of the vehicles to follow Alpha 1 deeper into Karabilah. As the column pushed west a few blocks, the enemy fire slackened. Then the lieutenant made another gutsy call. Avoiding the temptation of searching for an alternate route, he turned all the vehicles around, heading back east.

Certainly, there were some serious misgivings in that moment as the Marines wheeled their vehicles around and prepared to plunge back into the seething maelstrom they'd just come through. But no one balked. The column kept the same order as it made a U-turn, with Alpha 1 still in the lead, and headed back to the intersection:

There was no firing at first. I told Robbie, "We're good with the ammo," kind of to give him confidence. We were lead vehicle, heading into a sure ambush. He started firing when we were about a block away from the turn, into windows and roofs of buildings. The enemy started firing again, and Robbie's rate-of-fire picked up. I looked out my window and yelled to Jeff, "the turn's coming up!!"

—Scott Hauslyak[25]

Lamson strained to spot the upcoming left turn onto Emerald. Through the tunnel-vision of his NVGs, his view was again filled with smoke, tracers, and RPGs streaking by his windshield. Finally, the left turn was meters away. Amid the mayhem, he dimly heard Gass yelling, "Watch out, there's something there!" Then everything went dark.

As Robbie Gass later related, he was firing away when suddenly a pickup truck loomed out of the smoke on his right and slammed into the side of their Humvee. In that split second, Gass looked down to see a 13- or 14-year-old boy behind the wheel. "I remember feeling it hit the side of our truck and seeing that little kid looking up at me. Next thing, I'm picking myself off the top of the Humvee."[26]

The explosion from the suicide vehicle mushroomed up into a massive fireball. A few vehicles back in Alpha 3, Stann feared the worst. "I hear that explosion and the first thing that went through my head was, I just got five kids killed... And I get out of my vehicle, and I push [to their guntruck], to the point of friction."[27]

The blast could be seen and felt for miles. On the high ground south of town, Bravo Section watched the fireball boil up over the rooflines. To the north, hundreds of meters away where WarPig 1 maintained the blocking position, the power of the explosion was palpable. "We could actually feel the heat from it from where we were," says Ryan Masterson.[28]

GUNNER DOWN

Lamson came to lying in the street. He'd been blown out of the armored door on the driver's side. The front of the vehicle, from the windshield forward, was destroyed. "I didn't know what had happened," he recalls. "But we had drilled over and over on just this situation. Our gunner was down. I was shaken but OK, so I jumped up on top and grabbed Gass by his flak. Pulled him out, and we kind of rolled off the truck and I took him to the rear of the vehicle."[29] Running through enemy fire and confusion, Stann arrived at the blast site. In an interview years later, he described the scene:

> *I get there, and on top of it is this 22-year-old kid, Jeff Lamson, who's built like a No.2 pencil... How he's conscious, I don't know, but he's on top of it pulling our gunner out of the turret, who's got a piece of shrapnel in his head. Everybody's wounded, but Staff Sergeant Francis comes out and the whole side of his face is melted. And he's like, 'Sir, we're gonna be good. We're gonna be good." I was never more relieved in my life.*
>
> —**Brian Stann**[30]

The blast had warped the vehicle doors on Francis' side, allowing the fireball into the passenger compartment. "When I came to, I remember flames swirling in around the bent door, like the movie 'Backdraft'", he says. "I grabbed my rifle. The barrel was bent."[31] But the crew were all still alive. Francis and

Goldsmith were badly burned, and Hauslyak's leg was wounded by shrapnel. Lamson was banged up, but focused intently on pulling his friends out of the smoldering wreck:

> *[We're] still getting shot at... And there's bullets hitting... But man, to see Lamson. This kid, who actually had a little bit of an attitude at the time... hair's a little too long... But in this time of need, I'm telling you, he was saving lives. And it was so humbling, and so motivating, to see that.*
>
> **—Brian Stann**[32]

The most seriously hurt was Corporal Gass, who had a seven-inch piece of metal protruding from his forehead. It had penetrated the kevlar helmet and his skull, and clearly he needed immediate evacuation. Gass himself, however, was still unaware of his injury and no one wanted to inform him until they could get him to proper medical attention.

Meanwhile, the fight raged around them and the threat of yet another suicide bomber was very real. With incredible poise and command presence under fire, Stann set up a security cordon and directed the guntrucks and tanks to go weapons free to eliminate any opposition. He then got the wounded loaded into the M88 with its thick armored shell and coordinated for a CASEVAC bird.

Finally, the column started moving again up Emerald towards WarPig 1's perimeter. As they plodded north on the hardball road, more fire lashed at them from alleys and rooftops. Another suspicious vehicle appeared behind them, racing for the rear of the column. One of the tanks swiveled its turret and struck it dead on with a main gun round. The vehicle detonated in another fireball. The enemy had loosed another suicide attack against them.

Now they neared WarPig 1's perimeter and the LZ where the bird would be waiting, just a few hundred meters more. "As we climbed into the Mike 88, small arms fire was pinging off the side," recalls Hauslyak. "I was the last one in, and I was thinking, 'Thank God I'm in a tank now.' Then there was another big BOOM! and this one really knocked us around inside."[33]

Incredibly, the M88 had rolled over yet another large IED, which buckled the hull and knocked a track off. The recovery vehicle was now itself immobilized. Once more, Stann orchestrated the transfer of the wounded men. At the same time, WarPig 1 sent guntrucks to help the transfer and provide covering fire. A Cobra/Huey team had also arrived on station and was lashing the rooftops with withering fire.

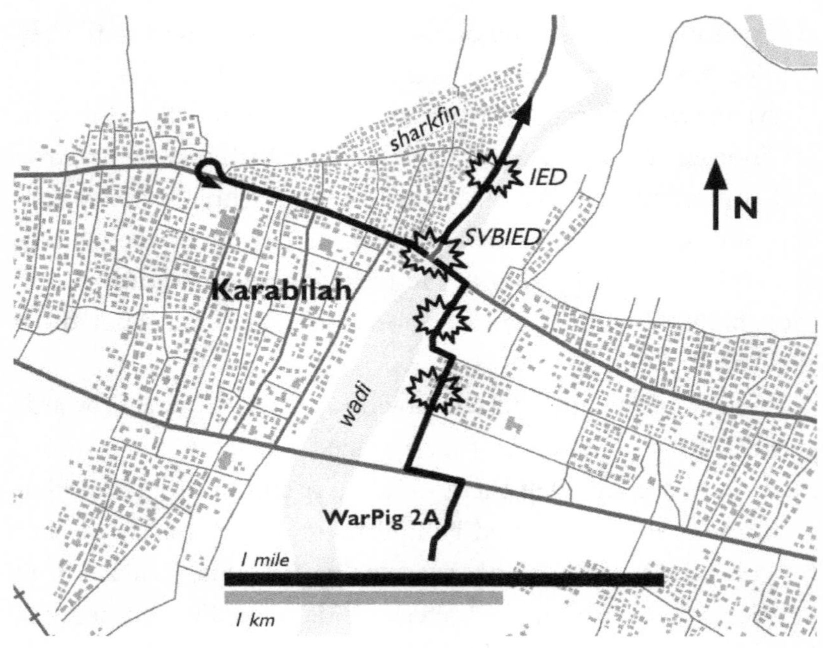

Finally, the wounded were loaded onto a waiting Blackhawk, and it lifted off. Strapped into the bird, the injured men watched as tracers arced up into the night after them. "When the helo took off, we took small arms fire. A couple rounds actually hit the bird," recalls Hauslyak. "And I could see a Cobra nearby firing down into the city. Then I remember the power of that Blackhawk, as it tilted forward and just zoomed us out of there."[34]

Throughout the harrowing event, Lieutenant Stann had shown exemplary leadership and the Marines under his command had responded with great bravery. Although Corporal Gass suffered a serious brain injury, the fact that anyone in Alpha 1 survived at all is amazing. Lamson reflects on his survival with wonder:

> *When I saw our wrecked truck later, there was a soda-can-sized hole in the windshield. A big piece of shrapnel had come through, right at my head height. I found it under the seat, a wicked chunk of metal. It should have killed me. I believe God saved me that night. It's the only way I can explain it.*
>
> **—Jeff Lamson**[35]

For his part as the Alpha Section Leader, Francis has often considered those events and the choices that were made under the stress of combat. "We missed that first turn, but if not, we'd have gone right into their prepared kill zone," he explains. "Later we found they had a well-thought-out, complex ambush set up, with sandbagged positions, fridge-sized IEDs and more SVBIEDs. But our passing by, then turning around and coming back from the opposite direction messed up their plan. It could have been so much worse."[36]

It was now early morning on May 10th, Day 3. To accomplish the original recovery mission, two of the M1 tanks chained up the immobilized M88 and the crippled tank and towed them back while it was still dark. They pushed right through the ambush site, this time without incident. Apparently, the insurgents had had enough for one night.

Lieutenant Stann and Alpha Section would stay at the blocking position, reinforcing Leahy and WarPig 1, until the end of the operation. For the wounded Marines, their recovery road was just beginning. For some it would be a long one, requiring a new kind of courage and the ability to focus on the positive. On that score, Scott Hauslyak was apparently off to a good start:

> *After Robbie Gass was evac'ed out, Francis, Goldsmith, and me were all in the same recovery room. Also, Josh Tucker, Alpha 2's gunner, who'd caught shrapnel in the arm. I was all doped up on morphine and was laying there, dead quiet, listening to the medical machines. Then I started chuckling. Someone asked what was so funny, and I said, "Can you imagine the bomber's muj buddies? They're thinking they're gonna kill a bunch of Americans, then all five of us badasses get out of the wreck. And they're like, "Damn! Those infidel bastards walked away!" For some reason we thought that was hilarious and everyone was laughing. It was just one of those weird moments.*
>
> —**Scott Hauslyak**[37]

17. CROSSING OVER

In the predawn dimness of 9 May, the various units of the main force were preparing to move. Some buildings in New Ubaydi were still smoldering, mute signs of the violent urban fighting of 8 May and the airstrikes during the night. After the unexpected delays of Day 1, Lieutenant Colonel Mundy knew it was imperative to cross the Euphrates and start sweeping Ramana. The Bridging Company had made repeated but unsuccessful attempts to connect the ribbon sections together to provide a useful span, but there was still no bridge.

"The previous night, I was pushing hard on the Army engineers," recalls John Day. "They came to me with the idea of using the sections like rafts. I said, 'Sure, just get us across already!' but it was too late to go that night. The force was smoked after 12 hours of combat. We'd go the next morning."[1] One of the large floating sections could ferry several loaded Humvees, or a single M1 tank. They would be pushed by the riverine tugs the engineers had brought with them. The improvised solution would take more time than driving across a completed bridge, but it would work.

Just before daybreak, the first raft was pushed across and vehicles rolled off onto the far bank. The crossing was unopposed.

At 0600, Lieutenant Nate Smith and Kilo Company's 2nd Platoon were at the river, ready to be ferried across. By 0730 they had pushed their AAVs through fields on the opposite bank and entered the small villages of Salman and Dughaymah. By 1200 they'd cleared this first battalion objective with no contact.[2]

As the morning progressed, the rest of the main force crossed without incident and pushed on to their objectives. Once the LAVs of Bravo Company were across, one of their vehicle sections dashed through farm roads up to the desert plateau that overlooked the whole valley. Getting a mobile screening force up on the heights was key to isolating the battlespace.

In one of the opening moves of 8 May, a platoon-sized element from 3/2's own Lima company had been helicoptered in to set up a blocking position on this high ground, near the village of Ar-Rabit at the west end of Ramana. But the element was withdrawn early on 9 May, due to the complications faced at the bridging site and in New Ubaydi. Leaving a platoon of infantry alone, with no heavy weapons or vehicles, just a mile from the Syrian border, was deemed too risky.[3]

Down in the valley, the force moved rapidly. Each cluster of villages was a numbered objective, and the units leapfrogged forward from one to another. Homes, gardens, and sheds were searched for weapons caches, and residents were asked if they knew where insurgents were. None were found. By 1630, Kilo's 2nd Platoon had reached the edge of Objective 2, the village of Khutaylah, and went firm. They'd reached the designated phase line and limit of advance for the day.[4]

The commander and his operations officer had been among the first to cross the river. They had been active all day, moving in the command Humvee from place to place, coordinating on the radios, and monitoring the operation first-hand:

At one point, I got a little too aggressive and had our vehicle forward of Kilo's lines about 500 meters. They had to call me to get back, so we weren't a friendly-fire risk. Then we went up on the plateau to the north. I always like to be on the high ground, to see what's going on. From up there, we could observe all of Ramana, and I could track the operation's progress... Later, at sunset, from the top of those cliffs we looked down on the river valley. There was a flock of white birds flying and, for a minute, it made you forget where you were, what was really going on down below.

—John Day[5]

SOUTH BANK

On the south bank of the river, the Marines of WarPig 1 and 2 still held firm by the Golden Gate bridge on the morning of 10 May. After the dramatic events of the night, Leahy and Stann had quickly determined that conducting a relief-in-place was not an option. WarPig 1 would stay in full force at the blocking position, as would WarPig 2 Alpha. Down to just a single tank, they wanted all the firepower they could muster.

By this time, the threat from the north bank was minimal. No incoming fire had been received from that quarter for some time. Accordingly, Leahy's two sections deployed northwest of Route Emerald, oriented primarily towards Karabilah. Stann kept his Alpha section, plus the tank, on the opposite side of the road facing south and east.

After pulling his friends out of their burning vehicle and seeing them evacuated, Jeff Lamson had remained with Alpha Section and was folded into Staff Sergeant Cherry's crew for the rest of the operation. He had salvaged as much as possible from the wreck of Alpha 1, pulling out demo charges and ammo that might be needed. After the sun came up on 10 May, Lamson remembers enemy fire coming from the edge of Karabilah.

"We had spotted the source, and Lieutenant Stann was talking the tank onto the target," recalls Lamson, "We had to back our truck out of the way so we wouldn't be in the muzzle blast when that main gun fired."[6] Incoming from that location was silenced around 0830, with four insurgents reportedly killed.

The enemy's zeal was starting to fade by this time, having spent the last two days attacking with little effect and clearly suffering many casualties in the bargain. In particular, the insurgents had little to counter the Marines' ability to call in airstrikes.

On Day 1, the enemy in Karabilah had unleashed a 12.7mm DShK heavy machine-gun (called a "dishka") from a rooftop in the sharkfin, targeting the guntrucks of WarPig 1. Lieutenant Leahy saw the fearsome effects as the burst slashed through his position:

> *The rounds stitched the ground right between two vehicles; it looked just like aircraft strafing trucks in old movies. It had to be directly south of my position. We figured it was hidden on a rooftop, in a little chicken coop structure. This matched the intel that there was a 12.7mm dishka or 14.5mm ZPU anti-aircraft gun in the area. The pilots were all aware of it.*
>
> —**Bryan Leahy**[7]

This was the type of weapon that might take down an aircraft, but apparently it only fired a few times. With Cobras on the prowl, and tanks looking for targets, perhaps the gunners decided to abandon it or move it. In any case, by Day 3 Marine close air support was dominating the engagement.

NORTH BANK

Across the river there was much less action. The main force was advancing from objective to objective, clearing villages with no contact. By afternoon, Khutaylah and Ushsh had been cleared by Kilo, and Lima 3/25 was just to the north working through a cluster of houses.

In the late afternoon, Kilo's 2nd Platoon along with LAVs of Bravo Company entered the village of Balujah and cleared it east to west. While no insurgents had been encountered yet on the north bank, caches had been found. In Balujah, 2nd Platoon discovered a suicide car bomb along with other IED-making materials, clearly indicating AQI bomb-makers had been there. The materials were blown in place and the Marines moved on.[8]

A new NCO joined Lima 3/25 that day. Staff Sergeant Kendall Ivy arrived from the RCT-2 staff, to replace Staff Sergeant Goodwin, killed two days earlier in New Ubaydi. Ivy would be the new Platoon Sergeant for Lima's 1st Platoon and brought a wealth of experience, including an influential tour as a senior instructor at the USMC School of Infantry. Many NCOs had rubbed shoulders with Ivy there and been positively affected by him. Lieutenant Colonel Mundy saw him as he arrived to meet his platoon and as they shook hands, the commander let him know the Marines needed his leadership.

News reports of another key event were proliferating on 10 May. That morning insurgents kidnapped Farhan al-Mahalawi, the Governor of Anbar. He'd been traveling from Al-Qaim to Ramadi, along with his son and four bodyguards, when unknown assailants took them. The captors reportedly called his family, demanding that U.S. forces leave the Al-Qaim area and release certain Zarqawi-associated prisoners. A coalition spokesman stated simply "We don't respond to insurgent or terrorist demands."[10]

For those in the know, the kidnapping highlighted the growing conflict between AQI and the Albu Mahal. As his name indicates, Farhan al-Mahalawi was a prominent member of the tribe and until recently had been Mayor of Al-Qaim, the same mayor who had met with Lieutenant Colonel Mundy and civil affairs Marines in March. With the grisly murder of Husaybah's police chief on 2 May, followed by the kidnapping of mayor/governor Farhan, AQI's intimidation campaign against the troublesome tribe was accelerating.

As darkness approached, Kilo Company's forward trace was just a mile from the Golden Gate bridge. Signs of WarPig's ongoing firefight could be seen and heard. Although they'd seen no combat since crossing over to the north bank, Kilo Marines were increasingly aware of the engagement on the south bank. "As we got closer, I heard a long, sustained burst from a PKM medium machine gun, an insurgent weapon," remembers Chris Ieva.[11] This was likely coming from the sharkfin area, aimed at WarPig guntrucks.

LINKUP

For the Marines at the blocking position, 11 May began like the previous three mornings, with incoming fire. Soon after daybreak, mortar rounds crumped into the fields around the two mobile assault platoons. Once again, the deadly game resumed, as guntruck crews shifted their positions to throw off the insurgent mortarmen while their own gunners searched for targets to engage. And as before, enemy fighters crept in closer through the wadi and other dead space areas to fire small arms or RPGs.

One particular building became the focus of attention. Through long-range optics, WarPig 2 could see frequent enemy activity around a gas station or maintenance garage about a mile away. Even though it had been hit before, insurgents could be seen entering the structure then emerging with weapons. Clearly, they were using the gas station as a cache or weapons staging area. Lieutenant Stann again called on the tank crew and they sent a main gun round slamming into the building. Smoke billowed out, but there was no satisfying secondary explosion.[12]

Later in the day, more insurgents were sighted at the gas station, prompting Stann to bring another weapon to bear. The shoulder-fired Javelin missile system gave mobile assault platoons a devastating punch against armored vehicles, even tanks. But it could also be used against fortified positions. Partly because of its cost, it was rarely fired against insurgents in Iraq, but the lieutenant judged this target to be worthy of special attention.

He called for Lance Corporal Lamson, who as an assaultman was trained on the Javelin.* For WarPig 2, having Lamson launch the missile was battlefield justice. It seemed right to have the remaining member of the Alpha 1 crew, who had

* The FGM-148 Javelin is a shoulder-fired, precision-guided missile system for use against armored vehicles, fortifications and other hardened targets. It can be used in the direct-fire mode or the top-attack mode, shooting up to around 500ft then plunging down on the target from above.

so narrowly survived the massive explosion two nights before, launch this $100,000 weapon at the jihadists who had tried to kill him and his friends.

Lamson and another assaultman, Lance Corporal Chris Gore, moved up onto the road to set up the system and acquire the target. "The Javelin is an amazing piece of equipment," relates Lamson. "I looked through the 4x view on the optics and locked onto a window. Once I was set, I pulled the trigger. It came out of the tube and dropped for a split second. Then whoosh!, it shot up and sliced straight down, right through the roof, and blew up inside."[14] No more activity was noted around the gas station for some time.

PASSAGE OF LINES

Meanwhile, Kilo Company advanced along the north bank searching for any sign of the enemy. The village of Albu Hardan was being cleared in the morning by 2nd and 3rd Platoons, augmented by tanks and LAVs. An Iraqi police station in the village was a reported insurgent position, and both the LAVs and M1s perforated the building, but no opposition was encountered. Lieutenant Smith's 2nd Platoon went firm about 500 meters east of the bridge, while Lieutenant Clemmey's 3rd Platoon actually pushed up to the bridge itself. [15]

Mundy and his forward CP had been moving each day, keeping pace with the clearing operations. By the afternoon of the 11th, the commander was in close proximity to the forward trace. Several reporters were also present. Given Operation Matador's scale and prominence, it had attracted national media attention.

Reporters from the Washington Post and LA Times were embedded with the force that day, but the most notable media figure was Fox News correspondent, author, and retired Marine Lieutenant Colonel Oliver North. North and a camera crew were accompanying Kilo Company, conducting interviews, and shooting video.

By 1600, Albu Hardan had been cleared and the force was ready to leapfrog forward. Lima Company 3/25 was tasked with securing Al Jaramil, the next village to the west, and prepared to execute a passage of lines with Kilo Company. In the waning heat of the afternoon the area was quiet, with no incoming enemy fire. In this relatively permissive environment several Marines took the opportunity to pose for photographs with Oliver North.

Suddenly everything changed. As the AAVs carrying Lima Company 3/25 passed through Albu Hardan on the dirt road leading west, there was a muffled explosion. A powerful IED had detonated under one of their tracs. Just minutes before, several other vehicles had passed through the same spot without incident. But as fate twisted that day, it was the third trac, carrying mortarmen, engineers, and 1st Platoon's 1st Squad, that triggered the IED. Sergeant Andrew Taylor was inside the AAV carrying 2nd Squad, just a few meters in front of the stricken trac:

> *Behind us there was an enormous 'Boom!' and huge black chunks flew overhead. Flynn and Porter were standing security and they both fell into our trac. Flynn was knocked out for a bit. I didn't know what it was at first. I thought we were being shot at.*
>
> —**Andrew Taylor**[16]

ENGULFED

Inside the vehicle, the results were catastrophic. Almost immediately the interior was engulfed in flames as the fuel ignited. Lieutenant Paul Croom, the RCT's public affairs officer, was at the rear of the troop compartment. "The vehicle leapt into the air, violently throwing us about. Everyone was flung upward. I came down hard on my right side," he described later. "The inside of the AAV turned orange and filled with thick, black smoke. I looked to the front of the troop cabin. All I saw was a wall of flames."[17]

There were only two available exits, the commander's hatch topside and the small personnel door in the rear ramp. As the confined space filled with choking smoke and searing heat, the Marines inside desperately tried to reach the hatches, but some remained trapped.

Subsequent events were traumatic, both for the survivors and all who witnessed the scene or heard the increasingly urgent radio calls. As men emerged from the burning AAV, some were on fire and others gravely injured. Despite their own wounds, several men reached back inside the inferno to pull others out. Sometimes they succeeded. Sometimes they did not. Soon the munitions inside began to cook off. Mortar rounds and small arms ammo started exploding as the merciless flames reached them.

Marines and corpsmen from all sides rushed to pull their brothers out and away from the hellish maelstrom, disregarding all hazards. There were numerous examples of extreme bravery as men defied the flames and increasingly dangerous cookoffs. One of these was Sergeant Dennis Woullard, the same Marine who had been wounded in New Ubaydi pulling men from the "death house." Stunned by the initial blast and wounded yet again, Woullard barely escaped from the burning AAV himself, then struggled to the rear hatch and pulled out several injured men. For the second time in three days, Woullard risked life and limb to save fellow Marines.

Men from other units reacted immediately, and their courage and professionalism helped stabilize a dire, horrific situation. Captain Ieva directed Kilo's 3rd Platoon to rush all corpsmen and qualified combat lifesavers to the scene. Lieutenant Clemmey and his men sprinted up the road and began to care for the wounded:

> *At first, we thought it was a controlled det... Then I heard the radio chatter, and someone said, 'Bring med bags now!' I grabbed my fire team, and we took off through the fields and ditches. Lieutenant Clemmey and his RTO [radio operator] were running too. We got there quick, but it seemed like forever. We ran up on people screaming, running around, a lot of confusion. It was surreal. I grabbed a kit and went to work.*
>
> **—Jeff Maniscalco**[18]

Meanwhile, Ieva worked the radios to call in CASEVAC birds, coordinate air support overhead, and direct other Kilo elements to secure the surrounding area. The battalion commander and his forward CP were also very close to the blast. "I had actually driven over the same spot," remembers Mundy. "We'd turned around and were headed in the other direction when the trac passed us. I don't think it was more than 50 to 75 meters behind us when the IED detonated."[19] Lieutenant Colonel Mundy, Sergeant Major Mennig, Gunner Vitale, and Chaplain Anderson went quickly to the scene and started helping with the wounded.

Crewmen from 2nd Platoon, Bravo Company, 2nd LAR, had gone ahead to form a cordon just west of the intersection. Now they hurriedly dismounted their eight-wheeled LAVs and ran back to do what they could. Their Platoon Commander, Lieutenant Sam McAmis, reached the stricken trac and helped get men out of the topside hatch:

> *The inside was full of smoke, and I could see a guy down there. He had his arms up, and I reached in and grabbed him. I had to cut the mag pouches off his chest, but I got him up on the deck. Then my guys helped me kind of 'crowd-surf' him down. It was Staff Sergeant Ivy, who I'd just met the day before. We pulled him over behind a nearby tree at the front of the vehicle and started to assess.*
>
> **—Sam McAmis**[20]

Finally, First Sergeant Gregory turned to Captain Ieva to say, "We have to call this, sir." Soberly, Ieva agreed and everyone was ordered back from the burning trac. The cookoffs made it too dangerous for any further rescue attempts, while the focus had to be put on saving Marines who had been pulled out. Several had life-threatening burns and needed to be evacuated immediately. [21]

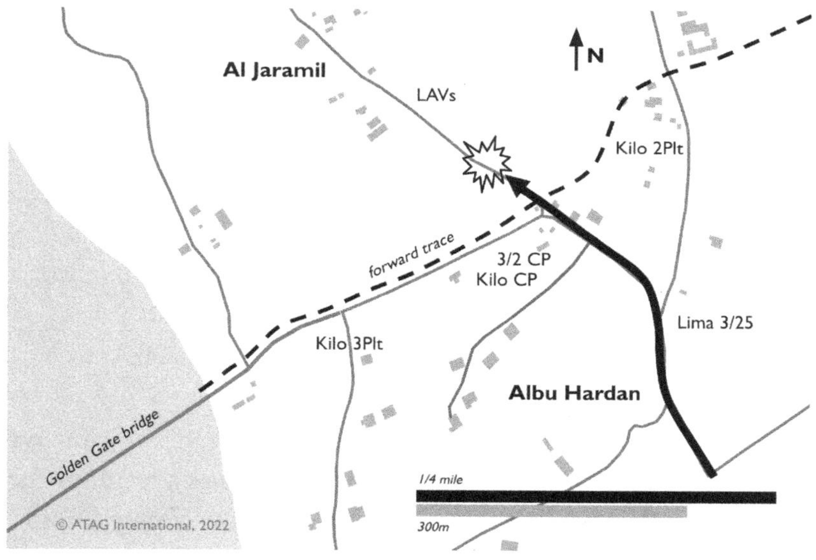

The CASEVAC process had fortunately begun just moments after the IED detonated. After seeing the initial blast and resulting flames, Ieva had called in an urgent CASEVAC request. The Army Blackhawk crews at Camp AQ launched and flew straight to the scene. "They got there very fast," remembers Ieva. "They were overhead in about eight minutes. My RTO and I had run up to the crossroads and had direct comms with the birds. There wasn't time for a standard 9-line brief, and I brought them directly into a field, right next to the road."[22]

After Lieutenant McAmis and other Marines pulled Staff Sergeant Ivy out of the trac, corpsmen worked to control the bleeding and stabilize him. But it became clear he was gravely injured and probably would not make it. McAmis stayed to help as best he could:

He'd been towards the front, and his legs and pelvis had taken the brunt of the blast. He was in a lot of pain, and the Doc gave him morphine. As that kicked in, he started talking, and he was talking about his wife and kids. It was a moment I'll never forget. I stuck with him, just talking, and listening, while we littered him down to the LZ and put him on a bird. After we had loaded him up, I sat down, totally spent. Sergeant Major Mennig asked me if I was wounded 'cause I had so much blood on me.

—Sam McAmis[23]

On the way to the Battalion Aid Station, Staff Sergeant Ivy expired from his wounds. Five others died also as a result of the blast or the flames. They were Lance Corporals Wesley Davids, Nick Erdy, Jonathan Grant, and Private First Class Christopher Dixon from 3/25's Lima Company and Lance Corporal Jourdan Grez, attached to Lima from 4th Combat Engineers.

Eleven others were wounded, and several needed specialized care for burns. Having already lost two KIA and others wounded in New Ubaydi, 1st Squad of 1st Platoon in Lima had now suffered nearly 100 percent casualties and was combat ineffective. The company's nickname, "Lucky Lima", now seemed more like a curse.

The rest of the force needed a pause. For many Marines around the blast site, the tragedy had exhausted their physical and emotional strength. They had been grim witnesses as six Marines died. Those closest risked their own lives to get them out, but the fury of the flames and exploding munitions eventually drove them back. On the north bank, Mundy ordered units to consolidate their positions after the CASEVAC was complete. Then 2nd Platoon, Kilo Company was sent ahead to Al Jaramil to secure the western flank.

Across the river, the men of WarPig 1 and 2 had witnessed the entire event from a distance. A thick column of black smoke rose over the wrecked trac, marking the location for miles around. They could see the flames and across their radios they could hear calls for help from Lima Company and transmissions from others directing the response. "From our position across the river, we hear every agonizing moment," describes Brian Stann in his autobiography. "I can do nothing. It is the most helpless, enraging feeling I've ever experienced. I have no way to get across the water." [24] This frustration and anger was felt by everyone at the river that day. It haunts many of them still.

Later that night, after darkness shrouded the Marines' movements, one of the bulky 7-ton trucks was brought up to the north side of the bridge. It was loaded with ammo, food, water, and other supplies for WarPig. The battalion Logistics Officer, Captain Frank Filler, and a junior Marine would take it across to the south bank. By then the bridge had been declared clear of IEDs, but its condition was unknown. The unarmored truck represented a large, juicy target for any lurking insurgents. "We had no idea if that bridge could hold the weight," recalls Mundy. "Captain Filler and I agreed they would keep their doors cracked open, ready to jump if the bridge snapped! That took some real courage."[25] Fortunately, other than some white-knuckle moments as they drove completely blacked out over the rusty bridge, the resupply went off without a hitch.

THEY KILL WITH A KNIFE

After 11 May, the intensity of the operation tapered off. At daybreak, Kilo Company began pushing forward again on the north bank, supported by the LAVs and the two tanks. Al Jaramil was cleared by the end of the morning, but with little to show for the effort.

On the south bank, however, the enemy was still engaging. Mortars hit the blocking position at mid-morning, and more action occurred later as WarPig 2 spotted enemy movement around the by-now-notorious gas station in Karabilah. Military-aged males were once again seen going into the half-wrecked structure and emerging with weapons and ammo. Evidently, even tank rounds and Lamson's Javelin strike had not destroyed the arms cache stored there.

Finally, Stann called for clearance to use heavier ordnance. Working through the ANGLICO team, he called for a fixed-wing airstrike. Just after noon, a pair of F/A-18s nailed the building with a 500-pound, satellite-guided bomb, achieving dramatic results. The gas station and its contents were converted into a pile of burning rubble. Even though more incoming rounds hit the blocking position later that day, enemy fire from Karabilah slacked off from that point on.

On the north bank, Kilo's 2nd Platoon began searching Ar-Rabit in the afternoon, and other Marines ascended the escarpment above the valley to search through a series of caves. There were reports that weapons were stored in them, but nothing of consequence was found. Meanwhile, the speedy LAVs patrolled the desert beyond the escarpment, but saw no suspect activity. There was strong evidence, however, that foreign fighters had indeed been in Ramana.

Down in the villages, locals came forward to describe how insurgents coming from outside Iraq had seized the area with an iron grip. They told of beatings and killings, and how jihadists targeted those who would not cooperate. The foreigners confiscated homes and property and kept residents from traveling across the river. One resident of Ar-Rabit, bearing scars he claimed were from being captured and tortured by the jihadists, spoke to an American reporter: "The terrorists frighten and hurt the people here," said the man, afraid to reveal his name. "They do checkpoints and patrols. Anyone they catch going to Al-Qaim, they will kill with a knife and throw him by the road."[26]

ON THE EDGE

On Friday morning, 13 May, the men of WarPig 1 had been living out of their guntrucks for six days straight. They stank of rancid sweat and spent cordite, with aching muscles from being cramped inside the Humvees for hours at a stretch. WarPig 2 Marines, and the crew of the remaining tank, were in similar condition. They were so used to enduring mortar fire that another enemy salvo that morning raised little concern. But a new threat soon got their attention.

A single rifle round clanged off the armor plate protecting Stann's gunner, Lance Corporal Josh Langston. After a time, another single shot barely missed the tank commander sitting up in his hatch. Over the next hours, several gunners were nearly hit by someone firing from the sharkfin. "We'd heard intel about a sniper coming in from Syria," recalls Leahy. "Whoever this guy was, he was disciplined. He hit the turret of the ANGLICO truck a few times."[27] Finally, a muzzle flash was spotted in a top-floor window. On command, the Marines opened up on the building in a withering barrage. No more rounds came from that location.

Two miles away in Ar-Rabit, Marines from Kilo and Lima 3/25 were scouring through the last of the named objectives at the far end of Ramana. The Syrian border was within view to the west. By now they had cleared hundreds of homes and were well-practiced in the drill. Lieutenant Smith received orders to establish a support-by-fire position near the river, and 2nd Platoon began setting up sandbagged positions on rooftops overlooking the Euphrates.

At first it wasn't clear why, but later they were ordered to scan the slow-moving river for any sign of small craft or movement. Apparently, reports had been received from above that the highest of high-value-targets, Zarqawi himself, was in the area and would try to escape the Marine dragnet by moving up the river. Smith and his men stayed on high alert for hours, but nothing was seen. The HVI lookout mission was called off later that night.[28]

RETROGRADE

Early the next morning, Day 7 of the operation, Lieutenant Colonel Mundy issued orders to prepare for retrograde, the return trip to base. By 0600 units on the north bank were moving back through Ramana, through the sleepy villages they had laboriously cleared over the previous five days and past the ill-fated intersection where the blackened hulk of Lima's burned-out AAV remained. The return trip was far swifter this time and the Army-installed ribbon bridge was ready for them. Two hours later, Smith's 2nd Platoon was rattling back across the Euphrates in their dusty tracs and set up facing Old Ubaydi.

That same morning, Lieutenant Leahy prepared to withdraw his platoon, along with Stann's WarPig 2 Alpha and the remaining tank from the blocking position by Golden Gate bridge. Rather than heading south through the Karabilah gauntlet yet again, Leahy decided they would take the narrow backroads west over to Camp Gannon. On Gannon, Stann's section could refit and then safely navigate back to Camp AQ through open desert.

The column formed up and began moving when it was light enough to see the road. There was a risk of getting stuck again, but a greater danger lurked in everyone's mind. There had been plenty of time for insurgents to bury IEDs under those soft dirt roads, anticipating the Marines would come back that way. That was a standard enemy tactic.

Ryan Masterson was again the gunner in the lead Humvee, as he had been back on 8 May, seven days and a lifetime ago. Now he would have to keep a sharp eye out to spot any sign of a freshly-buried mine or hidden artillery shell.

Just as they were about to roll, Gunnery Sergeant Harman appeared out in front. He stripped off his helmet and body armor, placing them on the hood of Masterson's guntruck. And with a terse, "follow me," he started jogging along the dirt track. Defying the enemy, the danger, and the regs, he took point for the column of armored vehicles and guided them out of the danger zone. Among the ranks of WarPig, "Gunny Harman's jog" has achieved semi-legendary status.

"I was in awe," says Masterson. "Here was this super Marine, leading us out of there along a road no bigger than a goat trail back towards Gannon, back towards safety."[29] Jon Maines also remembers Harman running ahead of the column all by himself. "He was intense, he could be a little scary. But he was a badass that morning, taking off his kevlar and flak and running us out of there."[30]

After a mile or so, Harman grabbed his gear, climbed back in a vehicle and the column pressed on. Within an hour, they were in sight of Trash OP. Masterson describes his feelings as they reached friendly lines again. "Right as we approached the OP, a bunch of India guys were there aboard their AAVs, and they started cheering us as we came back in, like we were heroes back from the brink. It was awesome. When we got closer, I could see my buddy Joey Habay yelling and waving at me."[31]

Corporal Edwin "Andy" Vera, of WarPig 2 Alpha, had survived the hellish ambush in Karabilah a few nights before and then several more days of combat. Born in Colombia, Vera had immigrated to the U.S. when he was young. That morning as the column passed by Trash OP, he caught sight of a small patch of color on the skyline:

> *When I was a young Marine, I had a Colombian flag in my room. One of my NCOs gave me a hard time about it. "So which flag will you fight for?" I answered the U.S. flag, and he said, "That's right, you're an American now." I realized he was right... Then, after Matador, when we got close to Gannon, I could see the American flag flying over the command post. And it was an overwhelming emotion for me. That flag is sacred to me. It means so much.*
>
> —**Edwin Vera**[32]

RESULTS

Most accounts of Operation Matador characterize it as a mixed success. The Ramana region north of the river was cleared for the first time in the war, but no major enemy strongholds were discovered there. It was widely reported that the insurgents had withdrawn before the operation. It was on the south bank, in Karabilah, Sadah, and New Ubaydi, where the enemy was encountered in force.

According to the official history, an estimated 144 enemy fighters were killed and 40 detained, while a significant quantity of weapons and bomb-making materials were destroyed or captured.[33] In those seven days, 3/2 and supporting units had pushed all the way to the Syrian border, clearing hundreds of buildings, at the painful cost of nine Marines killed and 39 wounded.[34] Then, despite the ground gained and cost borne, they swept back across the river to their bases.

But as their leaders well knew, any geographic gains were transitory. Without sufficient units to leave behind, the city blocks they'd cleared and the ground they'd covered would soon be infested by the enemy again. From the beginning, Colonel Davis and Lieutenant Colonel Mundy were under no illusions that Ramana could be held with the forces they currently commanded. They could clear but could not yet hold or build.

In other aspects, however, they had positively shifted the overall situation in the Western Euphrates River Valley. They had showed the insurgents and the population that the Marines would go where they wanted, when they wanted, despite determined opposition. And there was no doubt that AQI's plans and logistics had been disrupted. Caches were blown in place, car-bombs had been expended or destroyed, and AQI's materiel resources reduced.

Finally, there were well over 100 enemy fighters, perhaps many more, who would no longer be detonating IEDs, ambushing Marines, or murdering local civilians. While body counts were not seen as a measure of success, at some point, removing numbers of enemy combatants from the battlefield makes a difference, even in an insurgency.

Matador marked the first real combat for many 3/2 Marines and as such left an indelible mark on individuals and on the overall psyche of the battalion. The experience of being shot at with lethal intent, or being near the detonation of an IED, changes a man's worldview. Certain preconceptions about life are stripped away.

While Lance Corporal Kevin Smith had been the battalion's first KIA in March, in some respects his loss was experienced as an isolated event. But the loss of Philippon, Derga, and Goodwin in close-quarters combat, the fiery fate of six Marines in Lima 3/25 and so many inches-away close calls, made it crystal clear to all members of the battalion that death might be in the cards for any of them.

On the evening of 15 May 2005, while most of the supporting units were still at Camp AQ, a memorial service was held for the nine Marines who'd been lost. With an entire row of upended rifles lined up, helmets perched, and dog tags dangling, it was a sobering event for everyone there. Throughout the grind of the operation, there'd been no time for reflection or reverence. Now, in the slanting sunlight of a fading desert day, each man found his own way to say goodbye to friends, mentors, brothers.

CLOSING WITH THE ENEMY

I don't really think Matador went wrong, despite the problems we had. We went out looking for contact and we found it. From my standpoint, it was more effective to do these bigger ops, where we could stay out for a bit, gather intel, and engage the enemy if he showed. And we learned a lot in Matador. Mounting smaller "presence patrols" would just result in needless casualties. But in a large op like this, we could get more information on our AO and hopefully provoke an enemy response. We're Marine infantry. It's our job to close with and destroy the enemy and that's what we were doing.

—John Day[35]

The fight at New Ubaydi perfectly illustrates Day's point. While the enemy surfaced in an unexpected quarter, the Marines pivoted on a dime and moved quickly and with deadly force to meet them. Within hours, several dozen enemy fighters had been killed, many from long-range fires as they crossed streets or from the air as they attempted to flee the town and cross the river. AQI had attempted a large-scale ambush, only to have the tables drastically turned on them.

The same dynamic occurred in the Golden Gate fight, spread over several days. In some ways, the engagements fought by 3/2's two mobile assault platoons, WarPig 1 and WarPig 2, were the crux of the whole operation. The blocking position had found and fixed the main enemy stronghold, then eliminated many teams of insurgents with long-range fires and airstrikes. Moreover, WarPig 2's running shootouts with black-clad fighters and suicide bombers almost certainly engaged the headquarters of either a prominent AQI field commander or quite possibly Zarqawi himself.

WOUNDING ZARQAWI?

In fact, days after the conclusion of Operation Matador, a jihadist website announced Zarqawi had been shot in the lung during the recent fighting in the Al-Qaim district. In the media flurry that followed, the AQI leader was rumored to be at death's door, then only "lightly wounded." Eventually an audio message surfaced, from Zarqawi to Osama Bin Laden, assuring al-Qaeda's founder that he was still physically able to continue leading the fight in Iraq.[36] So while it can never be established for certain, there are multiple indications that Operation Matador, and WarPig 2 specifically, came close to killing the infamous terrorist and leader of AQI.

In several ways, the operation also drove the wedge deeper between the foreign fighters and the local forces of the Albu Mahal. The kidnapping of Fahad al-Mahalawi was a clear enough indicator of increasing tensions. In the weeks following Matador, Captain Frank Diorio and other India Marines started making tentative overtures to the tribe's militia group, or what they called the local insurgents.

"After that op, these guys wanted to talk," recalls Ryan Brummond, who commanded India Company's 1st Platoon in 2005, "They could see we were going after AQI, and I think Matador made the Hamza guys say, 'we gotta talk to the Marines'".[37]

The Marine Corps officially recognized two men for "conspicuous gallantry and intrepidity in action" during Operation Matador. Sergeant Dennis Woullard, Jr., the deputy sheriff and reservist assigned to 4th AAB, repeatedly risked his own life to pull fellow Marines to safety. He was awarded the Silver Star in November of 2006.

Lieutenant Brian Stann was pinned with the Silver Star in March, 2006. Stann's citation refers to his "zealous initiative, courageous actions, and exceptional presence of mind" during the multiple firefights he led his men through during Matador. But the citation only scratches the surface. In multiple interviews, men of WarPig 2 and other members of 3/2 universally described Stann as an exceptional leader, a man they were proud to serve with. For his part, Stann humbly writes, "I did not deserve such an honor. My platoon did. This was their award, not mine."[38]

18. ENGAGEMENT

Soon after Operation Matador, Lieutenant Colonel Mundy made one of his trips out to Camp Gannon. While India Company hadn't been part of the fighting in Ubaydi and Ramana, they were conducting small-scale operations when opportunities arose. As Mundy arrived, one of these missions was in the works. "A squad was going out to a house about two klicks out and they'd be out there alone," he recalls. He watched as the squad leader, Corporal Rashard Minnis, from India's 2nd Platoon, briefed the Op Order. "It struck me how calm this young Marine was."[1]

For his part, Minnis remembers the mission was business as usual. "We were going out into the city, where we thought there were bad guys," says Minnis. "I covered the plan, the critical vulnerabilities, and how we'd have to adjust if things went bad. But I wasn't putting on a show ... This was just ops-normal."[2] Still, he'd made a lasting impression on his battalion CO:

> *I had focused our training on the young leaders in the battalion. So, to see him talking about going out into enemy territory calmly, fully confident that he and his Marines could handle whatever was thrown at them, was motivating, inspiring really. That's the*

kind of thing I was most proud of. I never felt it was about me, the commander. It was about these young Marines and what they were capable of."

—Tim Mundy[3]

FOREIGN VS. LOCAL MUJ

The highly kinetic combat during Matador, and the accelerating effort by special operators to find Zarqawi and uproot his network, obscured another increasingly desperate fight going on in Al-Qaim. The red-on-red firefights that broke out just before Matador had continued during the operation. By the time it was over, the Albu Mahal had pushed foreign fighters out of key areas, including parts of Husaybah, and had openly split from Zarqawi and AQI.

This struggle was largely invisible to the Marines at Gannon and to the rest of the battalion, however. With few local contacts and tenuous connections to civilian officials, 3/2's leadership was only vaguely aware of the bitter feud. Most of the Marines simply called the two sides of this intramural conflict the "local muj" (short for *mujahideen*) and the "foreign muj" and saw both as threats.

While the 2 May assassination of Major Ahmed was the catalyst for the Albu Mahal's open combat against foreign fighters and their local allies, the conflict had been building for some time. It is difficult, so many years later, to pin the timing down but the 2010 interviews conducted by Dr. Knarr's team provide a rough chronology. Sheikh Sabah, along with his uncle and mentor, Sheikh Kurdi, described early developments and rising tensions:

There was tremendous patriotic resistance here in Al-Qaim... At first, al-Qaeda managed to get inside society here. Most people in this area considered al-Qaeda to be "the complete jihad." However, starting in mid-2004, al-Qaeda started doing some things in the area that the people didn't like.

—Sheikh Kurdi [4]

Local perceptions of the foreigners began to change as the jihadists increased their presence and power. According to Sheikh Sabah, al-Qaeda began bringing in hundreds of "terrorists", exercising harsh control over the area.[5] Other important players spoke about the turmoil of those days, describing the jihadists' escalating violence and depravity:

Al-Qaeda members are thieves and robbers...they don't have any respect for the people and used force to control them... that's why the first thing al-Qaeda did was to destroy the diwan... where all the tribes gather and conduct the annual meetings and other events. Al-Qaeda blew it up to stop the tribes from meeting and getting ready.

—De Hal Farhan[6]

Destroying buildings quickly progressed to destroying people. As early as the summer of 2004, the foreign fighters were unleashing terror tactics in Al-Qaim, including kidnapping and assassination. Sheikh Sabah related a particularly horrific atrocity committed by AQI:

Four members of one family—not from my tribe, from the Salmoni tribe—[were killed] in the middle of the street. They cut off their heads, and they put each head on the back of the body. This was in August of 2004 ... [Then] they came and put TNT on each body, and they called the family to come pick them up. When the family came at dawn, they exploded them ... They killed another eight, and they injured many others.

—Sheikh Sabah[7]

Ahmad Jelayan Khalaf recalled many similar incidents:

A lot of my friends were killed by having their heads cut off. It's like you wake up early in the morning and you go down the street, and you see four or five dead bodies with their own heads over their bodies. Three of my cousins were killed that way ... Sometimes we found only the head and the body had been tossed in the desert or in the river.

—Ahmad Jelayan Khalaf[8]

Such was the atmosphere when the sheikhs had their pivotal meeting with AQI emirs in early 2005. The Albu Mahal "negotiated with them to try to solve the security problem," stated Khalaf. But in response, AQI issued even more ominous demands. "Al-Qaeda asked for a list of tribal members," he continued, "[but] the sheikhs refused to provide the names [or meet] other conditions."[9]

Sometime after the meeting, the Mahalawis started moving to take control of Husaybah and other areas where they had presence. Just as India Company took over at Camp Gannon, the Albu Mahal were shifting their stance from energetically opposing the Americans to fighting the jihadist predators among them. Events in April all have to be viewed in this context. The East End Raid on 1 April, the establishment of Trash OP and the 11 April suicide attacks took place concurrently with efforts by the Albu Mahal to push out the foreign fighters.

According to Sheikh Kurdi's account, by mid-to-late April, the tribe had placed Major Ahmed into his position as the police chief in Husaybah. Presumably they were also sending their own armed men into the streets. This was happening around the same time as the shooting of a local on Market Street that Captain Diorio saw as an important indicator. The hidden conflict was starting to bubble up.

Rather than sending presence patrols and armored vehicles into this uncertain and volatile mix, India Company began looking for other ways to find cooperative locals, and perhaps to drive a wedge further between the people and the ultra-violent outsiders. One of their efforts was humanitarian in nature but had to be handled carefully.

During the 11 April attack, the truck bombs ruptured a water main in Husaybah, leaving parts of the city without running water and many residents suffering. The Marines received requests to repair the line, but the assets were not available. "I didn't have the capabilities to fix the water yet," Diorio later recalled.[10] But he could see there was an opportunity to send a message about who really had the interests of Iraqis at heart.

One night India Company loaded up several AAVs with hundreds of cases of bottled water. While Husaybah was slumbering, they drove to the affected sectors of the city and quietly distributed the water outside houses. "We put it on their doorstep in the middle of the night with no fanfare," said Diorio.[11] The gesture was largely symbolic, but it was an important one. From one of the gun positions on Gannon, Diorio peered out over a waking city to get a glimpse of residents' reactions. "Just as the sun came up, you could see [doors] open just enough to pull the water in," he related. "They wanted to make sure no one saw them getting help from us. That day we had people we had never talked to call the base. They said, 'Thank you for the water, and thank you for caring.'"[12]

FIRST BATTLE

In the meantime, however, AQI was cranking up the pressure. After the fractious meeting with the sheikhs and upon seeing Albu Mahal's defiant moves, the foreign fighters issued a death-list of key figures marked for assassination.[13] Major Ahmed was certainly one of the top names on the list and his gruesome assassination sparked open rebellion by the Albu Mahal. According to Iraqi sources, for the next two weeks (recollections vary), the tribe fought an extended battle against Zarqawi's forces:

> *The assassination triggered the first part of the war against terrorism in Al Anbar Province... against those members of al-Qaeda. The Albu Mahal tribe fought back and killed four members of al-Qaeda as retribution for Major Ahmed's death... They raided al-Qaeda's locations, captured a lot of weapons and ammunition.*
>
> **—Ismael Sha Hamid Dulaymi**[14]

> *This big fight... began on the 2nd of May 2005, and it ended about the 13th of May. The American forces in the region at the time played no part... during this first battle. Al-Qaeda couldn't drive the Albu Mahal tribe out of the area—the Albu Mahal kicked out al-Qaeda.*
>
> **—Sheikh Kurdi**[15]

> *After we pushed all the terrorists to Karabilah . . . we started patrolling to protect the area . . . We started running and ruling the city and trying to get it back to normal. The terrorists went to staging in Karabilah and Rummanah.*
>
> —**Ahmed Jelayan Khalaf**[16]

As pointed out by Sheikh Kurdi, however, there was no coordination between the Albu Mahal's tribal forces and 3/2 Marines as they pushed into Ramana. At this early juncture, the Marines had no mechanism for such coordination and no command guidance for engaging with the tribes. But slowly, haltingly, things began to change down at the company level.

REACHING OUT

Even before deploying, Captain Diorio had been reading reports from Al-Qaim. "I gathered a year's worth of INTSUMs [intelligence summaries], and I read them." His study only intensified once he arrived at Gannon. During turnover with Baker Company, he took further cues from his predecessor, Captain Nelson. "I watched Andy with piles and piles of INTSUMs that he would go through personally."[17]

This preparation and focus on intelligence paid off down the road. India Company not only inherited the reports, but Nelson's contextual knowledge as well. "Andy talked to me about what he thought and what he synthesized," said Diorio. For the rest of the deployment, "When I looked at new intelligence, I would always have that foundation."[18] Soon after the conclusion of Operation Matador, several pieces of this hard-won context clicked together:

> *One night I was going through a pile of INTSUMs... a stack of about 200 pieces of paper... It was basically given to me as worthless information to be honest, [just] chatter. And one of them was a summary about a local insurgent.*
>
> —**Frank Diorio**[19]

It was a recent report describing an unknown insurgent warning his group about a raid being launched from Camp AQ against foreign fighters. He had somehow been tipped off, but rather than trying to interfere with the Marines, he was telling his men to stand aside, to leave the Americans alone. As paraphrased by Diorio, he was saying: "Hey, if the Marines come against [the] foreign fighters, let them go. Let them hit these foreign fighters. We don't want them in our area."[20]

What others had seen as innocuous chatter; the company commander zoomed in on. "What I had was a guy taking leadership...giving orders, and I had a guy picking and choosing [sides]." As he turned this nugget of information over in his mind, the weight of it grew. It indicated there were local insurgents opposed to AQI, who might be approached as something other than enemies. For Diorio, it meant there was "someone else other than the people we were fighting...And I remember just staring at it for about an hour."[21]

With subsequent checking, it was confirmed that a raid had indeed been launched at the corresponding time and had met no resistance from local fighters. The report and the source checked out. At that point, Diorio turned to his interpreter and told him, "[Let's] get a message to this guy and tell him I want to talk to him."[22]

Naturally turning to their best local source, they called the

East End Lady. While she couldn't identify anyone herself, she provided other leads. Further calls were made to follow up, but none of the leads panned out. The outreach continued, though, as India Company tried another technique. Flyers were printed and distributed asking Husaybah residents to call the hotline with any information. It seemed like a futile effort.

Then, "one day we had someone call," relates Diorio. "She was actually a young girl, 16 years old." This was no cloak-and-dagger approach from a covert agent. According to Diorio's account, she was just a curious teenager. "I saw this flyer with the number on it," she said, "I just wanted to see what Americans sound like."[23]

It was a small break, but it was progress. Captain Diorio, Sergeant Jimmy, and others put their heads together to discuss how to cultivate this new contact. They didn't want to scare her off. "Don't ask her any tactical questions," said Diorio. "Don't ask for any information. Just talk to her."[24] A cultivation process began. The girl began to call the hotline almost every day to talk to Sergeant Jimmy and soon it was clear she had a bit of a crush on him. Again, patience was the watchword. At first, the daily phone calls were mundane conversations about daily life, but they were slowly building on the personal connection.

After about three weeks, it felt like the time was right to ask her for some valuable information. The hope was that she would have enough trust and could help identify the mysterious local insurgent leader. Diorio had his interpreter push to the next step:

> *[He] called her and said, "Hey, by the way, do you know who this [insurgent] is?" And she said, "Oh yeah, he lives here… my mom knows him. We live in the same area." So, we said, "Well, can you*

get his number without him knowing?" She said, "Yeah, I can get it." [25]

—**Frank Diorio** [26]

Sure enough, a few days later the girl called in and provided a new phone number for the growing contact list. By all indications, it was a direct line to an Iraqi insurgent who had likely fought against other American units and may have even been involved in attacks against India Company. By this time, it was late May or early June. "I sat on it for about three weeks," says Diorio. "At the time it just felt like it was still too close with everything going on. I wanted to get more atmospherics."

See **bastardsandbrothers.com** for notes, photos, maps, etc.

19. TARGET SOFTENING

After the conclusion of Operation Matador on May 14, 2005, a pressing question remained. Where had the enemy gone? There had been sharp engagements in New Ubaydi and all around the Golden Gate bridge. However, the main focus had been to sweep north of the river through Ramana and little had been found there. The insurgents had apparently melted away.

There were indications they had been forewarned, then dispersed to other parts of the district or withdrew across the border into Syria, ready to filter back in. It was clear the enemy was still active in the district, however. Mortar and direct fire attacks continued against Camp Gannon almost every day, while Kilo and WarPig's mobile assault platoons found further signs of insurgent activity.

A particular area stood out. Increased intelligence reporting indicated that AQI had set up shop in Karabilah, about four miles east of Husaybah with a population of about 60,000. It was also the traditional home of the Karabuli, one of the tribes considered allies of Zarqawi and his jihadist fighters.

The clashes that WarPig 2 had experienced as they drove through Karabilah during Matador were the most concrete evidence of a substantial AQI presence there. Lieutenant Stann's intense engagements against black-clad fighters employing AQI's trademark suicide tactics led to the conclusion that either a major AQI emir, or even Zarqawi himself, had established a base in Karabilah.

As this evidence mounted, RCT-2 and 3/2 planners began putting together a concept for another major operation. Collection was focused and more confirmation came in. Sources reported several safe houses, weapons caches, and facilities being used by the jihadis.

SEND IN THE REAPERS

In late May and the early part of June, the scout-sniper platoon played an important role in preparing for the upcoming operation. They began by executing reconnaissance & surveillance (R&S) missions to figure out where the insurgents were concentrated and what they were up to.

The first priority for these missions was to validate existing intelligence reports and establish a baseline for normal activity in the area. Even though modern aerial platforms have incredible capabilities and human sources can provide excellent information, there is no substitute for getting eyes-on-target.

Using high-powered optics, a well-trained scout-sniper team can derive a wealth of information through patient, persistent observation. Articles of clothing, equipment, weapons, vehicles, license plates, body language, movement patterns, schedules, facial features, and relative status among individuals, are all useful details that can be observed at long range.

And as these details from the scout-sniper teams are compiled, reported, and merged with other pieces of data, a very accurate intelligence picture can be built up. But putting teams into the right place at the right time is no easy feat. It takes careful planning, good coordination with other elements, and extraordinary physical and mental preparation by the men executing the missions.

Just days after Matador, one of these R&S missions was handed down to Reaper 4, probably on 18 May.[1] The surveillance target was a gas station along the highway running through the town of Sadah, about a mile east of Karabilah. Gas stations in Anbar were often used by insurgents to disguise their activity among the many vehicles coming and going, or to gain revenue by selling black market fuel or taxing an existing fuel-smuggling operation.

After mission prep, Corporal Aaron Smith along with Lance Corporals Roberto Mendez and Jeff Weaver were driven out to the Retrans outpost. Around midnight, Smith led the team as they moved unseen through the broken desert terrain about five miles to the edge of Sadah. They worked their way slowly to a gentle hill in an open area about 750 meters from the highway.

One of the first tasks was to set up their communications gear. Without good comms, they would be terribly vulnerable. If they missed two comms checks in a row for any reason, their SOP was to abort the mission. They set up a SATCOM set, and both UHF and VHF radios. Since a vertical antenna could give away their position, they carefully laid out antenna wires on the ground. The spot had enough "micro-terrain", small breaks or undulations in the ground, to conceal them in the prone position. The men settled in, maximizing each rock or fold in the ground for concealment, and placed weapons, water, and equipment within easy reach. They lay within inches of each other, close enough to signal with a nudge instead of talking, oriented outwards to cover 360 degrees. Pulling desert smocks over their head and torso broke up their outlines, blending their shapes into the earth. As daybreak came and the sun started to climb, they were invisible to anyone more than fifty feet away.

Harsh Conditions

Reconnaissance & Surveillance (R&S) missions in Anbar demanded uncommon physical and mental stamina. Lying prone for hours on end completely exposed to the elements could drain a man. The heat alone could be a real threat. Even in May, by midday the temperature was around 100 degrees with no shade. Staying hydrated was key. Taking care of bodily functions posed a different set of challenges, requiring creative solutions.

They would stay in this hide site for the next 24 hours, shuffling slowly at intervals as they rotated between positions to ward off boredom, mental complacency, and stiff muscles. One man was always oriented towards the gas station, "glassing" the area with high powered binoculars and making notes of all activity observed. The others scanned the rest of the circle for possible threats, while one also handled the radios, making necessary calls.

Threats could come in unexpected forms. Late in the day, Smith was peering through binoculars when he was startled by sudden movement in his peripheral vision. "This big green and yellow camel spider came hauling ass at me," he recounts. "I jumped up with an 'oh shit!', and the others got up on a knee and shouldered weapons. They thought insurgents were coming."[2] While amusing, even such a momentary lapse could compromise their position.

When darkness returned, the team broke down their gear, removed all sign of their presence, and rucked back out to Retrans. Nothing nefarious had been seen at the gas station or among the homes and buildings of Sadah. But their observations helped establish the environmental baseline for the area and a useful hide site had been identified.

POINT BLANK

Two weeks later, the picture had clarified considerably. More detailed intelligence showed AQI fighters ensconced in the center of Karabilah. Now the SSP's mission shifted to locate good infiltration routes and usable hide sites with views of streets and buildings the insurgents were reportedly using.

Just after midnight on 30 May, another R&S mission was launched, this one with a mixed team from Reaper 7 and 4. Corporal Pat Cassidy led the mission and Staff Sergeant Gallant came along to fill out an eight-man team. For higher-risk missions like this, they needed the extra firepower.[3]

They were inserted outside the city, behind a terrain feature about a mile south of the railroad tracks. Cassidy led them up to the berm where the rails ran, then the team moved into the scattered houses and dusty alleys. The immediate objective was to find somewhere with unobstructed views towards several key targets. But things didn't go as planned.

An urgent radio call came in and the COC told them to

go firm immediately. They were told special operators of Task Force 714 were executing a priority raid in Karabilah that night just a few hundred meters away, and Reaper's presence posed a real danger of friendly fire. An AC-130 gunship was already circling overhead, and the scout-snipers were directed to activate their infrared (IR) strobes. The strobes would identify them as friendlies for the gunship's night-piercing sensors. The team moved into an unfinished single-story house and set their security.

It was a sturdy, stone-walled structure with stairs to the rooftop. From there, they watched the Task Force mission unfold to their northwest. Flashes lit up the night sky and tracers crisscrossed through the air. The raid had kicked off a heavy firefight. Soon the AC-130 let loose, adding to the deadly symphony. This wasn't a good sign, as it meant more insurgents were rushing into the fight.

Next morning, the team remained holed up. They intended to resume the mission once night fell. Late in the morning, a silver sedan drove up the dirt road right past the house. It stopped a couple hundred meters to the northwest, where it was joined by a pickup truck. Both vehicles were carrying military-aged men and the Reapers observed them intently. Was this an enemy patrol searching for them?

They relaxed somewhat when the vehicles crossed the tracks and drove south away from them. Tension returned just minutes later, however, as gunfire echoed from that vicinity. They reoriented to defend against a possible attack from the south. But it was soon obvious that the shots were regularly spaced, indicating insurgent target practice or test-firing.

With the presence of weapons satisfying the Rules of Engagement (ROE), the vehicles could be engaged if they came back over the berm. Two plans of action were briefed. If the vehicles turned away from the house towards the northwest, the .50 cal rifle would be used to punch through the engine blocks, disabling the vehicles. Then the insurgents would be engaged at long range. If they turned towards the hide site, they would be engaged as they passed.

The firing soon stopped, and the silver sedan reappeared alone atop the berm. The pickup truck apparently left via another route. The car paused for a beat, then turned right, heading towards their hide site. Anticipation and adrenaline levels mounted as the car approached. They could hear the tires crunch on dirt and gravel when it drew close.

As the sedan passed by the front of the house at slow speed, the men on the ground floor opened up at point-blank range. Rising up from concealment on the roof, Weaver stood and unleashed even more devastating fire downwards. "They were immediately next to our building," recalls Weaver. "I was carrying a chopped SAW* and fired directly down through the top of the car. They really didn't have a chance."[5] The rounds struck home and the riddled vehicle rolled eerily for a few meters before stopping.

Cassidy and Smith cautiously approached while others covered. All six men in the car were clearly dead, spilling out when the doors were opened. But none appeared to be armed. For a sickening moment the team considered the implications. Jeff Weaver remembers Gallant muttering, "Good God, I'm going to prison." But when the trunk was pried open, all such concerns evaporated. It was filled with AKs, machine guns, RPGs, ammo belts, and grenades.

---

* A short-barreled version of the M-249 Squad Automatic Weapon (SAW)

They started site exploitation while calling for extraction. Assuming more enemy fighters would come to investigate, they had to work fast. The weapons were checked for booby traps then prepped for transport. The dead insurgents were photographed for later identification, their pockets checked for cell phones and documents, a grisly task. In the process, an instructive discovery was made. One of the dead men had a grenade rigged on his chest to detonate if a crude wire handle was pulled. The device was carefully disarmed, and the apparent suicide tactic was duly noted.

Meanwhile the men on the roof watched for threats, but none appeared. Within thirty minutes the guntrucks from WarPig rolled up. Dirty and exhausted, the scout snipers loaded up the captured weapons then piled in themselves.

The ride back gave them time to think. What if the vehicle had turned left instead of right? What if the driver hadn't pulled up right under their guns? What if there had been an IED rigged in the vehicle? But they'd definitely answered one question. They had confirmed that Karabilah was a viper's nest of insurgent activity that needed to be addressed.

HIDE AND SEEK

As May turned into June, temperature and tension were rising along the western Euphrates. On 31 May, fifty miles upriver to the east, near Rawah, a U.S. Army patrol found the body of the Governor of Anbar, and former mayor of Al-Qaim, after an unexpected firefight with his captors. He'd been held hostage by AQI since 10 May, and his death accentuated the already violent rift between the Albu Mahal and Zarqawi's foreign fighters.[6]

Nearer to Al-Qaim, an increasing spiral of violence was evident. On 2 June, a truck sped menacingly towards Camp Gannon. As the driver ignored all warning signs and then passed the "trigger line", Reaper 1 engaged, finally stopping the suspected suicide attack after multiple hits with a .50 caliber sniper rifle.[7]

In the predawn hours of 9 June, a pair of Cobra helicopters flying over the outskirts of Karbilah were fired on by at least two heavy machine guns. The crews reported hostile fire from 12.7mm machine guns or 14.5mm anti-aircraft guns. Later that same day, Marines found the dead bodies of five Iraqi men at a crossroads just a few miles from 3/2's base at the train station. They'd been beheaded or shot in the head.[8]

Meanwhile, the plan for cleaning out Karabilah was being prepared. A key preliminary step would be what the Marines called "target softening." It would involve two composite Reaper teams executing their riskiest mission yet, requiring stealth and skill as they pushed in close to observe insurgents in the city.

One team would insert on the southern edge of Karabilah, led by Sergeant Carlos Rosario. Accompanying Rosario's team would be Lieutenant Habenicht and the battalion's senior FAC, Captain Edwards, to coordinate airstrikes. The second team, led by Corporal Cassidy, would move further north along the large wadi. This northern team would be especially vulnerable, positioned within the insurgent-held part of the city. WarPig 2 would be their extraction force and fire support if things got dicey.[9]

In the early morning darkness on 11 June, the two teams were inserted then proceeded on foot. All went smoothly as they slipped in from the desert to their hide sites. Rosario's team set up in a three-story house just south of ASR Jade, where they had unobstructed views along two north-south streets. Cassidy's team navigated down the wadi and went firm in an abandoned house with good views along east-west streets near the city center.

When daybreak came, they watched Karabilah come awake. "Once we were set up, it was kind of eerie," remembers Carlos Rosario. "The kids were all gone in the morning, like the residents knew we were there and that something was going to happen."[10] Evidently, no one tipped off the insurgents, however. The morning passed uneventfully while the scout-snipers observed their surroundings and made range cards. These were filled in with target data for quick reference. Working with the southern team, Habenicht and Edwards checked and rechecked their communications and determined what air assets were available.

The first opportunity to hit the enemy presented itself around noon. For some time, Rosario's team had been patiently watching a group of insurgents manning an ad-hoc checkpoint. They were brandishing weapons, stopping cars, and basically strutting their stuff in the street. When over a dozen of them entered a nearby building and no civilians could be seen, an airstrike was called in.

From nearly five miles up, invisible from the ground, the pilot of a U.S. Air Force F-16 confirmed the target and released a single GPS-guided, 500-pound bomb. The bomb took several minutes to slice through the air, automatically adjusting its trajectory as it fell. Over the radio, Edwards called out the countdown to impact.

In a sudden flash the bomb exploded, flinging a column of earth, rocks, and masonry high into the air. A second later, the blast wave reached both Reaper teams with a dull boom. When the dust cleared, the structure had collapsed, the men inside likely shredded or buried.

To the south team, it seemed like they'd kicked over an anthill. Multiple insurgents scurried out into the street with some entering and exiting other buildings. "We could tell they were organized," says Rosario. "They went right into recovery mode, getting bodies out, clearing rubble...The AQI guys were serious fighters. I noticed two in particular. One had a muscular build, in good physical shape with ammo belts across his chest. The other was packing RPG rounds on his back; I could tell they were flechette rounds."*

After more minutes passed several men carrying AKs and RPGs congregated into a group. When they entered another structure, a second target was designated. As before, precise coordinates were passed to a jet orbiting high above. Soon another bomb slammed into the building with similarly dramatic results.

Again, multiple armed men boiled out of adjacent buildings. Some got into a white car and sped away. But with both Reaper teams scanning overlapping fields of view, the vehicle was soon located again, parked near a designated safehouse. A laser-guided bomb destroyed the house, but the car escaped again.

Over the next few hours, the scout-snipers essentially conducted a deadly game of hide-and-seek, tracking small bands of insurgents as they appeared, calling in precision strikes whenever possible. Given their vantage point overlooking several enemy-occupied structures, most of the strikes were called in by the south team.

---

* The presence of specialized RPG rounds was further evidence that these were not just local Iraqi insurgents.

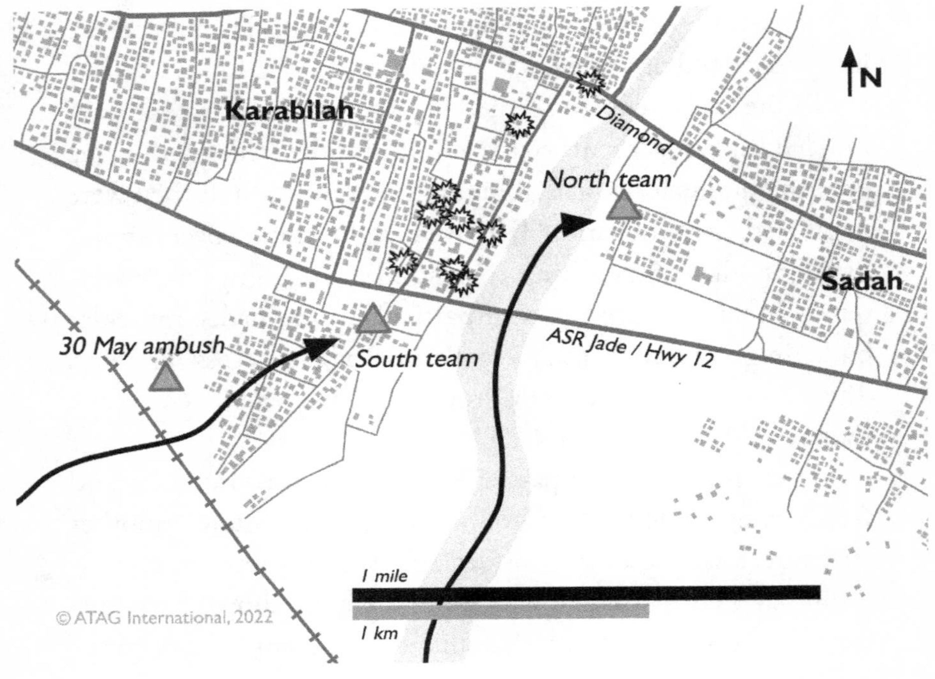

Several other buildings were destroyed with armed insurgents inside, resulting in at least a dozen more enemy killed. The white car was eventually blasted by a laser-guided Hellfire missile, launched from a Cobra. Through it all, the Reapers kept a low profile, never taking a shot, patiently waiting for another chance to rain down death from above.

HELL OUT OF DODGE

As the afternoon progressed, however, the enemy began to figure out what was happening. About 5:30pm, several mortar rounds suddenly impacted near the southern team's hide site. It was obvious they'd been spotted. Sergeant Rosario determined it was too dangerous to stay and pulled his team back south of the train tracks to be picked up.

Meanwhile, the north team remained hidden by the wadi. Soon after Rosario's team pulled out, Cassidy's team spotted at least two other targets which were converted into rubble by precision-guided bombs. At that point, the north team had been holed up in the abandoned building by the wadi for over 16 hours. Aaron Smith and Jeff Weaver were downstairs on security when suddenly Weaver hissed urgently across the team intercom. "There's a guy right here!" An insurgent was lurking right outside the house:

> *I motioned to Jeff and whispered that if the guy looked in the window, we'd grab him, pull him in and shoot him with our 9mm pistols jammed against his chest to quiet the shots. When we saw his shadow in the open window frame we tensed up for the grab. But he walked away. We had to make our exit before more insurgents tightened the noose.*
>
> —**Aaron Smith**[11]

Cassidy rallied the team and they silently gathered up their gear then stacked next to the front door. The insurgent was just outside, a few feet away. With a hand signal, they flung open the door and flowed out, weapons at the ready.

The insurgent was caught completely by surprise. He had a chest rig with grenades and an AK in his hands but had no time to even raise his weapon. The first man out the door delivered two pairs of controlled shots that toppled the man backwards over a low brick wall, where he disappeared from view. Remembering the rigged grenade found on an insurgent's body a few days before, the Marines tossed a frag over the wall to ensure the man was dead. The noise was sure to attract attention, so they kept moving:

> *Our break contact movement was harrowing. The gunfire and grenades gave up our location and the jig was up. We were in the middle of a densely-populated town with no support on station. There was vehicle traffic, foot traffic all around, and armed insurgents looking to take us down. The six of us were loaded down, and it turned into "a Mogadishu mile" situation in broad daylight. Our only bet was to get the hell out of Dodge and out to the open desert.*
>
> —**Aaron Smith**[12]

The first leg of their escape route took them down busy streets, and a few times they actually had to fire warning shots to get cars to stop while they jogged through an intersection. They then dropped into the wadi, leapfrogging forward to cover each other. The west edge of the wadi loomed some 30 feet above them. Any gunman there would have a clear shot on the six struggling scout-snipers.

They moved as fast as possible, but adrenaline and extreme physical exertion were rapidly sapping their energy. The temperature still hovered around 100 degrees and each man was loaded with 60 pounds of body armor and gear, plus a 70 or 80-pound ruck. With aching legs, scorched lungs, and sweat pouring from under their body armor, they finally found cover and stopped, still a half-mile short of the extraction point. Assuming that insurgents would be appearing soon, they prepared to fight.

It was an immense relief, then, to see a dust plume and hear the rumble of engines coming up from the south. Knowing fellow Marines were in trouble, Lieutenant Stann had disregarded the plan and pressed north with WarPig 2's Humvees, each with a crew-served weapon. Within minutes, the exhausted men were bundled safely aboard and the guntrucks headed back to Camp Al-Qaim.

The target softening operation had been a classic application of scout-snipers leveraging stealth, battlefield awareness, communications, and precision airpower. Enemy behaviors and reactions had been closely watched, and detailed observations were fed into the ongoing planning cycle. Moreover, an estimated 30 to 40 insurgents had been killed, a platoon's-worth of enemy fighters taken off the battlefield. AQI's command and control had also been severely affected. Most important, in just a few days, brother Marines would be launched into Karabilah on a major operation. Undoubtedly, Reaper's actions leading up to that operation saved Marine lives.

20. TIP OF THE SPEAR

With Karabilah now clearly established as an AQI stronghold, RCT-2 concentrated forces for another large clearing operation. The new mission was named Operation Spear and the force assembled included most of the same units that had conducted Matador. It was set to launch on 17 June.

Coming only seven months after the Second Battle of Fallujah, stories of the vicious house-to-house fighting there had percolated throughout Marine units in Iraq. Many Marines viewed the upcoming operation as "Fallujah-Lite" and anticipated determined, even suicidal, resistance. They geared up accordingly.

Kilo Company and Lima Company 3/25 would again provide the core infantry companies, fighting alongside each other once more. An additional rifle platoon was also available this time. 3rd Platoon of 3/2's own Lima Company would be another maneuver element in the operation with the callsign "Beowulf." WarPig 2 and 3 would be on hand to screen and support, along with LAVs and several Abrams tanks.[1]

The operation would also feature two key force magnifiers. The first was a company of Iraqi Army troops, assigned to work with Kilo. The company came from the Iraqi Army's 4th

Brigade, 2nd Battalion and with it came a supplemental name for the operation, *Rhome*, the Arabic word for spear. Ieva decided to fold the Iraqi platoons in with his 3rd Platoon, led by Lieutenant Joe Clemmey. He had high confidence in Clemmey's abilities and had him integrate each of his three squads with one of the Iraqi platoons, forming a combined Marine/Iraqi unit.[2]

The second force magnifier was more kinetic. Knowing that main streets had been seeded with IEDs, 3/2 brought in specially-equipped AAVs with mine clearing line charges, known as MICLICs. These consisted of a long, explosive rope attached to a rocket that could be fired up and over a minefield or obstacle. Once the line was stretched out on the ground, an electrical charge would set off the C4 explosives, resulting in a massive detonation that would clear a lane 30 feet wide and 300 feet deep.

At the leadership level, there was hesitation about both measures. While integrating Iraqi soldiers into the operation helped the overarching strategic objective of building up Iraq's Army, there were questions about their tactical proficiency and will to fight. Meanwhile, the plan to use MICLICs in a city raised concerns of collateral damage.

LOCKED ON

At grunt-level, though, there was little thought about such matters. As they prepared to assault Karabilah, most Marines figured that additional forces and firepower could only help. For their part, they concentrated on loading mags, prepping demo charges and getting ready to defeat a tough, remorseless enemy while staying alive.

In the final hours before launch, the atmosphere was electric. At the squad level there was palpable excitement at the chance to close with the enemy. "We knew we would get more action than normal, and we were pumped," remembers Ian Norris, a machine-gunner in Kilo. "We were more locked on ... We just wanted to take the fight to the enemy and kill as many of them as we could ... That's why we went into the infantry. You knew the chances of taking casualties was higher. So, you had to be in the right mindset. On top of your game."[3]

The operation began at 0300 on the 17th, as columns of vehicles rolled out into the darkness then navigated across a dozen or so miles of desert to the southern outskirts of Karabilah.[4] While the infantry units set up, the LAVs and guntrucks took up support-by-fire positions on the flanks.

Just before first light, a key support asset began to play its unique role. The Army Tactical Psyops Team fired up their vehicle-mounted speakers, broadcasting into the still morning air. The pre-recorded message called for residents to leave the city and demanded that "enemies of Iraq" put down their weapons.* With the speakers blaring and armored vehicles massing on the city's outskirts, most of Karabilah's residents fled or found shelter. By the time the shooting started, most buildings were empty, the streets deserted.

* From Hearts and Mines: A Memoir of Psychological Warfare in Iraq, by Russell Snyder. This book is an intriguing first-hand account by a member of the Army Tactical Psyops Team that supported 3/2 in 2005.

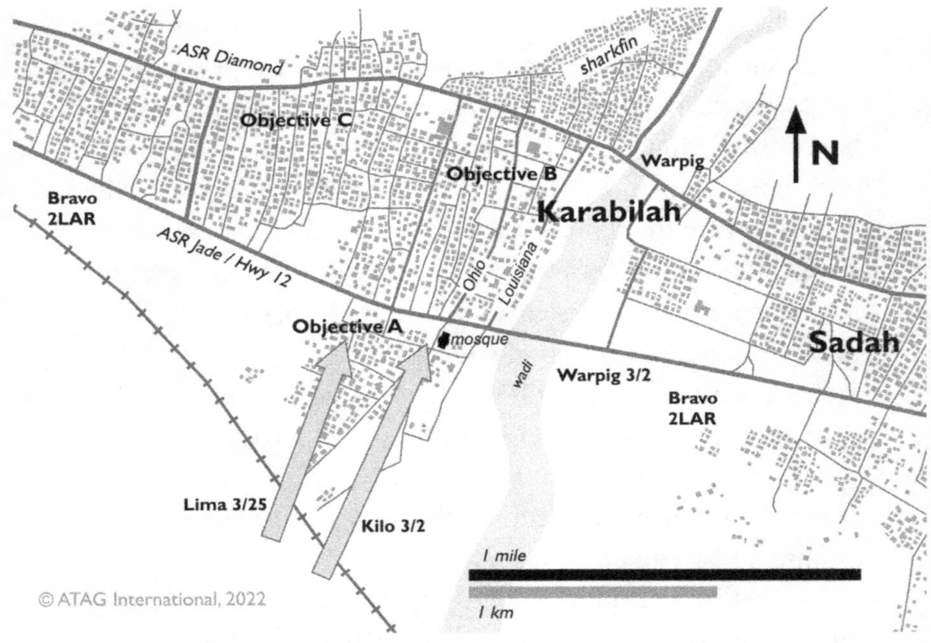

BATTLEFIELD DIPLOMACY

The less-built-up southern sector of Karabilah, south of the highway known as ASR Jade, was designated as Objective A. As the sun rose, Kilo Company dismounted and began to clear each home and building. After they had established supporting positions, Lima 3/25 was sequenced in on their left flank.

There was little significant action during the opening hours as both companies searched houses. Explosions from grenades and demolition charges punctuated the morning. The Marines had been briefed to destroy any vehicle they thought might contain explosives or be used to construct a car-bomb. They interpreted that guidance liberally, and soon the skyline was marked by multiple columns of drifting black smoke.

The relatively permissive situation changed, though, as units reached buildings adjacent to the highway. Sporadic enemy fire started coming in from across Jade. The most prominent structure in that sector was a gold-domed mosque. According to the ROE, Iraqi troops had to lead the way when clearing a mosque. Clemmey's integrated Marine/Iraqi formation was given the task.

Entry was unopposed and the mosque was quickly cleared. Small arms and ammo were found. As was so often the case, insurgents had been using a holy place to store weapons. Some of the Iraqis went to the roof where they came under fire from across ASR Jade. They took cover beneath the parapet, not daring to even peek over the edge. This prompted some impromptu battlefield diplomacy by one of 3rd Platoon's squad leaders, Lance Corporal Brian Newton.

Emerging onto the rooftop, Newton saw about twenty ISF soldiers cowering there. Not one was returning fire, and no one appeared to be in charge. Nearly an entire platoon of infantry was pinned down. Newton would have none of this and started to take rough remedial action. Completely disregarding the incoming rounds, he strode upright from man to man, yelling at the top of his lungs, cursing, grabbing, smacking helmets, and pushing the Iraqis to be men, get up, get online, and engage the enemy.[5]

From a nearby rooftop, Captain Ieva watched as Newton went to work. "In a few minutes, he had the whole bunch up and shooting. It was amazing and motivating," he recalls.[6] By refusing to let the Iraqi soldiers stall and setting a personal example, Newton set the tone. There would be no hunkering down.

WE MEAN BUSINESS

Clearing through Objective A took most of the morning and by noon all elements of 3/2 and 3/25 were online along the south side of ASR Jade. Ahead there were 100 to 150 meters of open ground to cross. How to get Marines across it without getting shot or blown up now became the question. Overwhelming firepower would be the answer.

Whenever insurgents fired from hidden positions on the north side of the highway, the response was swift and massive. In several instances, enemy snipers were engaged by tanks. As he overlooked the area north of the mosque, Ieva judged that the time was right to push across. He expected AQI fighters would be dug into buildings on the other side, waiting to trigger hidden IEDs or open up on his men.

Again, the psyops team blared warnings for civilians to clear the area. Meanwhile, a combat engineer trac rumbled into position, lurching to a stop just in front of the gold-domed mosque and facing directly down the dirt street called Ohio. The MICLIC launcher arm was raised into firing position.* If by some chance insurgents were watching, they could hardly imagine the fury that was about to be unleashed.

Lieutenant Colonel Mundy gave approval and moments later the 5-inch rocket hissed up into the sky, leaving a squiggling, corkscrew trail of blackish smoke with the white line-charge arcing behind, then falling neatly along the street. A few seconds later, the charge was detonated. "That was the biggest

* The M58 mine clearing line-charge is a 350-foot rope encased in bundles of explosives. Every foot of rope carries five pounds of C4, totaling almost a ton. Originally designed to clear a path through a minefield and obstacles, combat engineers sometimes used them to clear IED-infested city blocks.

explosion I had heard or felt up to that point," describes Matt Moore, a platoon sergeant in Kilo. "I was inside an AAV about 200 meters away, with my hatch almost all the way shut. It was open just enough to see out. I felt the shockwave in my chest when it came through."[7]

For all the Marines within sight, that first MICLIC detonation down route Ohio was awe-inspiring. Certainly for those on the receiving end, it must have been a significant emotional event. After echoes from the explosion faded, there was surreal quiet. But Ieva wasn't done with the MICLIC yet. Immediately after the first detonation, he had the engineers reposition one block to the east on route Louisiana.

Within fifteen minutes another concussion rippled down the street, toppling walls, shredding trees, and shattering glass. At least one secondary explosion resulted, meaning a car bomb or buried IED had been set off. Others were likely disrupted without detonating. Many of the men who cleared Karabilah over the next few days credit the decision to use MICLICs with intimidating the enemy and ultimately saving Marine lives:

> *That sent a message of "we mean business."... The muj had a choice to make. Stay and fight us or get out of Dodge. No question that it saved lives in the long run. If we simply went across the ASR without those softening blows from the MICLICs, our fight would have been more fierce.*
>
> —**Matt Moore**[8]

As the dust cleared over, 1st Platoon bounded by squads across ASR Jade. They cleared the first row of buildings adjacent to the highway and set up support-by-fire positions on the rooftops. Now the process of clearing objectives B and C, the main areas of Karabilah, could begin.

I'M A TANK!

At this point the armored machines of Alpha Company, 1st Tank, commanded by Captain Lance Langfeldt, began to play their part. Six tanks were on hand to provide direct fire support. Four from 2nd Platoon, under Lieutenant Danny James, and the headquarters tanks of Langfeldt and his XO, Lieutenant Tony Davis. They used the callsign "Tiger."

As the infantry crossed Jade, the tanks accompanied them. Whenever AQI fighters tried to stand their ground, a tank opened up with its coax machine gun or fired high-explosive, anti-tank (HEAT) rounds from the main gun. Directing this firepower required strict, detailed procedures. The tanks were under terminal control of the infantry, meaning it was the platoon and squad leaders who were responsible for positively identifying targets and approving fires.

For clearing buildings, the pre-briefed SOP was for a squad to talk the tank onto the target via the radio or just yelling up to the commander in the hatch. Then the squad leader would fire tracer rounds to mark the spot they wanted breached. The tank would confirm the breach point with a burst from the coax. Once confirmed, the tank would send two main gun rounds through the breach and a third into the upper story, if present.

The effect of HEAT rounds inside a structure was devastating. Even to the Marines outside, the concussion was truly impressive. Multiple rounds hitting the right places would collapse a building. Although the M1A2 is impervious to almost all direct fire, in the tight confines of city streets it can be threatened if enemy fighters get close enough. And as had been demonstrated during Matador, a large IED can injure or even kill the crew. The key to tanks' survivability in urban terrain is to operate as a combined arms team, with infantry in close proximity.

The two tanks of the headquarters section were emblazoned with black, skull-like "punisher" logos on the turret. Langfeldt's crew had dubbed their tank "Penetrator", while Davis' crew named their machine "Iceman", stenciling the names onto their main gun barrels. Kilo Company had already worked with Alpha's tanks several times. "Lance was awesome. Absolutely fearless," recalls Chris Ieva. "The guy would stay heads-up in the hatch to maximize visibility and battlefield awareness. But that left him exposed."[9]

At a certain point, a narrow street blocked Langfeldt's tank from getting to where he was needed, so he had his driver take a different path. "Lance just drove through a wall, went up 200 meters and banged a left," says Ieva, who was watching from a balcony a few blocks away:

> *As he draws up by 1st Platoon, a vehicle-borne IED went off, just 30 meters from his tank. A van with multiple arty rounds, and I can hear it go off, whump!, whump!, whump!' The tank stops in a cloud of dust. I call "Tiger, Tiger, are you OK?" Lance must have got his bell rung, cause it took some time but then we hear him, "I'm OK! I'm a tank! I can do this!"*
>
> —**Chris Ieva**[10]

Using tanks in close quarters came with risks, though. One squad's close call is a vivid example. "We got ahead of the tanks and into a house where everything but the front door was locked or barred up," remembers Ryan Lusby, from Kilo's 1st Platoon. As Lusby stood inside, a tracer round came sizzling down the hall, nearly hitting him. With sudden terror, Lusby and his squad mates realized a tank had marked them as insurgents:

> *We pretty much all thought we were gonna die. The scariest thing was hearing that turret move and point the main gun right at us. I stuck my head out and screamed at them. Guys were trying to break through a barred window, knowing if we ran out the front we would get lit up. Finally, someone got comms to the tank and called, "Friendlies!" The tank commander got out and came inside looking like he had seen a ghost. Said he'd been a second away from firing.*
>
> —**Ryan Lusby**[11]

Another event turned tragic when civilians were on the receiving end of tank fire. As 3/2 pushed into the city, Marines in Beowulf Platoon reported contact while clearing a house. Shots were fired at close quarters. They quickly withdrew and, rather than taking the risk of re-entering, the decision was made to call up a tank.

On a nearby rooftop, however, men in Kilo's 2nd Platoon had a different vantage point and they spotted a family inside the house. Frantically, they tried to call off the tank, but it was too late. Two 120mm rounds were fired into the structure. When Marines subsequently entered the house, they found no insurgents but came upon the bodies of two small children killed by the blasts. Nearby, their mother lay grievously wounded.

All Marines involved followed the Rules of Engagement and took precautions. But still civilian lives were lost. Evidence was found that someone had indeed fired AK rounds from inside that home. While no one had been seen fleeing, Captain Ieva personally found an AK in the courtyard and recently ejected AK shell casings in several locations. His working theory was that an insurgent had fired from within and escaped before the house was hit. Fanatical AQI fighters would often hold Iraqi families hostage in their own homes, using them as human shields as they fired against coalition troops. The hard truth is that urban combat puts innocents in mortal danger.

"That incident shook several of us up," recalls Sean Gregory, who was also on the scene. "I've got daughters myself, and that event was probably the hardest thing to go through besides losing our own KIA. I remember Sergeant Major Mennig was there, and he respectfully covered the bodies."[12] The injured mother was evacuated out to Camp Al-Qaim, and then on to Al-Asad to get advanced care.

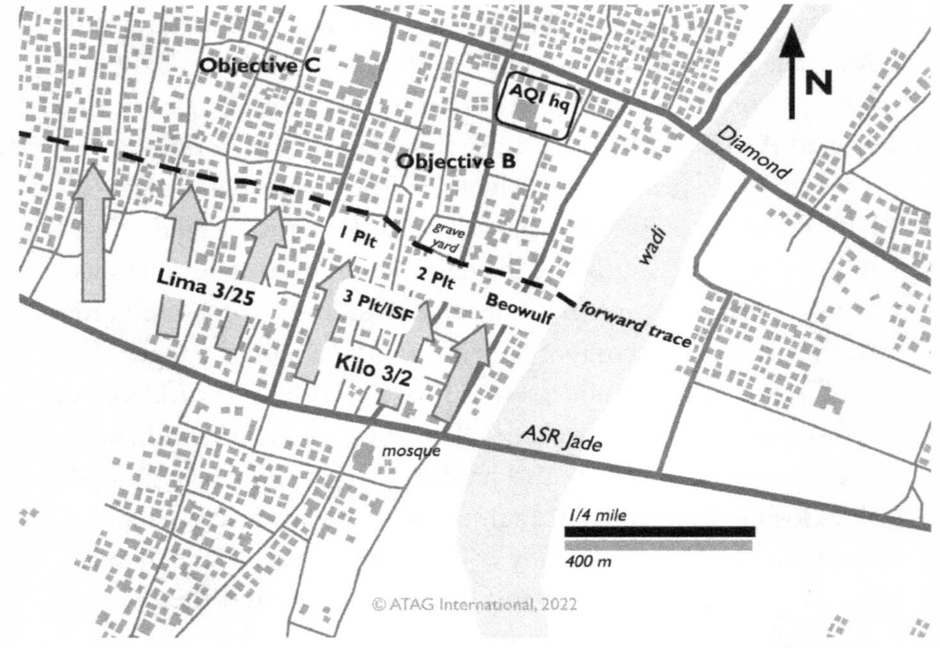

ON TRACK

As Day 1 of the operation came to a close, Mundy was pleased with the progress. The two rifle companies were across ASR Jade and had cleared well into Objectives B and C. The Iraqis embedded with Kilo's 3rd Platoon had performed adequately, particularly after Corporal Newton's very hands-on leadership.

The MICLIC detonations had gone off without a hitch and the combined arms machine was firing on all cylinders. Infantry, tanks, AAVs, psyops, and aircraft were all working well together, giving the enemy no chance to consolidate. Casualties had been minimal, with two Marines injured when an IED struck an AAV early in the morning. Civilian casualties had also been light, despite the family hit by tank fire.

Now the forward trace ran along an east-west line, running roughly across the midsection of Karabilah. Lima Company 3/25 had acquitted themselves well on the far left flank and stayed linked to Kilo's 1st Platoon. On the far right, Beowulf hugged the wadi that ran through the eastern part of the city.

Kilo's 3rd Platoon, with most of the Iraqi soldiers, had been back-clearing through Objective A, searching more thoroughly for arms and munitions after the other platoons pushed up. In the center, 2nd Platoon set in for the night on the south edge of the city's graveyard. They were within sight of the next day's main objective, a complex of buildings and an underground bunker used by AQI. The Marines were tired, sweaty, and dirty, but their anticipation for the next day's fight was high.

NIGHT OPS

At night the action shifted into a different mode. Platoons consolidated into buildings, going firm for the night. They would remain in close proximity, providing mutual support around an intersection or along a street. Locations were picked for the cover and protection they provided, fields of fire from the rooftops, and the control of key terrain. In a city like Karabilah, that meant controlling the streets.

Squads set up rotating shifts to man security watches and perform communications and observation duties. Those not on watch would inspect and prep their gear, reload mags, and choke down an MRE. Corpsmen checked on each Marine, making sure they were hydrated, and their feet were healthy.

Then the grunts might grab a couple hours of sleep. It was a strict standard, however, that for an hour at dusk and again at dawn, platoon and squad leaders would conduct "stand-to", bringing their men to 100 percent readiness.

For the scout-sniper teams of Reaper, however, nighttime was hunting time. Working in close cooperation with the FACs, the snipers would use the darkness to carefully insert into selected hide sites. Then, just as they had done in the target softening operation, they searched for insurgent locations and worked through the FACs to either get a better airborne view of the position or call in a strike.

In some ways, it was easier for aircraft to identify targets when it was dark, since almost all friendly ground units were occupying known positions for the night. Any uncoordinated movement observed in or around the city would immediately attract attention. And if insurgents fired at night that attention would be swift. Helos would swoop in to attack, lashing out with a stream of .50 cal or 20mm rounds, or a fighter jet would deliver a guided weapon. Seconds later, a large fireball would blossom over the rooflines and a concussion would shake windows and walls.

DOWNTOWN

As dawn broke over Karabilah on 18 June, the Marines were already moving from house to house again. Kilo Company moved north through the dusty streets and narrow back alleys towards the city center, expecting to encounter more determined resistance. Led by Lieutenant Smith, 2nd Platoon worked their way along Ohio and Louisiana. This was the area where most of the

AQI safehouses had been identified, some of which had been struck by the airstrikes of 11 June. Smith and his platoon were advancing right through the center of the enemy-held area.[13]

They had been training hard to perfect their urban combat tactics and were exploiting every possible advantage to minimize their exposure to enemy fire or IEDs. They used the lumbering AAVs with their bulky, angled front ends to push open locked metal gates or topple cinderblock walls so the grunts could enter. Where possible, they avoided the street altogether by moving from one structure to another using "mouseholes" blasted through the walls. When insurgents were detected in a building, the tanks punched main gun rounds into the structure, pulverizing the interior.

Throughout the morning, 2nd Platoon pushed north as quickly and smoothly as possible before the onset of the withering midday heat. They were clearing north of the graveyard towards the center of town, leap-frogging from building to building towards the complex of structures designated as AQI's main compound. Although they weren't getting contact, Sergeant and squad leader "China" Chinatomby, accompanied by a Reaper team, found an enemy sniper's hide site, complete with expended brass from a Dragunov sniper rifle. Somebody had been watching them.[14]

For Smith, the lack of contact was good news. It meant their tactics were working, his Marines were using the urban terrain smartly, and the enemy weren't being given any chance to engage them. To their left, however, at least some insurgents chose to stand and fight.

BRASSED UP

In the area to the west of the AQI complex, Lieutenant Bullock's 1st Platoon was clearing in a methodical and deliberate manner. Captain Langfeldt's command tank maneuvered close in to provide direct fire support. Above the city, Cobra gunships circled menacingly, waiting for targets. Lieutenant Clint Cummings, the Weapons Platoon commander, was coordinating the rotary-wing air support.

Meanwhile, Ieva had moved on foot, along with his RTO and security section, to what he perceived was a critical point. "That was always my preference, and sometimes it got me a little too far forward," he says. "If it weren't for those guys around me, Smith, Older, Collare, Dean, I wouldn't have made it through that tour. They were very protective, would jump in front of me. True heroes."[15]

As he moved through the urban maze, the company commander found himself ahead of 1st Platoon and dangerously exposed. As he crossed from one side of a street to the other, an insurgent hidden in a house suddenly opened up on him full-auto.

"I had gone one block too far and got brassed up,"[16] recalls Ieva. "The guy missed, but I went down hard and was pinned against a wall. Kevin Collare, my self-designated bodyguard, and my command team were across the street, and I was looking back at Bullock's position." To his front was a two-story house with at least one insurgent inside:

> *From where I was pinned, I set up a play over the radio, coordinating a time-on-target strike on the house. When I called the brevity code "Arrow", Langfeldt pushed his tank up, Cummings popped up*

a couple of Cobras, and one of his squad leaders threw a smoke grenade. That lured an insurgent to peak out, and I heard a sniper shot. Bullock talked the tank onto the breach, while the Cobras detected the target, and I approved a Hellfire strike. As the Cobras are setting up, Langfeldt's tank fires its coax and Bullock confirms the exact spot for the breach. Langfeldt yells, "On the way!" and fires the first 120mm round low through the breach. And from where I'm pinned, I'm looking back as it all unfolds.

The second tank round goes. I see Bullock's assault squad stiffen. They know the third round's coming. One Marine does the sign of the cross. The sound and pressure of a tank main gun in an urban environment is punishing, like getting punched. The third round fires, and they go. The rest of 1st Platoon opens up with suppressive fire. I hear rounds snapping by. The first fire team starts their rush towards the house. Second team follows, then the third. Across the street from me, I see Collare pop out and start shooting. Then I hear frags in the building and shooting. I can hear an AK firing inside.

I make my rush. Chris Dean, my RTO, follows, lugging the radio. As we start moving, I hear the lead Cobra call "shotgun" as it pumps out a Hellfire. The missile streaks directly over my head and strikes the target to my front… We close the distance to the house, and I announce entry and step inside. It's a bloody mess. Gore spattered everywhere, dead enemy in the courtyard. The squad leader reports the house cleared, no casualties. The Marines are jovial and laughing. Not because of the enemy dead. But because they rushed headlong into the abyss and dominated. They did their job. Did it well.

And because I'd gone one block too deep, I got to observe my men from the enemy's perspective. They were tight, technically sophisticated, and fearsome. Fighting block to block, integrating fires from tanks and helos. I was so proud of them. As I'd watched their rush, the thought came to me, "There's no replay of this awesome sight, no ESPN, no record of their heroics. It's just us." Which is why when I got brassed up, they'd actually cheered. Because I was there with them, watching them run into that abyss, defeating their fear by pushing it away.

And in the split-seconds between the suppression and their rush, I'd felt myself shift gears emotionally. From extreme empathy, a heartbreaking love, into a hard-edged apathy. We needed that house…I needed them to go. If you care too much, they don't go.

—Chris Ieva[17]

See **bastardsandbrothers.com** for notes, photos, maps, etc.

21. THE HARD EDGE

Approaching midday, Kilo's 2nd Platoon prepared to clear the walled AQI compound and an abnormal quiet settled on the immediate area. Beowulf was brought up on the right flank to support by fire, with a view over the wall. Captain Langfeldt and Lieutenant Davis drove their tanks into a rubble-strewn open area south of the compound, main guns oriented on the wall. Once all was set, the breach command was given.

The lull was shattered as "Penetrator" sent a round slamming through the south wall, leaving a gaping hole. The round also set off a secondary explosion, generating flames and yet another column of thick black smoke. Langfeldt had his gunner pump a few more rounds through the breach, trying to set off any IEDs set inside the buildings.[1]

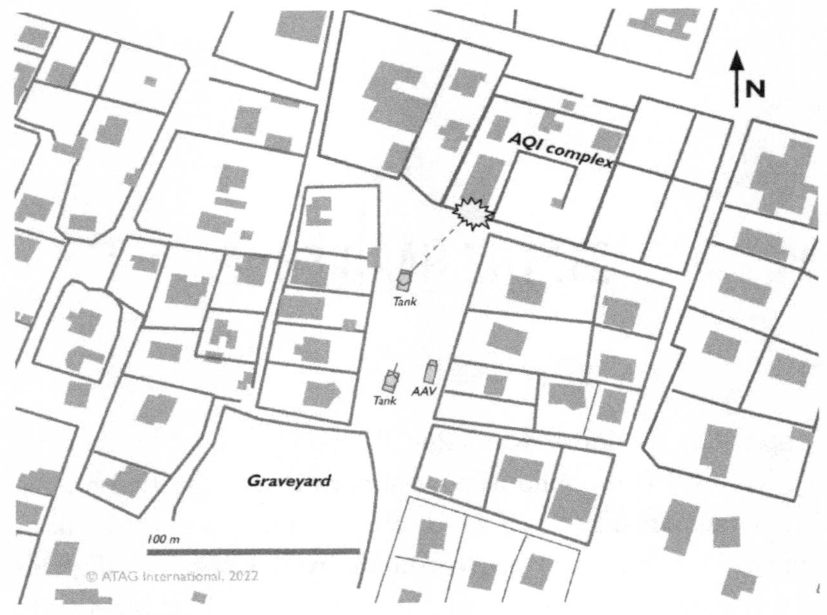

TREASURE TROVE

Finally, Marines rushed through the opening on foot and began clearing the buildings. They were tense. Each hallway, each room entered, posed the threat of sudden death, as this was the core of AQI's presence in the city. They soon discovered multiple signs of the enemy's presence, including an assembly area for car bombs with explosives, wires, electrical components, and several vehicles that had been at least partially prepped as SVBIEDs. Other rooms yielded ammunition and weapons caches, and another had clearly been used as a classroom with drawings on the wall showing how to fire RPGs, how to set up ambushes, etc.

The key discovery was a room set up as a kind of "in-processing center" for foreign fighters. There were passports, documents, and written logs listing the jihadists that had passed through. It was a treasure trove of intelligence, and within minutes digital photos were being taken of the documents, starting the "sensitive site exploitation" phase.

A building in the compound's northwest corner raised suspicions, and supporting fire was called for. From a rooftop south of the wall, one of the Beowulf squads fired an AT-4 rocket and suppressed with machine gun fire. Marines from 2nd Platoon followed, including Lance Corporal Matt Gundlach. "We stacked outside, prepped a grenade, threw it in, and rushed in. The sulfur and smoke choked us," he describes. "Then we heard voices in the next room. I don't know why we didn't throw a grenade in there too, but it was good we didn't...We stormed in. There were four guys sitting there all handcuffed, beaten and starved. We had no idea who they were at this point, but we immediately started giving them MREs".[2]

The prisoners were bound, blindfolded, and bore the marks of horrendous beatings and torture. Lieutenant Smith moved quickly to the building and as he entered the room was confronted with a macabre scene:

> *We found two border guards and there were two teenagers from one of the local tribes, apparently held as hostages. They were handcuffed and had been beaten with rebar and subjected to electric shock. Some were injected with motor oil. They'd soiled themselves when we'd hit the building, and we quickly brought in the terps and the corpsmen to care for them. They were very grateful to be rescued, as just moments before they were sure they were going to die. In another room, we found where they'd probably been*

tortured. The windows had been painted black, and there was a hook in the ceiling with a rope where people would be hung up. The whole thing was pretty gruesome.

—Nate Smith[3]

It was another stark reminder of the enemy's sheer ruthlessness. While these prisoners had been spared an ugly fate, there was no telling how many others had been kept here. The blacked-out interrogation room bore mute witness to the horrors that had been inflicted there.

More discoveries made it plain that 3/2 had scored a major intelligence find. There were weapons, including 12.7mm heavy machine guns and a slew of RPGs, along with stacks of black uniforms, cell phones, CDs, several computers, and hard drives. This was AQI's reception center for suicide bombers and fighters coming from across the Middle East.

Its importance was immediately apparent. There were documents on AQI's organization, confirmation of foreign fighters and methods for bringing them across the border. Some of the documents had instructions on what to do with hostages, how to secure them and how to value them for ransom.[4]

Colonel Davis, who had once again set up his forward CP at Camp AQ, decided he needed to see it for himself. He grabbed several intel personnel, loaded onto a vehicle, and headed directly to Karabilah. Meanwhile, Captain Ieva received instructions to allow an embedded CNN reporter and video team to enter the compound. They were given full access and even sat with the rescued prisoners and interviewed them.

From his perspective, however, Nate Smith thought all the commotion was dangerous. The CNN crew had been let in before the entire compound was cleared, and he was worried that without proper tactical precautions, his men could be put in jeopardy. An unseen booby trap, a hidden insurgent, or an incoming mortar round could change everything in an instant. "It was all becoming kind of a dog-and-pony show" he recalls, "I was checking my guys, getting them into position in case something happened. Then we heard a firefight flare up on our left flank. There was a really long burst, which was unusual. Something had just happened."[5]

GOING BACK IN

Just a few blocks to the northwest, 1st Platoon, led by Lieutenant Bullock and Staff Sergeant Matt Moore, were clearing north towards ASR Diamond. They were moving deliberately, keeping mutual support, and posting Marines on commanding rooftop positions. On the far left, the platoon's 3rd Squad was charged with maintaining contact with 3/25 Lima Company. Moore, the platoon sergeant, was positioned with them to ensure that was the case. Advancing on the right flank was 2nd Squad and in the center was 1st Squad, led by Sergeant Chase Roth.[6]

Lieutenant Tony Davis and the crew of "Iceman" were providing direct fire support. Their tank was locking down an intersection, positioned to control the roads north and east. Davis was heads-up in the hatch manning the .50cal machine gun. He'd been baking in the sun for a couple of hours. Some fifty meters behind him, the Marines of 1st Squad were working slowly up the street, clearing each house as they went.[7]

Davis was startled when he noticed an old man in a white *dishdasha* standing right in front of the tank. Somehow, the man had managed to appear out of nowhere. He was repeating a phrase in Arabic and gesturing back across the street towards one of the larger houses. Davis motioned aggressively at him to move back and called for an interpreter to come up. "I didn't know what he was saying, but he was distraught," says Davis. "The terp goes to talk to him, and then the guy shuffles off over to the house. I call the squad leader over and tell him there's an old man in there."[8]

With the presence of at least one non-combatant in the building, the clearing procedures used so far in Karabilah would need to be modified. Tanks wouldn't be breaching this particular structure. Soon Lieutenant Bullock had moved over to the location to set up the clear.

Behind the house to the west, 3rd Squad took rooftop positions looking into the backyard and windows of the target house. To the south, a team was sent to a neighboring two-story residence, then Roth's squad was brought up to prepare for entry. Bullock briefed them about the old man inside and instructed them to use "flash-bang" stun grenades instead of lethal frag grenades. Then the lieutenant joined his men. He'd be going in with them.

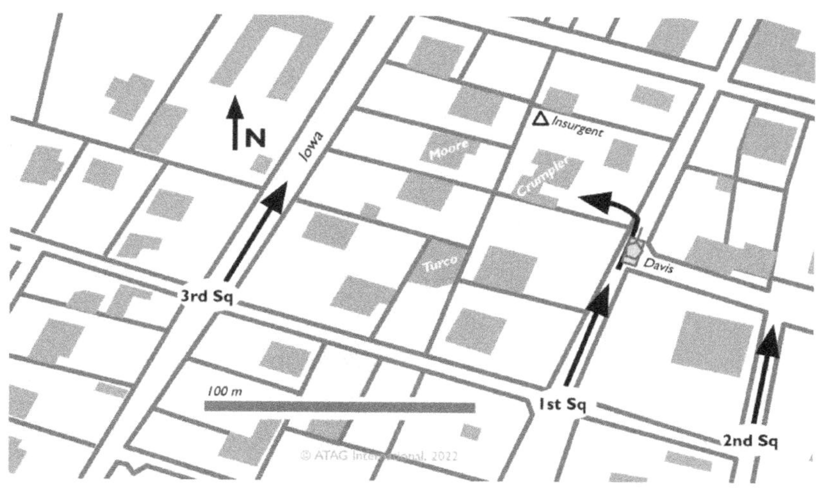

Entry into the house was quick and uneventful. From the front door on the south side, they entered into a large central foyer, with several side rooms opening into it. Opposite the entry and to the right was a stairway leading to the roof. The squad immediately broke into teams, fanning out to clear all the ground-level rooms. The old man was quickly found and brought to the foyer. He kept repeating, "No ali-baba! No ali-baba!" the Iraqi slang term for insurgents.

As the first floor was called clear, a fire team stacked next to the staircase. SAW gunner Joe Garrity began to take the point even though his bulkier weapon wouldn't be ideal in the confines of a stairway. The dark, narrow staircase made two 90-degree turns to the right as it rose to the roof. As Garrity moved into position, Adam Crumpler, armed with his lighter M203, stepped up and said, "It's OK, I got this."

As the stack started up the stairs, the old man suddenly yelled out in Arabic then bolted out the back door. Just as Crumpler took the first few steps up, a burst of full-auto erupted from the unseen shadows of the stairwell and at least one grenade, probably two, came bouncing down the steps. In a split second, the room exploded into smoke-filled chaos, with more shooting and pained cries of, "Corpsman up!"

Magnifying the suddenly nightmarish scene was one of the freakishly improbable occurrences that happen with regularity in combat. Lance Corporal Pat Jackson was carrying an AT-4 rocket strapped across his back. As all hell broke loose, this weapon was struck by a hot grenade fragment or bullet, igniting the rocket motor. In a blinding flash of flame and smoke, it accelerated and actually penetrated the ceiling. Matt Moore remembers that instant with amazement. "Brian Richmond and I were posted up on the roof next door," he recalls. "When the firing started, we both saw the AT-4 punch up through the roof and then spit and sputter out. I'm not sure where it finally landed, but we could not believe our eyes."[9]

Inside the house, it was bedlam. No one could tell what had happened, or even see across the room. But clearly the enemy was in close proximity. In the dense smoke from the grenade blasts and the near-simultaneous AT-4 ignition, Bullock tried to take stock of their situation:

> *We can hardly see. I took cover in the nook under the stairway, so can't see anything on the stairs. I never saw an insurgent and didn't know how many there were or where. Clearly, we needed to get out, to regroup and assess. Marines were already pulling back through the front door. To get there, I'd have to cross the room. I count to three, then dash across to the door, not knowing if I'd get shot.*
>
> **—Marc Bullock**[10]

The lieutenant consolidated the squad outside. Three of his Marines were wounded, including Jackson who had severe burns on his legs from the AT-4 ignition and a bullet wound in his arm. "It was still very chaotic, the comms were all garbled," says Bullock. "We were concentrated on security and setting up the casualty collection point, and I started a headcount. Then I get the call that we're one down. I say, 'Who's down?' and hear that Crumpler's unaccounted for. He must still be inside."[11]

Several of the men present and others who heard the radio traffic remember the tension at that moment. A Marine was still somewhere inside a house with an unknown number of enemy fighters. Lieutenant Bullock's voice came across the frequency, clear and unequivocal. "I'm going back in to get him." Tony Davis recalls, "That was one of the bravest things I've experienced. He was determined."[12]

Bullock grabbed Sergeant Roth and they went back through the front door into the smoke and debris-filled foyer. "We didn't know if bad guys were in there waiting for us. Or if Crumpler was alive or dead. I just knew we had to find him," says Bullock. "Then we saw him, slumped at the bottom of the stairs. And when I got to him, I could tell immediately he was dead. He'd been hit right in the forehead, just under the rim of his Kevlar. We also saw his weapon was missing."[13]

Several blocks away, Kilo's First Sergeant Gregory was monitoring the increasingly tense transmissions on the tactical frequency. "The call came through, somebody was down in 1st Platoon," he recalls. "I took Gunny Linch and Sergeant Nelson and took off running through the streets. That was probably a dangerous thing. There was no telling if there were enemy in the area, but I had Marines in trouble."[14]

The radio crackled again with urgency. "I've got a bad guy in the bushes!" called Corporal Frank Turco, who was tucked into the rooftop overwatch position just south of the house where Crumpler had been hit. The insurgent, wearing camouflage pants and a tactical vest with several grenades, was crouching in some vegetation behind the house. Turco could see a weapon in the man's hands and an M203 slung across his back. Apparently, he'd fled from the house through a back or side door, taking Crumpler's weapon as a trophy. Turco sighted in on him just as he looked up, then put him down with well-placed shots.

By this time, Staff Sergeant Moore had sprinted over to join his lieutenant, and together with other Marines they brought Crumpler's body out to the casualty collection point. First Sergeant Gregory met them there, and with great care and as much tenderness as possible, they placed Crumpler into the back of an AAV for transport back to Camp Al-Qaim. Struggling to hold back a surge of strong emotions, Sean Gregory gently reached over to close Adam's eyes.

Several of Crumpler's squad mates, his best friends, took his death particularly hard. Moore had to physically shake one young Marine back to the reality of the fight. "Now's not the time," he said, looking him in the eye. "We're still in this. We have to carry on."

News of the loss rippled quickly across the airwaves and by word of mouth. Word spread that the old man had baited 1st Squad into an ambush, and that Crumpler's killer was clearly a dark-skinned, non-Iraqi fighter, reportedly from Sudan. Crumpler was popular in the ranks, known for his quick smile and friendly, joking personality. But rather than causing debilitating grief, his death seemed to galvanize Kilo Company, honing their combat instincts to a hard edge.

PERMISSION TO ENGAGE

Despite the casualties in 1st Platoon, the force needed to push on. The objective for Day 2 was to reach ASR Diamond and set in along its southern side. 2nd Platoon cleared the last row of buildings just north of the AQI compound, and Beowulf pressed forward on their right flank, clearing a school that lay east of the compound.

As Marines reached the ASR, a new threat emerged in the form of a truck bomb barreling down the road. Machine gunners with 3rd Platoon, Sergeant Jorge Zamora and Corporal Jesse Ybarra were emplacing their machine-gun on a rooftop when they spotted a blue water truck moving towards their position. They loosed a stream of 7.62mm rounds at the truck, and watched several males jump from the vehicle and scatter. Lance Corporal Andrew Morrison, a rifleman, also opened fire on a man carrying an AK.

The truck kept rolling, however, until they concentrated fire on the tires and engine. The vehicle finally lurched to a stop and began to burn. At least one of the men lay dead in the street. Minutes later, an Abrams tank put a HEAT round into the truck. The resulting secondary explosions confirmed it had been rigged as an SVBIED.[15]

Back on the left flank, Staff Sergeant Moore was still in an overwatch position. One of his main concerns was keeping tabs on the progress of 3/25 Marines from Lima Company as they worked through Objective C. A long, north-south street dubbed "Iowa" comprised the boundary between 3/2 and 3/25. Unit boundaries are always potential trouble areas. As Moore and squad leader Brian Richmond scanned across Iowa, they spotted a threat to Lima 3/25:

> *We could see 3/25 clearing in their sector and just ahead of them were four or five insurgents, running in and around a mosque. They were setting up to ambush the Lima guys. I called it in over the radio to Captain Ieva, to coordinate fires into 3/25's area. He came back and gave permission to engage. I had our fully-automatic weapons hold fire, since friendlies were so close, and I wanted very precise fires. Then we opened up, six to eight Marines firing M-16s and M-4s from about 200 meters. We hit them hard, killing or wounding them, and totally disrupted the ambush. That got Lima's attention. At first their CO was angry that we had engaged into his AO, and personally came to our rooftop to see what had happened. But when I gave him the binoculars and he saw an insurgent's body in some bushes really close to his Marines, he thanked us.*
>
> —**Matt Moore**[16]

The smoke-smudged sky reddened as June 18th drew to a close, and the vicious Anbar heat started to subside. At the end of a hard-fought day, each platoon and section found mutually-supporting positions in structures with good fields of fire. As the Marines went firm for the night, the forward trace now overlooked ASR Diamond and the neighborhoods of the sharkfin on the other side.

DECEPTION

All units started prepping and moving again before dawn on 19 June, getting ready to push across Diamond. The intensity of the action had dropped off, but the sharkfin area was an older section of the city with close-packed houses and even tighter streets. It was assessed as the reserve area for the enemy, and several safe houses and weapons caches had been identified.

As the morning progressed, the MICLIC was brought up and prepped by the combat engineers, just as in the crossing of ASR Jade on Day 1. But now Captain Ieva came up with a new way to use the fearsome weapon. Instead of actually launching line charges, he orchestrated a tactical deception. The engineer AAV, the tanks, and other vehicles were positioned, and the pre-launch procedures followed, but this time it was all for show. The intent was to draw insurgents out and make them vulnerable.[17]

Several blocks to the west, 1st Platoon was still holding firm in a building on the south side of the highway. Ieva's deception play unfolded to their right but was obscured from their view. To their front they had commanding fields of fire up, down and across ASR Diamond. As they watched, two men emerged from an alley across from their building, walking casually towards the east. One man had an AK, and the other was carrying an RPG. "They were just ambling along, not moving tactically," recalls Moore."[18]

From rooftop positions, 1st Platoon watched in bemused curiosity as the two insurgents passed directly in front of them on the other side of the highway, barely 25 meters away. "It was like they were on a morning stroll" says Bullock. "Obviously they hadn't spotted us. Had no idea we were there. One guy had an RPG over his shoulder like a fishing pole, and the other was carrying a machine gun by the handle, like a briefcase."[19]

After the initial surprise of being presented with such an easy target, Bullock gave the order and his Marines opened up, quickly killing both insurgents. Apparently, the MICLIC deception play had indeed flushed them out, right under the guns of 1st Platoon.

HOLD POSITION

Weather conditions soon caused a delay, however, so no units crossed into the sharkfin. High winds had kicked up, a common occurrence during Iraq's hot summer months, and the blowing dust severely reduced visibility. While this was a mere annoyance for grunts on the ground, it was a no-go situation for the helicopter crews supporting them. And with the CASEVAC birds grounded at Al-Qaim, the COC issued the order for units to hold position until the weather improved.

However, sometime during that night or in the early morning of Day 4, an interesting aerial mission occurred which many Marines remember. As they stood watch atop various buildings, they heard a low-pitched, droning sound of turboprop engines. Suddenly, out of the darkness, loomed a large four-engine aircraft at extremely low altitude. Marc Bullock swears he could see rivets on the plane's underside as it passed overhead. Chris Ieva also has a vivid memory of the incident:

> *It came in from east to west, towards Syria. At first I thought maybe it was a special ops AC-130 gunship that had been hit and was crashing. It was so low. As it came in, the muj started shooting at it. And we started trying to engage them as they fired. It was surreal. For a minute it was like something out of Normandy in '44. The night sky was lit up with tracers, and you can see the underside of this big airplane. Can hear the engines. And then I see leaflets. It*

was a leaflet drop. They fluttered down all across the city, and then the aircraft turned south and was gone.

—Chris Ieva[20]

One of Kilo's terps grabbed a leaflet and translated it. It was a warning to locals that coalition forces were coming, which was odd since Marines had been in Karabilah for three days at that point. The intended purpose of the leaflet drop remains unclear, but apparently it was an information operation planned higher up the food chain.

THE SHIRTLESS ONES

On 20 June, Day 4, the operation started winding down. From the campaign-level perspective, this is where the ongoing challenge for Colonel Davis and RCT-2 was clear. In the summer of 2005, there were never enough units on hand to establish a sustained presence in a city like Karabilah. The forces that had concentrated in support of 3/2 now needed to recover, refit, and prepare for upcoming missions. As a result, clearing operations in the sharkfin were abbreviated.

The rifle platoons were by this time reaching the limits of their tactical endurance. Three days of strenuous effort in 120-degree heat exacted a toll. As fighting units, they needed an operational pause. The logistical and other requirements of modern ground combat units are extensive, and much coordination is needed to keep units effective. Resupply requirements include ammunition, batteries (which can be critical), food, and water. Water alone can be a significant limiting factor.

The other reason for ramping down was the enemy's

departure from the fight. In retrospect, it appears that by Day 4 the foreign fighter cells had decided to live to fight another day. Their leaders had likely fled early in the battle, but now the fighters themselves would abandon the field. The weather hold was lifted that morning, and preparations began for the push across ASR Diamond. The Army psyops soldiers once again cranked up the loudspeakers, calling on all residents to leave the area and warning enemies of Iraq to surrender or suffer the consequences. What followed was an interesting demonstration of both the frustrations of fighting an irregular, insurgent foe, and the Marines' strict adherence to the rules of engagement and laws of armed conflict.

Sometime after the psyops broadcasts began, several batches of men emerged from the streets and houses on the north side of the highway. They were all unarmed and had either removed their shirts or pulled them up over their heads, as the broadcasts had instructed. They were young and fit, some wearing tactical-style clothing. Obviously, these were the elusive AQI fighters the Marines had been hunting from block to block and exchanging shots with. Now 15 to 20 of them were in plain view.

But because they were unarmed and following the psyops team's instructions, there was no legal rationale for engaging them. They simply came out onto ASR Diamond, walked east across the 51 bridge and melted into the town of Sadah. Near the east side of the bridge, WarPig had vehicles in a support-by-fire position, but they weren't prepared or manned to stop and detain that many individuals. In essence, a group of the enemy executed a "surprise retreat" to escape. Ieva relates his reaction:

To be honest, I hadn't expected that. We couldn't light them up. Possibly we could have moved to intercept, maybe using the Iraqis with 3rd Platoon, but it took us by surprise. And to try that would have meant putting my guys at risk, not knowing if there were more bad guys in the sharkfin that might open fire or set off IEDs. So, we just watched them cross the bridge. Very frustrating to have the enemy in our sights and let them go.

—**Chris Ieva**[21]

But while the enemy showed craftiness, the event also demonstrated the discipline and training of 3/2 Marines. "Consider this with respect to our ROE compliance," Ieva continues. "The enemy had sufficient faith that we would follow our own rules, and in a way trusted us enough, that they walked out right under our guns."

INTO THE SHARKFIN

Soon after the "shirtless ones" walked across the bridge, Kilo's 1st and 2nd Platoons advanced across Diamond with no opposition. Entering into the far west corner of the sharkfin, Lieutenant Bullock reoriented 1st Platoon's squads towards the east and proceeded to clear the smaller homes that were prevalent in this neighborhood. Meanwhile Lieutenant Smith led 2nd Platoon across into the eastern part of the sector. Soon evidence was discovered that AQI had indeed been holed up there. 2nd Platoon found two arms caches. The smaller one contained Syrian medicine, sleeping pads, and pita bread that was still warm. It was clear that insurgents had just left that location by climbing a nearby wall.

It was also clear that if they'd stayed, an assault on the position could easily have cost Marine lives. There were two RPGs, prepped in their launchers and ready to fire, and an RPK machine gun with a belt of armor piercing ammo that could slice through kevlar and SAPI plates. "I took away a big lesson learned from that," says Smith. "By exercising good clearing procedures, we gave them no chance to engage us. It showed that we always needed to be doing the right thing, and when we did, they'd run rather than fight."[22]

Rather than going house-by-house through all of the shark-fin, 1st Platoon was directed to several potential safe-houses and cache locations that had been identified. No further contact was encountered and not much was found. The sector was apparently devoid of any opposition, and retrograde operations soon began. Units started pulling back, loading onto tracks and other transport for the short trip back to Camp Al-Qaim.

USED CAR CLEARANCE

One particular target needed special attention, however. In the northwest part of the city, on the edge of Lima 3/25's sector, was a large area of open ground with multiple vehicles. Intelligence reports had previously identified this as a potential target, and tagged it as a "VBIED facility", in other words, a car lot full of car bombs.

Alpha Company's tanks were selected as the tool for the job. Langfeldt and Davis' tanks were joined by a third for the mission. To avoid IEDs and other threats, they proceeded north into the open fields beyond the city, then west. They approached the lot from the north side of Diamond, with at least one helicopter and a UAV overhead to observe and support. As they rolled into the designated area, they spread into a rough V-shaped formation. They could see no human activity, but inside and next to the vehicles, they could see wires, propane tanks, extra gas tanks, and other IED-associated paraphernalia.

The tanks pumped 120mm rounds into each vehicle, shredding their aluminum skins and setting some aflame. There were some secondary explosions as IEDs hidden within were set off. In short order, AQI's "used car lot" was converted into a junkyard, with blasted pieces and parts scattered across the dirt and columns of black, oily smoke shrouding that part of the city. It wasn't a particularly glamorous mission, but those car bombs wouldn't be used against coalition resupply convoys, markets in Baghdad, or schoolchildren in Ramadi. Once more scanning for threats, the three hulking machines withdrew back towards the center of the city to team back up with the infantry.

MESSAGES

While the operation officially lasted until June 22, 2005, the next two days were quiet. There were a few more arms caches found and detonated in place and a few more houses were cleared, but the main activities now involved recovery and retrograde back to Camp AQ or other bases. An exception to this was yet another mission for the psyops team.

In coordination with the COC and the staff at RCT-2, the Army psyops experts now planted preplanned messages for the locals, and for the foreign fighters of AQI. Paper handbills in Iraqi-dialect Arabic were placed throughout the city, where residents could read them or take them home. They contained "wedge" messages, carefully crafted to counter jihadist propaganda. Some messages were spray-painted as graffiti, often denigrating the manliness and fighting prowess of AQI.

Another part of this psychological operation was aimed directly at the insurgents themselves. Some of the handbills and graffiti were placed specifically so returning AQI fighters would see them, especially wherever ammo had been found. These messages taunted and ridiculed the insurgents. It was all part of the wedge approach to undermine the enemy's confidence, find any crack between them and the local populace, and pry it open a little further.

BREATHING SPACE

In the official history of Operation Spear, the Marines estimated 47 enemy fighters were killed and one detained. Only one Marine was killed in action and six wounded. Eight others suffered so-called non-combat injuries. Since most residents fled their homes during the fighting, civilian casualties were likely low. There is no official record, but by all accounts probably between 10 and 20 Iraqi civilians were killed and/or wounded.

A total of 24 suspected vehicle-borne IEDs were destroyed, along with two other explosive devices. Numerous arms caches were discovered, and most were blown in place. As a measure of the kinetic intensity of the fighting, 210 tank main-gun rounds were fired and 23 fixed-wing airstrikes were conducted, not to mention the two MICLIC line charges detonated.

The operation's impact can be debated. There was no effort made to establish permanent presence in Karabilah, to follow the "clear" with "hold" and "build" phases. So, among some Marines from 3/2 and other units there remains a level of frustration. Warriors never like to think the dangers they endured and the sacrifices they made were wasted.

Clearly, many of the AQI fighters had escaped. Some of those same bitter enemies would have to be faced again in months and years to come. In fact, just five months later, Karabilah would have to be cleared again. The city center was heavily damaged during Spear, which hardly set the stage for economic or political progress. To the contrary, the massive firepower unleashed was probably counter-productive when viewed through the classic counter-insurgency lens.

However, the summer of 2005 in western Anbar was far from a classic counter-insurgency situation. AQI and its tribal allies were in full-contact mode, attempting to establish a safe haven. Their fighters were wearing body armor and uniforms, and were armed with heavy-caliber weapons, armor-piercing rounds, and almost unlimited quantities of explosives.

They had refined their methods for launching horrific suicide car-bomb attacks, learned to entrench themselves in mini-bunkers within a house then shoot assaulting troops in the face. They were kidnapping, torturing, and viciously killing any locals who opposed them or who they suspected of cooperating with the government.

Very much like Fallujah in late 2004, Zarqawi's jihadist network had dug into the Al-Qaim region and would not be dislodged without a fight. On the continuum of military operations, Marines in western Anbar were not conducting population-centric stability and security operations. They were engaged in a combined-arms battle to seize a contested area from a well-armed enemy. The outcome was still very much in question.

In that context, then, Operation Spear was a marked success. AQI's regional headquarters and hub in its foreign fighter smuggling operation was displaced. RCT-2 had won operational breathing space as it shuttled overstretched forces around to handle other situations. It also demonstrated to residents in the surrounding towns, especially Karabuli tribesmen, that AQI could not stand toe-to-toe with the Marines.

During an interview after the operation, Colonel Davis did some expectations management in his answer to a reporter's question: "It would be a misnomer, talking about sealing the border. You're not going to stop everything that's coming through. I don't think [this operation is] a backbreaker [for AQI]. This is just continual war."

Perhaps most important, the intelligence take from the AQI compound in the center of the city was a big win with far-reaching consequences. For starters, the RCT-2 staff was quick to capitalize on the information-operations opportunity, and rapidly announced to the global media the hard evidence confirming that foreign fighters and suicide bombers were flowing into Iraq from Syria. This had been a hotly-debated question, with important political dimensions. The public discovery of multiple foreign passports, a well-organized in-processing center, rosters of suicide bombers, training documents, and proof positive of an active al-Qaeda affiliate in Iraq, settled that question definitively.

Moreover, the intelligence would feed into the quickly expanding SOF targeting machine run by Task Force 714. Soon after Operation Spear, the Task Force mounted its own behind-the-scenes surge of special operations units in Anbar, pushing teams out west to take on AQI closer to the border. And throughout Iraq, the operators running nightly capture/kill operations would quickly start crunching through the names discovered by Kilo Company in Karabilah.

EULOGIES

After sundown on June 21st, Marines, Navy corpsmen and other personnel gathered at Camp Al-Qaim to pay their respects and bid final goodbye to Adam Crumpler. After a few words from Chaplain Anderson, and short eulogies from Crumpler's closest squad mates and friends, Marines knelt for a moment of silence. They bowed close-shorn heads to remember a brother warrior who gave his life fighting beside them.

Two days later, on June 23rd, another eulogy of sorts was posted to various websites. The statement purported to be from Abu Musab al-Zarqawi himself, commemorating the death of one Abdullah Muhammad Rashid al-Rashoud, a Saudi-born member of al-Qaeda. Al-Rashoud was one of the most-wanted men in Saudi Arabia, and a known terrorist leader. According to the letter, he had recently crossed from Syria into Iraq to wage jihad.

Al-Rashoud had allegedly been killed by an American airstrike somewhere in the Al-Qaim area, quite possibly in Karabilah. Perhaps he had planned on driving a car bomb into a crowd of innocent civilians. Perhaps he joined AQI to coax others into such heinous acts. But it appeared his designs were thwarted by an action in support of, or related to,

Operation Spear. There would be no gathering of his friends, and there would be no burial. His body was most likely broken and scattered by a U.S.-made 500-pound bomb, never to be recovered.

22. GRAY ZONES

Woven into the story of successive Marine battalions fighting to stabilize western Anbar are subtle threads revealing the mostly-unknown history of special operations in the same area. There were two parallel campaigns in the WERV, one conducted by conventional forces and one by special operations forces. The full history of SOF operations in that timeframe is still not publicly available, but enough details have been released to show the outlines of what the "operators" were doing in and around Al-Qaim.

The term Special Operations Forces refers to a range of different units and organizations. These include acknowledged units operating under the same authorities as conventional military forces. The U.S. Army's Special Forces, the vaunted Green Berets, are among them.*

While capable of a wide variety of missions, including direct action raids, the Green Berets specialize in working "by, with, and through" a host nation to train and advise military and other forces. In Iraq, the Special Forces' main role was to develop

* The terms Special Forces (SF) and Special Operations Forces (SOF) should not be confused. The Army's Special Forces are just one part of the wider U.S. Special Operations Forces community.

select Iraqi units, known as Iraqi SOF or ISOF. When they conducted direct action missions, it was almost always alongside the Iraqi units they were training and advising.

After being withdrawn from Anbar in mid 2004, Special Forces ODA (Operational Detachment-Alpha) teams were coming back in 2005. Within RCT-2's battlespace, this first entailed training and advising a 34-man Iraqi reconnaissance unit often called Shawanee Scouts, or Shawanee SOF. Colonel Davis suspected that most had been members of Saddam's Republican Guard but acknowledged their proficiency. "They were real good ... They were disciplined and they knew what to do."[1] This small unit and their advisors worked with 3/2 several times. But in mid 2005, no ODA had yet connected with the Albu Mahal tribesmen that were fighting against AQI in Al-Qaim.

Another highly-trained unit working in western Anbar at that time was categorized by the Marine Corps as "special-operations capable", although it did not formally fit in the SOF world. The 1st Force Recon Company was attached to RCT-2 during 2005 and conducted many direct action raids across the regimental AO. Sometimes these were done in conjunction with 3/2 or other units and sometimes on their own. In essence, 1st Force Recon was Colonel Davis' in-house direct action unit.[2]

OTHER COALITION FORCES

On February 20, 2005, Army Rangers and operators from a special task force had set up a roadblock near the river somewhere between Ramadi and Rawa, according to author Sean Naylor.[3] They had reliable information that a senior AQI leader would pass by any minute and were in position to intercept and capture him. They waited tensely, then waited some more. Just when they decided their tip was bad and prepared to leave, the target vehicle raced through. As the operators scrambled to pursue, Rangers at a second site down the road took aim, ready to shoot. But without positive ID on the occupants, they weren't cleared to fire.

When the vehicle shot past, the Rangers could plainly see Abu Musab al-Zarqawi inside "staring wildly" back at them. The operators sped after him in a high-speed pursuit, while a drone tracked their moving target from above. The vehicle's driver turned into a nearby town, where Zarqawi exited the vehicle and fled on foot. Maddeningly, at that exact moment the drone's camera suffered a glitch and zoomed out to a wide view. By the time it could be refocused, the most wanted man in Iraq had disappeared. It was one more frustration in the intense manhunt for AQI's murderous leader. In early 2005, it seemed that every time coalition forces got close to cornering Zarqawi, he would somehow slip away.

The organization with the specific mission to kill or capture Zarqawi and dismantle his network went by many names and numerical designators. It is well-documented that Major General Stanley McChrystal commanded Joint Special Operations Command, or JSOC, the U.S. military's premier counter-terrorism force, from 2003 to 2008. In his autobiography, he calls his forward-deployed command Task Force 714, TF 714 or just the "Task Force."[4] The same designations will be used here.

According to McChrystal and expanded by numerous other sources, Task Force 714 included several special mission units, including the Army's elite commando unit and the top-tier Navy SEAL unit. These were often called "Task Force Green" and "Task Force Blue" respectively.[5] Added to the mix were the Army's elite 75th Ranger Regiment and the 160th Special Operations Aviation Regiment, known as the "Nightstalkers." Collectively, the Task Force and its special mission units operated under different authorities than conventional military forces. Their mission was to capture or kill the highest priority terrorist and insurgent targets, not just in Iraq but Afghanistan and elsewhere.

The units that almost snagged Zarqawi in February were part of Task Force 714, and in 2005 they were stepping up efforts in Anbar. As he describes, earlier in the year McChrystal had made a key decision. He realized that while his highly-trained teams of operators were "energetically tearing away" at the AQI network, the situation was still worsening overall. "I believed that failure in Iraq was tangibly close," McChrystal wrote. "Al-Qaeda essentially controlled stretches of the western Euphrates River Valley. It needed to be stopped."[6]

SNAKE EYES

By May, McChrystal had met with General Casey, the commander of coalition forces in Iraq, to express those concerns and his intent to surge TF 714 forces into Anbar and the WERV. Casey had agreed and committed to start allocating more conventional forces out west. Following this meeting, which evidently occurred just before Operation Matador, McChrystal sent a personal message to General John Abizaid, the four-star commander of U.S. Central Command. He captures part of this message in his memoir: "I'm going to send us out there in greater numbers, and I think it is going to be very dangerous. I think it is going to be bloody. And so, I am steeling everybody for greater casualties."[7]

McChrystal also described a meeting with leaders of his sub-command in Iraq. These experienced operators had reservations about the SOF surge out west, where they would operate further from support and against an enemy they knew was ready to fight to the death:

> *The meeting wasn't easy... The Green leaders sat with still faces. Only their eyes moved, alternating between me and the whiteboard where I wrote and drew a map of Iraq. Until this point, TF 714 had drawn up targeting decks, not maps: We executed missions; we did not wage campaigns.*
>
> —**Stanley McChrystal**[8]

Despite the operators' quiet reservations, they began aggressively executing the plan, which was named "Operation Snake Eyes".[9] To plus up, a "second squadron of Green" was deployed to Iraq while more "SEALs and aviation" assets were brought from Afghanistan, according to McChrystal.[10] Sean Naylor writes that these forces were designated "Task Force West" and launched their first missions out of Al-Asad in May 2005.[11]

The dangers involved were soon evident as the Task Force started to take casualties. Sergeant First Class Steven Langmack died at the end of May, after a raid somewhere in Al-Qaim. He was struck down by small arms fire, according to McChrystal, while "entering a fortified enemy position." This appears to be the same raid that diverted a 3/2 sniper-scout mission by Reaper as they probed into Karabilah on May 30. Then, on June 17, the first day of Operation Spear, TF 714 lost two more men in the Al-Qaim area. Master Sergeants Mike McNulty and Bob

Horrigan were killed "in close-quarters combat with tenacious enemy fighters," according to McChrystal.[12]

These were heavy blows in a tight-knit family of warriors. Green hadn't lost anyone killed in action since 2003 and hadn't suffered two KIA on the same mission since the infamous "Blackhawk Down" incident in Somalia in 1993. The loss of these highly-experienced men, well-liked and respected in their teams, "hit the unit like a shudder," writes McChrystal.[13] Yet the Task Force's raids in Anbar continued and accelerated. They were racing to dismantle Zarqawi's network, and kill or capture him, before his merciless campaign of terror could dismantle Iraq.

As more SOF units moved west in July, TF 714 set up a forward base at the "industrial rail depot" near the phosphate plant, according to McChrystal. "At this critical, tough post we installed one of our most talented commanders," he states in his memoir, and describes how "Green teams, Rangers, and SEALs worked alongside the Marines."[14] For the rest of the deployment, 3/2 Marines would often share their battlespace with the Task Force. Periodically, they would be involved in supporting SOF missions by screening, setting an outer cordon, or escorting the operators to or from a location. At other times, 3/2 units received support from SOF assets, particularly from airborne platforms:

> *They were very easy to work with and usually just asked us to clear out of an area they were going into. They'd often ask to have attack helos on call or my QRF ready to assist... Most of the time they didn't need it. They were definitely professionals, and I appreciated our working relationship built on mutual respect. And they seemed to enjoy working with Marines. We all left egos at the door and just focused on getting the job done.*
>
> **—Tim Mundy**[15]

KICKING DOORS

The special unit operators weren't the only ones executing raids, however. Now more than halfway through the deployment, 3/2's battle rhythm was humming along. Each day and most nights, elements pushed out from Camp Al-Qaim looking for hidden insurgents and their leaders. Now with a firm understanding of both the physical and human terrain, and a sharpened picture of where and how the enemy was operating, these missions were paying off.

Kilo Company along with WarPig 2 and WarPig 3 from Weapons Company, were fully engaged in the battalion's own targeting cycle, conducting frequent raids and searches in towns and villages along the river. Just as the SOF commandos were going after their deck of high-tier AQI targets, 3/2 had its list of local insurgent cell leaders and suspected bomb-makers. Even before Operation Spear this had been the case, but the pace accelerated in late June and early July.

In particular, under the guidance of Captain Phillips, WarPig started to come into its own as a force capable of independent operations. WarPig 2 and WarPig 3 each had seasoned combat leaders at the helm and their Marines were battle-tested, organized into smoothly-functioning vehicle crews. A series of missions during this timeframe demonstrated their capabilities.

On June 4th, the two mobile assault platoons left Camp AQ in predawn darkness heading towards the Euphrates. Their objective was the farming village of Ashshia, just east of New Ubaydi on the far side of the river where an insurgent bomb-maker had reportedly set up shop. A rickety pontoon bridge connected Ashshia to the south bank, but it would not support the weight of WarPig's guntrucks. While it was still dark,

WarPig 3 crossed on foot without incident. "Dogs were barking, flashlights came on. People were sleeping outside their houses," recalls Jonathan "Penny" Penland. "We didn't detain them but herded them off to one side while we started searching."[16]

Out on the bridge, combat engineers and EOD Marines made an important find. Several pontoons held weapons and explosives. The bridge itself was an arms cache, hiding cases of ammo, RPGs, several machineguns, and over 100 rockets, including large 122mm rounds. Marines had to climb down into the dank innards of the pontoons to take out the deadly contents. Some were nearly overwhelmed by noxious fumes. Stacked among the weapons were bags of home-made explosives. "We found rocket propellant, which looked similar to fettuccine noodles, but larger," described Gunnery Sergeant Chuck Yannizzi, the EOD Team Chief. "We pulled bag after bag out. They were clearly building their own rockets."[17]

All weapons and explosives were taken from the pontoons into the desert and destroyed in a controlled detonation. The large arms cache confirmed that the area needed attention. Interestingly, the 122mm rounds and home-made propellant were hard evidence supporting Gunny Yannizzi's theory that foreign fighters were launching rockets at Camp AQ from north of the river. Use of non-standard propellant would explain why the rockets typically fell short.

WarPig Marines launched further independent missions after Spear, picking up the pace, and racking up results. On 3 July, a predawn raid into Sadah netted one of the battalion's HVIs, a bombmaker for AQI that specialized in assembling the dreaded suicide vehicle bombs.[18] The first locations they hit were "dry holes", but someone gave them a new house where they rolled up the bombmaker and his son. They'd reacted on the fly to new information and quickly exploited it, much like Task Force operators did against their targets.

The next morning, on July 4th, another WarPig mission rolled up on one of the irrigated farms 10 miles west of Camp AQ. The Marines began a cordon and knock operation just as the sun started rising, and soon found signs of insurgent presence. At one house, a sizeable stash of food and medicines was found. Out back, several small white tents were set up. "We detained a guy. At first he said he didn't speak English, but it was clear he was supporting insurgents," recalls Penland. "Later he spoke up in perfect English and said, 'I'm a doctor. I went to Yale. The insurgents come to me and I have to help them'".[19] Apparently, wounded insurgents had been treated there after Operation Spear.

OUTLAW

A few days later, on 8 July, WarPig returned to Ashshia with a larger-scale search operation dubbed Operation Outlaw. This time, helicopters were used to insert WarPig 2 and WarPig 3 across the river. "We got up at O-dark early and did a detailed pre-mission walkthrough," remembers Henry Sowell of WarPig 3.[20] The two platoons with attached EOD and engineer teams would insert on the far bank northwest of the pontoon bridge, then sweep south and east through the fields. Cobra/Huey teams would be overhead and Captain Edwards, the senior FAC, would be on the ground handling close air support requests. For this mission, the battalion commander would have an unusual perspective. Lieutenant Colonel Mundy would monitor progress from overhead, aboard one of the Hueys instead of in the COC.

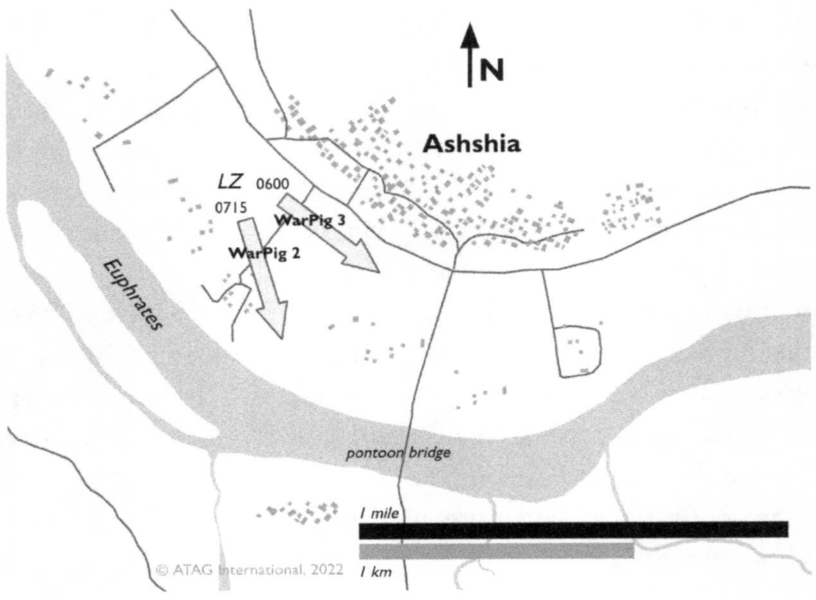

Before dawn, the first lift took off from Camp AQ and minutes later deposited WarPig 3 just outside the village. WarPig 2 followed in the second lift. "When it was light enough to see, the squad leaders got everyone on line," relates Sowell. The palm trees, heavy undergrowth and the helicopter ride reminded them of a scene from Vietnam. "At first we were tense 'cause we didn't know what to expect." Sowell continues, "We started searching, with every fifth guy or so carrying a little orange flag so we'd have a visual on each other and stay on line. The vegetation was really thick, and it was a large area."[21] When anything suspicious was spotted, they would mark it with a flag and call up a mine clearance or EOD team to check it out. It was slow, methodical work.

But within a couple of hours, the search hit paydirt. Hidden under the palm trees was a sizeable weapons cache. Scores of artillery shells and more rockets were uncovered. Two vehicles were also found, a fuel truck and a tilt-bed cargo truck. The fuel truck was of major concern since it could be converted into a fearsome SVBIED. The other vehicle was an intriguing and worrisome find. The bed of the truck had been modified with a false bottom to hide several large tubes. Inside the tubes were at least two 122mm rockets. The truck's bed could be mechanically tilted up, elevating the launch tubes into firing position. Insurgents had produced an improvised mobile rocket launcher capable of delivering an impressive payload.

In another location, Gunny Yannizzi's EOD team came across more weaponry. Buried near the sandy river bank they unearthed a 14.5mm anti-aircraft gun. This type of weapon could fire bursts of exploding rounds that could do serious damage, especially to helicopters. An insurgent group with access to this kind of firepower was a significant threat.

And soon enough enemy fighters responded. After the cache was found, WarPig 2 started to take fire. "We were out in the open when shots came in," recalls Kyle Miller. "It was coming from across the river to our south. There were some pre-dug fighting holes on our side and we jumped into them."[22] Then, as RPGs came streaking across the water, WarPig 2 called for supporting fire. In minutes, 81mm mortar rounds were impacting on the south bank and the insurgents faded away. The attack helos also found enemy movement across the river. Edwards had set up on a rooftop where he had good visibility, and controlled strikes against insurgent targets near New Ubaydi. Hellfire missiles slammed into a vehicle carrying weapons and armed insurgents at a house.[23]

The search went on without further incident until the

afternoon. At the cache site, captured weapons and munitions were piled together and blown in place. The fuel truck and tilt-bed rocket launcher were destroyed as well. As the Marines prepared to leave, a separate LZ was set up in an open field for the extraction. But as the big CH-53s approached, small arms fire broke out. Apparently, insurgents had filtered through the farms and groves behind the Marines and were now in position to engage.

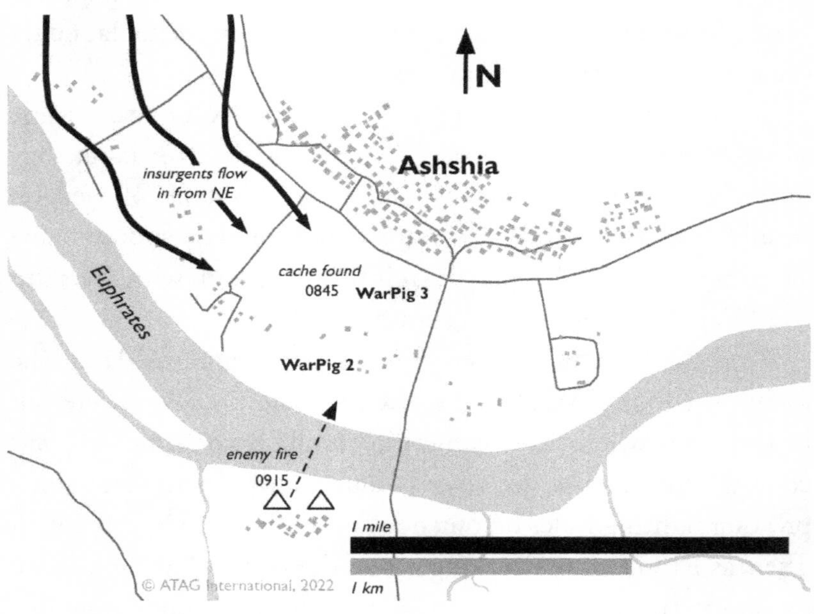

TIME TO GO

From his rooftop perch, the FAC, Captain Edwards, could hear the rattle of a firefight breaking out to his north. He and four others left the farmhouse and headed for the LZ. They'd moved only a hundred meters when AK rounds started snapping by. Enemy fighters had slipped into the house they'd just left and were firing at them.

Edwards hurriedly worked the radio to bring in a Huey-Cobra team for immediate support. Gunny Yannizzi was crouched next to him and watched as a Cobra banked in aggressively. "Hey, he's aiming right at us!" Yannizzi called out, concerned they were about to be lit up by their own aircraft.[24] But at the last second the pilot kicked rudder and let loose on the house. "When I saw the Hellfire impact that house, I figured it was time to go," Edwards recalls. "We sprinted to the bird, and as we took off the 53s took some small arms fire."[25]

Some WarPig 3 Marines had a similar experience. Approaching the LZ for pickup, they could also hear the enemy open fire:

> *We staged at the edge of an open field, about 150m from the helos, then ran across to get to them. It was a crazy moment. I'm not sure the 53 crews knew they were getting shot at, but we could tell they were taking fire. We could see the first helo getting shot at. They came in from the east to the LZ, then we took off to the west, right over where the insurgents were shooting from.*
>
> **—Henry Sowell**[26]

The attack helos prowled over the area, suppressing any position where hostile fire had been observed. Again, the air cover provided by the Cobra and Huey crews was a decisive advantage. All personnel were successfully pulled out by 1600, with

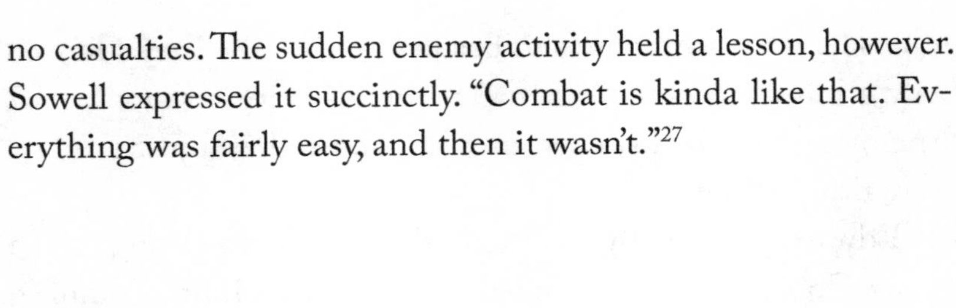

no casualties. The sudden enemy activity held a lesson, however. Sowell expressed it succinctly. "Combat is kinda like that. Everything was fairly easy, and then it wasn't."[27]

See **bastardsandbrothers.com** for notes, photos, maps, etc.

23. TRUST

While the pace of Marine and special ops raids accelerated in June and July 2005, important developments were unfolding at Camp Gannon as well. During this same timeframe, Captain Frank Diorio was finally able to make contact with the local forces fighting AQI in and around Husaybah. This came through patience, a growing list of local Iraqi contacts, and Sergeant Jimmy's ability to cultivate those contacts. While exact dates for certain events are unavailable, the rough chronology can be pieced together.*

By late May or early June, Diorio had acquired a phone number for a suspected leader in the Albu Mahal tribal militia. Very likely, the man was a "local muj" that Marines had been battling since 2004. At this time in the war there was no program for tribal engagement at battalion or company level. In fact, standing coalition guidance frowned on dealing with militias. All the way up the chain of command, the emphasis was on building the new Iraqi Army, not forming or assisting local militias, particularly in Sunni areas. With no specific authority to start talks

* The primary sources for this chapter are Frank Diorio's published interviews with IDA's Awakening Project and the Virginia Military Institute (VMI).

with suspected insurgents, Diorio was understandably hesitant to dial the number. Moreover, Operation Spear occupied most of 3/2's attention during mid-June, making it prudent to wait, gather more information, and think things over.

Eventually, though, he gave the go-ahead to make contact. It was probably around the end of June, about three weeks after they'd acquired the man's phone number.

It must have been an interesting conversation. After hanging up, the interpreter said, "Yeah, he wants to meet." It was an important step. But agreeing to meet was one thing. Actually meeting in the middle of a three-way combat zone was quite another. "We tried the cloak and dagger, middle of the night... He was afraid we were going to shoot him," Diorio explained. "We tried another place [but] he didn't get there in time, and we left. We didn't feel good about being there."[1]

Apparently there were several aborted attempts to meet over the next few weeks. Captain Diorio, First Sergeant Brazeal, and other India leaders debated the risks involved. There were many open questions. Who was this guy? What were his group's motivations? Were they infiltrated by AQI sympathizers? No matter how many precautions were taken, there was the distinct possibility that any surreptitious rendezvous could be an ambush. The impasse was only broken when the Iraqi called the hotline himself:

> *Finally, he called one day, and he said, "Come into the bank and arrest me." And I said, "What do you mean?" He said, "Just come into the bank. I'll be there at one o'clock. Come and arrest me."*
>
> —**Frank Diorio**[2]

The bank was a prominent building just off Market Street,

only a short distance from the platoon positions at the ING compound. The front side was within the Marines' fields of observation and fire, but it could also be entered discreetly from the back. The scout-snipers of Reaper 1 would carry out this unprecedented daylight mission, not to engage a target but to facilitate a conversation. That conversation probably happened on 15 July, based on the known dates of other events.

THIS IS YOUR TOWN

At the agreed-upon time, the snipers went to the bank. Anthony Cunha, part of Reaper 1, was on the mission. "We had good cover from the ING, so we weren't too nervous," he recalls. But as Cunha pulled security, it was definitely a strange experience. "There was an Iraqi tribal guy just 10 or 15 feet from me. He had an AK and was also pulling security for his guy. We were just staring at each other, sizing each other up."[3]

According to Diorio's account, the snipers "arrested" the leader just as he had suggested, and temporarily put wrist restraints on him. They then walked him over to a dilapidated building on or near the ING compound. Captain Diorio and First Sergeant Brazeal were nearby waiting. Across the radio came the call, "Sir, we got him ... He's waiting for you, but everyone looked really mad in there."

The slightly-built captain, in full battle rattle and flanked by several burly Marines, entered the ad-hoc meeting hall. "It was very surreal," recalls Diorio. "It was a bombed-out building. The roof was gone. There [were] remnants of the SVBIED."[4] One of the men flanking India's commander that day was First Lieutenant Ryan Brummond of 1st Platoon. When he initially heard about the meeting, he thought, "We're going to talk to guys with guns? These guys who were shooting at us not too long ago?"[5]

On later deployments in Afghanistan, Brummond learned to deal with tribal fighters, but this was a new and strange situation. "We let them bring in a couple of armed security guys, which was weird," he remembers. "But we had layered security, outside and inside. I was standing behind the captain, a few feet away. He and the Iraqi sat down on a couple of cinder blocks."[6] This strange key leader engagement proceeded without a table, chairs, or even the traditional pot of tea, just two combat leaders looking each other in the eye, with Sergeant Jimmy translating:

> *He was about five foot, two inches and on a good day I'm about five seven ... He said, "So, the Marines let short people be in charge too." And I said, "I guess so. I guess so." So that kind of broke the ice a little bit. I very quickly got a feel that this [was] a man sitting in front of me who was taking leadership, and I should just be as frank with him as possible. So basically, we just started talking ... I said, "Here's the deal. This is your town ... We have no intention of taking over your town. We're here, and we'll stay here until there is peace ... That's our mission. But unless there's peace and people can live in safety and security, we are not leaving. Once that's achieved, you can assume that we're going to leave. But not until that happens." And he said, "Well, it is our town." And I said, "Well, would you like to have a part in making it that way?" And he said, "Absolutely."*
>
> —**Frank Diorio**[7]

They talked for about ten minutes. Diorio knew he was operating beyond any guidelines or precedent. It wasn't at all clear how the two might help each other, but plainly the man hated the foreign fighters. They had killed members of his own family. "It was kind of a gray area, but I knew I had something that I had to work with," recalls Diorio. At one point, he turned and asked Brummond for his platoon's annotated map. "They started working things out, right on that map," recalls Brummond. "Here are the good guys. Here are the bad guys. I didn't recognize it at the time, but this was the local 'G Chief', just like in classic Special Forces doctrine."[8] As the meeting wrapped up, Diorio looked his counterpart in the eye and bluntly summed up the situation:

> *The last thing I said to him was, "I think it would be best if you don't trust me. And I promise, I don't trust you." And he smiled, and he said, "That's the most honest thing I've heard in the last two years." I said, "OK, then we'll go that way"... We shook hands, and we left... I knew I couldn't make any promises. I didn't have the authority to do that. We didn't even say what we were going to do. We just agreed to not trust one another. We looked at each other and said, "This is what I believe, and this is what you believe and how you want this place to go. We're working towards the same thing."*
>
> —**Frank Diorio**[9]

The man's real name has never been revealed, but India Company called him "Falzi."* He was a leader in the Hamza militia. Sources vary on his background, but most say he had been an officer in either the Iraqi Army or, more likely, the Border Police. Despite his diminutive stature, he was confident and had the presence of a man who'd seen combat. It was unclear

* According to Frank Diorio's interview in Awakening, Vol IIIA, Falzi did not survive the war

how many men he led, but at that time the tribe could probably muster one or two hundred armed fighters.*

That meeting in the wrecked building was a pivot point. An open line of communication was now established between India Company and the Albu Mahal and the two key commanders had sized each other up. Over the next days and weeks, they began to warily test the new relationship to see if it would hold weight.

About four days after the meeting, Falzi called in to warn of an imminent attack on the Marines. He claimed thirty AQI and allied fighters were preparing an attack that night against the "forward position" on the north side of the city. He used a local nickname for the outpost, but he was plainly referring to Trash OP. It was a specific warning, implying that he was somehow able to get inside information about enemy plans.

But given the source, there was serious deliberation about how to react. Could this be an attempt to mislead or divert attention? Was it a way for an enemy to observe the Marine's reactions? How far could India Company really trust the "local muj"? Diorio realized that if something went wrong, if Falzi turned out to be unreliable or actually hostile, he would be held responsible. Ultimately, though, he figured it was smart to act on the warning and had platoon and squad leaders beef up their posts and ensure their men were alert.

Sure enough, a significant attack occurred that night, probably 19 July 2005. Trash OP was fired on from four separate locations along the north edge of Husaybah.[10] The battle position was hit by machine guns and RPGs, but the Marines were ready, and no one was hurt. Instead, three enemy fighters were

* Just a few months later, this force was officially numbered at 278 men

recorded killed. The information had been right on the money. In a follow-on phone call, Falzi pointed this out, telling Diorio "I was right, wasn't I?" Diorio acknowledged, "Yes, you were."[11]

KIND OF AN UNDERSTANDING

Soon after, there was a chance to return the favor. India received intelligence that insurgents from a rival tribe, allied with AQI, were planning a revenge attack. Fighters from the Salmoni tribe had been part of the failed attack and may have lost some men. Somehow they had discovered that the Mahalawis had tipped off the Marines. "[From] east of us in Karabilah, the Salmonis were going to come into town" describes Diorio, "to pay a visit to the Albu Mahal tribe, and pay them back for warning us." This time the warning went the other way:

> *We said, "You're going to get attacked tonight in this area." And he said, "OK."... And that night they got attacked. But he set up his forces where the [enemy's] entry point was... and it was another lopsided event.*
>
> —**Frank Diorio**[12]

This was a good start, but Diorio still knew he was on shaky ground. Going by existing rules, "we shouldn't have even had that relationship," he realized. He also knew he needed to ensure that his leaders were aware of these developments. "I reported up to higher that this was going on," he recalled.[13] The information was passed up through the battalion, to the RCT, and on to division level. Slowly, this tentative cooperation with an armed tribal force grew in scope and significance:

We just let it go that way for a while... This [was] still all brand new... They would call me and say, "Foreign fighters [are] coming to attack us tonight... We're going to have weapons two streets away from your base." I [would say] "O.K. But if one round comes [at] my base, we're going to [return] fire."... In the middle of the night, we could see this firefight going on but... no rounds came towards us... [Then] he [would call] later on. "Was that OK?" [I'd say] "Yes, that was fine." It was just kind of an understanding so that we would build trust.

—Frank Diorio[14]

24. WHEREABOUTS UNKNOWN

Towards the end of July 2005, most of 3/2's Lima Company was finally liberated from security duty at Al-Asad and rejoined the battalion. Captain Sean Hankard was heartened to get closer to the action as the bulk of his company boarded helicopters for the lift out to Camp AQ. "Lieutenant Colonel Mundy wanted us back and the regiment had found another way to fill the security requirement," he recalls.[1] Lima's 3rd Platoon, however, would still be "Beowulf", the regimental reserve and QRF

Arriving at the base in Al-Qaim, Hankard noticed signs of strain. "When we got there, the battalion was tired,"[2] he remembers. One of the challenges faced by combat leaders and experienced warriors comes when their deployment winds down. As home gets closer with every day marked off the calendar, keeping their edge requires sustained discipline and psychological toughness. And as grunts have learned over and over, a lack of focus in the final stretch can be lethal.

As July blurred into August, the end of the deployment was in sight. But operations continued apace. Kilo and WarPig continued their targeted raids to roll up bomb-makers and key insurgents whenever they could be identified. Lima Company's arrival prompted discussions on how to best employ them as they began orienting to the battlespace. "We did some initial missions," says Hankard. "Route clearance, a raid with Kilo Company, a sweep down to ASP Wolf."[3] The battalion leadership discussed rotating Lima out to Gannon to replace India, but by that time the contacts India had cultivated with Falzi and the Albu Mahal were morphing into a tentative, but potentially important, relationship.

Yet another regimental operation was on the planning board that would involve elements of 3/2. With the preliminary name of "Lightning Strike"[4] this was to be a large-scale sweep through one more suspected insurgent hideout, the town of Anah. On the first day of August, however, fate yanked the operation in a different direction.

OVERWHELMED

Below the massive Haditha Dam, the Euphrates turns south to wind its way through what the Marines called the "triad" or "tri-cities" area. Haditha and Haqlaniyah lay on the west bank, connected by flimsy pontoon bridge to Barwana on the east bank. These riverside communities were infested with insurgents, which 3/25 had been battling on and off for months. On August 1st, the battalion had sent three scout-sniper teams on a mission to counter the increasingly accurate threat of 120mm mortar fire against the battalion's base at the dam. They were inserted during darkness into the open desert area south of the dam and east of the river. For operational reasons, two of the three-man teams combined early in the morning to occupy a hide site on high ground overlooking a wadi. Around midday, the third team heard an unexplained burst of small arms fire from that direction. After receiving no response to multiple radio calls, the third team moved on foot to check on their fellow snipers. The battalion also scrambled the designated QRF. Approximately an hour later, both elements reached the hide site where they discovered a bloody and harrowing scene.[5]

It was obvious the six snipers had been overwhelmed by a well-armed group of attackers. Five Marines lay dead, hit multiple times at close range by small arms. But a sixth, Corporal Jeffrey Boskovitch, was missing. There were drag marks and tire tracks indicating he'd been taken off the small hill and put into a vehicle.[6]

This was the nightmare scenario that haunts every commander, every service member, and every military family. A brother Marine was unaccounted for, assumed to be either desperately evading or in the hands of a depraved and merciless enemy. Like a pulse of dark energy, the grim news traveled almost instantaneously through battalion and regimental comms networks, radiating out and up through other units and higher headquarters.

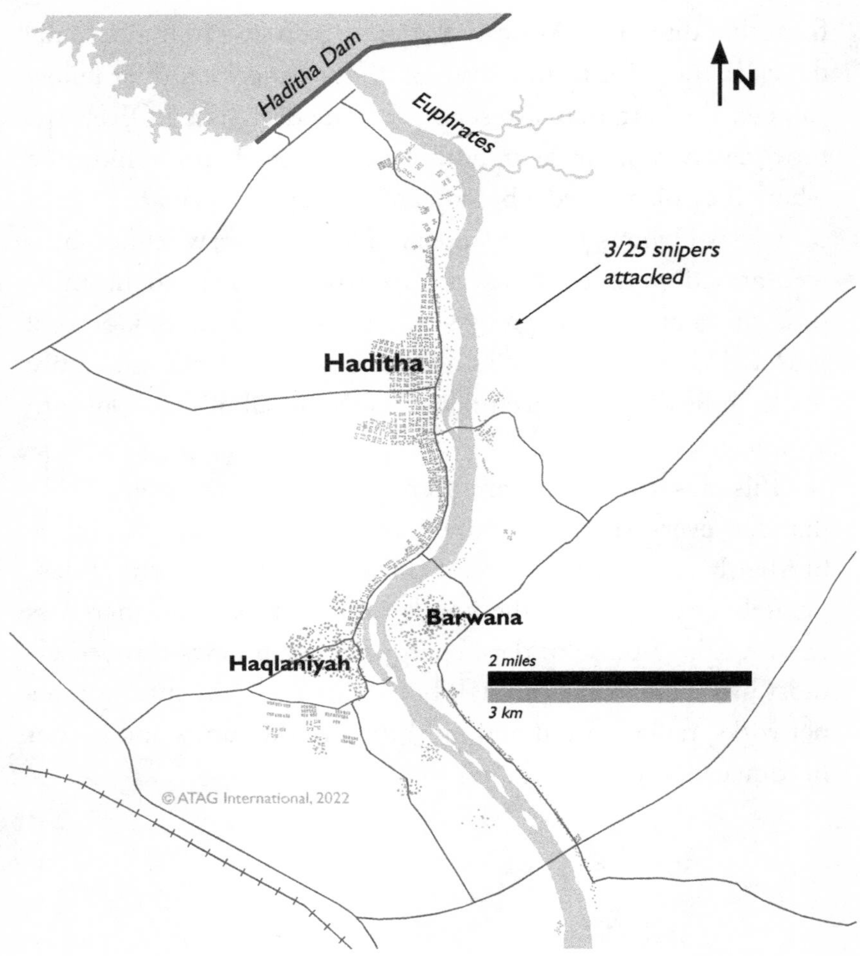

The military acronym that applies to such situations is DUSTWUN, typically pronounced "dustwon" It stands for "Duty Status and Whereabouts Unknown." It is a preliminary categorization, before determining if the individual fits into other status columns such as "Absent Without Leave" (AWOL), "Unauthorized Absence" (UA) or "Missing in Action" (MIA).

As such, it is a stilted, bureaucratized way of saying, "we don't know where they are." It also antiseptically, perhaps intentionally, obscures the underlying and terrifying implications.

On 1 August those implications became all too real. That afternoon and evening, 3/25 watch officers at the dam picked up disturbing indications from conversations among the local populace. As Colonel Davis later recalled, "We received information [from insurgents] that 'We've got an American. We're going to behead him on Haqlaniyah Bridge.'"[7] In a military culture where the oath to never leave a fellow warrior behind is a sacred duty, and in a fight against foes known for using cruelty as twisted propaganda, the situation called for maximum effort to recover the missing Marine. Military units all across Anbar were alerted and began spinning up for action. The search for Corporal Boskovich suddenly eclipsed all other priorities:

> *The RCT planners were going into overdrive thinking, "How are we going to get him? How can we save this Marine?"... We shut down the AO. We started getting information coming in from all the different intel sources."*
>
> —**Stephen Davis**[8]

Units pushed out to lock down key intersections and seal all avenues out of the tri-cities. Motorized riverine craft sped from their berths near the dam to aggressively patrol the river, and at least one of the craft took and returned fire. It was a race against time. Smaller insurgent cells in Iraq were known to "trade up" high-value captives to larger, better-funded groups that would certainly pay a large sum for a captured U.S. Marine. Every possible action would be taken to prevent that from happening. At this high-pressure moment, one of the resources Colonel Davis turned to was the SOF Task Force. With the close working relationship he had fostered between RCT-2 and the special mission units, this was a natural choice:

> *The Task Force element at Al-Asad immediately agreed to support in any way they could. They brought greater abilities and resources, ISR in particular, and aided in rapidly locking down the AO. We already had liaison personnel in their ops center and together we quickly formed an operations cell specifically to coordinate all efforts and information for the search.*
>
> **—Stephen Davis**[9]

Meanwhile, insurgent propaganda efforts were also ramping up. With surprising speed, a grainy video surfaced on the known jihadist websites. It had been shot that day and uploaded to the Internet just a few hours after the attack. The footage showed black-clad attackers tactically advancing on the snipers' position, then cut to masked men displaying American-made weapons, including sniper rifles, spotter scopes, body armor, and other U.S. military gear. Another scene showed an insurgent cutting the dog tag from a dead Marine's neck. Certain details in the video provided positive identification that the gear had come from the 3/25 snipers. About the same time, the radical jihadist group Ansar al-Sunnah claimed credit for the attack, although such claims were often suspect or inconclusive. At that time in the war, Ansar al-Sunnah was a separate entity from AQI but shared the same extreme Islamist ideology and ultra-violent methods.

Later that night, insurgents themselves called into the 3/25 tip line spewing further dark threats. It was impossible to verify what they said or judge what their motivations were. Perhaps they were trying to initiate negotiations ... or were just taunting the Americans. Then a last, bone-chilling call came in, remembers Davis. "They said we could find our Marine on route Grizzly near a well-known intersection outside of Haqlaniyah."[10] The lead was passed to the Task Force and their assets moved quickly to confirm the information and put boots on the ground to secure the site.

In the predawn hours of August 2nd, 2005, the corporal's body was recovered and brought by helicopter to Al-Asad airbase. "I was there when the Blackhawk brought him in," says Davis, in a voice thick with emotion. "The whole special mission unit formed up on the flight line as they brought out my Marine covered in an American flag. It was a tribute to professionalism, duty, and sacrifice and something I'll never forget."[11]

A medical examination revealed no signs of torture or mutilation, according to Davis.[12] It was clear that Boscovitch had been mortally wounded in the initial engagement and must have died shortly after being hit. There was also evidence the insurgents had actually cleaned his body, showing a modicum of respect for a fallen foe.*

While their rationales can only be supposed, they must have realized there was no further value in exploiting the situation and that they were about to be relentlessly hunted. Ultimately, they left the body behind where it could be found and left the area. Once the missing sniper was recovered and positively

* Although Ansar al-Sunna quickly claimed responsibility for killing the 3/25 snipers, the preponderance of evidence indicated that the actual attackers were part of the nationalist-oriented 1920s Revolution Brigade. As shown in the insurgent-made video, the tactics used in the assault and the manner in which they laid out the captured weapons exhibited previous military training. It was well-known that many 1920s Brigade fighters had served in elite Iraqi military units. Their relatively respectful treatment of the fallen Marines' bodies was another indicator.

identified, the DUSTWUN declaration was terminated. It had been a long, nerve-wracking fourteen hours since Corporal Jeffrey Boskovitch had been reported as unaccounted for, his whereabouts unknown.

RARING TO GO

Recovering Boskovitch did not close the books on the episode, however. Across the regimental AO, forces were being readied to flood the Haditha triad. The scale of the reaction would be much larger than mounting patrols and raids. The previously scheduled operation to clear the town of Anah was completely redirected. Within hours, Colonel Davis and his staff turned the RCT planning cycle on a dime to bring every resource to bear. All forces poised to launch Operation Lightning Strike were given new orders and new objectives, and the operation was renamed Quick Strike.

Meanwhile, every possible source of information and local contact was being tapped, scouring for information on who was responsible for attacking the snipers. By morning, word was out across the tri-cities area; the Marines were coming in force and would be turning over every rock to find anyone involved in attacking their brothers:

> *Where I'm from, we have a certain way of doing business. You hurt one of mine and I'm coming after you. That's what was going through my head after the sniper episode. This was very personal, and everyone wanted to go in there and show what happens when you attack the Marines. But early in my career, a mentor had taught me that you had to separate emotion from the fight. Yes,*

we were going into those towns to root out the enemy, but we were going to do it without losing our cool, without breaking the ROE.

—Stephen Davis[13]

The core of the operation would be 3/25, buttressed again by 3/2 and several other augmenting forces. At the dam and other bases in AO Denver, preparations for the mission kicked into high gear. Camp AQ was a frenzy of activity on August 2nd, as 3/2 and its supporting units readied to move towards Haditha with as much combat power as they could muster. All across the base, Marines scrambled to prep vehicles for extended operations. Meanwhile, commanders and senior NCOs hunched over maps and computer screens to finalize load plans, communications plans, ops orders, and all the minutiae required for movement to their objectives and making contact with the enemy.

As in previous operations, Kilo Company and the two mobile assault platoons, WarPig 2 and 3, would be linchpins of the battalion's part in Quick Strike. But this time, two more units were available. Most of 3/2's Lima Company would be part of the lineup and after being cooped up at Al-Asad, they were raring to go. "This was Lima's moment," recalls Sean Hankard, "Our opportunity to get into the fight."[14]

Additionally, 3/2 would link up with an Iraqi SOF unit and their U.S. Army Special Forces advisors at the objective. The efforts to build up the new Iraqi Army were beginning to bear fruit with more and more Iraqi soldiers, often called *jundis*, coming through the training pipeline. Both the quality of their training and their unit-level leadership had made incremental improvements. That progress could be seen in the field. In May, there had been no Iraqi participation in Matador. In June, Iraqi troops had augmented 3/2 during Spear, folded into Kilo Company. Now in Quick Strike an Iraqi company would participate alongside 3/2 as a separate maneuver unit.

DESERT DASH

With several such fast-react missions under its belt, Kilo Company was already primed and ready to move. In the weeks before Quick Strike, Kilo's leadership prepared for multiple scenarios. "I give great credit to my XO, John Hayes, First Sergeant Gregory, and Gunny Linch. They had developed pre-planned, three-day battle packages for several possible operations, including Haditha."[15] With that head-start on mission planning, Kilo began pushing out of Camp AQ early in the afternoon of August 2nd, accompanied by the guntrucks of WarPig 3 under Lieutenant Gabe Diana.

Just a few hours later, 3/2's Lima Company and its attachments were good to go. Lieutenant Colonel Mundy, Major Day, and much of the battalion's battle staff were ready to move as well. Just before sundown, a long column snaked out of Camp AQ. Leaving the base, the convoy was over a mile long[16] but soon each element formed into a separate task group according to their objectives. The imperative was to get to their designated launch positions by morning, ready for action. As always, the IED threat was a major concern, so they stayed off the main roads and pushed through the desert.

Measured in a straight line, the outskirts of Haditha lie about 70 miles east from Camp AQ. But factoring in the terrain and the need to keep unit integrity as they moved meant the trip took several hours. It was a kidney-bruising, dust-filled, bone-jarring ride, particularly for Marines riding in the back of 7-ton trucks. They huddled on the hard benches, struggling to breath as they were inundated in clouds of fine talcum-powder sand that got in their eyes, ears, nose, mouth, and every crevice. "It was brutal for those guys in the back," says Hankard. "Whenever we finished a trip with a 7-ton, it was like a scene from 'Mad Max'. They looked like sand-covered statues."[17]

While it avoided IED-laden roads, heading cross-country had its own inherent dangers. Vehicle accidents, especially rollovers, could be just as lethal as mines or roadside bombs. Drivers had to keep a sharp eye out for ridges or sudden drop-offs. Likewise, taking a wrong turn or missing a landmark could put a single vehicle or an entire column in the wrong place at the wrong time, with potentially catastrophic results. Despite the hazards, over 130 vehicles[18] carrying most of 3/2 pressed on through the desert towards their designated attack positions.

See **bastardsandbrothers.com** for notes, photos, maps, etc.

25. RIVER CITY

By the early morning of 3 August 2005, the battalion was poised for Operation Quick Strike. Kilo Company and WarPig 3 were staged in the desert southeast of Haditha, opposite an area called Bani Dahr. Lima Company and WarPig 2 were in position just west of Haqlaniyah. Just to the south of Lima 3/2, the Iraqi SOF company was ready to clear the industrial area and worker residences of the K-3 oil pumping station.

Across the Euphrates, which runs north and south as it flows by Haditha, 3/25 was in position to the east of Barwana. Lima Company 3/25 and supporting elements were the main effort on that side of the river. Meanwhile, a mobile assault platoon and other elements from 3/25 were on the west bank, just below the dam, ready to clear south and link up with Kilo 3/2 in Haditha.

Together, around 1,000 Marines formed a belt around the tri-cities and come dawn would begin constricting inwards towards the center, to find and engage any insurgents that dared oppose them. They would also be searching for any evidence or information that might lead them to the cell that had killed the sniper teams.

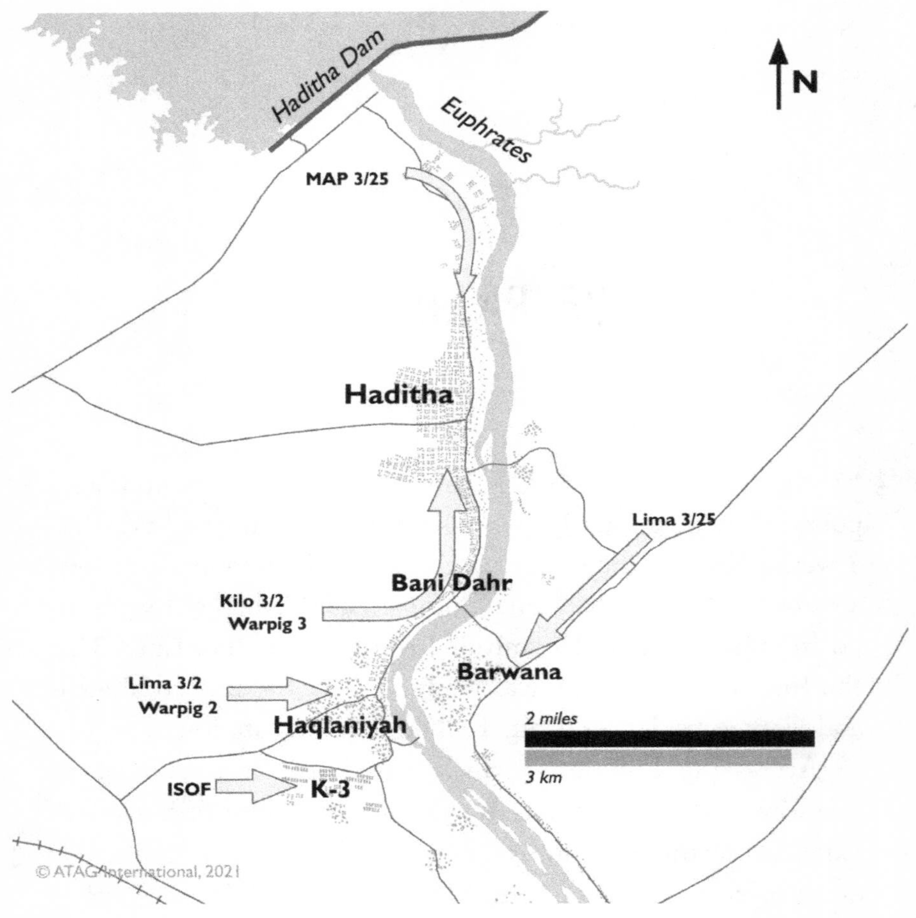

From their jump-off positions outside Bani Dahr and southern Haditha, 3/2's Kilo Company began pushing into those areas in the dim pre-dawn light. For this operation, Captain Ieva implemented a different tactical approach to the task of urban clearing. Rather than using a predictable advance, lining up platoons outside the city's west edge and sweeping east to the river, each platoon was assigned a zone they would clear in a hub-and-spoke manner. Using this approach, Kilo penetrated into the neighborhoods in separate smaller columns, seizing control of key buildings and intersections before most residents were even awake:

> *By this time, our platoon and squad-level leaders were mature and seasoned. We'd seen combat and knew our stuff. I was confident they could handle this more decentralized approach, which required good communications, management of fires, and situational awareness.*
>
> —**Chris Ieva**[1]

From these initial strongpoints, they began radiating patrols outwards, probing, and searching for armed military-aged-males. "It was an ink-blot strategy" describes Ieva, "to penetrate, go after known HVIs or caches, control key terrain, then conduct platoon level raids or nuanced, mutually supported clears to bait the enemy and generate intel."[2]

As they did so, they exhibited their own brand of messaging. Just before the operation began, Captain Ieva directed all Kilo Marines to don face paint and fix bayonets. "We were letting everyone know we were deadly serious," says Ieva.[3] Brother Marines had been ambushed and the killers had bragged about it. Now the Marines were there in force, combing the streets in full battle-rattle, looking for the perpetrators and daring any would-be insurgent to take a shot.

IMPECCABLE TIMING

Captain Sean Hankard and Lima Company 3/2 had pulled

together at a staging location enroute. Right before making the final drive to their objective, the commander brought his platoon leaders together for a huddle near his vehicle. "I didn't really give pep talks. I always had a just-the-facts delivery for those moments."[4] Just at that point, his radio operator passed him the latest intel update. It specified that their planned route to Haqlaniyah would likely have an increased number of IEDs and mines:

> *The timing was impeccable. It came in literally as we were mounting our vehicles. There was nothing I could do about it ... we just didn't have time to adjust the plan. I just told them, "Look sharp and we'll execute immediate actions if someone gets hit." ... We just had to put our heads down and go.*
>
> **— Sean Hankard** [5]

Fortunately, no hidden explosives were encountered as they made the last leg and took up positions outside Haqlaniyah. At first light they were facing northeast alongside the main road leading into town. On their far left flank, WarPig 2, along with two M1 tanks, established a support-by-fire position. In the center was 1st Platoon and the company CP, and to their right was 2nd Platoon. "We got our vehicles online, AAVs, Humvees and 7-tons, and dismounted," remembers Hankard. [6]

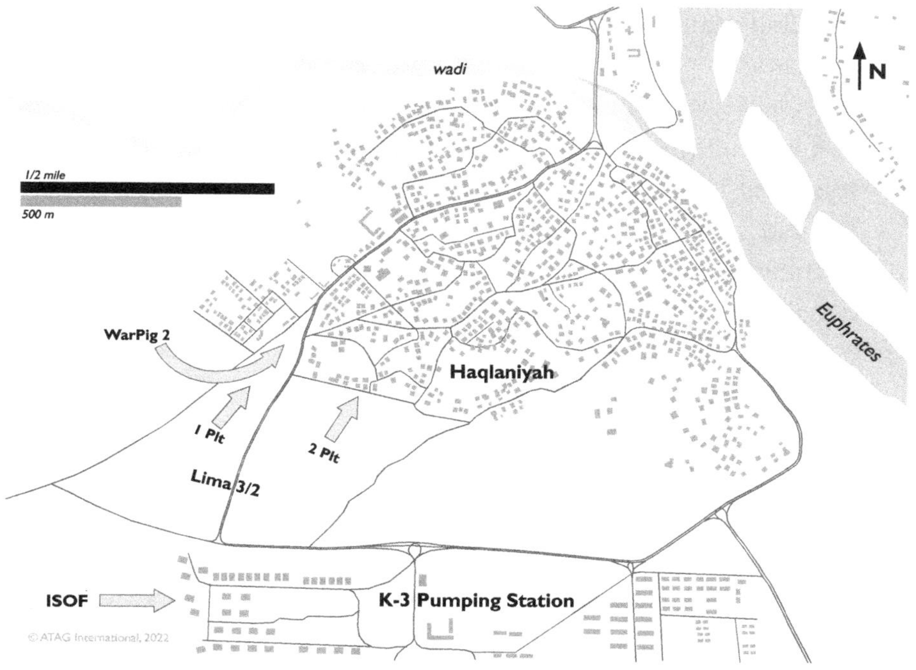

Everything seemed quiet for a few minutes. "Then I started hearing popping noises," says Hankard. "At first I didn't realize we were getting shot at."[7] For the captain and many of his men, this was their first exposure to hostile fire. But any hesitation lasted only a moment before their training and decisiveness overcame it and the two rifle platoons bounded forward. Once Marines reached the first buildings, the sounds of contact increased. As the rattle of small arms fire intensified, Hankard directed WarPig 2 to advance and put suppressive fire down the main streets and against any enemy positions located. He watched as Lieutenant Stann led a section of gun trucks forward and heard their heavy crew-served weapons clattering as they engaged. With that support, 1st and 2nd platoons seized the edge of Haqlaniyah and pushed forward.

"Once we got into the outer buildings, the enemy pulled back," Hankard remembers. "There were a few scattered shots inside the town, but nothing much. We found some bloody bandages, but the bad guys were gone. It was like chasing ghosts."[8] After the opening excitement, Lima 3/2 proceeded systematically with the remaining task, clearing block by block towards the river.

In Hankard's view the resistance had been relatively light, just a smattering of small arms and a few RPGs in the opening moments of the assault. But he later heard a different account from Sergeant Major Mennig, who had gone in with 2nd Platoon on the right flank. Mennig had watched mortar rounds impact near the Marines as they dismounted and began to advance. This illustrates a universal truth about combat. Each participant experiences its intensity and danger from different perspectives, which can vary from others greatly.

Lance Corporal Terry Hudson, from Prospect, Ohio, certainly had a unique perspective that morning. He was leading a three-man gun team attached to 2nd Platoon, working from aboard a 7-ton truck as the assault began. The machine-gunner, Lance Corporal Ronny Tomasetti manned a cupola-mounted 240G on the vehicle, while Hudson and Private First Class Brian Lewis were dismounted a few feet away.

Standing with his M-16 angled down at the low ready position, Hudson heard the distinctive boom of an RPG launch. He had no time to react. When the propellant of an RPG round ignites, it pushes the conical warhead through the air at about three football fields per second. And as it leaves the launcher, four stabilizing fins snap open, increasing the round's total diameter to about 18 inches.

This one came in directly from Hudson's front and either the warhead itself or one of the fins actually struck his rifle. In the blink of an eye, the glancing blow shattered the rifle's foregrip, sliced a chunk out of Hudson's left thumb, then carried past into the desert behind where it exploded about 100 meters away. Dazed, Hudson didn't know what had happened. "I couldn't see my thumb at first, but there was a burning feeling. It felt like someone had hit it with a hammer."[9] His rifle was non-functional, but amazingly, his right hand still held it firmly by the pistol grip.

A corpsman rushed over and as he bandaged Hudson's wounded hand, reassured him that his thumb was still attached, and he would be alright. Slowly Hudson realized how narrowly he'd escaped death. Had the warhead fuzed on impact, he would have been blasted apart instantly. Moreover, the angle of the strike meant the RPG's scythe-like fins had come within inches of slicing through his body.

With the trademark twisted humor of combat Marines, Hudson and his thumb quickly became the subject of ribald and merciless ribbing. It began as the irrepressible First Sergeant Joe Rovnak came over to check on the situation. After seeing no one had sustained serious injuries, Rovnak asked wryly, "Hey Hudson, thumbthing wrong?" then taunted him with a big grin and two thumbs up. "When the RPG went off and Hudson yelled 'corpsman', my heart sank," recalls Rovnak. When I saw his face I recognized a little shock. Figured a good poke of fun would bring him around."[10] Other Marines quickly piled on with incessant thumb jokes and puns. Hudson took it all in stride, just glad to be alive. With a useless rifle and a ball of blood-soaked gauze on his left hand, he was soon on a CASEVAC bird to Al-Asad.

BARWANA

Across the river, 3/25's Lima Company moved in towards their objectives. Under the command of Major Stephen Lawson, Lima 3/25 had seen heavy action ever since arriving in Iraq. The reservists had acquitted themselves well but had paid a bitter price in casualties. Their unofficial nickname "Lucky Lima" had evaporated after Operation Matador, when they had lost eight men killed and numerous seriously wounded. In late July, they'd lost another Marine and a Navy corpsman.

Lima 3/25 knew Barwana well from previous experience. In April, they'd engaged in an extended shootout with insurgents near the pontoon bridge and expected to have contact there again. For Quick Strike, the company was reinforced with a platoon from Kilo 3/25, a section of tanks, and another of wheeled LAVs. As they left their jump-off position heading into Barwana, several LAVs went first, then the massive M1 tanks, rotating their turrets to spot any hostile targets. The rifle platoons followed, loaded once again into lumbering AAVs.[11]

Captain Christopher Toland, 3rd Platoon's Commander, was in the lead trac. At about 6:30am, the AAVs turned down the main route leading into Barwana, onto a paved road that had already been crossed by multiple armored vehicles and declared clear. As Toland later related in a documentary, "After I took that right, probably, I don't know, about 50 or 75 meters, maybe 100 meters, there's a massive explosion. It was so big I thought for sure it had hit my amtrac."[12] A huge IED had been command-detonated directly under the third trac, flipping the 30-ton AAV upside down, breaking it in half and engulfing it in a huge fireball. All but one of the 15 men inside were killed.

The driver survived, severely wounded but thrown clear of the twisted wreckage.

Other vehicles dashed in to recover the driver and look for other survivors, but it was obvious no one else could be saved. In a hellish instant of smoke and flames, 11 members of 3rd Platoon's 1st Squad, three AAV crewmembers, and an Iraqi interpreter had died, 15 men total.[13] A thick column of black smoke rose into the morning air, marking their death. The event occurred in the flat, open terrain just outside of town, in plain view of their fellow Marines arrayed around them. The sight is burned forever into the memories of the many who witnessed it.

The task of clearing Barwana remained, though, and the company pushed on even as they reacted to the devastation. Some choked back tears. Others had to check their anger as they dismounted and began to clear houses on the edge of town, gruffly questioning anyone they encountered. Clearly some residents in those homes would have seen the placement of such a large IED, or observed the triggerman, but as usual, no one knew anything about it.

Lance Corporal Travis Williams had been alongside Captain Toland in the lead trac when his closest friends were destroyed just yards behind him. He'd been pulled from the ill-fated vehicle for radio duty just before the mission began and was now the 12th and last surviving member of 1st Squad. After the cataclysmic event, Williams was on a rooftop overlooking the wreckage, wrestling with bitter frustration, anger, and grief. "I was looking back at the accident site and I saw guys go out there with blankets to cover up the body parts" he recalled. "All I wanted to do was shoot anything that was moving. If it wasn't in desert cammies, you know, it was going down. And I got up there, and stayed up there, just crying…The closest guys that I ever had as friends are all dead."[14]

Despite the morning's pain and loss, Lima 3/25 and supporting units pushed on to secure the pontoon bridge and cleared through the town. There was a short and inconclusive firefight with unseen insurgents, but otherwise they encountered no substantial enemy activity. Most of Barwana's occupants had left or remained hidden and little weaponry was found during the searches.[15]

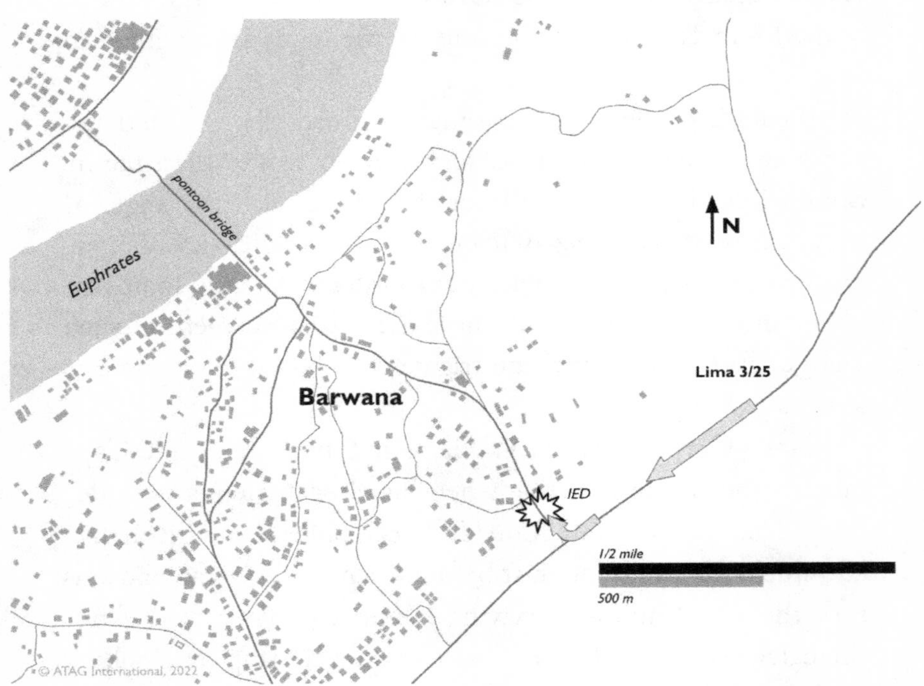

WHO'S SHOOTING AT MY MEN?

Back on the western bank, the operation continued as 3/2's companies cleared in their zones. In Bani Dahr and Haditha, Kilo company's hub and spoke tactics were successful as each platoon radiated outwards from their initial positions. Then the Kilo Marines spread through surrounding city blocks, unpredictably appearing on street corners and rooftops. Any insurgents trying to oppose them couldn't tell where the Marines might appear and had to worry about being ambushed themselves. Aside from a few scattered shots, Kilo Company met little opposition.

After the initial firefight at the edge of Haqlaniyah, Lima 3/2 met similarly light resistance. The company used a more typical "squeegee" approach, clearing west to east in a linear fashion. Squads searched each building while maintaining mutually-supporting positions. An embedded reporter was with them that day and observed Sergeant Major Mennig going house to house and sweating right alongside his junior Marines. The reporter described a scene that played out countless times during the war, as Mennig questioned an Iraqi man. When he asked where the insurgents were, the man said armed fighters would drive through the town market, crammed into three or four cars. "But where are they now?" Mennig pressed. "They all fled town," came the answer. "Then who is shooting at my men?" Mennig responded.[16]

The operation continued for the next seven days, officially concluding on August 10th. While not as intense when compared to Operations Matador or Spear, each of the companies involved turned up concrete evidence of insurgent presence. Significant amounts of explosives and IEDs were discovered, including 300 artillery shells, 23 IEDs, and nine vehicles rigged as bombs. Another trend emerged from the operation as Marines encountered several buildings wired with explosives. Fortunately, these "building-borne IEDs" were identified and destroyed with no casualties, but clearly the enemy was hoping to bait the Marines into confined deathtraps.[17]

Captain Hankard was satisfied with the way his men had handled themselves. At one point during the operation, he met up with Lieutenant Colonel Mundy who had come to check how Lima 3/2 was doing. "We talked for a bit, and I told him our team had done well," says Hankard. "We'd had contact and our guys had kept their heads under fire. They did their job, and I was proud of them."[18]

Lima Company Marines also recovered some American-made military equipment, apparently taken by insurgents after the attack on 3/25 snipers. It was a significant lead in the ongoing search for the attackers, but also gave Hankard a small glimmer of what the future might bring in Haqlaniyah:

> *An Iraqi man, a civilian, brought it to us. It wasn't much, an IR strobe, a map, and some personal effects. But it showed he was trying to help us. We'd already cleared his house without finding the equipment, so he didn't have to bring it to us. He must have thought it was safe to cooperate with us. The HET guys went over to question him about it, but it occurred to me that there were people here who would work with us if given the chance.*
>
> —**Sean Hankard**[19]

After his razor-close brush with an RPG round, Lance Corporal Hudson spent a week or so at Al-Asad nursing his injured hand, then eagerly returned to be with his buddies in Lima 3/2.

They were also glad to see him back, and gleefully unleashed a new round of thumb jokes to celebrate his return.

MEAN STREETS

Viewed superficially, Operation Quick Strike surely seemed to some as yet another inconsequential "hit-and-leave" sweep along the restive river valley, and a particularly costly one at that. But on closer inspection, there were promising threads woven into the story. First, there were finally enough adequately-trained units in the new Iraqi Army to start making a difference out west. Iraqi soldiers were integrated into the operation as units and performed credibly and competently on both sides of the river. "It showed how effective you could be with the Iraqi Forces," explained Lieutenant Colonel Mundy. "[For them] it is very obvious when something doesn't look right. [An] American would have completely missed it, because he's just not used to looking at it."[20] A much larger Iraqi Army presence in AO Denver and in Al-Qaim was just around the corner.

Also, the RCT-2 campaign plan was starting to produce clear results. In late June, the city of Hit had been secured after Operation Sword. Kilo Company 3/25 and an Iraqi Army company then established combat outposts (COPs) right in the city. It was the first time RCT-2 elements cleared, then stayed. At the southern end of the Hit-Haditha corridor, then, Marines and Iraqi Army troops were actually holding and starting to build. But good news in one place meant bad news in another. As occurred so often in Iraq, when insurgents were defeated or suppressed in one area, they surged somewhere else. This helps explain the stepped-up insurgent activity in the triad during August.

In October, after 3/2 and 3/25 had rotated back home, Haditha, Haqlaniyah and Barwana would again be the focus of RCT-2's attention. Operation Rivergate saw Marines and Iraqi Army troops building joint combat outposts (COPs) in the triad, finally establishing a permanent presence there, as had been accomplished in Hit. In the mean streets of Haditha, however, tragedy struck again on November 19, 2005, when Marines from 3rd Battalion, 1st Marines suffered a lethal IED attack against a routine resupply mission. The bomb blew the front end off one of their vehicles, instantly killing a popular Marine. His squad mates responded by aggressively clearing nearby buildings, and unarmed Iraqi civilians were killed in the process. The notorious incident became a major controversy, tagged by the media as the "Haditha massacre."

The Marines of 3/25 knew those same mean streets all too well. Some had patrolled over the exact same ground where the November incident later occurred. Certainly, after losing the snipers on August 1st, followed by the IED strike two days later, they also knew the raw emotions, the vengeful instincts, that can surface after such violence. To their everlasting credit, however, they kept those primal instincts in check and conducted themselves with professionalism and restraint.

By the end of July, 3/25 had already experienced heavy casualties with 27 KIA to that point. The unit had been the subject of multiple press stories, which invariably highlighted their losses. Then, in just three days at the beginning of August, they lost 21 more. By the end of the deployment, 3/25 and attached units had lost a total of 48 Marines and Navy corpsmen, the highest number of killed-in-action for any battalion in the Iraq War.

When a deployed American military unit suffers a death or serious injury a "reduced communications" (RC) protocol is enforced to prevent the identities of stricken personnel from being prematurely broadcast by the media or passed by unit members to their own contacts back home. This is done primarily to safeguard servicemembers' families, who should never hear of a loved one's death through unofficial, quite possibly inaccurate, sources.

This means when a Marine is killed or gravely wounded overseas, the deployed unit goes offline for several days, with morale phones and internet stations shut down until the affected next-of-kin have been officially notified. This can be nerve-wracking for families as they wait for news, hoping and praying it doesn't come with a knock on the door.

During the first week of August, 2005, initial reports of multiple deaths in an Ohio reserve unit in Iraq hit the families of 3/25 like a tidal wave. They had to wait in agony as the maddeningly vague news stories proliferated. Unable to check on their loved ones directly, many family members checked on each other and shared strength and comfort. Meanwhile, uniformed pairs of Marine Corps casualty assistance officers and chaplains began to fulfill their somber duty.

Thousands of miles away in Anbar, personnel assigned to RCT-2 and its component units could not let their families know they were alive and unhurt. Until all casualty notifications were completed, they remained under the blackout requirements of Reduced Communications, more commonly called "River City."

See **bastardsandbrothers.com** for notes, photos, maps, etc.

26. BACKLASH

During July and August, the blast-furnace heat of western Iraq tries to suck life and spirit from any living thing. Under an unrelenting sun, daytime temperatures often top 120 degrees. Sweltering under their kevlar helmets and the added weight of armored vests, men manning posts at Camp Gannon, the ING and Trash OP struggled to stay alert as the heat constantly drained their bodies of water and energy. Alertness and full body armor were absolutely necessary, though, as they were still taking fire almost every day, sometimes several times in a single day.

While India Company's engagement efforts with the Albu Mahal had begun to show results, much of Husaybah was still in hostile hands. By this time, India Company had mapped out in some detail the areas controlled by the Hamza tribal militia, and those where insurgents allied with AQI held sway. Falzi's men and the Mahalawi forces held about half of the city, concentrated in the center and southeast sectors bounded by Market Street on the north, the railroad tracks on the south, and East End Road. The sectors closest to the Marine positions, however—including the 440 neighborhood, the blocks by West End Road, and the west end of Market Street—were controlled by the Salmoni tribe and foreign fighters. To the east, in the H&K Triangle, AQI and their allies from the Karabuli tribe had control.[1] For India Company, then, these geographic realities made providing actual support to the Hamza fighters a tough challenge.

It was challenging for the 3/2 staff and RCT-2 headquarters as well. The idea of a Marine rifle company or battalion forging, then managing some kind of battlefield alliance with a Sunni tribe was outside the proverbial box in 2005. While high-level Marine officers had made a series of overtures to prominent sheikhs living in Jordan, these had not produced anything tangible at the tactical level. Moreover, for nearly every coalition unit in Iraq, the process of unraveling the tribes and their labyrinthine interrelationships was just beginning.

"Understanding the tribes was discovery learning for us," recalls Chris Starling. Beyond his role as RCT-2's operations officer, Starling had also been given the task of tribal engagement throughout AO Denver. "I was familiar with the basic layout of the tribes in Western Anbar, but it's easy to paint them all with one broad Sunni brush. Then we learned different tribes controlled different activities; border checkpoints, smuggling routes, construction, food distribution, and more . . . That was new to me." During one of his trips out to Al-Qaim in February 2005, Starling was briefed on a map of known tribal territories, a seemingly random colored mosaic. "At that point we were still viewing them more like ethnic neighborhoods," he recalls. "At first we didn't really comprehend the depth of tribal loyalties and, more importantly, how influence and control were wielded."[2]

The outbreak of red-on-red violence before and during Operation Matador shifted Starling's perception. "We saw tribes fighting against each other, fighting against foreign fighter influence. It dawned on us that those colored maps mattered," he remembers. "Maybe we could leverage greater influence in some of these enclaves." But operationalizing that knowledge was a different issue. "Part of our doctrine was to win hearts and minds, so in the beginning we were trying to treat all tribes equally. We weren't trying to form alliances, really. We knew we wanted to talk to the sheiks. Some had fled to Jordan, some were still in Iraq. But it was a hard puzzle to figure out. Who was the enemy? Who was on our side? And why?"[3]

There was plenty of suspicion to go around. The sheikhs were masters at double-talk, maneuvering in the middle ground, and playing all sides. From the Marines' perspective, dealing with them always posed the danger of being used to settle old scores, or worse, deceived into actually supporting the most dangerous enemies. In Colonel Davis' view, then, the Albu Mahal were not necessarily the victims they portrayed themselves as, particularly in early 2005. "Some of these guys had been fighting against us since our RIP/TOA in March," Davis recalls, "They weren't always distinctly opposed to Zarqawi and his guys."[4]

While officers at higher echelons worked on the tribal engagement puzzle, it was down at the company level where the realities had to be worked out. For the grunts sweating out every day at Camp Gannon, it had become obvious which side was trying to kill them and which side they should support. Sometime after Captain Diorio's face-to-face meeting with Falzi, India Company conducted a squad-sized raid outside Husaybah, probably in mid-July, that highlighted the nuances of dealing with the "local muj."

According to Diorio's account, an RPK machine-gun was found at the target house. Standing rules allowed Iraqi households to have one AK-style rifle in their home for self-defense, but this was a full-auto, belt-fed 7.62mm weapon and the squad promptly confiscated it. A day later, a call came into Gannon. Either Falzi or another Hamza leader was on the line. He said, "Hey we need that [weapon]. That protects us from the attacks we're having," recalled Diorio, who responded, "That's out of the ordinary. We want to keep that." But the man pressed back, "I'm telling you; it would mean a lot to us if we kept it."[5]

This posed a serious dilemma. They wanted to build the relationship, but just how far could India Company trust this Hamza force? Would the RPK just be turned back on them in a few days? Diorio talked it over with some of his junior Marines:

> *My squad leader said, "Sir, we need to give it back." And I said, "But I have the burden of knowing this could get turned around on you guys... I'm going to think about it." I talked to higher [battalion leadership] a little bit. I asked if we have authority to give it back, and they said, "Yeah."*
>
> **—Frank Diorio**[6]

The captain's answer back to the Hamza fighters was, "We're going to give it back to you, but if I see any automatic fire coming this direction, we're coming back to your house and we're going to take the RPK and everyone in the house." Apparently this rough-hewn battlefield compact was honored. "We gave it back and never got a single round towards us [from] that way," recalled Diorio.[7]

In retrospect, up to that point the intramural fighting between the Albu Mahal and their tribal rivals was a fairly low-intensity affair resembling a gangland turf war, but with fully-automatic weapons and mortars. While the Mahalawi sheikhs claimed they had "kicked out al-Qaeda" from Husaybah back in May,[8] that didn't refer to members of other tribes who lived there. The Salmonis, in particular, still had their strongholds and some foreign fighter cells must have remained with them.

The center of the city, in particular, was a shifting and confusing patchwork. Certain blocks were controlled by Salmoni tribesmen while others were held by the Hamza fighters of Albu Mahal. By late summer, red-on-red skirmishes were breaking out regularly in Husaybah. During the day Marines would hear gunfire echoing over the rooftops, as bursts of small-arms fire erupted. At night, tracers arced back and forth between the neighborhoods.[9]

Certainly not all the fire was directed inside the city. Trash OP, the ING compound, and Gannon itself continued to take incoming, usually from the Salmoni-held parts of the city. By this time, Marines on Gannon had been through so many firefights that getting shot at had become routine, which could lead to dangerous inattention. "One night I went out to the piss-tubes, and I had one of those little red LED lights," recalls Ryan Brummond. "A bullet whizzed by me in the dark, a few feet away. I dropped to the ground and killed the light."[10] In his journal, Chris Nothstine writes of a similar near-miss that got his heart racing:

> *Two nights ago, it was 98 percent visibility, and I was on post from 2100-0100. Well, at 0100 I left post. I was on the rooftop and apparently skylined myself. Then, CRACK! It was pretty freakin' close.*
>
> —**Chris Nothstine**[11]

Other incidents were more serious than single pop-shots

and showed the vulnerability of posts facing the city, exposed to darting enemies firing from street corners and hidden positions just blocks away. On July 22nd, India's 3rd Platoon was attacked as they executed a relief-in-place at the ING compound. Suddenly, AK and machine-gun fire lanced through the position. A squad-sized group of insurgents was firing from a few blocks down Market Street. The grunts fired back furiously to drive them away, but an RPG round sizzled in and exploded, wounding two Marines.[12] Based on the weapons used and the number of attackers, the 22 July attack likely involved a foreign fighter cell operating in the Salmoni-held sector.

As Diorio described the end of July and early August 2005, "There was a lot more foreign fighter influence coming into the city…the Salmoni tribe had joined up with foreign fighters to fight the Albu Mahal." This definitely made the situation more volatile. But from Diorio's perspective, the dynamic had also shifted in an important and positive way. "We started seeing a lot of kinetic activity that wasn't towards us," he recalled. "The Albu Mahal [were] now basically feeding us information and working with us. And at this time, we had gotten approval to work with them."[13]

It was still an open question whether engagement with the Mahalawis was worth the risks. Were they cynically manipulating the situation? Could trying to support them get Marines hurt or killed? Would they just end up siding with AQI after all? These were valid concerns being weighed up and down the command chain. But at this juncture, a crucial event provided evidence that something positive was unfolding.

"One night we heard this huge firefight in the middle of the city," related Diorio.[14] Based on other sources, it was likely a few hours after midnight on 4 August 2005. Marines saw the

Husaybah skyline light up as intense small arms fire erupted from the blocks controlled by the Albu Mahal, the same part of town where their main contact lived. This was no hit-and-run skirmish. The fire was sustained, and tracers blossomed out in all directions. Some rounds arced towards the Marine positions, intentionally or not.

In the midst of the conflagration the hotline rang. It was the wife of one of the Hamza leaders. "Her house was getting attacked on all sides," Diorio recalled. There was desperation in her voice, and she was calling for help. Specifically, she was asking for, almost demanding, that American helicopters provide her tribe's militia, the "local muj", with air support. A cascade of thoughts and implications rushed into Captain Diorio's mind:

> *[This was] another surreal moment... After [all my] fire support classes, and after all [our discussions] of who has terminal authority [for airstrikes], I had an insurgent's wife telling me to send helicopters... And at that moment I knew I had buy-in. They felt like we had that kind of relationship.*
>
> —**Frank Diorio**[15]

But sending attack helicopters into such a situation was clearly impossible. It was a dense, urban environment. There were no defined targets, and no way to pick out hostiles from friendlies. The most likely result would be the deaths of innocent civilians. Even if valid enemy targets could be identified, Captain Diorio knew he wouldn't get "authority to request helicopters to support people who claim they are no longer insurgents... This was still very new to everyone at headquarters," he recalled. "Even if I tried to explain it, it probably wouldn't make a whole lot of sense."[16]

But a flat refusal would wreck the groundwork that had been so carefully laid and destroy the trust painstakingly built. Clearly it was a life-and-death situation for Mahalawi tribesmen on the ground. Their lives and their families' lives were at stake. "I also knew that they were getting attacked," Diorio explained. "I had to do something, but I wasn't sure what."[17]

In this crucial moment, out on the edge of the war in a beleaguered outpost, under stress with seconds ticking by, a Marine company commander found a way to tread a very thin line. "About every other night we had a patrol done by helicopters, trying to [counter] IEDs that were in the city," remembers Diorio. "They basically flew the same route... So I just asked the [duty officer], 'Hey are we having a patrol tonight?'" Sure enough, the counter-IED birds would be on station in the next half-hour.[18]

As the helos were inbound, India Company's COC contacted the lead pilot to make a delicate arrangement. Top priority of course was to keep the aircraft out of unnecessary danger. "There's a firefight going on in the city, just so you're aware," Diorio remembers telling the pilots, but went on to ask, "We'd appreciate it if you could continue but please stay in the periphery, continue doing your patrol." The crucial area of the city was identified, and the hoped-for effect explained. According to Diorio, their answer was, "OK, we'll stay above and beyond, but we'll make sure that we can be heard."[19]

Meanwhile, a call was made back to the militia leader's distraught wife. Across the phone line, the rattle of AK fire could be heard in the background. "I said, 'They're on their way.' and she said, 'OK.' And we could still hear the fight continuing," described Diorio. The ploy was definitely a gamble. The leader's house might still be overrun by enemy fighters. He and his wife might be killed, and the tribe might blame the Marines. The minutes ticked by anxiously. After about an hour, the phone rang again. It was the woman calling back, as Diorio described:

> *She was screaming into the phone, "It worked! They fled; they ran away once they heard your helicopters. Thank you for sending the helicopters." And I said, "You're welcome."*
>
> —**Frank Diorio**[20]

CONVERGENCE

Several other developments were converging in August as 3/2 neared the end of the deployment. First, the coalition was about to triple or even quadruple conventional forces in the Al-Qaim area. The battalions' hard-fought operations through spring and summer had made it clear to the chain of command, all the way up to General Casey, that more manpower and resources were needed in the far west of Anbar. Securing the border near Al-Qaim and dislodging AQI's strongholds there would be high-level priorities in what RCT-2 called the "second semester." Another battalion was set to relieve 3/2 in early September and their advance team was already on the ground.

The unconventional side of the fight was ramping up as well. The special mission units of TF 714 were accelerating their raids near Al-Qaim and along the Euphrates. By all accounts they were finding plenty of AQI-related targets.[21] And now, after leaving the province in 2004, the Army's Green Berets were back in Anbar looking to work with indigenous forces. At the end of July, Major Martin Adams of 5th Special Forces Group began setting up a command element (ODB) at Al-Asad to oversee activities of three ODA teams.[22] Captain Jim Calvert led ODA 582 and arrived in Camp AQ in mid-August. In a later interview, he described the team's mission and their first trip out to Gannon and Husaybah:

> *The original mission was basically "Make Things Better. Do tribal engagement and make [it] a better place for the Iraqi people." So, it was a very broad mission, which is great for an SF team... To get the lay of the land... we took a long convoy ride [with the Marines] through the desert from the base at Al-Qaim to Husaybah... It was so bad; we couldn't go back that night... which was a surprise... There was sniper fire, machine gun fire, indirect fire, and a mine strike... It was like, "Welcome to Al Anbar."... Right away you knew that this was different than most places in Iraq.*
>
> **—Jim Calvert***

Additionally, personnel from civilian organizations were intensifying their activities in Anbar that summer. The military referred to them as "other government agencies", or OGA. They supported special operations but also worked independently on their own priorities. That summer, enigmatic figures were showing up in Marine ops centers, typically in khaki pants and polo shirts and using only their first names.[23] "We learned a lot from them," says Chris Starling. "At one point I remember Colonel Davis, myself, and a couple of OGA folks leaning over the hood of a vehicle with a map. Their contacts in the Albu Mahal tribe were sending them enemy locations. It was a guy with a beard and a woman correlating these enemy positions to tribal

* From interview in Awakening, Vol IIIA; "Jim Calvert" is a pseudonym which the IDA interviewers were asked to use for attribution purposes.

territories. She was very optimistic and well informed about the tribes."[24] The OGA types showed up at Camp Gannon as well. "I wound up getting visits from other government agencies asking if they could come to Husaybah and meet with our sources," recalled Frank Diorio.[25]

The fourth development flowing into the event stream was enemy-driven. The Albu Mahal's nascent alliance with 3/2 Marines had become a major thorn-in-the-side for AQI. Not only was the Al-Qaim District, particularly Husaybah, key terrain for the jihadists' supply lines, it was important symbolically. Abu Musab al-Zarqawi and his terror-minded emirs knew that if they allowed a Sunni tribal rebellion against them to grow, it could spread rapidly. But the former prison enforcer was determined not to let that happen. By August, 3/2 was regularly picking up rumors that AQI had something in the works. "The Salmoni tribe was gaining more and more support from outside influences and foreign fighters," Diorio recounted. "The rhetoric was they were going to come and teach Albu Mahals a lesson for working with the Americans."[26]

FEAR AND FIRE

As the sun set on 12 August 2005, the grunts of India's 1st Platoon were on post at the ING compound. Behind layers of sandbags and ballistic glass, they looked over their gun barrels into the restive city of Husaybah. Corporal Luis Maxwell, a squad leader, had just checked one of the rooftop positions and quipped to another Marine, "It's been a slow day. I wish we had something to do."[27] Just as he turned away and took a few steps, an RPG round slammed into the building, followed immediately by withering enemy machine-gun fire. Suddenly there was lots to do.

Deeper inside the compound, Lieutenant Ryan Brummond and Platoon Sergeant Chris Reith were in the ING's makeshift command post when they heard the gunfire erupt. "It was a very intense, heavy barrage of small-arms fire," remembers Reith. "It didn't rise gradually, like most engagements. It was like an ambush had been triggered."[28]

In those first crucial moments, the fight was in the hands of Corporal Maxwell and his fire teams. "I knew I was in charge until the lieutenant or platoon sergeant took over," he says, "And the enemy was very aggressive on this one. They were so close." The 21-year-old squad leader started directing traffic, coordinating with the other two squads. "My guys were engaging, I could hear the MG fire, and I got on the radio. I told Marconi to get his guys into the supplementary positions. Then I sprinted to the CP and told Mitchell to have his guys ready to run ammo."[29]

Lance Corporal Derrick Herndon was hunkered down in the position on top of the "Vet" building when the attack kicked off:

> *I recall the first 'splack' on the glass right in front of my face. It scared the shit out of me! ... Most of our posts had ballistic glass, from Humvee windshields. Ours was horizontal and about 2 inches thick. I was behind that glass with Phil Butcher who was on the 240G ... There were lots of enemy. Double digits. They were getting really close, in the dirt area to our south ... I was engaging targets with my M-16 and tracers, using my "suicide mag" loaded with all tracer rounds, walking them onto targets to mark them for Butcher ... When the adrenaline hits, you don't feel fear or anxiety. You're just totally focused.*
>
> —**Derrick Herndon**[30]

The attackers were using excellent fire and maneuver tactics and concentrating their fires, unlike previous fights. "Usually, they'd hit us then slink back to the east side," recalls Brummond. "But that night they got in really close on the northeast, east, and south. They had what we called a dangerous distribution."[31]

Lieutenant Brummond and Sergeant Reith soon pushed out to manage the fight which was unfolding on several axes. "There were about 25-30 enemy fighters, about a platoon-sized element," Reith remembers. "They were trying to breach the wire and obstacles and we came close to blowing the claymores we had set up. We pulled ammo from the platoon reserve and had guys run it out to the posts."[32] Out on his exposed rooftop post, Herndon remembers getting ammo delivered while under fire:

> *There were lots of RPGs coming in. Some were hitting right below us. Our sandbags were being shredded. The air in the post was full of choking dust…Just then Habay ran up there to give us more ammo. As he came in the post, an AK round came through between the glass and the sandbags. I saw it burn by and thought for sure it had hit him. It came right by his head.*
>
> —**Derrick Herndon**[33]

Lance Corporal Joey Habay, from South Lyon, Michigan, had crowded into the cramped space behind the gun. A former linebacker, his 6'2" 240-pound frame almost filled the post. "I bent down to link in a new belt, and felt a 'crack' by my head," he says. "I looked up, and dirt was falling out a hole in the sandbag right over my head. Herndon yells, 'Are you OK?' and I yelled, 'Just keep firing!' and went back for more ammo."[34]

Chad "Doc" Martin was in the CP room with Private First Class Peter Macko when the fight exploded outside. In the unit's pre-arranged reaction plan, Macko was part of Martin's assigned security to get the Doc to where he was needed in case of a serious assault. Before that night, there had been a bit of friction between the two. With Martin hailing from Texas, and Macko from New York, they had frequently exchanged verbal jabs. But all rivalry was put aside as the bullets started flying. Grabbing his med kit, rifle, and a radio he knew the lieutenant needed, Martin joined Macko by the door and they braced themselves to rush outside.

"We could hear all the gunfire, guys yelling." recalls Martin. "Macko looks back at me and says, 'You ready?' then he started to go." But as Macko pulled open the no-frills plywood door, Martin had a sudden prompting. "I just knew he was in danger, and I reached out and yanked him back."[35]

That moment is seared into Pete Macko's memory. "I was gonna look out to see where fire was coming from," he says. "My foot was already on the threshold when Doc pulled me back just as two tracers snapped right by my face. If he hadn't grabbed me, I'd have been dead."[36] They took a jittery pause inside the doorway, and Macko asked, "Why did you grab me?" Martin answered, "Dude, I don't know." Then, with his face just inches away, Macko looked Martin in the eye and said, "Doc, you just saved my life!"

Still, they needed to get out that door and over to the Vet building. "We gotta get over there. If someone's gonna get hit, it'll be over by the lieutenant," said Martin. "If we're not dead yet, we're not dying tonight." They gathered themselves and charged out the door to cross about sixty yards of open courtyard, exposed to enemy fire. "It was crazy. There were tracers all over the sky. An explosion lit up the courtyard and debris went flying," Martin recalls. "I was running as best I could, but weighed down with gear and with my rifle in both hands, I was worried I'd trip. When I looked at the ground there were puffs of dust, bullet strikes at our feet. For some reason, in the middle of all that I remember seeing a little child's shoe in a heap of trash."[37] Through the chaos, they made it across and after a few more close calls, Doc Martin and the radio arrived safely at the point-of-friction on the rooftop.

Combat vets say firefights have a rhythm, a syncopation of violence that can be understood by those with experience. About 10 or 15 minutes after the initial spasm, 1st Platoon could tell the engagement was tapering off. They had fended off the initial assault, reinforced their positions, and called for mortar support. "We had a little time to breathe," recalls Luis Maxwell. "We made sure we had our geometries, interlocking fires."[38] By that time, illumination rounds from Gannon were bathing streets and alleyways in their harsh light, stealing away the shadows where the enemy could hide. While desultory firing continued from the city, the insurgents began to withdraw.

As the night grew quiet, the Marines assessed their status. No one had been hit, but only by the thinnest of margins. The concentrated enemy fire had literally eaten away at the crude rooftop bunkers, shredding the outer layer of sandbags and gouging into the timbers and ballistic glass. "After the fight, there were dozens of bullet impacts in our glass," recalls Derrick Herndon. "We couldn't see through it anymore."[39] As soon as the shooting stopped, the Marines set about rebuilding their posts, hauling up new sandbags from below and getting ready for whatever would come next.

Clearly, the attackers had been of a different caliber. And under the withering barrage, some had come close to penetrating into the compound, which would have been disastrous. "These guys knew what they were doing," says Chris Reith. "With their intensity of fires, their use of plunging fire from MGs, they were obviously a better-trained enemy."[40]

Months before, Brummond and 1st Platoon had taken on the project of improving the ING compound's defenses, so the lieutenant was justifiably proud of his men's performance on August 12th. "It was Sergeant Reith and the squad leaders, Heath Mitchell in 1st, Luis Maxwell with 2nd, and Will Marconi in 3rd Squad, who had made the right preparations, who made the difference." Still, the ING was a known vulnerability, protruding into the city as it did. "That south side especially kept me up at night," Brummond recalls.[41]

Everyone sensed there were more dangers coming. With the end of the deployment excruciatingly close, they would have to stay razor sharp if they wanted to get home in one piece. "I consider that night as the beginning of AQI's push," explains Brummond. "The foreign fighters were massing their forces in Husaybah, gearing up for something ... and we knew they had us under close observation."[42]

Two meaningful artifacts of the 12 August 2005 firefight remain today. The bullet-scarred ballistic glass from the rooftop bunker that protected Lance Corporals Butcher, Herndon, Habay, and others from a hail of hostile fire, is now displayed at the 3/2's headquarters on Camp Lejeune. The other artifact is more significant in the long run. Chad Martin, the corpsman with the Texas swagger, and Pete Macko with his brash New York accent, who at first annoyed the hell out of each other, are now lifelong friends, bound together forever in a moment of fear and fire overcome.

See **bastardsandbrothers.com** for notes, photos, maps, etc.

27. VENGEANCE

Even with the deployment drawing to a close, 3/2 continued to apply pressure on the enemy. Day and night, elements of Kilo Company and the mobile assault platoons launched from Camp AQ and ranged across the AO, conducting raids and looking for signs of insurgent presence. By this time, both Kilo and WarPig were experienced raid forces using refined tactics, techniques, and procedures.

The pre-dawn raid described in the opening chapter was a typical, if dramatic, mission during this time-frame. On that night, 17 August 2005, Kilo Company's 1st Platoon was the designated raid force, led by First Lieutenant Bullock. "When word came that one of our top HVIs had popped up, we were the ones to go," says Bullock.[1] The platoon quickly assembled and briefed up on the objective; a notorious but elusive bomb-maker. Highlighting the target's importance, a Predator UAV would provide real-time support overhead.

The platoon moved by vehicle to an insert point about a kilometer from the town, dismounted, then patrolled stealthily into the objective. Bullock remembers it was quiet as they reached the target and set up an outer cordon to isolate the house. Other Marines, Joe Poulter and Buddy Miller among them, stacked outside and placed a breaching charge. "We normally used extra C4," says Bullock, "to ensure the breach and increase the shock effect. It definitely worked that night."[2] Breach and entry happened without a hitch and the Marines quickly flooded the house.

But as Miller and Poulter went up a stairway to the roof, things suddenly went sideways. Stepping onto the roof first, Miller spotted a man hunched to his left and stepped towards him, gesturing for him to get down. Instead, the man stood up. Even in the dark, Miller could sense his angry defiance. "He was glaring at me, like he was boring holes in my eyes."[3] Closing the distance, Miller grabbed the man's shirt and tried to force him down. That started a dangerous dance:

> *He pulled back, grabbing my left wrist with one hand and my rifle barrel with the other... I hit him in the face with my fist, but he didn't go down. He was bigger than me and stocky. Then he lowered his head and was swinging wildly at me, pulling on the rifle, and moving forward. I kept both hands on my weapon trying to pull it from his grip. We ended up against the low wall at the edge of the roof, and he almost pushed me off.*
>
> **—Buddy Miller**[4]

Meanwhile, Poulter rushed over and grabbed the man from behind, trying to pin his arms back. Now the three men were locked in an adrenaline-fired struggle to control a lethal weapon. Miller finally snatched his rifle free but tripped and went down to one knee. From just six feet away he brought his muzzle up but hesitated, worried about hitting Poulter. Then he saw a good angle and aimed in. "I shot the guy in his left shoulder, high up," he describes.[5]

The shot toppled both men over onto the rooftop. "When Miller fired I was still on the guy's back," says Poulter. "He fell over backwards, right on top of me. For a second I thought I'd been hit too. There was blood on me, but it wasn't mine. There was a woman up there too, and she started screaming and wouldn't stop."[6]

By this time, Lieutenant Bullock and other Marines had come up and were trying to sort through the commotion. Back in the battalion COC, staff officers were clamoring for updates. They'd watched the struggle unfold on the Predator's live video feed and wanted to know what had happened. Captain James Keller in the ops section feared the worst. "At first it looked like a Marine had gone off the roof," he remembers.[7]

Details became clear moments later. Both Poulter and Miller were unhurt. The wounded man was positively identified as the notorious bombmaker, making the mission a success. But disaster had been narrowly avoided. The insurgent had indeed tried to take Miller's rifle and had almost thrown him off the roof. Miller's deliberate shot to the man's shoulder was actually a restrained response to a deadly threat.

Furthermore, the Marines found a belt-fed machine gun on the roof, loaded with black-tipped armor-piercing rounds and aimed directly at the stairway. The weapon could have shredded any Marine coming up the stairs, but for some reason the insurgent hadn't fired it. "I think our breaching charge rattled him," says Bullock. "Miller and Poulter had just enough time to get up there before he could get behind the gun."[8]

After the shooting, a corpsman tended to the wounded bombmaker while Bullock called for a CASEVAC bird. Because of other threats in the area, however, they would need to evacuate him by vehicle. Within minutes the platoon pulled out of the house, taking the captured bombmaker with them as they exfiltrated back to the insert point where they mounted up and drove back to Camp AQ.

On the ride back, Miller was uncharacteristically quiet. He was doing some soul searching. "I was trying to make sense of what had happened," he says. "Why did that guy fight with his hands when he had a machine-gun? It didn't add up. I've thought about it many times since. I don't think the breaching charge explains it . . . It felt like someone, a guardian angel, was protecting me that night."[9]

When the platoon returned to base, Captain Ieva went out to meet them. He'd monitored the video feed and radio calls, so knew it had been an intense mission. He also knew he needed to bring Bullock into the ops center to explain what had happened on the roof. The capture of an HVI, the chaotic rooftop struggle, and a detainee with a gunshot wound had generated lots of questions.

As he emerged from the COC, Ieva could see Bullock and several of his men gathered behind a Humvee. He was conducting an immediate post-mission debrief, according to the guidelines Ieva himself had set. "That was part of our SOP," says Ieva. But as the captain approached, his lieutenant held him off. "Bullock held up his hand, and told me, 'Sir, I'll be right with you, I'm conducting my debrief.' I was a little put off but couldn't get too mad. He was following my own directions. He was being a professional, taking care of business and making sure his men were OK. I wanted to honor that."[10] As he waited, Captain Ieva scanned across the Marines' faces and observed their demeanor:

These were hardened warriors who'd seen a lot and done a lot. And they were wound pretty tight. You could see it in their eyes, how they carried themselves. That moment drove home to me that I needed to take steps, conscious efforts, to prepare them for redeployment. They needed to be ready to leave the war behind, to return back to their families and back into the world.

—Chris Ieva[11]

ZARQAWI IS LOOKING AT US

By mid-August 2005, 3/2 had begun the relief-in-place (RIP) with the next unit to assume responsibility for Al-Qaim, 3rd Battalion, 6th Marines. The 3/6 advance team was already doing right-seat, left-seat missions to get a feel for the AO. They were learning quickly and would soon be mounting missions of their own.

Other personnel were also keenly interested in what was going on in the district. Chris Reith remembers receiving an interesting visitor one day, probably just after the 12 August firefight. "This guy was brought out to the ING, out to one of the forward posts," he recalls. "He had a beard, just a pistol, and wore old-style desert tri-color cammies." Reith gave him a quick rundown of recent attacks and what the Marines faced every day. "The guy was cool and collected. He was there to get eyes on the city." But when he started talking about actually entering Husaybah, Reith was alarmed. The visitor had no security detail, just an interpreter. "He started talking about walking over to the bank, and I tried to talk him out of it." Undeterred by the sergeant's warnings, the two enigmatic figures left ING and slipped into the city. "I didn't see when they came back," says Reith.[12]

Another intriguing incident occurred during this timeframe illustrating how uncertain the situation was and the difficulty of sorting out who was who in a confusing battlespace where various shadowy actors were operating. According to recollections of Marines in India Company, one day they received reports of an unidentified armed "technical" vehicle* moving around in the area outside Husaybah. Marine attack helicopters soon spotted the truck and one of the pilots remembers the encounter:

> *I look down and see a white pickup with an MG mounted in it. It's a technical. They weren't reacting to us at all, which was kinda weird. We called it in ... Finally, we got word back, 'go ahead and take it out'. So we [attacked] with a Hellfire. The missile went right through the truck, out the other side and blew up in the dirt. Didn't kill anyone. Then the guys got out and ran off. My wingman re-attacked with a TOW, and that blew it up, but the whole time the situation didn't seem normal.*
>
> **—Steve Held**[13]

The next day, a call came into Camp Gannon. As Mike Hodd relates, "Our tribal source called in and complained, [saying] 'Hey you blew up our truck that your guys gave me!'"[14] Where the truck came from is open to speculation, but clearly other coalition forces and agencies were providing some kind of support to the Albu Mahal but had not yet worked out effective coordination and identification procedures.

---

* Multiple Marines at Camp Gannon. Irregular forces in the Middle East, Central Asia and Africa frequently mount heavy machine-guns or other large weapons in the bed of a pickup or light truck. Such vehicles are commonly known as "technicals."

Additionally, based on the observations of the Marines at Gannon, Husaybah was attracting more attention from the special mission operators of TF 714. On some nights they would hear the distinctive sound of a multi-engine AC-130 gunship orbiting over the city, then watch as an angry stream of tracers stabbed down from the darkness.[15] In at least one incident, India Company was given a heads up that unidentified other forces would be in their area. "One night we were directed not to fire to the east for any reason," remembers Derrick Herndon. "Then two or three 'Little Bird' helos came in flying low, right down Market Street."[16] Soon afterwards they flew back the other way, according to Herndon.

The targets that night can only be surmised, but several sources were aware that al-Qaeda in Iraq was gathering strength, preparing for something in Husaybah. According to Sheikh Kurdi, the Albu Mahal's on-the-ground leader, AQI had been "gathering all its fighters from other provinces" since they'd lost ground to the tribe in May. "A lot of them came to [the Al-Qaim] region."[17] India Company had received indications that hundreds of AQI fighters were massing, and one of their interpreters warned that local sources were telling him, "Zarqawi is looking at us. He's coming at us."[18]

This rise in enemy activity in late August was hardly a coincidence. Throughout the war, insurgent forces proved adept at exploiting "seams" in coalition plans, structures, and timetables. Turnovers between units constituted such a seam. Certainly, AQI had many ways to monitor and gather information on Marine operations, especially at Camp Gannon, and were aware a new unit was arriving. In retrospect, it seems obvious that AQI's leadership, perhaps Zarqawi himself, had waited for a chance to strike just as 3/2 started to hand off the AO.

For India Company, that handoff included sending Captain Diorio back to North Carolina a couple of weeks early as part of 3/2's advance team. Nominally, the team's role was to make necessary preparations to receive the battalion's main body as they returned to Lejeune, but Lieutenant Colonel Mundy and his staff also wanted to get Diorio home before his wife delivered their first child.[19]

As the heat waves subsided following another scorching day, probably late on 23 or 24 August, Captain Diorio passed command of India Company into the very capable hands of his executive officer and departed Camp Gannon[20]. For the next several days, he would be trapped in a frustrating no-man's land as he transited Camp AQ and Al-Asad, awaiting air transport to the States. No doubt he was anxious about his wife and unborn child, but it was also excruciating to leave his Marines, knowing the threats they still faced.

AQI'S SURGE

On August 25, 2005, the proverbial excrement hit the fan. Now years removed, it is difficult to piece together the exact sequence and timing of events. But the overall pattern of the story is clear. Foreign-led jihadist forces of AQI, accompanied by tribal allies in the local area, surged into Husaybah to seize control, intimidate the local populace, and take revenge on the defiant Albu Mahal.

This fight would go well beyond the gang-style shootouts of previous weeks, both in the numbers of combatants and the intensity of the combat. From Marine sources, they estimated that several hundred AQI fighters were involved. With typical exaggeration (sometimes called "Iraqi math"), the Mahalawis talked of defending against "thousands." But there is no doubt the Hamza militia was heavily outnumbered and outgunned. As Sheikh Sabah, who was in Jordan at the time, later recounted:

> *On Thursday night [25 Aug], al-Qaeda attacked Husaybah. My tribe had 65 armed men. And there were about 4,000–5,000 of them [AQI]. They were stationed in Karabilah and Ramana near the Syrian Border, and they were attacking Al-Qaim [i.e. Husaybah] from all directions... Most were of foreign, Arab nationalities.*
>
> —**Sheikh Sabah**[21]

While the sheikh's math on enemy forces is dubious, the number of Albu Mahal fighters he cites correlates closely with a first-hand source*. With only around 60 armed men in Husaybah, the Hamza militia faced an overwhelming force.

Sometime that same day, most likely after dark, a convoy of TF 714 vehicles was making its way towards the Syrian border. Based on the recollections of 3/2 Marines and other limited information, the special operators were headed to Camp Gannon, from where they would launch a direct action raid in the area. Given their mission profile and the situation at the time, they had probably identified a key AQI target, perhaps several, in or near Husaybah.

But they never got the chance to execute. Just a few miles from Gannon, one of their specialized armored vehicles struck

---

* One of the original Hamza militia leaders was Mukhlis Shadhan Ibrahim al-Mahalawi who was evidently in Husaybah during the August battle. "We were 68 individuals fighting the terrorists," he stated in his interview in Awakening, Vol IIIA. This closely matches the "65 men" mentioned by Sheikh Sabah.

an IED or anti-tank mine with devastating effect.[22] Several men were killed and others seriously hurt. The mission was called off and all effort turned to evacuating the wounded. According to Department of Defense announcements, Sergeant First Class Trevor Diesing, and Master Sergeant Ivica Jerak, assigned to the U.S. Army Special Operations Command, and Corporal Timothy Shea, of the 75th Ranger Regiment, were killed in action on 25 August. A fourth man, Sergeant First Class Obediah Kolath, also with Special Operations Command, died of his injuries three days later.[23]

Whether their mission, if executed, could have changed the course of subsequent events can only be guessed at. A successful SOF strike against AQI leadership at that particular juncture may have disrupted their plans. But given the numbers of enemy fighters massing in the area, it seems more likely the operators would have run into a buzzsaw of determined opposition, generating even more U.S. casualties.

STREET FIGHT

As the sun came up on 26 August 2005, AQI's forces in Husaybah were advancing on the Albu Mahal-controlled blocks from the west, north, and east.[24] There are no first-hand accounts of this fighting, but street-level violence between irregular forces follows typical patterns. Armed men cluster at the street corners, sheltering behind buildings and cars until one or two rush forward. In Husaybah, black-clad jihadists would have been at the front of the attacking forces, firing RPGs and light machine-guns. Those on the defensive end usually fire a few rounds then flee before they can be cut off. But when no retreat is possible, especially if men are defending their homes and families, the fight gets vicious.

From Camp Gannon on the west end of town, the Marines could plainly hear the rattle of small arms fire and the booms of RPG launches echoing across the city. Obviously this was more than a skirmish. The Marines were taking fire as well. In several incidents starting early that morning, insurgents fired at the ING, Trash OP, and posts at Gannon. Sometimes black-clad fighters were spotted darting down the alleys a few blocks away.[25] It seems AQI had enough forces on hand to make a concerted push into the center of Husaybah while also engaging India Company, probably to keep them occupied and out of the fight.

Meanwhile panicked calls cascaded into Camp Gannon from Hamza militia contacts and other sources among the Albu Mahal. The tribe was asking for help against an overwhelming enemy.[26] Some India Marines wanted to enter the city, knowing that the locals they had been tentatively supporting were now under assault. But several factors made that an unworkable option.

For one, the RIP process had already begun and the company's ability to launch an ad-hoc offensive action was impaired. Additionally, there were strong indications that AQI was planning another attack on Camp Gannon. "We had reports that AQI knew that certain posts were vulnerable and were taking surveillance photos," Hodd remembers. "They were developing thorough intel on us."[27] Given the close assault of the ING just two weeks before, and of course April's triple suicide attack, such reports kept India focused on repelling any threats.

Finally, without knowing exactly where the AQI forces were in relation to the "good guys", pushing Marines into the city would only put them at high risk with little prospect of success. In close urban terrain there was high potential for killing innocent civilians or destroying the very tribesmen they were trying to protect. All this was understood and discussed between India Company leaders, Mundy and the 3/2 staff, and with RCT-2 headquarters.[28] There would be no ground intervention. Looking back, the decision not to launch India Company or another element of 3/2 into Husaybah at that time makes sense.

CLEARED HOT

There were other measures at hand, however. As the fighting intensified through the day, one of the Marine's most reliable local sources, the East End Lady, called in to report a large group of AQI fighters, over one hundred, in an abandoned hotel in Husaybah. The Marines had nicknamed this prominent, two-story building the "yellow hotel." Cross-checking her information with other sources and working up the chain of command, it was confirmed that the building, with its 50-60 rooms, had been taken over by AQI as a safehouse and staging area. This presented a lucrative target. Diorio remembered that "Colonel Davis was involved. [Lieutenant Colonel] Mundy was involved. They were all read into what was going on. They were sending up the request for airstrikes."[29]

By this time, it was clear the Hamza militiamen were being mauled. "They [were] getting beat back," said Diorio, "pushed to one corner of the city, the southeast part of the city."[30] Meanwhile, their leader, Falzi, was barricaded in his house, besieged by AQI fighters. "The fighting [in Husaybah] was tooth and nail, [but] the Albu Mahals were losing," Colonel Davis told an interviewer. The situation called for fast, out-of-the-box thinking. "We were trying everything we could to keep them in the game," recalled Davis.[31] The RCT-2 Commander turned to his air officer, Major Lister, to coordinate an unconventional approach. As Lister recalls:

> *Colonel Davis brought me into his battle-cab, and there was this large guy in civvies and a full beard. The colonel asked me, "Can you conduct a strike on a target if you can't physically see the target or the aircraft?" I said, "Sure, that's a Type-2 or 3 strike." Then he says, "What if someone else calls in the target?" I said, "Yeah, we can do that".*
>
> —**Mark Lister**[32]

In a later interview, Davis elaborated. "We had Mahalawis in downtown Husaybah on cell phones, identifying locations." These so-called "muj JTACs" would call back to an ops center at Al-Asad…"talking to the OGA representative and relaying target information."[33] Lister fills out more details on how the strike was coordinated:

> *There's a 'muj JTAC', on the other end of the phone. He's talking to the bearded guy who speaks fluent Arabic. The muj gives bearded-guy the target, and [he] gives it to me. Then I put a two-seat FAC-Airborne [an F/A-18 jet with a digital targeting pod] over Husaybah… I could see the feed [from the pod] to the Rover [laptop]. I could see the right building and talked the jet onto the target. So, the targeting chain was: The muj JTAC on the ground, to the bearded guy, to me with the Rover, then to the F/A-18 with the pod."*
>
> —**Mark Lister** [34]

In the mid-afternoon, a formation of Marine F/A-18s flew high over Husaybah. With digital targeting data shared from Lister and the FAC-Airborne overhead to provide visual cues, they hit their aimpoints on the yellow hotel with devastating accuracy. After the first bombs hit, the unidentified ground observer continued reporting what he saw, providing first-hand battle-damage assessment (BDA).[35]

"The bearded guy was still talking to him after the bombs hit," says Lister. "The observer reported more AQI in or near the hotel, and I could see and confirm everything on my screen." The F/A-18s pulled around for more attack runs, launching more guided bombs, along with Maverick missiles and 5-inch unguided rockets to kill as many "squirters" as possible. The estimated toll was 40-50 enemy fighters killed from the air.[36]

The strike on the yellow hotel also laid down a marker. For everyone in Husaybah, "It was obvious that the Albu Mahal had forward eyes that were working for the coalition," explained Diorio. "[AQI] couldn't blend in anymore, because the locals could tell them apart and the locals were giving up information on them."[37] Over the next few days, the same unconventional targeting methods would be used several times to hit concentrations of AQI in and around Husaybah. "That [was] definitely unorthodox," said Davis, while adding ... "To ensure that we were always within the ROE, I had a lawyer next to me for every targeting decision."[38]

DESPERATION

27 August—The foreign muj came in and are currently murdering everyone in town. Bullets are impacting all over our base. It's total chaos... Lots of close calls for me in the last few days.

—Chris Nothstine[39]

Despite losses in the air strike from the previous day, AQI continued advancing through Husaybah, squeezing the Albu Mahal and Hamza militia into a smaller and smaller sector.[40] Meanwhile, insurgents continued to trade fire with Marine positions overlooking the western part of the city. India Company and its attachments fired back whenever they had a clear target and monitored the situation as best they could, fully expecting some kind of larger attack. A steady stream of calls came in from locals reporting the ongoing violence and asking for help.

For men manning the posts, it wasn't clear what exactly was happening, but they knew it wasn't good. "We heard the foreign fighters were cutting heads off in town," remembers Pete Macko. "One night we saw an AA gun [heavy machine gun] open up, but not at us. I looked at Mitchell and said, "What are we gonna do when they turn that thing on us?"[41] The combat diary of Jordan Bogart, a corporal and vehicle commander with WarPig 1, shows another grunt's-eye view of how the Marines at Gannon understood developments in Husaybah and the danger they were still under:

27 August—I'm out at BP Harman [i.e., Trash OP] for a change. There has been constant fighting in the city... We got a report this morning that the local muj has been defeated and the entire city now belongs to the foreign fighters. And their next move is to try and take over BP Harman. We have been doing a good deal of fighting as well. I was in the turret of the Mk19 truck and had a bunch of bullets whizz by my face, and returned fire into a tower, most likely killing the men shooting at me. And this morning we took fire from another building. I again returned fire. Am not sure if anyone was killed, but we have not received anything from that spot since. It is now 2pm and all we can hear is machine-gun fire and explosions coming from the city. Yesterday we had F-18 Hornets drop 500-pound bombs in the city on specific targets. This place went from being the best it has been in two years to the worst it ever was in a matter of days.

—Jordan Bogart[42]

More airstrikes were conducted on 27 August and on the next several days whenever a suitable AQI target could be identified.[43] At the street-level these aerial interventions made little difference, however. The jihadists and their tribal allies pushed the Mahalawis back, and tales of murderous atrocities accompanied their assault. "One time a mom called in," remembers Mike Hodd. "She was saying 'help us! Help us!' and said they'd just killed her 16-year-old son."[44]

There is no direct record of the fighting or the barbarities of the jihadists, but members of the tribe have since told of murder, rape, and torture. Five years later, Sheikh Sabah still had trouble discussing such things with interviewers. "It was a very difficult time," he expressed. "It really hurts me too much for me to speak about it."[45] In those 2010 interviews, the Mahalawis mention one detail that shows the desperation of their struggle. AQI apparently knew where the key tribesmen lived and specifically targeted their homes. According to Sheikh Kurdi, "al-Qaeda blew up the houses of 41 Albu Mahal tribesmen, using propane tanks."[46] Most of these residences were probably unoccupied, but perhaps not all.

Any of the tribesmen's family members captured were subject to heinous treatment. "Al Qaeda kidnapped a lot of old people and tortured them, because they were from the Albu Mahal tribe," said Ahmad Khalaf. "One of these old guys was my father. He was more than 73 years old and because I am his son, they took out one of his eyes."[47]

Reports from U.S. journalists (filed from Baghdad) confirm AQI's brutality in Husaybah and provide indirect reflections of the ugly realities. Call-in sources told of men being executed in the city center by Zarqawi's fighters and described the bullet-riddled body of a young woman with a sign reading "a prostitute who was punished." Other stories from that timeframe report AQI-aligned insurgents kidnapping and killing over thirty Albu Mahal members.[48]

As they look back and remember those turbulent days, many 3/2 Marines, those with a limited perspective on the situation and those with more detailed knowledge, express frustration at not being able to do more to help the tribe withstand AQI's onslaught. Especially for those in India Company, they were watching as the progress they had made with the Albu Mahal and the locals unraveled. Today some are philosophical, knowing the practical options were limited. Others regret being "held back."[49]

By 28 August 2005, the battle was essentially over. In the southeast corner of the city, the Albu Mahal were holding onto a small area, according to briefing slides from that time. But the tribe was evacuating any family members that had not fled already. Accompanying them was a general exodus of civilians leaving Husaybah to get away from the jihadist spree of killings and violence. Marine helicopter crews overhead could see caravans of civilian vehicles leaving the city.[50]

At this juncture, a crucial event occurred that had a large effect on both Sunni tribal leaders across Iraq and high-level coalition decision-makers. Just after the sun rose, probably on 28 August, Marines on watch at Trash OP spotted movement through the early morning haze. From the north edge of the city a group of military-aged males walked out towards them, without weapons, some bearing ragged flags of truce.[51]

Pete Macko, who had nearly been shot at the ING compound just two weeks before, held his fire as the men approached. "It was weird. First one guy came down the path towards us. Then more guys came, all unarmed military-aged males. Some had white flags," remembers Macko. "Someone fired a warning shot [to halt them], and we called it into the COC. We didn't know what to do at first. The HET guys and terps came out to find out what they wanted."[52] The men were members of the Hamza militia, disheveled and exhausted after days of fighting. Meanwhile, their leader, Falzi, was calling in saying, "These are my people; please help them."[53]

This was unprecedented and Lieutenant Hodd, the acting company commander, had to make a quick decision. With more clusters of men approaching the OP, he directed the Marines there to allow them inside the outer HESCO perimeter.[54] Eyewitness accounts vary on the numbers that came, but it was somewhere between 30 to 60 men. With the obvious danger of a suicide bomber hiding among them, they were searched, restrained, and remained under hyper-vigilant Marine eyes while they were at Trash OP. Soon AAVs drove out and they were shuttled over to Gannon, then processed as if they were detainees. The Marines who guarded them and the corpsmen who gave them medical attention say they were haggard, but friendly, and immensely grateful for being rescued.[55]

A flurry of communications ensued as Hodd coordinated with battalion and the 3/2 staff worked the issue with RCT-2. The decision was passed down to let the Hamza fighters stay and recuperate within Marine lines for a short time. There were stringent coalition rules for keeping detained Iraqi personnel at a forward base and violating them could have serious repercussions. Normally, detainees held at Gannon were transferred within 24 hours to the battalion's certified detention facility at Camp AQ. But as these men had not been actually detained for hostile acts, they fell into a gray area. Several layers of command considered courses of action, and eventually Hodd was directed to release them and facilitate their evacuation.[56]

At this time, the lieutenant was also authorized to provide some concrete support for the tribe. Stored in Camp Gannon's armory were several thousand rounds of 7.62x39mm ammunition, which could only be used in AK-style weapons. It was from captured insurgent arms caches or part of leftover Border Guard or ING stocks. With approval from above, India Company prepared to transfer this cache of ammo to the Albu Mahal. While it came too late to matter in Husaybah, it could help the Mahalawis defend themselves from further AQI assaults.[57]

By then the Marines were aware that many Albu Mahal refugees from Husaybah had fled to the small desert community of Akashat, about 75 miles to the southwest, where they were being sheltered by kinsmen living there. A traditional stronghold of the Mahalawis, Akashat became the natural fallback position for displaced families and defeated tribal fighters. This remote, sand-blown refuge would soon figure prominently in the defiant tribe's ongoing saga.

A few hours after midnight on 29 August, a convoy of AAVs and guntrucks left Camp Gannon and navigated carefully through the terrain a few miles outside Husaybah. Huddled in the back of the AAVs were the Hamza militiamen, with India Marines alongside them. In his journal, Nothstine wrote a brief account of the mission. "[We picked up] a bunch of Phalsee's [Falzi's] men. Then we drove out to the desert south of the city. We fed, watered, gave them free smokes ... and 3,000 rounds."[58]

Luis Maxwell remembers a few more details. "They looked like they'd been through hell, but they were super friendly to us," he says. "One guy spoke a little English and was smiling, pointing at our weapons and naming them."[59]

Upon reaching a designated point, the Marines stopped, set up security, then waited. Sitting there in the dark, the grunts were understandably a little tense. "Prindle was our SAW gunner in back of the trac," recalls Maxwell. "I told him, 'Hey if anything happens, don't go cyclic' [i.e., uncontrolled fire]."[60] Soon a few vehicles appeared, probably Toyota pickup trucks. Evidently they came from the south, from the direction of Akashat. Terse greetings were exchanged in the dark and India Company's erstwhile guests were turned over to their fellow tribesmen along with the much-needed ammunition. At a nameless, featureless point in the desert, combat-tested Marines of 3/2 and battle-worn Hamza fighters wished each other well, then parted ways, melting back into the night.

While these events occurred in tragic circumstances, they formed a moment that many Marines and other informed observers now believe was an historic inflection point. For the first time in the Iraq War, a prominent Sunni tribe, which just a year before had been an active part of the insurgency, was now fighting tooth-and-claw against AQI and openly asking for help from the Marines and the coalition. To Frank Diorio, it was amazing that the Mahalawis acknowledged India Company "as their rescuers, in broad daylight with their hands up ... That was the point where the entire city, the foreign fighters, AQIZ, saw the Albu Mahals say, 'The Marines are our help.'"[61]

LAST BLOOD

The overall situation in Al-Qaim remained dire, however. Al-Qaeda in Iraq had gathered fighters from across Anbar and beyond, flooding them into the district. Now they had seized Husaybah and re-infested Sadah, New Ubaydi, and other areas as well. For 3/2, the most dangerous next step the enemy could take would be to mount another large-scale attack on Camp Gannon.[62] There were credible indicators that foreign fighters were planning to do just that, and the Marines were taking every possible measure to prepare.

But the concentration of enemy forces also presented opportunities. In the farm fields northeast of Husaybah was a large, ornate residence and associated compound. The Marines called it the "mansion" or "palace", and 3/2 had reconnoitered it before without incident. Now it became a focus of attention all the way up the chain of command.[63] As fighting in the city raged, a local Iraqi source had called in claiming "hundreds" of foreign fighters were staying there.[64] Another lucrative air target had emerged.

At Al-Asad, Major Lister began the coordination work for an RCT-controlled airstrike. He soon became aware of other sources indicating that one of Zarqawi's main lieutenants, or emirs, was at the mansion. There was also speculation that

Zarqawi himself might be there. Watching a drone feed of the target, Lister could see a well-organized group of guards, patrolling inside and outside the perimeter. It was a strong sign that someone important in AQI's hierarchy was inside.

Just after midnight on 30 August, four GPS-guided bombs hit the mansion, collapsing most of the structure in on itself. Follow-on strikes delivered still more precision weapons, until the building was assessed as totally destroyed. Dozens of AQI fighters were probably killed, never seeing the aircraft that delivered the bombs.[65]

Just two days later, another group of enemy personnel attracted unwanted attention. On September 1, 2005, Corporal Anthony Cunha of Reaper 1 was in a dusty hide site just south of Husaybah. He was on a joint mission with a newly arrived scout-sniper team looking for enemy activity. Early that morning they observed multiple armed men, dressed in all black, entering and exiting the defunct train station on the south edge of Husaybah.

This was a known arms cache location, and as the snipers watched from over a mile away, the insurgents set up security and went into one of the rusty train cars. "Through the spotting scope we could see guys loading crates of some type," remembers Cunha. "We also noticed one of them was carrying an M249 SAW, and others had M-16s."[66] Cunha and everyone else on the mission were acutely aware that only weeks before, snipers from 3/25 had been ambushed and insurgents had taken their weapons.

The scout-snipers called in the activity, requesting an airstrike. It took time and further coordination up the chain to get the strike OK'd, probably due to collateral damage concerns. The snipers insisted they had eyes-on the target, though, and eventually the strike was approved. Around midday, F/A-18s checked in on-station and dropped multiple bombs. Cunha watched as guided weapons slammed into the train station and blasted the nearby locomotive and railroad cars. Over 20 enemy fighters were assessed as killed.[67]

Did the U.S. weapons observed really come from 3/25? Were those insurgents somehow connected to the snipers killed in Haditha? There was no way to tell, but Cunha and others on the mission felt they'd struck a blow on behalf of their Marine brothers lost. The 1 September mission was 3/2's last lethal shot against AQI, the murderous, implacable enemy they'd fought for seven long months, one last measure of vengeance delivered against the black-shrouded killers.

See **bastardsandbrothers.com** for notes, photos, maps, etc.

28. REDEPLOYMENT

The first days of September seemed to lengthen for the men of 3/2. Now their replacements were on the ground in full force, taking the lead on missions. To Staff Sergeant Timothy Hanson from Kilo Company, they seemed to have their act together. "It's good to see a unit coming in that has a lot of experience," Hanson told a reporter.[1] But to Lance Corporal Jeff Maniscalco, the new guys seemed a little jumpy. "They were definitely nervous, you could tell," he recalls. "Then again, we were probably just like that seven months before."[2]

Nervousness was warranted, however. On 1 September, at almost the same time that Reaper 1 was calling in airstrikes outside Husaybah, Marines from 3/2's Lima Company traded shots with insurgents near Al-Qaim town. The following day they received mortar fire in the same vicinity. In a raid three days later, WarPig found and destroyed a suspected IED shop, and several cars hidden under a farmer's haystacks. Locals claimed insurgents planned to convert them into SVBIEDs for use against the Americans. On 5 September, a convoy was hit by small arms fire just outside Camp Gannon, followed by yet another mortar attack against the camp itself.[3]

While no Marines were hurt, these were vivid reminders

that danger still lurked. "I still felt like anything could happen," says Maniscalco. "A mortar or rocket attack. Someone trying to hit the main gate or get inside the wire."[4]

For those at Camp Gannon, each of their final days was fraught with tension and a strange mix of emotions. They'd lived through hell, been attacked hundreds of times, survived a storm of suicide bombers, and through it all had forged unbreakable bonds. For some, knowing they were leaving it behind brought an odd sadness. The night before they were due to pull out, Sergeant Chris Reith and Lieutenant Ryan Brummond stood together on a post. "We were looking at a clear desert sky," recalls Reith. "I was going home to my wife and a new baby daughter I'd never seen. But I said to him, 'I don't want to go back'. And he said, 'Yeah, I know what you mean'".[5]

The next day, September 6th, Lieutenant Hodd organized the convoy that would take most of India Company back to Camp AQ. Marines from 3/6 had already taken charge. Gannon and Husaybah were their responsibility now. In a moment of reflection, Hodd looked around the dusty camp where so much had happened. "I spotted one of our squad leaders, Roy Mitros. He was leaner and meaner with dust all over him, but he was the same dedicated Marine. A warrior. And we were all dirty and haggard, just like those Baker Company Marines seven months before. But we were just as professional as when we showed up. Now even more so."[6]

As men started boarding a line of 7-ton trucks and other vehicles, Corporal Marlon Garcia, chief of the 81mm mortar section, gathered his team. He pulled out the Cuban cigars First Sergeant Brazeal had presented to Hellfire section months before, after their well-aimed counterfire had destroyed an enemy mortar team:

> *Standing by the mortar pits I told them, "We've been through the shit together, we've fought for each other. We're leaving part of our souls here. Now we are bound as brothers for life." We were still gathered together when we started to take small arms fire. That kind of ruined the moment. We went to condition 1, rifles locked and loaded. Somebody said, "I just wanna go home!" But we had to shift back, get ready for a fight.*
>
> —**Marlon Garcia**[7]

As men boarded the vehicles and scattered shots zipped overhead, a strange sound rose over the noise. A Marine from 3/6 was playing Scottish bagpipes, honoring the departing warriors with soulful, lingering strains. "That was totally motivating," recalls Garcia. The long ordeal was almost over.

But not quite.

The enemy had one more parting shot for India Company. Just a short distance from the south ECP and still within sight of Gannon, an up-armored Humvee struck a buried mine or IED. The detonation tore off a front wheel. No one was seriously hurt, but the vehicle had to be recovered, disrupting the entire movement. To the Marines' great frustration, they turned around and re-entered Camp Gannon.

After one last restless night at the edge of a hostile city, they reformed the convoy the next day. Departure went smoothly this time and after another dusty ride they arrived at Camp Al-Qaim. For men who'd been under constant threat, the larger base seemed like a different world. "Camp AQ was strange for us," remembers Reith. "Everyone was wearing clean cammies, were well fed, and had their weapons in condition 3 (chamber empty)."[8]

All battalion missions were soon turned over to 3/6 and in those last days Lieutenant Colonel Mundy met with each of his companies. The CO thanked his men, expressed his great pride in them, and gave a rundown of all they'd accomplished. While there is no record of those talks, he shared similar thoughts in his final phone message to the families back home:

> *I want to try to express to the families and friends of Marines and Sailors of 3/2 just how proud I am of your men. They have operated and fought in one of, if not the, toughest areas in the Al-Anbar Province. This province is also the worst in the country by far, and the enemy your men have faced daily are the hardest of the hard core. We are fighting fanatical terrorists in this area and we have found evidence of their presence through documents and weapons we've captured, and we've looked them in the face after we've killed them and they fought us. Abu Musab Zarqawi himself has slipped in and out of this area to rally his forces, usually because they have suffered another humiliating defeat at the hands of your men.*
>
> *It has been my privilege, and the highlight of my career to lead this battalion in combat in this area, and against this enemy. Nothing came easy to 3/2 out here. The success we enjoyed was possible because of the professionalism, hard work and proficiency of your Marines and Sailors. They were innovative in how we fought the enemy. They varied their routines. They learned from what the enemy did. They rehearsed, they prepared, they trained. They were vigilant. They lived up to the reputation of Marines who have fought long before us. And I hope you share my pride in what they have accomplished. They are U.S. Marines in every sense of the word, and I thank God I had the opportunity and honor to be their commanding officer.*
>
> *As of today, 3/2 will have turned over all missions to 3/6 and*

I wish them the very best in continuing the tough work ahead. India Company has now returned from Camp Gannon and over the next four days, 3/2 Marines and Sailors are moving from Al-Qaim to Al-Asad, staging for our eventual return home. I will remain here until the 10th, at which time responsibility for this area will be turned over to Lieutenant Colonel Alford, CO of 3/6. With that, this chapter of the Betio Bastards history closes, and we only have about one week to return home to all of you. Your men will return home carrying their heads high, and well they should. They're the best in the world. I look forward to seeing you again soon.

–**Tim Mundy,** transcribed from the recorded phone call

On 10 September 2005, the formal transfer of authority was held with a no-frills ceremony. Lieutenant Colonel Mundy presented the American flag to Lieutenant Colonel Alford and with it the formal responsibility for the AO. Most of the battalion had already helicoptered to Al-Asad, however, leaving in groups over the previous few days. Jeff Maniscalco recalls his helo ride out:

They left the back hatch of the chopper open as we took off... I was glad to be leaving but sad at what we all had experienced. Nobody really talked and I was thinking, "Thank God I made it, I hope I never have to go back!" I felt like I accomplished something good by not dying.

—**Jeff Maniscalco**[9]

Once at Al-Asad, they could enjoy the luxuries and had time to relax. "It was pretty chill," says Maniscalco. "You could walk around without your rifle."[10] Amazingly, there were stretches of green grass and Steve Sims remembers the exquisite feel of it under his bare feet. Even Camp Cupcake's enticements didn't satisfy for long, however. Everyone was impatient to get home. Getting military airlift out of Iraq was notoriously unreliable, more so than flying in, but most of 3/2 waited only a few days at Al-Asad before catching their flights out.

In Kilo Company, Captain Ieva and First Sergeant Gregory wanted to give their men a head start on transitioning from the war back to home and family. To aid that process, they held a short formation just before boarding the aircraft. Ieva stood and spoke briefly of warriors leaving the battlefield behind. "I wanted to prepare us symbolically and emotionally," he explains. An aviation squadron had erected a Japanese-style torii gateway by the flight line. "Before we boarded the plane, I had the company cross under it, like ancient Romans under an arch, a symbol of leaving the profane and crossing back into the sublime. I thought it might help."[11]

The return to Camp Lejeune worked in reverse of their deployment journey. Military cargo aircraft flew them to Kuwait where they boarded chartered airliners. The transatlantic flight included a refueling stop in Shannon, Ireland, where, to their surprise, airport pubs were open. For better or worse, the constraints of General Order 1 did not hold outside the U.S. Central Command's area, so drinking alcohol was allowed. Many 3/2 Marines recall overindulging in dark Irish ale, with predictably raucous results. Some remember nothing of their onward flight from Shannon.

The chartered airliners had staggered arrival times at MCAS Cherry Point, North Carolina, so the battalion did not arrive all at once. As each plane landed, the men transferred onto buses for the drive to Lejeune. Justin Randolph, a Private First Class in Kilo at the time, remembers that drive as "the longest bus ride of my life. I just wanted to get home."[12]

Unloading from the buses, each planeload of Marines hustled into the battalion area to turn in weapons and gear, then assembled on the manicured "quad" by the headquarters building. With minimal formality, they were brought to attention, saluted, then dismissed. There, at long last, they finally rushed into the arms of their waiting families and loved ones. For the battle-worn men, coming home meant picking their lives back up and refocusing on family, career decisions, and routine details. That transition wasn't always easy as they readjusted back to normal. There were many restless nights.

John Schneekloth was impatient to see his wife and hold the son he'd never seen but had to wait a few more days as they were staying with her parents out of state. Once he started his leave, he flew out to be with them. "When I finally got to hold Jacob for the first time he was five months old and was looking at me sort of like, 'Who is this guy?' and I was just smiling ear to ear." That moment began shifting his priorities. "I'd been through the gauntlet once and never regretted it but had new obligations at home. I decided to get out soon after that."[13]

For Chris Ieva, it was great to be back but there were ups and downs. "Suddenly I was back in my life," he relates. "My son, Fiori, who could barely walk when I left was now a full-fledged toddler and my wife was about to deliver our daughter, Alexandra. But I was uneasy having so much extra time on my hands. I felt I should be doing something all the time. My brain was still on overdrive, analyzing everything, thinking about the next deployment. I'd hear a helicopter and think about the nearest LZ. I was always switched on."[14]

Due to airlift issues, Lieutenant Colonel Mundy, Sergeant

Major Mennig, and a few other senior staff members returned a few days after the main body, arriving to very little fanfare. "I was met by my family, but our reunion was short because life goes on and my oldest daughter had a tennis game that afternoon," he remembers. Sitting in the bleachers watching a high school tennis match just hours after returning from Iraq, he had to make a sudden switch from combat commander to father:

> *"My son had a bad stomach ache, so I had to take him home," recalls Mundy. "When we pulled into the driveway I hurried to get him into the house. But just as I was getting him out of the car, he upchucked onto the seat, the driveway, and me! It was one of those 'Dad moments' that keeps you humble and was definitely a reality check that I was back to my life in the U.S. My neighbor, a good friend and also a battalion commander, was working on his lawn right next door. He couldn't help but see the humor and irony and said, 'Welcome home, war hero!*[15]

Chris Reith, like others who had been at Gannon, had a tougher adjustment period than most. "We only had about a week from being in combat to shopping at Walmart," he says. "When we went on post-deployment leave, I had guys calling me to check in from wherever they'd gone. More than a few mentioned it was strange to be back home, back with family, and missed being with the platoon and in Iraq."[16]

Upon their return from leave, the battalion began spinning up their training regime once more. But the effects of their recent experiences persisted. Down the street from the battalion area on Camp Lejeune, a weapons range was in use frequently. Even weeks after being home, and knowing there was no real threat, the sudden staccato flurries of small arms fire would prompt automatic flinch responses as Marines instinctively crouched for cover.

29. AWAKENINGS

As 3/2's battle-worn veterans focused on picking their lives back up and moving forward, they occasionally heard about events in western Anbar, but not in detail. Surely for some it seemed their efforts had been futile. Judging by the headlines, stability in Iraq was further away than ever.

For those leaving the service, the 2005 deployment would be the last of their military career. Those staying in geared up for yet another pump. Some, sent to other battle zones in Iraq or Afghanistan, would see even more intense action than they'd experienced during that spring and summer. No wonder, then, that most have not fully recognized the impact they had. But looking back these many years later, an objective eye can see that 3/2's fight for Al-Qaim set the stage for many successes that followed, successes that were built on their work and sacrifice.

HELL HOUNDS

As 3/2 left Al-Qaim, it was replaced by another battalion with a proud history. The 3rd Battalion, 6th Regiment (3/6) was dubbed "Teufelhunden" (hell hounds or devil dogs) by the Germans in World War I. This was their third deployment since 9/11. Commanded by Lieutenant Colonel Dale Alford, 3/6 had recently returned from the Taliban-infested eastern provinces of Afghanistan and were well-versed in counter-insurgency methods.

During India Company's last days at Camp Gannon, Alford traveled there to see the situation for himself. Joey Habay remembers when the incoming commander came into one of the bullet-scarred perimeter posts. At that point Husaybah had been overrun by AQI:

> *I was out on P8 with Butcher and Pele when the First Sergeant brought Lieutenant Colonel Alford out... I told him about all the attacks and how we'd usually get hit with small arms fire. Just then, three rounds hit the ballistic glass. Smack, smack, smack! We didn't even jump, and he just kinda looked at us. "Well don't let me stop you!" he said, and we started firing back with the 240.*
>
> —**Joey Habay**[1]

Alford and his staff had bold plans. He had already been to Al-Qaim in July for his pre-deployment survey and had talked about how 3/6 would operate in the AO. "We came up with a plan to move into [Husaybah], come hell or high water," said Alford. "I remember telling Colonel Davis, 'I'm moving into the city.' He [was] like, 'Alright big boy, we'll see you when you get back.'"[2]

But Alford would also have the combat power he needed to execute that plan. In the last part of 2005, more forces were plugged into RCT-2, including U.S. Army battalions as well as a brigade of Iraqi soldiers. In the spring, Colonel Davis had commanded just 3,200 personnel. By the fall of 2005, he could leverage a force of over 14,000.

This would have big impacts in Al-Qaim. All of 3/6's rifle companies would be available and the RCT could draw on others for large operations. Additionally, the new Iraqi Army was finally ready to play. The training, certification, and formation process had been gaining momentum. As 3/6 began its deployment, the Iraqi 1st Brigade of the 1st Division was assigned to Anbar and one of its battalions was sent to Al-Qaim.

AKASHAT

In the first days of September 2005, as 3/2 was turning over to 3/6, Lieutenant Colonel Starling from RCT-2 embarked on a unique mission. He boarded a helicopter bound for Camp Korean Village, the Marine base outside of Rutbah, 130 miles southwest of Al-Asad. Accompanying him was one of the bearded OGA men that were working behind the scenes in Anbar that summer.[3]

Their objective was to meet with a leader of the Albu Mahal, see what aid the tribe might need, and assess their willingness to officially side with the coalition and the Iraqi government. By this time, says Starling, "We'd gained a real understanding of the depth of the tribes and their influence." A good chunk of this understanding came via 3/2's backchannel contacts with the Hamza militia and the Albu Mahal. Now RCT-2 and higher levels of command were seeing that "whole tribes could be turned."[4]

The two Americans met with a personal representative of Sheikh Sabah. The leading topic of discussion was how to protect the tribe from further AQI depredations. At that point, many tribesmen and their families had fled to the dusty mining town of Akashat. There the tribe had set up a makeshift refugee camp to house hundreds of men, women, and children. They needed food, water, and other supplies to ease their suffering.

This was a critical moment. Certainly, the Mahalawis were in desperate straits, willing to make whatever deal they could to ensure their survival. But they had also decisively turned against the destructive vision of the jihadists and had already shown they would risk their own lives to fight AQI. From all available evidence, that discreet meeting led to the first officially-sanctioned battlefield cooperation between a Sunni tribe and the coalition.

After the meeting, things happened quickly. Starling arranged for convoys to take supplies and humanitarian aid out to Akashat, including engineers to dig a well. A security zone was established to prevent AQI from advancing on the town. With the open terrain and limited roads southwest of Husaybah, the zone could be patrolled from the air. "We under-promised and then over-delivered," says Starling.[5]

Very soon, perhaps just hours after the meeting, an Army Special Forces ODA team landed outside Akashat. This was Captain Calvert's ODA 584, with his mission to "make things better." They brought a medical team, set themselves up in an old clinic, and announced, "Anybody who needs medical care, line up!"[6] While the medics worked, other ODA members made contact with Albu Mahal sheikhs and Hamza militiamen. They found them willing to join forces with the American military and Iraqi government in some capacity. These were the first concrete steps towards forming a unique and ground-breaking unit.

The foundations for those steps had been laid far up the food chain. In this same timeframe, the Mahalawis were leveraging their own political connections. Representatives of the Albu Mahal and Albu Nimr tribes had met with Iraq's Minister of Defense, Sadun al-Dulaymi, about forming a Sunni-manned Iraqi Army unit to fight in Anbar, according to declassified documents. Members of the Hamza militia reportedly welcomed the idea.[7] Sheikh Sabah also described such a meeting with al-Dulaymi, stating, "I went to visit him in Baghdad. The U.S. Deputy Ambassador and the British Ambassador were there during the meeting . . . Within a week, the Americans and [our] trainees reached Akashat."[8]

On the coalition side, General Casey, Commander of MNFI, was also very involved in the discussions on forming a unit of Albu Mahal tribesmen. Davis recalls that Casey fully supported the initiative, describing it as "General Casey's baby."[9] The idea of working with the Albu Mahal and the effort to "flip" the tribe had finally gained high-level approval. On 15 September, General Casey and Defense Minister Dulaymi signed a Memorandum of Understanding (MOU) allowing the formation of a tribally-based unit in Al-Qaim.[10]

DESERT PROTECTORS

The Casey-Dulaymi memo effectively transformed the Hamza fighters into the first approved Sunni militia unit. They would be called the "Desert Protectors." The name was an oddity, implying some kind of border patrol function. But their implicit mission was to fight against Zarqawi's AQI and help secure the Al-Qaim area.

Today there is ongoing debate about the significance of the program, with some claiming it had negligible impact.[11] Others, however, point to its early successes and trace its long-term effects. To be sure, the Desert Protectors got off to a modest start. "This wasn't a big game changer at the time," recalls Davis.[12] Nevertheless, it was an important landmark.

Calvert and his ODA set up a recruiting and vetting process in Akashat and soon had the first batch of tribesmen ready for training. The first 20 to 40 men, only a platoon's worth, were flown to Habbaniyah for three weeks of rudimentary military training. "These guys were treated like rock stars, this first little platoon," recalled Major Adams.[13]

Soon more men became part of the Desert Protectors, nearly all from the Albu Mahal tribe. During this first phase, around 270 men were vetted, inducted into the Iraqi Security Forces, and put into a training pipeline. The unit did not officially fit into either the Iraqi Army or the Iraqi Police controlled by the Interior Ministry. Defense Minister Dulaymi described them as "neither fish nor fowl"[14]. Figuring out where and how to best utilize the newly-minted Desert Protectors, some of them clearly former insurgents, was a challenge.

"At that point we looked at what's the best way to employ these guys," recalled Calvert. The initial decision was to use some for so-called low-visibility reconnaissance operations and assign the rest to work alongside the Marines. Working as "scouts" they would bolster 3/6's area knowledge and help identify foreign fighters and other insurgents.[15]

TAKING IT BACK

While the Desert Protectors were being formed, bigger wheels were in motion. On October 1, 2005, 3/6 kicked off Operation Iron Fist with all companies clearing east to west through Sadah and the eastern sector of Karabilah, up to the large wadi. However, this was just one of several operations being sequenced along the Euphrates, to secure the upcoming Iraqi constitutional referendum on October 15th.

Operation River Gate, RCT-2's main priority at that time, was another large operation in the Haditha-Barwana area. It began a few days after Iron Fist and this time the objective was to seize and hold, not just conduct another sweep. To keep the RCT's operational focus, Colonel Davis had 3/6 hold position along the Emerald wadi while River Gate proceeded. "[Alford] would have probably taken all of Al-Qaim if I would have let him," Davis later recalled. "I said, 'You've got to slow your operation down ... I need you to phase this thing.'"[16]

Although 3/6 constrained its advance for the time being, it hardly remained inactive. Alford pushed units out of Camp AQ, establishing the first of several new platoon-sized outposts or battle positions. This was part of the plan to move closer to the population. Alford's Kilo Company, commanded by Captain Brendan Heatherman, established two outposts in Sadah. "The number one thing we needed to do," recalled Heatherman, "was [make] connections with the local populace ... We just went out and began talking with people."[17]

The battle positions would soon house Iraqi soldiers as well. Just as Iron Fist wrapped up, a battalion of the 1st Iraqi Brigade arrived at Al-Qaim.[18] Grunts and *jundis* began living and operating side-by-side in these bare-bones outposts. While most of the Iraqi soldiers were Shiites or Kurds, viewed by Sunnis with suspicion, their presence lent legitimacy while doubling or even tripling the number of troops available.

STEEL CURTAIN

The constitutional referendum was held on October 15, 2005, with a reported 22% of Anbar's eligible voters casting ballots. While still the lowest participation rate among Iraq's provinces, it was a vast improvement.[19] With the referendum wrapped up, the time was right for RCT-2 to turn its full attention to Al-Qaim.

By this time, AQI had basically occupied Husaybah, Karabilah, New Ubaydi, and outlying areas. During their assault in August, the jihadists hung Zarqawi's black and yellow banners along the streets and reportedly posted a sign on the entrance to Husaybah declaring "Welcome to the Islamic Republic of Qaim." Residents described AQI fighters roughly enforcing strict Islamic law, beating men for drinking alcohol, and burning CD stands and beauty parlors.[20] During the referendum, they placed cameras to record anyone trying to cast a ballot, effectively shutting down the vote in Al-Qaim.[21]

In the first days of November 2005, a massive task force began assembling, readying for the largest Marine Corps operation in Iraq since Second Fallujah. The force was built around 3/6 along with 2/1, temporarily assigned to RCT-2. More U.S. units were brought in, and all three battalions of the Iraqi Army's 1st Brigade were dedicated to the operation. All told, this eight-battalion force plus attachments numbered 2,500

U.S. Marines, sailors, and soldiers, joined by 1,000 Iraqi Army troops.*

Added to the mix would be about 120 newly-minted Desert Protectors. Just weeks after losing their battle against AQI and rival tribes, the Mahalawi tribesmen were coming back as a small, though significant, part of this force. But there was precious little time to fold them in. Captain Calvert and the ODA rushed to "explain to the units who these guys were . . . the benefits that they came with, and the possible side effects."

On the plus side, Calvert said they were "a tremendous asset . . . to have members of that city, members of that village with you. When you took an element of American and Iraqi Security Forces with a Desert Protector . . . it definitely went a long way for hearts and minds." On the minus side, "You have [Albu Mahal] guys who lost family members," Calvert explained. "You have to keep a close eye to make sure there aren't reprisals or revenges for past actions."[22]

Operation Steel Curtain began on 5 November, with 3/6 and 2/1 emerging from clouds of dust near Gannon then entering Husaybah from the north and west.[23] The city was cleared block-by-block over seven days during the first phase. This time, though, they would leave a lasting presence. New battle positions were set up in Husaybah, manned jointly by 3/6 and Iraqi soldiers. More were built in and around Karabilah when that was cleared. It was all according to 3/6's strategy. "It is just protecting the population," related Lieutenant Colonel Alford.

---

* See The Battle for Al-Qaim, USMC History Division, 2013, p24. In the fall of 2005, The 2/1 Battalion Landing Team was the ground combat element of the 13th Marine Expeditionary Unit (MEU), the operational reserve for U.S. Central Command. Committing 2/1 for Steel Curtain shows the importance of the operation to the coalition.

"[We've] got to live where the population is . . . get into the people, kick the bad guys out, establish ourselves and stay."[24]

The second phase began on 14 November, with 2/1 and the U.S. Army's 3rd Battalion, 504th Parachute Infantry Regiment (3/504), pushing into New and Old Ubaydi respectively. Just as 3/2 had experienced back in May, the Marines of 2/1 fought dug-in insurgents house-to-house in New Ubaydi for the next several days. 16 November was the deadliest day, when five Marines were killed taking a fortified house.[25]

When Operation Steel Curtain concluded on 22 November, all key population centers in Al-Qaim had been cleared, 139 insurgents were killed and 256 individuals detained, at a cost of ten Marines killed in action and 59 wounded.[26] This time the ground gained would be held. Thirteen platoon-sized battle positions had been left behind, manned by Marines and Iraqi soldiers. They covered Husaybah to New Ubaydi south of the river, and AQI's old stomping grounds in Ramana on the north bank.[27]

As an official assessment described, "AQI's ability to carry out operations in the city was severely degraded and the group was forced underground. AQI lost its ability to coordinate attacks in the city, to support insurgent activity further east, and to use the area as the capital for their notional state."[28] Colonel Alford's description was more succinct. "We just saturated and swallowed up the Al-Qaim region and made it where the bad guys could not operate" he explained.[29]

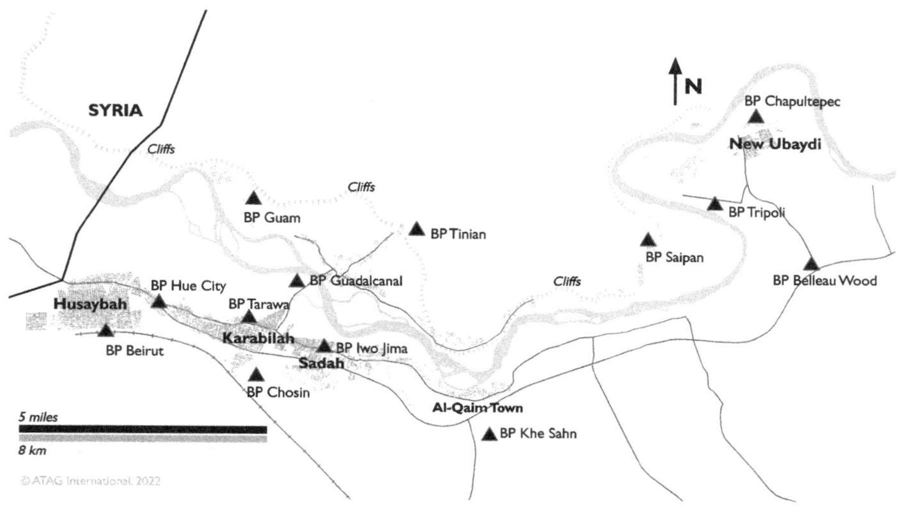

The operation also marked an important shift in Iraq's convoluted tribal politics. The Albu Mahal was now openly allied with coalition forces. More Mahalawis were being recruited into the Desert Protectors, which had played a small, but significant role in liberating Al-Qaim from AQI's murderous grip. As Alford said in a 2010 interview, "They went in and they took out al-Qaeda, very selectively and very discreetly, in the early stages of us moving into Al-Qaim."[30]

BANNER DAY

On 30 November 2005, eight days after Operation Steel Curtain ended, a podium was set up in downtown Husaybah. Out in the street, Iraqi soldiers were formed up in ranks and files. Off to one side stood a formation of U.S Marines. Other Marines, alert and ready for any trouble, provided security. Sitting behind the podium were high-powered VIPs, including Iraqi Brigadier General Al-Khafaggi representing the Ministry of the Interior, Dr. Saadoun al-Dulaimi, Iraq's Minister of Defense, and General George Casey, MNFI Commander.[31] Also on the podium were the architects of the operations that had allowed this event to occur; Colonel Davis, Lieutenant Colonel Starling, and Lieutenant Colonel Alford.

Up front and parallel with the Iraqi Army soldiers was another formation. A platoon of Desert Protectors stood ready for review in their recently-issued boots and sand-colored fatigues. There had been a last-minute scramble to get them matching headgear. "Right before we got started, our sergeant major acquired black knit watch caps for all of them," recalls Starling, "So they'd look as squared-away as possible[32]

The Iraqi national flag was raised, and the VIPs spoke. "This is a historic day for Iraq," said Minister al-Dulaimi, standing at the podium. "I will not forget this day. The insurgents are no longer controlling the border."[33] The words didn't matter as much as the fact that there, standing united on a battle-scarred stretch of Market Street, were Iraqi soldiers, U.S. Marines, and former tribal fighters. Some behind-the-scenes symbolism was playing out as well. "We intentionally held that ceremony right in front of what had been AQI's headquarters in the city," says Starling. "It was our way of publicly poking them in the eye."[34]

After the ceremony, General Casey met in private with his battlefield commanders and confided to Davis and Alford, only half-jokingly, "I never thought you guys could take that back." Davis replied without missing a beat, "We never thought we couldn't."[35]

PROGRESS

A true turning point had been reached in Al-Qaim. Attacks on the Marines and other violence subsided. The rebuilding of civil government and the economy began. "We started to turn the corner," described Captain Rich Pitchford, commander of 3/6's Lima Company. "There were shops opening up. The people were content, and things were getting back to business."[36] Lieutenant Colonel Alford established weekly city council meetings and began meeting regularly with the sheiks of all the tribes, not just the Albu Mahal. A new mayor of Al-Qaim, Farhan De Hal Farhan was appointed and soon he became a key partner for stabilizing the district.*

Marines even started to buy meals from local food kiosks and vendors. "It was like [going to] a pizza joint. You could order sheep kabobs," recalled Alford. "But what else did you really get? You got intelligence ... Marines began to meet the old ladies ... [They] would tell them who was bad and who needed to go because they wanted their town cleaned up. They wanted a better life for their kids ... So, the Marines began to figure out who was who and they would patrol from meal to meal."[37]

On 15 December 2005, Iraq held its second general election since the 2003 invasion, this time to select a new parliament. Across the country, voter turnout was remarkably high at around 80%. The big story, however, emerged out of Anbar. Eleven months earlier a mere two percent of voters in the troubled province had cast ballots. But by December, the situation had shifted dramatically, and Anbar's voter participation surged

* The new mayor, Farhan De Hal Farhan should not be confused with Raja Nawaf Farhan who was mayor, and then became Governor of Anbar for a short time before he died in a firefight north of Rawah between insurgents who had kidnapped him and U.S. Army soldiers.

to 86%, the highest of any other province.[38] Some 23,000 votes were cast in Al-Qaim District, according to a press release. Even in Husaybah the lines at the polling stations snaked back for blocks. It was a positive sign that Anbaris, and Sunnis overall, were ready for political participation instead of obstructionism and violence.[39]

Clearing Tal Afar

In late 2005, the coalition was also enjoying another key success In Nineveh Province, north of Anbar. Concurrent with the arrival of 3/6 in Al-Qaim, U.S. Army and Iraqi soldiers conducted "Operation Restoring Rights" in September to secure the key city of Tal Afar. Sitting astride the other main insurgent ratline from Syria, Tal Afar was the gateway to Mosul, Iraq's second-largest city. There the US Army's 3rd Cavalry Regiment (3rd ACR) and its commander, Colonel H.R. McMaster, partnered with Iraqi forces, built combat outposts in the city, and worked closely with local leaders. These were essentially the same counter-insurgency techniques used by Lieutenant Colonel Alford and 3/6 in Al-Qaim, employed at a larger scale.

The signs of progress only multiplied after that. In February, the Iraqi 1/1 Brigade was replaced in Al-Qaim by the newly-established 3/7 Brigade, formed mostly of Sunni soldiers. This helped immensely to build trust and confidence among the local population. Many of the unit's members were recruited from the Albu Mahal or other tribes. "That was a huge piece," related Alford. "Over a thousand men in the brigade were from the Al-Qaim region ... the sheikhs committed men to it, and then they committed men to the police force."[40] The brigade commander was Colonel Ismail Shihab al-Mahalawi, cousin to Sheikh Sabah. His brother, Colonel Jamal, commanded the growing police force.[41]

A key leaders' conference was held in Al-Qaim on 26 February. Sheikhs from each tribe attended. At one point, Colonel Ismail stood to speak. Specifically addressing those sheikhs who had been siding with the foreign fighters, he confronted them face-to-face:

> *Are you with me or with al-Qaeda? Whoever is not with me, is with al-Qaeda ... I know every one of you. I even know how many of you have helped the foreign fighters ... I know you well. Don't try to deceive me ... We are the new Iraqi Army. We are not the National Guard that al-Qaeda found an easy target.*
>
> —**Ismail Shihab al-Mahalawi**[42]

With all the bloodshed that had come before, this was not just theater. Colonel Ismail knew he was a target for AQI assassins and might be betrayed by certain sheikhs in that room. For their part, some of those sheikhs knew the Colonel and his troops might soon be kicking in their doors if they continued to support the jihadists.

In March 2006, 3/6 was replaced by another battalion, 1/7, under the command of Lieutenant Colonel Nick Morano. The battalion had fought in Al-Qaim in 2004 and now found the area changed dramatically. "We [could] move around the battlespace without a whole lot of enemy activity," Morano recalled. One of his main objectives was to rebuild the police.

"The police [could] tell you exactly who the bad guys were by name and what houses they were in," said Marano.[43]

During 1/7's tenure, police stations were established in each sector and the number of policemen in the AO rose dramatically to 1,200. Many of them came from the Albu Mahal tribe and the Desert Protectors.

Al-Qaim transformed radically in 2006 . "Coalition operations in western Iraq had decisively shifted the balance of power in the area away from AQI and back towards the Iraqi government," stated an official analysis.[44] What had been one of the most violent districts of Anbar, where al-Qaeda in Iraq had ruled through torture , beheadings, and suicide bombers, was now the most peaceful. Markets were open, kids were back in school, blue-shirted Iraqi police patrolled the streets , and U.S. Marines munched on lamb-kebabs from the kiosks.

That spring, a reporter from the London-based Financial Times spent several days with 1/7 and wrote admiringly of the new realities in Al-Qaim. His article glowingly portrayed the district as "an oil spot of stability" where "cooperation of the tribes [keeps] the region safe" and graffiti in Husaybah read "No to takfiris [terrorists]" and "Long live the Iraqi Army." [45] The article was published on May 5, 2006, not quite a year after Day 1 of Operation Matador when three brave Marines were lost going house-to-house in New Ubaydi.

THE WAR GOES ON

The peace breaking out in Al-Qaim, however, did not immediately spread to the east. While there was a brief spate of optimism among the coalition, Zarqawi and his jihadist minions would again stoke the fires of violence and tragedy. After Operation Steel Curtain, scores of AQI leaders and fighters filtered over to the province's eastern districts to reconstitute. Consequently, in the first two months of 2006, the locus of the struggle in Anbar shifted back to the Haditha triangle and especially Ramadi.

In January, Zarqawi formed a new umbrella group called the Mujahideen Shura Council. This was an effort to put an Iraqi face on his extremist network while still allowing AQI to dominate the Sunni-based insurgency. Accompanying this move was a violent counter-stroke against Ramadi-area tribes trying to cooperate with the government.

Earlier that month, AQI struck a hard blow when a suicide bomber killed 56 Iraqis and two Americans at a police recruiting drive at the Ramadi glass factory. Until that ghastly attack, the recruiting drive had been hugely successful. Then came a wave of assassinations against sheikhs and the leaders of competing insurgent groups. Under such pressure, the nascent tribal movement in eastern Anbar crumbled. Meanwhile, Zarqawi, AQI and the Mujahideen Shura Council moved aggressively to control Ramadi, declaring it the capital of a new Islamic emirate, just as they'd done in Husaybah.

Then, with one atavistic stroke on February 22, 2006, Zarqawi managed to plunge much of the rest of the country into a period of ugly, ruthless intercommunal violence. On that day a team of AQI fighters blew up one of Shiite Islam's holiest sites, the al-Askari mosque in Samarra. In retribution, Shiite militia groups quickly struck back against Sunni mosques, masked death squads began roaming Sunni neighborhoods, and morgues filled with mutilated bodies from all sides. This was the sectarian civil war Zarqawi had wanted to spark.

Once again, Iraq appeared on the edge of total breakdown, but this time the chaos lasted for months. The coalition scrambled to tamp down the violence and U.S. troops often found themselves in the middle, under attack from both Sunni and Shiite groups. The successes in Tal Afar and Al-Qaim faded into the background. In Anbar, attention was focused on the critical struggle for Ramadi where day and night hundreds of AQI-led fighters engaged American soldiers, SOF operators, and Marines amid rubble-strewn streets and blasted buildings. The Battle of Ramadi raged through the spring and summer of 2006 with no end in sight.

On June 7, 2006, two precision-guided bombs dropped by a U.S. Air Force jet slammed into a safehouse outside Baqubah, finally putting an end to the sheikh of the slaughterers. But while Zarqawi was dead, the reign of terror he had initiated continued under its own twisted momentum. Another jihadist, Abu Ayyub al-Masri, was named as AQI's new emir. An Egyptian, al-Masri was one of Zarqawi's earliest associates in Iraq and reportedly had been involved in smuggling suicide bombers in from Syria and down the Euphrates Valley ratline.[46]

On August 17th, a high-level Marine report provided a hard-eyed assessment to U.S. leaders. Issued by the senior intelligence officer at MEF headquarters, the report stated that "U.S. and Iraqi troops are no longer capable of militarily defeating the insurgency in al-Anbar." The most pessimistic parts of the Devlin Report were leaked, then widely touted by media talking heads. They seemed to confirm that Anbar was beyond hope and therefore the Iraq War was probably already lost.[47]

THE BIG FLIP

Under the surface, however, unseen currents were stirring that would soon produce a tide of positive change. While AQI had murdered key Sunni sheikhs and co-opted certain tribes, there were others still actively fighting against them. By this time, several powerful tribes and subtribes in Anbar were sworn blood-enemies of AQI. Previously suppressed through murder and intimidation, by the fall of 2006 they were reconsolidating and finding new leaders. At least 13 tribes were categorized as "the most anti-AQI", by coalition analysts.[48] Additionally, the split between the various Sunni resistance groups, such as the 1920s Brigade, and the religious extremists was wider than ever. Just as the situation in Ramadi seemed the darkest, the tables were already starting to turn.

Within days after the Devlin report on Anbar was issued, a major tipping-point occurred in Ramadi, prompted by yet another heartless murder and AQI's own anti-Islamic conduct. In an outlying area of the city, the Albu Ali Jassim tribe had been battling AQI cells through the summer while recruiting men to join the police. Their leader, Sheikh Khalid Araq, was a former Iraqi general with influence among Sunni nationalists. On August 21st an AQI hit team killed Khalid, his son, and a nephew. They then dumped the sheikh's decapitated body in the desert, preventing his family from properly burying him according to Islamic teachings. This triggered an outraged response.

On August 31, 2006, sheikhs from several tribes met to declare a united front against AQI, calling themselves "Anbar Revolutionaries." Among them was a brash, 34-year-old black-marketeer and smuggling ring-leader, Sheikh Abu Sattar of the Albu Risha tribe. He had previously dabbled in the insurgency while also performing contracts for the U.S. military. But after his father and older brother were killed by AQI, Sattar became the openly anti-AQI leader of his tribe. Seen at first as a bit-player and the tainted leader of a minor tribe, Sheikh Sattar soon proved he had courage, political skills, and armed power behind him.

In the same period, U.S. forces in Ramadi had begun to rack up tactical successes. The U.S. Army's 1st Brigade Combat Team of the 1st Armored Division (1/1 BCT) arrived in June, taking over the AO just after the death of Zarqawi. The 1/1 BCT, also known as the "Ready First", was commanded by Colonel Sean MacFarland and had been involved in securing Tal Afar. Now MacFarland led a composite force of Army and Marine battalions and a task unit of Navy SEALs. But while the Ready First mounted aggressive combat operations, they also actively reached out to talk with tribal leaders, drawing on lessons learned in Tal Afar and Al-Qaim.

MacFarland and several of his officers became key actors in the Battle of Ramadi and supporters of the burgeoning tribal revolt against AQI. One of MacFarland's battalion commanders, Lieutenant Colonel William Jurney, led the 1st Battalion, 6th Marines as it defended the Government Center and cleaned out Ramadi's toughest sector. A young Army Green Beret, Captain Travis Patriquin, was MacFarland's civil affairs advisor and the main liaison with the sheikhs. Patriquin, who spoke Arabic, developed a personal friendship with Sheikh Sattar and his family. His influence and popularity among the sheikhs were so great he was adopted into the Albu Risha tribe.

The combination of Sunni tribes standing up to AQI, supported and fostered by the forces of 1/1 BCT, finally broke the insurgents' hold on Ramadi. On September 14th, with endorsement from Colonel McFarland, Sattar and forty other sheikhs publicly declared they were allying themselves and their tribes with the coalition to fight against AQI. They called their movement the *Sahawa al-Anbar*, or Anbar Awakening Council, which included 17 tribes, among them the Albu Mahal. This was the Great Awakening, the mass "flipping" of the Sunni tribes, that transformed Ramadi over the next few months and swept across the rest of Anbar.

After Sheikh Sattar's pronouncement, tribesmen in Ramadi and elsewhere flocked to join the police, while others formed armed, quasi-official emergency response units (ERUs) to patrol the streets. The results were immediate as insurgent attacks dropped 50 percent just in September. A key victory came in November, when foreign fighters gathered to attack the Albu Soda tribe in the suburb of Sofia (or Sufiyah). After the tribe called for help, a U.S. Army battalion actively intervened with tanks and airstrikes, killing 68 AQI fighters and saving the tribe. By the time the Ready First rotated out of Iraq in early 2007, the number of police in Ramadi had mushroomed to almost 3,000 with another 3,000 Sunni tribesmen manning local ERUs. Insurgent attacks were down 70 percent while an estimated 1,500 insurgents had been killed and an equal number detained.[49]

The key players of the turnaround in Ramadi during 2006 are now in the history books. Colonel Sean MacFarland rose to the rank of Lieutenant General in the Army, retiring with three stars. Lieutenant Colonel William Jurney, commander of 1/6, became a three-star Lieutenant General in the Marine Corps. Sadly, the two men at the very center of the story would not live to see its conclusion. Captain Travis Patriquin, called "Hashim Abu Risha" by the tribes, was killed by an AQI-emplaced IED in December of 2006. At his memorial service in Ramadi, Sattar and senior Anbari sheikhs sat in the front row next to Colonel MacFarland, a symbol of the unlikely alliance Patriquin had helped bring to life. Travis earned a different kind of star, one that still shines brightly in the hearts of his combat brothers and his Iraqi friends.

Months later, Abdul Sattar Abu Risha was also killed by an IED on 13 September 2007, almost a year to the day since he had put his own life on the line by announcing the *Sahawa al-Anbar.* After many unsuccessful attempts, the killers of AQI had finally found a way to assassinate their nemesis, though it was too late to stop the movement he had sparked. Upon his death, his brother Ahmed took the reins of the Awakening Council, proclaiming, "Although they killed Sattar, there are a million Sattars in Anbar."[50]

PIVOT POINTS

The Sunni Awakening paved the way for the coalition's surge in 2007. At the end of 2006, the dramatic turnaround in Anbar was a crucial factor in President Bush's decision to reinforce the effort in Iraq. On January 10, 2007, he announced a new strategic direction in the war, including the deployment of five additional brigades and 30,000 troops under a new commander, General David Petreaus. The U.S. president specifically mentioned that in Anbar Province, "Tribal leaders have begun to show their willingness to take on al-Qaeda. And as a result, our commanders believe we have an opportunity to deal a serious blow to the terrorists."[51]

Cursory accounts of the Iraq War often blur the Awakening

and the Bush/Petreaus surge together or fade the former into the background. But in fact, months before the first surge brigades had even deployed, the turning of the Anbari tribes shifted the momentum in the coalition's favor. Today it is clear the surge would never have happened without the Awakening.

Likewise, the Marines' multi-year campaign along the upper Euphrates, and its interplay with tribal politics, set up the success of the Anbar Awakening Council. The critical events that unfolded in Ramadi and eastern Anbar in late 2006 were preceded by key turning points tracing back along the Euphrates River Valley to western Anbar.

While there are numerous accounts about the Ready 1st Brigade, Sheikh Sattar and the Ramadi Awakening, they give short shrift to preceding events. Some mention early efforts to engage tribes or refer to "proto-awakenings" further west, but those are treated as if they were failures or disconnected from what came later in Ramadi. That interpretation is incorrect, however. What happened out west earlier in the war, particularly in Al-Qaim in 2005, formed a tightly-connected chain of events that led to a seismic turnaround.

The appearance of 3/2 in that chain came at a vital hinge on the timeline. Zarqawi and his allies had just become al-Qaeda's franchise in Iraq and had zeroed in on Al-Qaim as their base of operations. There they intended to establish their first territorial caliphate. So, while it was little understood at the time, 3/2 deployed directly into the boiling center of a gathering storm.

Over the next seven months, the Betio Bastards met that turbulence head on, disrupting AQI's plans, dispersing their forces and, yes, killing hundreds of enemy combatants. An overworn cliché about counter-insurgency (often coming from the sidelines) is the claim that, "You can't kill your way out of an insurgency." But there is a flip side to that platitude. A well-armed insurgency can certainly kill its way into power. There is, then, a phase in a counter-insurgency campaign when the kinetic battle must be fought, when violent means must be taken to clear the way for less-kinetic approaches.

The battlespace 3/2 entered in February of 2005 was fully kinetic. The roads were laced with IEDs, every vehicle was a suspected suicide bomb, and each room a Marine cleared might mean getting shot in the face. There was little room for the security and stability operations their pre-deployment training had stressed.

The battalion's primary weapon in that kinetic fight was Kilo Company. Captain Ieva and First Sergeant Gregory had prepared their Marines for high-intensity combat, building excellent leadership teams in each platoon. Kilo was the core infantry unit in all major operations in 3/2's AO and was leveraged by RCT-2 in several operations along the Hit-Haditha corridor. The company also ranged all across Al-Qaim, executing raids against high-value targets and neutralizing arms caches. Without Kilo Company's aggressive stance, tactical proficiency and its many successes in killing or capturing die-hard foreign fighters, other successes that 3/2 and RCT-2 enjoyed would have been less impactful, or would not have occurred at all.

Likewise, Weapons Company and its mobile assault platoons played vital roles in the maneuver battle, often operating independently. Reaper's scout-sniper teams and the Forward Air Controllers also brought devastating precision firepower to bear against the enemy. So, while 3/2 did not kill its way out of the insurgency in Al-Qaim, its actions directly removed scores—even hundreds—of dangerous enemies from the battlefield, including key insurgent leaders. On two occasions, apparently, the battalion even came close to killing or capturing Zarqawi himself.

Moreover, The Betio Bastards forged a path for the success of units that followed. The hard battlefield lessons they learned informed other units that followed. In particular, their leverage of intelligence at the company level, innovative employment of precision air strikes, and close cooperation with special mission units set patterns that would later become standards for conventional U.S. forces.

At the same time, 3/2 also broke new ground on the non-kinetic side, through India Company's engagement of the Albu Mahal and the Hamza militia. Certainly, the Marines led by Captain Frank Diorio and First Sergeant Don Brazeal were also in a very kinetic fight as they defended Camp Gannon. They fended off suicide bombers, endured mortar attacks, and had almost daily firefights. All told, India and its attachments had over 300 engagements during the deployment, which certainly killed many insurgents.

But India Company achieved its most important and long-lasting impact not through firefights, but by reaching out to the Albu Mahal. Now a full colonel, Frank Diorio remains a soft-spoken leader who pushes accolades and recognition to those he leads. He is reluctant to take credit, always looking out for "his Marines." Of those at Gannon, he told an interviewer, "It wasn't me...it was lance corporals and corporals...they came to me with strategic-level ideas...They had the awareness. They were the ones who said, 'Don't shoot' when they had every right to shoot."[52]

Nonetheless, it was Diorio's idea and initiative to engage with shadowy individuals who were considered enemies at the time. He took a path fraught with risk, not only to his career but to the physical safety of his men and himself. That initiative led step-by-step, one tentative agreement after another, to India Company and 3/2 loosely cooperating with the Albu Mahal as they resisted domination by foreign fighters. The tribe finally turned openly to the Marines for safety and assistance as AQI surged into Husaybah. Diorio himself admitted he had doubts at that difficult time, initially thinking the effort had failed. But he went on to express:

> *As we continued to think about it, we thought that this is the tipping point that every counter-insurgency needs... you [had] a Sunni tribe... sided with coalition forces, sided with India Company, sided with the Marine Corps.*
>
> —**Frank Diorio**[53]

While some may argue this was not *the* turning point in Iraq, it was certainly a crucial juncture where the event-chain pivoted in a new direction. The Special Forces' mission to Akashat and the Desert Protectors grew directly from that pivot point, which in turn led to Albu Mahal tribesmen operating alongside 3/6 Marines and the momentous flag-raising ceremony in Husaybah. Soon thereafter, AQI was effectively neutered in Al-Qaim, the district was relatively peaceful, and hundreds of tribesmen joined the new Iraqi Army and the police as the Desert Protector program transitioned.

Consider whether those events could have occurred had Frank Diorio *not* sat down with Falzi, or if India Company Marines had *not* built a trusting relationship with the Albu Mahal. What would have been the result had they ignored the tribe or engaged them with firepower instead of talk? The choice to build trust with suspected enemies began a flow of positive effects downstream. The long-term impact of that decision is revealed by looking closely at the connections between the Albu Mahal's awakening in Al-Qaim and subsequent events in Ramadi.

In late 2005, the Desert Protector program was enjoying good publicity. And by early 2006, word of what was happening in Al-Qaim had spread through the intertribal grapevine, the person-to-person network that was all but invisible to Americans. Tribes in and around Ramadi certainly knew about the Albu Mahal's relationship with the Marines out west. Ironically, AQI's own actions energized this information sharing. After fleeing Husaybah, some Mahalawi families and Hamza fighters sought refuge with friendly tribesmen on the outskirts of Ramadi. While there, they almost certainly shared harrowing stories of AQI's barbarous acts and the contrasting benefits of cooperation with the Marines.

There is also a particularly strong connection through Sheikh Sattar's own tribe, the Albu Risha, which shared common lineage and affinity with the Albu Mahal.* The Albu Risha tribe had offered assistance to the Mahalawis as they were fleeing Husaybah in August of 2005. Moreover, one of Sattar's uncles was none other than Minister of Defense Sadun Dulaymi. Dulaymi was also a senior figure in the Albu Risha tribe and the chief proponent for the Desert Protectors in the Iraqi government. Clearly Sheikh Sattar was well aware of the Desert

* The principal reference for this section is the study by Dr. Bill Knarr, The 2005 Iraqi Sunni Awakening: The Desert Protectors Program, Oct 2015, published by the Joint Special Operations University (JSOU). This is the seminal work connecting the Albu Mahal and the Desert Protectors to the subsequent Awakening in Ramadi.

Protectors and probably had kinsmen who had joined them. By 2006, he was asking U.S. military personnel in Ramadi how to join the program.*

Sattar also knew Sheikh Sabah personally. Before the Anbar Awakening Council was announced, Sattar traveled to Jordan to meet with him. The two discussed the Albu Mahal's experience fighting AQI and ways the tribes could rally to defeat them in Ramadi, according to Sabah. "I was teasing him by telling him that I would send the Albu-Mahal tribe to him and see what they could do," recalled the sheikh. "So he answered me, 'I will show you what I can do myself!'"[54] Just weeks later, there were Mahalawi sheikhs in Ramadi standing alongside Sattar and other tribal leaders as they declared The Awakening that would soon make such an impact.

The landmark Awakening Project, commissioned by the Marine Corps and headed by Dr. William Knarr, documents these connections and highlights their importance. "The movement that started in Al-Qaim was not 'localized' as some would contend; it was part of a larger movement that spread throughout Al Anbar," writes Knarr. "The Ramadi awakening was a significant part of that effort—not the start of it."[55]

Other key participants agree. "The Anbar Awakening, from my assessment, began out west and kind of rolled east," stated Lieutenant Colonel Morano of 1/7, who experienced an Al-Qaim in 2007 that had been amazingly transformed.[56] Sheikh Kurdi, the Albu Mahal leader at the center of so many

---

* In the spring or summer of 2006, Sheikh Sattar specifically asked to join the Desert Protectors during a meeting with an officer assigned to the Navy SEAL unit in Ramadi, Task Unit Bruiser. The unit's commander, Jocko Willink, describes this in a Jocko Podcast episode; "Unraveling 7", 19oct21.

key events, expressed the same view with a bit more flare; "The sun of freedom rises in the west!"[57]

The Marines of 3/2 were not merely the unit with their boots on the ground as that sun began rising, they actively shaped that ground so that it could rise.

HALLOWED PLACES

On a cool October morning I found myself on a pilgrimage of sorts. Having finished up a research trip to Quantico and meeting Colonel Mundy for the first time, I needed to make another visit. It was too early to find a florist, so I stopped at a grocery store to buy a simple bouquet. I chose orange and yellow flowers in a modest vase. I had to prop them up in the passenger seat so the vase wouldn't tip over as I drove north on I-95.

An hour later I parked at Arlington National Cemetery, checked to see that the flowers weren't wilted, lifted them from the vase and began walking. A morning mist clung to the ground, caressing the impeccably straight rows of white stone in soft, ethereal tendrils. The rows seemed endless; my footfalls too loud.

Arlington's section 60 is set aside for service members who died in Iraq and Afghanistan. Covering just 14 acres, it has a different feel than the rest of the 600-acre expanse. On any given day there are dozens, even hundreds, of visitors to section 60. They often linger in family groups, including children. The headstones there are more generously adorned with flags, letters, stuffed animals, small pebbles, and of course, flowers.

I had arrived early enough to be alone as I located specific plots. Winding through the graves, I found the first one I was looking for; Lawrence Robert Philippon, Lance Corporal, U.S. Marine Corps. I touched the cool marble, offered a silent prayer, and leaned a few blooms against his headstone. Nearby I found others who'd been killed in action in Al-Qaim during 2005. Awkwardly, I realized I hadn't brought enough flowers. I gingerly rationed them out to give each stone a splash of golden-orange.

For anyone with a scintilla of conscience, it is impossible to come away from such hallowed places without pondering the purpose behind the sacrifice they enshrine. Leaving Arlington that day, I knew the conclusion of this book would necessarily raise gut-wrenching questions. Why did Americans have to die in Iraq? What were they fighting for? What did they accomplish? These questions are all the more daunting since popular opinion and prevailing political winds hold that the Iraq War ended in failure. Grappling with that mischaracterization is beyond the scope here, but a short attempt to correct the record is warranted.

By the end of 2009, the corner had been turned militarily in Iraq. The remnants of AQI had been defeated and decimated. Iraqi Shiite militias were marginalized, their leaders jockeying for political power rather than fighting in the streets. Violence across the country had declined steeply and kept declining. Unfortunately, subsequent political decisions at the highest levels in the U.S. and Iraq essentially threw away the progress that had been made. The premature withdrawal of remaining U.S. forces in 2011 set the stage for ISIS, the ultra-violent reincarnation of AQI, to plunge Iraq back into war. Politicians turned a hard-won victory into a loss.

Strategic rationales and political arguments dissolve to vapor, though, when talking to a gold-star mother of a Marine who lost his life far from home. The "why?" question floats persistently, intrusively even, whether spoken or not. Behind her gracious smile she wants to know, "Why did my son die in Iraq?" In response I can only offer what I believe is the most true answer, although the incomplete truth of it provides scant comfort.

When her son fell, he was exactly where he wanted to be, fighting alongside his brothers, making a stand against a dark tyranny festering in a violent corner of the world.

30. THE FALLEN

Mercifully, the United States has suffered relatively few casualties in our recent conflicts when compared with past wars. The American military lost 3,490 killed in action during Operation Iraqi Freedom, between March of 2003 and the end of August 2010, the timeframe commonly thought of as The Iraq War. To take a sheer statistical approach, this works out to about forty killed per month, just over one per day throughout the war. Placed in historical context, this loss rate pales alongside wars and battles of our past.*

But the men and women killed in Iraq were not statistics. Their lives were not aggregated numbers to be crunched for historical analysis or exploited for political purposes. And the word "mercifully" does not occur to a family when the knock on the door comes. Each of those 3,490 names was a son or daughter, a husband, a wife, a parent, a sister, or a brother. Every

* The American Civil War was by far the United States' costliest conflict, with over 600,000 military deaths. In a single day at Antietam, over 3,500 Union and Confederate soldiers died. During World War II, in just ten desperate days during the Battle of the Bulge, about 5,000 American soldiers were lost along Elsenborn Ridge. And at the height of America's involvement in the Vietnam War during 1968, nearly 17,000 U.S. servicemen were killed in action, about 46 per day.

one of them had boundless potential which was suddenly cut short. Each loss left a jagged hole in the hearts of their loved ones and friends, their units, and communities. Yes, the shard-like edges of that loss can soften with time, but the hole will always be there.

The fact that 3/2 suffered only three killed during 2005 is striking, given the combat the battalion experienced. In one sense, it is a credit to the unit's high tactical proficiency, professionalism, and excellent leadership. But another factor also stands out. In each case where 3/2 lost a man, he had consciously put himself at risk to protect his fellow Marines and to "close with and destroy the enemy in close combat." Whether his final act was kicking a door, moving to the front of the stack, or manning the gun, these young men literally put themselves in the line of fire. They embody the highest values of the Marine Corps, our country, and of higher powers as well. As the timeless verse testifies, "Greater love has no man than this, that a man lay down his life for his friends."

KEVIN SCOTT SMITH, LANCE CORPORAL, USMC

Born 28 September 1984—Killed in Action, 21 March 2005, Al-Qaim, Iraq (age 20). Laid to rest in Vale Cemetery, Springfield, OH.

Kevin Smith was born in Springfield, Ohio, to Ronald Smith and Kathy (Wilburn) Smith. His young life unfolded along typical patterns in middle America. He grew up playing baseball, picking out tunes on his guitar, and tinkering with cars, especially his 1993 Toyota Celica. By the time he was a student at Kenton Ridge High School, he was doing well academically and was in the Spanish National Honor Society. His teachers described him as thoughtful and well-behaved. But at some point after the 9/11 terror attacks, he chose to leave the well-traveled path to serve his country in a time of war. In his senior year, he signed on the dotted line and reported to bootcamp in August of 2003.

Seven months later he checked into 3/2, in February 2004, as a fully-qualified infantryman and soon deployed to Guantanamo Bay, Cuba for several months. Upon return, he was assigned to the security platoon. He fit well into that small unit and was recognized for his diligence and determination to do the job right. "Kevin seemed more mature, more poised," says A.J. Lomando, one of his closest friends in the platoon. "He was tall, about six-foot-two, and was a good runner. He was duty-driven and objective-oriented," remembers Lomando. "One time our squad did something wrong, and the NCOs had us run from the barracks to French Creek and back with a telephone pole. It was like six miles. Other guys were dropping out and in the end it was just me and him carrying that log. Somebody offered to give him a break, but he wouldn't give it up. He was determined to finish."[1]

That determination was noticed and once deployed to Iraq, Kevin was selected as a vehicle commander, leading the crew of one of the platoon's guntrucks. "He was an exceptional leader, who really took care of his fellow Marines. I was the gunner he relieved that day, putting himself at risk to give me a rest," Lomando recalls, his voice turning low. "I'll never forget him and can only imagine what he'd be today. He gave his life so I could live. I resolved that when I got back I wasn't going to squander that."

LAWRENCE ROBERT PHILIPPON, LANCE CORPORAL, USMC

Born 20 March 1983—Killed in Action, 8 May 2005, New Ubaydi, Iraq (age 22). Laid to rest in Arlington National Cemetery, VA, Section 60, plot 8181.

From West Hartford, CT, Larry Philippon was a star hockey and lacrosse player in high school. The world of northeast collegiate sports seemed to be his trajectory after graduation. But something else was stirring in him. In 2003, he came home from Central Connecticut University and declared he was joining the Marines. Both his father, Ray, and his mother, Leesa, had served in the Army but never actively encouraged their son to join the military. Larry signed up to be an infantry Marine, expressly because that's where he would be the most likely to see combat. After bootcamp, though, he was "volunteered" to be in the ceremonial Marine Color Guard in Washington D.C., based on his six-foot, four-inch frame and impressive bearing. He was hardly pleased about it, however, and persistently requested assignment to a front-line infantry unit. He told his parents, "I didn't sign up to be a pretty boy."

That persistence finally paid off and he was assigned to 3/2's Kilo Company a few months before the battalion deployed. Quickly selected by the NCOs as a fire team leader, he initially encountered friction with squad mates who had more experience as infantry grunts, but his positive attitude, quick smile, and willingness to take on any task promptly overcame their reservations. One of his closest friends in the squad became Emmanuel "Nelly" Nelson. They seemed like an unlikely pair on the outside; the tall, white college athlete alongside the tough black kid from the streets of Detroit. But during many 12-hour guard shifts together they found common ground. "We spent a lot of time together, and Philippon knew I was a spiritual person. We would talk about God, about our families."[2]

Mother's Day is painful for the Philippon family, especially for Leesa, who lost her oldest son that awful day in 2005. They are Christians, strong in their faith, but the whole month of May is tough as they remember Larry and lend each other spiritual support.

Each year on Memorial Day weekend, Ray and Leesa make a trip down to Arlington to visit Larry's grave. On the first of these visits they happened upon Brenda Cheney, mother of Staff Sergeant Anthony Goodwin from 3/25, also lost on 8 May during Operation Matador. "She was sitting by Anthony's grave when we walked up," recalls Leesa. "We instantly bonded, cried, and hugged each other." Among the hallowed rows of white stone markers, they mourned together and forged a tight, heartfelt relationship. Since then, they've also established close friendships with the parents of Dustin Derga and several other gold-star families. "We stay in touch, especially on our difficult days," says Leesa Philippon. "As we say, its family from the core to the Corps and forever."[3]

ADAM JOHNSON CRUMPLER, LANCE CORPORAL, USMC

Born 31 August 1985—Killed in Action, 18 June 2005, Karabilah, Iraq (age 19). Laid to rest in Kanawha Valley Memorial Gardens, Glasgow, WV.

Adam Crumpler was born in Loma Linda, CA, but was raised in Campbell's Creek outside Charleston, West Virginia by his grandparents, Hubert and Emma Lou Johnson. Despite a rough start as an infant and the early death of his mother, he had a healthy and active childhood. He played Little League baseball and football, and pulled daredevil stunts on skates, bikes, and snowboards. As a preteen, he discovered martial arts and enjoyed the challenge, structure, and discipline as he advanced from level to level. One of his goals was to open his own martial arts studio. Another goal was to become a Marine, like his grandfather. Hubert R. Johnson was a WWII Marine who served in the Pacific and landed on Iwo Jima. Adam idolized him and would sit on the porch swing listening to his stories. Early on, Adam resolved to follow his grandpa's legacy into the Corps.

While he was still just 17, attending Riverside High School, he signed up for the Marine Delayed Entry Program and was eager to enlist right after graduation. After finishing boot camp and the School of Infantry, he was assigned to 3/2 and Kilo Company. In the barracks, he made friends easily and was known for joking around with his squad mates and new-found buddies. Whenever he had a free weekend, he'd bundle into a car with a few others and head up to his grandparents' house. "Many Saturday mornings, I'd get up and cook for a house full of Marines," says Emma Lou. "They'd be scattered all over the house and were from all over the country. Some had never even had biscuits and gravy. I loved 'em all."[4]

Adam met Joe Faw during infantry training and the two became fast friends. "He was like the brother I never had," says Joe. "He was always joking around, and everyone knew he was always up to something." Many of his squad mates remember Adam's sense of humor and mischievous nature, but there was no nonsense when it came to his job. "He was always serious on missions," Joe recalls. Right before Operation Spear, Adam confided to Joe that he'd sent a letter home detailing his own funeral plans. "It was like he had a premonition, like he could feel it coming."[5]

Joe was clearing rooms in the same house when Adam went down in a maelstrom of gunfire and flame. "Afterwards, I was that young Marine that Staff Sergeant Moore had to calm down when they brought Adam out," he recalls. "When I saw my friend, I broke down. Staff Sergeant Moore told me, 'We gotta continue the mission, Faw. That's what Adam would want', and he was right…Adam was always about doing his duty, for his family and his country. My own Mom kind of adopted him. After he died, she told me she had the feeling Adam would be my guardian angel, that he'd always have my back. I served two more times in Iraq and came back OK, so I guess she was right. I miss him all the time."

FALLEN FROM 3/25 AND SUPPORTING UNITS IN 2005

3rd Battalion, 25th Marines, composed almost entirely of reservists from Ohio, paid a tragic cost in lives during 2005. During several operations in Al-Qaim and the Hit-Haditha area, Marines from 3/25 and 3/2 fought together. It is therefore fitting to honor 3/25's losses here:

Bryan J. Richardson, Corporal USMC, KIA, 5 March 2005

Michael B. Lindemuth, Lance Corporal USMC, KIA, 13 April 2005

Joseph S. Tremblay, Corporal USMC, KIA, 27 April 2005

Aaron N. Cepeda, Sergeant USMC, KIA, 7 May 2005

Lance T. Graham, Lance Corporal USMC, KIA, 7 May 2005

Michael A. Marzano, Sergeant USMC, KIA, 7 May 2005

Jeffrey L. Wiener, Petty Officer Third Class USN, KIA, 7 May 2005

Dustin A. Derga, Corporal USMC, KIA, 8 May 2005

Anthony L. Goodwin, Staff Sergeant USMC, KIA, 8 May 2005

Wesley G. Davids, Lance Corporal USMC, KIA, 11 May 2005

Christopher R. Dixon, Private First Class USMC, KIA, 11 May 2005

LCpl. Nicholas B. Erdy, Lance Corporal USMC, KIA, 11 May 2005

Jonathan W. Grant, Lance Corporal USMC, KIA, 11 May 2005

Jourdan Lin Grez, Lance Corporal USMC, KIA, 11 May 2005

Kendall H. Ivy II, Staff Sergeant USMC, KIA, 11 May 2005

David N. Wimberg, Sergeant USMC, KIA, 25 May 2005

Ricardo A. Crocker, Major USMC, KIA, 26 May 2005

Dustin Birch, Lance Corporal USMC, KIA, 9 June 2005

Daniel Chavez, Lance Corporal USMC, KIA, 9 June 2005

Brad D. Squires, Corporal USMC, KIA, 9 June 2005

Thomas O. Keeling, Lance Corporal USMC, KIA, 9 June 2005

Devon P. Seymour, Lance Corporal USMC, KIA, 9 June 2005

Joseph P. Goodrich, Staff Sergeant USMC, KIA, 10 July 2005

Ryan J. Kovacicek, Lance Corporal USMC, KIA 10 July 2005

Travis L. Youngblood, Petty Officer Third Class USN, KIA, 21 July 2005

LCpl. Christopher P. Lyons, Lance Corporal USMC, KIA, 28 July 2005

Andre´ "Dre´" L. Williams, Corporal USMC, KIA, 28 July 2005

Cpl Jeffrey Boskovitch, Corporal USMC, KIA, 1 August 2005

LCpl Roger Castleberry, Lance Corporal USMC, KIA, 1 August 2005

Nathaniel S. Rock, Sergeant USMC, KIA, 1 August 2005

David J. Coullard, Sergeant USMC, KIA, 1 August 2005

Daniel N. Deyarmin, Lance Corporal USMC, KIA, 1 August 2005

Brian P. Montgomery, Lance Corporal USMC, KIA, 1 August 2005

James R. Graham, Sergeant USMC, KIA, 1 August 2005

Eric J. Bernholtz, Lance Corporal USMC, KIA 3 August 2005

Christopher Jenkins Dyer, Lance Corporal USMC, KIA 3 August 2005

Aaron H. Reed, Lance Corporal USMC, KIA 3 August 2005

Michael J. Cifuentes, Lance Corporal USMC, KIA 3 August 2005

Nicholas William Baart Bloem, Lance Corporal USMC, KIA 3 August 2005

Timothy M. Bell Jr., Lance Corporal USMC, KIA 3 August 2005

Grant B. Fraser, Lance Corporal USMC, KIA 3 August 2005

William Brett Wightman, Lance Corporal USMC, KIA 3 August 2005

Edward August "Augie" Schroeder II, Lance Corporal USMC, KIA 3 August 2005

Justin F. Hoffman, Sergeant USMC, KIA 3 August 2005

David K. J. Kreuter, Sergeant USMC, KIA 3 August 2005

Bradley J. Harper, Sergeant USMC, KIA 3 August 2005

Kevin G. Waruinge, Lance Corporal USMC, KIA 3 August 2005

David S. Stewart, Corporal USMC, KIA 3 August 2005

FALLEN FROM U.S. SPECIAL OPS FORCES, IN AL-QAIM DISTRICT, 2005

Stephen M. Langmack, Sergeant 1st Class U.S. Army, KIA, 1 June 2005

Robert M. Horrigan, Master Sergeant U.S. Army, KIA, 17 June 2005

Michael L. McNulty, Master Sergeant U.S. Army, KIA, 17 June 2005

Trevor J. Diesing, Sergeant 1st Class U.S. Army, KIA, 25 August 2005

Ivica Jerak, Master Sergeant U.S. Army, KIA, 25 August 2005

Timothy M. Shea, Corporal U.S. Army, KIA, 25 August 2005

Obediah J. Kolath, Sergeant 1st Class U.S. Army, KIA, 25 August 2005

See **bastardsandbrothers.com** for notes, photos, maps, etc.

31. THE STRUGGLE

The war does not stop when the deployment is done.

—**Kevin Collare**[1]

While precision weapons, body armor, and advanced battlefield medicine have dramatically reduced the number of American troops that die in combat, the human costs of combat go far beyond the number of flag-draped caskets. For every Marine killed in action in Iraq, there were approximately ten others wounded. While most returned to duty after treatment, many could not. When high-velocity bullets, armor-piercing projectiles, and powerful IEDs don't kill those they strike, they often inflict life-altering injuries.

Recovery typically involves repeated medical procedures, surgeries, skin grafts, and possibly the fitting of artificial limbs. Subsequent rounds of physical therapy can be painful ordeals. To complicate matters, those wounded can find themselves hooked on prescription pain medications and fighting to beat addiction. The notorious bureaucracy of the Veterans Administration, mountains of paperwork, and a system that too often seems stacked against them, pose another set of challenges. For some 3/2 Marines, the sustained courage required to fight back from their wounds exceeded the bravery they showed on the battlefield.

EDDIE RYAN

As he was loaded onto a dustoff helicopter on April 13, 2005, Corporal Eddie Ryan began a long, painful, yet miraculous journey. The friendly fire incident that tragic day caused him life-threatening and life-long brain injuries. From Iraq, he was flown to the Army Hospital in Landstuhl, Germany while his family traveled from the States to join him. "We were told we'd probably be saying goodbye," remembers Eddie's father, Chris, a rock-jawed former heavy equipment operator from Yonkers who had also served in the Marine Corps Reserve.[2] The Ryans are a close-knit family, strong in love and faith. As doctors battled to save him, Eddie's mother, Angie, spent every possible moment by her son's bedside, a constant prayer in her heart.

After five days in Germany, Eddie was flown to Bethesda Naval Hospital in Maryland. He was in a medically induced coma to minimize brain activity and reduce swelling. "There was no guarantee he'd ever wake up," recalls Chris, but their son again surprised the doctors and began breathing on his own. The staff called him the Miracle Marine. Slowly, the Ryans could see their son coming back to the world.

It would be a tortuous path, however. After Bethesda, Eddie was moved to the VA hospital in Richmond, Virginia where conditions were not the same. The staff was overwhelmed by the numbers of traumatic brain injury (TBI) cases, mostly from IED attacks. "We had to push to get him the attention he needed," his father recalls. "I'd say, 'This is my son!' They even called security on us once." But the Ryans are a force to be reckoned with and would not be denied. Soon other families joined them in demanding better care for their wounded warriors. Together, they brought enough pressure to bear that the VA's protocols for TBI treatment were updated.

Eventually, with bipartisan involvement from Congress, Eddie was transferred to Helen Hayes Hospital in West Haverstraw, a national leader in rehabilitation and recovery from brain injury. There he received top-notch physical, occupational, and speech therapy. "He started talking again, putting sentences together. That was huge," remembers Chris.

In the summer of 2006, after some 16 months of operations, recovery, and rehab, the Ryans took their son home to Ellenville, New York where they began a constant regimen of care and therapy. Since then, he has made slow, incremental improvement and they work tirelessly each day on multiple fronts to help him keep moving forward. Eddie will never recover fully. The damage from his injuries is too extensive. But his attitude is positive, and he and his family keep pushing every day for small victories. Each step is its own miracle.

The family moved to Lake George, New York in 2011 to be closer to a hospital and more outdoor activities. Sergeant Eddie Ryan, the Miracle Marine (he was promoted while recovering), is now a well-known figure in Lake George. "The community here is super supportive," says his father. "They've really wrapped their arms around him. It's just incredible." Many of Eddie's Marine brothers stay in contact as well, part of an extended family. Former Reaper teammates or other 3/2 veterans will call or drop by when they can.

"When life throws you a challenge, have faith in God. He'll send angels to help." says Chris. "We've had so many incredible experiences. People we've never met will come into our lives, and just want to help. It's amazing." Each year on 13 April, the Ryans, along with close friends, caregivers, and veterans celebrate Eddie's "Alive Day." They talk with Eddie, share stories, cry a little, and laugh a lot. They buoy each other up and give thanks for another year together. Then they carry on.

ROBBIE GASS

After his guntruck was hit by a suicide bomber during Operation Matador, Corporal Robert Gass left Al-Qaim with a jagged piece of metal stuck in his forehead. Military doctors performed his first craniotomy while he was still in Iraq, removing the shrapnel and patching his skull. He was then flown to Landstuhl, Germany. His brain injury treatment was further complicated since he'd been severely burned in the blast.

After being stabilized, he was flown to Brooks Army Medical Center, Texas, for treatment of burns on his abdomen, hands, and face. Subsequently he was transferred to a VA hospital in Tampa, Florida, to begin treatment for traumatic brain injury. "By that time, I was ready to go home," he says. "I was tired of not being able to walk, talk, or even write."[3] Soon after, he was medically retired from the Marine Corps and went home to South Carolina. While receiving sporadic therapy from the VA, healing largely came with time. His brain gradually rewired itself, and old abilities slowly returned.

Emotional recovery took longer, however. "For a while, I lived on the wild side," Gass remembers. He met his wife during that time, but their life was chaotic. "I was drinking a lot, doing crazy things." Together, they decided to turn things around and sought spiritual support. They began attending a church and turned their lives towards God. Private support groups also helped, such as Operation Heal Our Patriots, a faith-based program in Alaska for wounded vets. "We've had many blessings since our trip to Alaska," he says.

Through another vet-founded program, Mission 22, Gass received hypobaric oxygen therapy for his TBI, which has had noticeable effects. "I'm calmer now, and better at communicating." While his injury will have life-long effects, and his speech is measured with frequent pauses, Robbie Gass concentrates on his family and raising two little girls. "I have so many blessings," he says. "My wife Brittany is great. I feel like God put her in my life. And along with her, our focus is on my faith and our family."

Psychological wounds can run even deeper than physical ones. Each man brought home the indelible sights, sounds and smells of war, the rampant highs and lows. Coming back into society, or even to garrison duty, is often a jarring transition. Many who return to civilian life feel isolated, alone. "We don't view things the same anymore," explains Kevin Collare. "After you've seen death up close, been with it, beside it, embraced it even ... things just look different. Most people can't understand what you understand." Returning combat vets often experience sleepless nights, disorientation, frustration, anger, depression, and a sense of guilt. Guilt for not being "over there" where others are fighting. Guilt for not having done enough. Guilt for having survived, while brothers did not:

> *I've witnessed hell on Earth. I've seen and experienced some of the most horrific and immoral things the human race is capable of unfold right in front of me. I only served for four years, but it*

seemed like a lifetime. While you're immersed in the warrior culture... most things roll off your back like water off a duck. But what happens when you take a warrior out of that element?

—Jon Maines[4]

TRAVIS KERN

Wounded in Operation Matador when a 7.62mm round tore through his leg, shattering bone, Travis Kern was soon on a MEDEVAC back to the States. It took six months of treatment, battling infection and several operations, before the wound healed. He couldn't return to full duty, however, and was medically discharged in 2006. Two years later, while undergoing treatment at the VA, a small chunk of metal was discovered lodged behind his knee next to an artery. Doctors said it was too risky to remove, so it remains in his body to this day. He still carries emotional scars as well. "I don't think I'll ever get over losing Philippon. It should have been me on that door when he was killed. It should have been me. Survivor guilt is a bitch, and for years I punished myself. I've learned to deal with it, to keep up my hope and faith. But sometimes I just have to take it day by day."[5]

In more recent years, the U.S. military, the Veteran's Administration, and the healthcare system overall grew more aware of challenges faced by returning vets. Better approaches and programs have been developed. But in 2005, the nation was still learning how to bring these warriors home. Many who served with or alongside 3/2 in Al-Qaim had a tough transition afterwards. "Everyone left a piece of themselves in the sand," wrote Jon Maines in a heartfelt essay to fellow veterans. "It affected each of us differently... Some have suffered through the loss of a brother. I've experienced it, and it's like a piece of me went with them. Others struggled with the moral aftermath of taking human life... Some moved on immediately into successful positions, but still found themselves struggling. Lots of us, including myself, didn't realize we had issues we were dealing with."

Too often, combat veterans self-medicate with drugs or alcohol to suppress memories and emotions that can well up within. But trying to bottle up such feelings leads to further problems. Jon Maines goes on to describe the inner turmoil that he and many others have been through:

> *The "bad memory dam" you tried keeping closed for so long cracks open and starts a flood. It's overwhelming. I've been there, many times over. This is where the depression starts to set in. You sink to your lowest low... the darkest mental hole you've ever been in, and that becomes the focus and center of your life. It feels like the most impossible place to leave, as if there's no escaping... It eventually comes to a point to where you're tired of fighting with yourself every day just to open your eyes and roll out of bed.*
>
> **—Jon Maines**

For a few that downward spiral has been fatal. Nationwide, too many veterans are taking their own lives, with devastating consequences for families and friends. The grim statistic of "22-a-day", derived from the numbers of veterans (of all eras) who commit suicide each year, has been widely cited. It marks an alarming trend and 3/2 veterans have not been immune. Sadly, more Marines from the battalion's 2005 deployment have been lost to self-induced causes, including suicide, than were killed in action in Al-Qaim. Each such loss ripples painfully through circles of warrior brothers, prompting further soul-searching and redoubled efforts to support each other.

OVERCOMING

The vast majority of 3/2 veterans, however, have pushed on through whatever challenges they faced and came out the other side. "The big thing is to realize that real men do ask for help," urges Scott Hauslyak. "If you think you need help, get help. Talk to someone who will listen. Find something, anything, that you feel good doing. I do a lot of hunting and enjoy the outdoors. That works for me. And when it gets tough, I think 'I'm not gonna let them win.' I'm not gonna give up this many years later."[6]

A message to my brothers

Combat did not define who we are. It was a turning point in our lives, no doubt, but it is not the reason we ultimately exist. We have more life to live, more things to experience. War was not the end of the road. Find a healthy outlet, an alternate purpose. "Adapt and overcome." For some, your family gives you strength. For others, it may be donating your time to help others. It may be a hobby you're passionate about, or you just want to be a better man for the woman you love with everything you have ... You have the rest of your life in front of you. Do it for the guys who are no longer with us, because that's what they would have wanted.

— Jon Maines

These men reach out to each other to talk and reminisce, to fortify one another when spirits flag. "I know my brother Marines will never abandon me, leave, quit, or fail when the storms come and the waters get rough," says Chris Reith.[7] They maintain their ties through phone calls, social media, small get-togethers, and unofficial unit reunions. Back with their brothers, they can relax and share stories of life, love, and loss, and continue to provide mutual support. For many, that ongoing support has been a great strength, a source of healing.

Some have traveled harder roads than others, but by and large they have picked up and moved forward. And while they will always have those moments when something stirs up the still waters from deep inside, they've learned to focus their energies and make positive contributions to their families, professions, and communities. They are not victims. They are not broken. Their wartime experience made them wiser and stronger. One of the Corps' iconic leaders has stated his own perspective on post-combat, post-deployment recovery:

> *For those who close on the enemy, who seek out, close with to kill the enemy, it is a very atavistic, primitive environment and there is post-traumatic stress for anyone who's been through it. There is stress, no doubt about it... But it does not have to be post-traumatic "disorder" or "syndrome." You don't have to come at it from a position of illness. You can come at it from a position of wellness, from a position of growth as a human being... There is also something called post traumatic growth... I recognize the grim realities. I don't recognize the limited potential of the human being when they come out of that.*
>
> —**General James Mattis, USMC (retired)**[8]

This outlook is prominent among the 3/2 veterans interviewed for this book. One, who as a 19-year-old grunt, amazingly escaped unscathed from the fiery blast from a suicide bomber, today expresses sentiments echoing those of the famous general, perhaps even more eloquently:

> *We are tougher than we give ourselves credit for. This lesson has allowed me to move ahead when I did not think I even had the strength to stand. Being a Marine, being at war and coming home, tested my mind, body, and spirit to its very depths. And proved to me that no obstacle is unconquerable, no trial is unbearable, and no test is too difficult to endure. You can push one more time, take just one more step, and then another. Today I remind myself to keep moving forward to completion, as Paul says in 1st Corinthians.*
>
> *This really started that day long ago, as we recovered from the suicide bomb that hit our guntruck and I saw the fist-sized chunk of metal that came through my side of the windshield. It ended up under my driver's seat instead of tearing into my torso, as all who saw it agreed it should have. That day is when I grasped the fragility of life and knew I had to take advantage of each and every day. Now I focus my attention on my calling; to help and encourage others, to be the best husband and father I can be for my wife and four children. To love, guide, encourage, while making great memories. Life still has its difficulties, they are just different, and I still draw on those lessons so painfully learned years ago.*
>
> **—Jeff Lamson**[9]

Of the 3/2 vets who stayed in the Corps, many became leaders, mentors, and examples to a new generation of Marines. And of those who rejoined civilian life, a good portion gravitated into fields centered on service of one kind or another. Many have found careers as first-responders, in emergency medicine, or in police and fire departments. Others are now teachers, therapists, or counselors. Still others volunteer in various capacities. Their service, their pursuit of purpose, propels them and they have discovered that helping others heals their own wounds too. Included here are just a few examples:

NOAH ANDERSON

During Operation Spear, Noah Anderson's position was hit by multiple volleys of enemy mortar fire. One round exploded just meters to his front, lancing a piece of shrapnel into his helmet and permanently destroying the hearing in his left ear. He finished the 2005 deployment but was diagnosed with degenerative hearing loss and left active duty in 2006. "It was hard for quite a while," Noah says. "I was hard on myself."[10] Fighting bouts of depression, anger, and survivor guilt, at first he coped through alcohol and retreated into himself. At a certain point, he reached bottom and realized he was damaging his family and loved ones.

Through his family's support, he found a healing path through ultra-marathon running and began to turn things around. In 2016, he teamed up with award-winning filmmaker Tim O'Donnell to produce "The Last Time I Heard True Silence", a moving documentary about his running and post-deployment recovery. Since then, he has made several extreme distance runs to raise awareness and funding for wounded veterans, including Sergeant Eddie Ryan, forging a close friendship with the Ryan family in the process. He also holds frequent volunteer workshops for veterans from all branches and eras to help them through their own struggles. "That's the most rewarding thing I do now," he relates. "We just talk things out." Reflecting on being a Marine, undergoing combat and his own struggles, he says, "I used to see it as a negative, but I've changed my mind on that. It's made me much more resilient, able to focus on moving forward."

EMMANUEL NELSON

Wounded alongside Travis Kern during Matador, Emmanuel "Nelly" Nelson, returned to duty and deployed with 3/2 again in 2006. After that tour, he got out and struggled with sleeplessness and anger. Eventually, though, he went to college and found his calling. He earned an MA in Social Work from Wayne State University. Even before finishing his degree, he worked as an intern with the VA and after graduation volunteered to help homeless veterans find shelter.

Since 2016 he's been a licensed Master Social Worker working as a substance abuse therapist in the Detroit VA Center. "I really enjoy working with vets, and feel at home with them," he says. "I've got tough memories too, feelings of isolation. But sometimes we've gotta do things we don't want to do, like doing pull-ups to build our strength. I give them the tools, and motivate them to reach out, to socialize, ask for help. They're the ones that have to do the work, I just show them that I care. And it feels good to see them a year later, and they're doing good."[11]

NATHAN SMITH

Nathan Smith, commander of Kilo Company's 2nd Platoon, deployed again with 3/2 in 2006, first as Weapons Platoon commander in Kilo, then 1st Platoon commander in India Company. After two very tough combat tours, he rotated out of 3/2 to the Marine Corps Security Forces Battalion in Bangor, Washington. "That was my time in the wilderness," he says. He had his own struggles with what he'd been through. "I decided to get out, but wasn't sure what to do," Smith remembers. "Nothing appealed to me. I lost weight from the stress."[12] But as he left the Marines in mid 2010, he found a new and rewarding job helping other veterans. Brian Stann contacted him about working with a small non-profit organization called Hire Heroes USA, based outside Atlanta. "I trusted Brian, and if he was involved I wanted to be part of it." Smith eventually became the chief operations officer and the two made a good team:

> *We focused on finding veterans, our clients, meaningful careers, not just jobs. The emphasis was on quality over quantity. We were very personalized, very "high-touch." When I came on board, we were annually helping less than 100 clients find jobs... We didn't want to just push people through a website to rack up numbers.*
>
> **—Nathan Smith**

Slowly, steadily, they built a highly-effective organization that helped veterans and their spouses find positions that were a good fit, emphasizing meaningful engagement and integrity of the process. Large institutional donors took notice, and their reach and reputation grew. "At first, I did a lot of transition workshops myself," says Smith. "I'd work with a guy, and he'd walk out with new found confidence, clutching a resume that conveyed real value in the marketplace. It was highly rewarding to see how truly transforming that was for them."

Hire Heroes now has a nationwide presence, with a growing permanent staff and hundreds of volunteers. "Over the years, we had some 3/2 guys come through and they told us about the positive experience they had with our transition specialists," says Smith. "That was what Brian and I always wanted." After nine years of growth, Smith was recruited as COO for a financial management firm. "My time at Hire Heroes helped me see that what I'd done in the military was really valued. The fundamentals I'd learned in the Marines, the experience leading people, were applicable anywhere."

*****

In the opening of the 21st century, one small sliver of the American population was called on to enter a myriad of nameless battlegrounds, some even more remote and desperate than the ones described in these pages. That segment wore uniforms from all the services. They were men and women. They were active-duty, reservists, and national guardsmen. They willingly picked up the burden, again and again and again.

Today they are our friends, coworkers, and neighbors. You probably won't recognize them at first glance, because they usually don't talk much about their wartime experience. But if you know what to look for, you might pick one out. He's the middle-school teacher that calls his students "sir" and "ma'am." She's the single mom and city alderman that looks you straight in the eye and shakes your hand with a prosthetic. He's that guy in the back of the gym with the watchful gaze who always stands for the national anthem. If you look closely you may see a certain look in his eye, a quiet ripple of the things he's seen and the brothers he's known. And if you call him a bastard he will smile and say, "You bet your life I am."

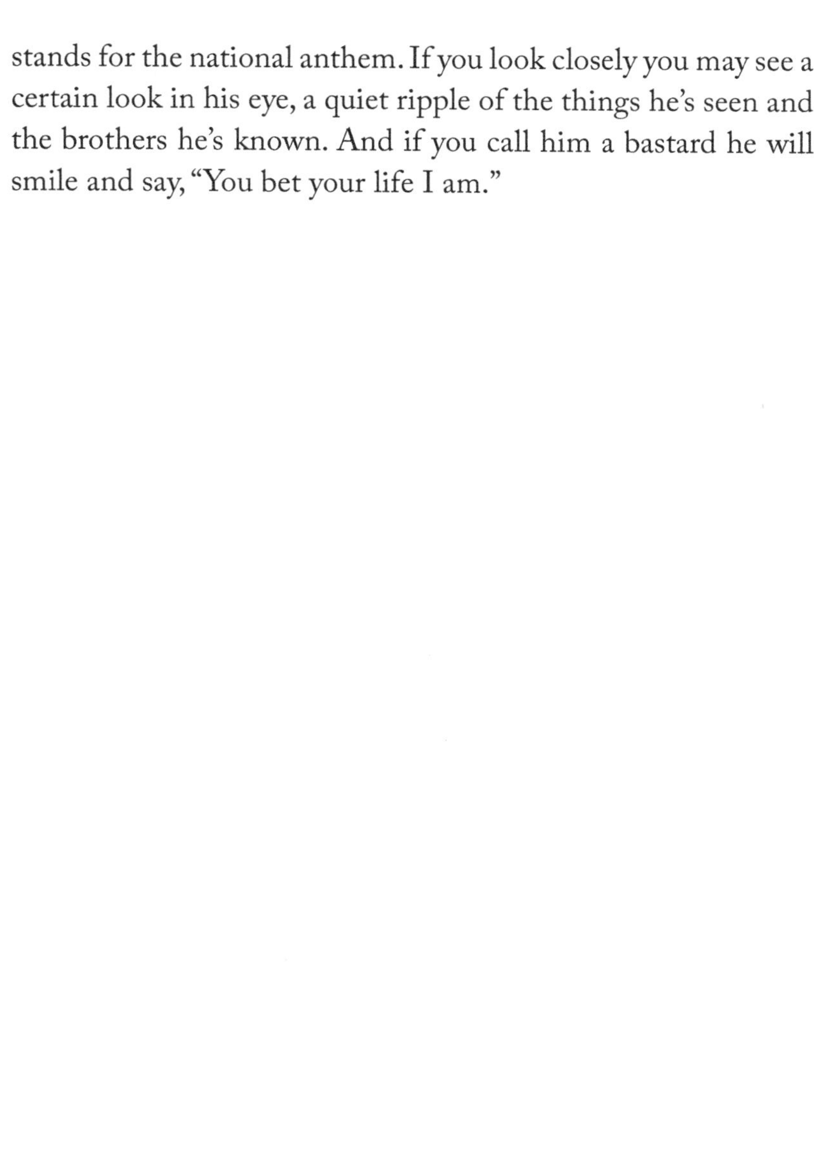

ACKNOWLEDGEMENTS

Like a boot Marine fresh out of Parris Island, I launched into this project knowing just enough to be dangerous. Fortunately, a host of guides and mentors hammered me and the book into a useful shape.

First to Cindy, the love of my life, fearless adventure partner, front-line editor, and sanity-checker, thank you for your patience, your faith in me and the courage you have loaned to get me through the tough slogs.

Then to Bob Babcock and the team of professionals at Deeds Publishing, who were instrumental in bringing the book to life. Thank you for recognizing the power and beauty of this story. And to Anthony Cunha for introducing me to Bob and his team.

To all the combat veterans who shared amazing experiences and sometimes their pain with me, I am humbled and honored by the confidence you placed in me. Thank you barely suffices. Without you I could never have produced an account of such depth, scope, and spirit. Your voices are the beating heart of the book.

The foremost example has been Chris Ieva, who tutored my pogue ass and opened countless doors. His warrior spirit shines on many pages. Chris, you've been indispensable. Without the raw, honest emotions you shared, showing me what the book could be, it would have been a lifeless tome.

Many others I interviewed were equally open, confiding in me and even calling me a brother. Special thanks to Jesse Bedia, Robbie Gass, Matt Gundlach, Travis Kern, Jeff Lamson, and Jon Maines who gave me a glimpse of those still waters that run so deep. Mike Hodd and Don Brazeal helped me peel the onion, layer by fascinating layer, of the India Company mafia. Likewise, Jeff Weaver, Aaron Smith, and Anthony Cunha pulled back the camo nets to give me a peek inside the shrouded world of scout-snipers.

Other key sources added perspective and layers of vital context. Tim Mundy, Stephen Davis, Chris Starling, and "Rock" Lister spent hours enduring my ceaseless questions, providing operational-level perspectives and the command-level view of complex events. Thank you for your patience and wise advice.

A huge thanks to Nate Smith, Chris Nothstine, Andrew Taylor, Scott Bunker, Jason Ellis, Jordan Bogart, and Michael Ledbetter, for trusting me with their journals, personal accounts, and combat logs. The matchless detail and all-important dates they contained allowed me to reconstruct key events while faithfully portraying emotional highs and lows.

To Leesa and Ray Philippon, Emma Lou Johnson, and Chris Ryan, I remain forever in awe of your courage, grace, and faith in the face of tragedy. Heartfelt thanks to you for allowing me to better know your Marine. May God bless your family.

GLOSSARY

.50 cal–The M2 .50 caliber heavy machine-gun, nicknamed the "Ma Deuce".

1/7–1st Battalion, 7th Marine Regiment

2nd LAR or 2LAR–2nd Light Armored Reconnaissance Battalion

3rd ACR–3rd Armored Cavalry Regiment (U.S. Army)

3/25–3rd Battalion, 25th Marine Regiment

3/6–3rd Battalion, 6th Marine Regiment

3/7–3rd Battalion, 7th Marine Regiment

7-ton–U.S. military truck, aka the Medium Tactical Vehicle Replacement (MTVR)

AAV–Assault Amphibious Vehicle, fully tracked personnel carrier. Also called "amtrac" or "trac"

AC-130 Spectre – Heavily-armed U.S. Air Force gunship, usually used to support special operations

Accelerants – Equipment, weapons, money, and personnel that "accelerate" an insurgency. Alternatively, ingredients added to an improvised bomb to increase its power and lethality

AH-1 Cobra – U.S. Marine attack helicopter

AK – Series of Soviet-designed rifles used by insurgents; AK-47, AK-74, AKM, etc.

Amtrac – Nickname for Assault Amphibious Vehicle (AAV), aka "trac"

ANGLICO – Air Naval Gunfire Liaison Company, specialized Marine unit that coordinates airstrikes and long-range artillery fires

AO – Area of Operations

AQI – Al-Qaeda in Iraq. Extremely violent terrorist/insurgent group led by foreign jihadists fighting in Iraq. Previously known as the Organization of Monotheism and Jihad *(Jama'at al-Tawhid wal-Jihad)*, abbreviated as JTJ. AQI eventually morphed into ISIS (Islamic State of Iraq and Syria).

ASP – Ammunition Supply Point, aka ammo dump

ASR – Alternate Supply Route

AT-4–Unguided, single-shot 84mm rocket fired from the shoulder

AV-8B Harrier–U.S. Marine attack jet. Can take off and land vertically

Battlespace–Any area of conflict or combat; airspace, seaspace, etc.

BAS–Battalion Aid Station

BCT–Brigade Combat Team

C4–Military-grade plastic explosive

CAAT–Combined Anti-armor Team. Precursor to Mobile Assault Platoon

CAG–Civil Affairs Group

CAS–Close Air Support. Methods and missions to support ground troops in combat from aircraft

CASEVAC–Casualty Evacuation. Initial transport of wounded personnel to a medical facility

CBR–Counter-battery radar. Small radar able to pinpoint the source of mortar or rocket fire

CCP–Casualty collection point

CH-53 Sea Stallion – U.S. Marine heavy-lift helicopter

CH-46 Sea Knight – U.S. Marine and Navy medium-lift helicopter

Clear – Sweeping a large area, or entering a building to eliminate any threat

Coalition – Also called the Multi-national Force-Iraq (MNF-I). The combined military forces of the United States and allied countries that operated in Iraq during the war. Did not include Iraqi forces.

CO – Commanding Officer

COC – Combat Operations Center. Equivalent of a Tactical Operations Center (TOC) in the U.S. Army

COP – Combat Outpost. Similar to a battle position, but more permanent and developed

Combined Arms – Method of warfare combining the strengths of different unit types and weapons

Corps – The U.S. Marine Corps, or a high-level command in the U.S. Army or other militaries

Counter-battery fire – Friendly artillery or mortar fire against the sources of enemy indirect fire

CP – Command Post. General term for command facilities at various levels. Can be static or mobile.

CPA – Coalition Provisional Authority. The U.S.-led coalition's civilian leadership component

CW3 – Chief Warrant Officer 3. Advanced-level expert in technical and tactical areas

Direct Action – Short-duration strikes, raids and offensive actions to seize, destroy or capture designated targets. A primary mission of special operations forces

Direct Fire – Fire from rifles, machine-guns or any weapon firing straight at the target

DShK – Soviet-designed 12.7mm heavy machine-gun. Aka "dashika"

DUSTWUN – Duty Status or Whereabouts Unknown

ERU – Emergency Response Unit. Local Sunni tribal forces that allied with the coalition. Early version of the Sons of Iraq program

Echelon – Refers to level of command, as in "higher-echelon" leaders

ECP – Entry Control Point

EFP – Explosively Formed Penetrator. Highly lethal form of

IED that punches a slug of molten metal through armored vehicles. Almost exclusively used by Iranian-backed Shiite militia groups

EOD–Explosive Ordnance Disposal

Firm–Marine infantry term for temporarily holding a building or good defensive position

Flak–Marine slang for kevlar body armor, refers to obsolete "flak jackets"

F-16 Fighting Falcon–U.S. Air Force multi-role fighter jet

F/A-18 Hornet–U.S. Marine Corps multi-role fighter/attack jet

FAC–Forward Air Controller

FO–Forward Observer

FMF–Fleet Marine Force, designator for a Navy corpsman assigned to support Marines

GRG–Ground Reference Graphic. Detailed map superimposed on satellite imagery.

Guntruck–Common nickname for an armored Humvee mounting a machine-gun or heavy weapon

H&S–Headquarters & Services

H&K Triangle–The area that joined the cities of Husaybah and Karabilah

HEAT–High Explosive Anti-tank

HET–HUMINT (Human intelligence) Exploitation Team

HESCO–Folding barriers used at almost every coalition base. Filled with dirt and rocks, they protected against incoming fire, mortar impacts and suicide attacks. Developed by Hercules Engineering Solutions Consortium.

HOG–Hunter of Gunmen. Graduate of Marine Corps Sniper School

HM1, HM2, HM3, HMC–Hospital Corpsman 1st, 2nd and 3rd Class and Chief Hospital Corpsman

HMLA–Helicopter Marine Light Attack

HUMINT–Human Intelligence. Collection and management of information from human sources.

Humvee–Common nickname for the High Mobility Medium Wheeled Vehicle (HMMWV)

HVI–High Value Individual, sometimes called High Value Target (HVT)

Incoming–Any type of fire aimed at your position. Direct or indirect fire.

IDF – Indirect Fire. Fire from mortars or rockets that arcs into the air then down onto the target

IR – Infrared. IR systems can detect targets in darkness or bad weather

IED – Improvised Explosive Device

IO – Information Operations

ING – Iraqi National Guard, an ineffective Iraqi force, disbanded in 2005

INTSUM – Intelligence Summary

ISF – Iraqi Security Forces. General term for Iraqi military personnel

ISIS – Islamic State of Iraq and Syria, also called the Islamic State of Iraq and the Levant (ISIL). This notoriously violent group grew out of the defeated remnants of Al-Qaeda in Iraq (AQI).

ISOF – Iraqi Special Operations Forces

ISR – Intelligence, Surveillance and Reconnaissance

JAM – *Jaysh al-Mahdi*, aka Mahdi Army. Large Shiite militia group in Iraq

Javelin – FGM-148 man-portable guided anti-tank missile

JAG–Judge Advocate General. Military lawyer. Can be assigned at various levels of command

JTAC–Joint Terminal Attack Controller

JTJ–Organization of Monotheism and Jihad, or Unity and Jihad *(Jama'at al-Tawhid wal-Jihad).* Terrorist/insurgent group that was a precursor to Al-Qaeda in Iraq (AQI)

Kevlar–Marine slang for a kevlar helmet

KIA–Killed in action

LAV–Light Armored Vehicle. Fast eight-wheeled armored vehicle used by the Marine Corps, mostly in Light Armored Reconnaissance (LAR) Battalions

LZ–Landing Zone

M1A2 Abrams–Main battle tank used by the U.S. Army and Marine Corps in 2005

M203–Single-shot 40mm grenade launcher attached to an M16 rifle

M240–7.62mm medium machine-gun. The common M240G model is nicknamed the "Golf"

M249–5.56mm light machine-gun, aka Squad Automatic Weapon (SAW)

M88 Hercules – Fully-tracked heavy armored recovery vehicle

MAC – Mobile Assault Company

MAP – Mobile Assault Platoon

MAGTF – Marine Air-Ground Task Force

MEDEVAC – Medical Evacuation. Onward transport of wounded to a more advanced medical facility

MEF – Marine Expeditionary Force. Large, Corps-sized war-time force of multiple units

Moto – Marine slang for "motivated" or "motivating"

MAW – Marine Air Wing

MCAS – Marine Corps Air Station

MEU – Marine Expeditionary Unit

MICLIC – Mine Clearance Line Charge

Mk19 – Mark-19 40mm automatic grenade launcher

MG – Machine-gun

MRE – Meals-Ready-to-Eat

MSR – Main Supply Route

NCO – Non-commissioned officer

NVG – Night Vision Goggles

OCS – Officer Candidate School

ODA – Operational Detachment Alpha. Field team of Army Green Berets

ODB – Operational Detachment Beta. Command team of Green Berets

OGA – Other Government Agency

OIF – Operation Iraqi Freedom. Official name for the invasion and occupation of Iraq, 2003-2011

OP – Observation Post

PIG – Professionally-instructed gunman. Marine scout-sniper who has not graduated from sniper school

PGM – Precision-guided munition

PKM – Soviet designed medium machine-gun often used by insurgents

POI – Point of impact of an indirect fire attack, i.e., the point where a mortar round or rocket hits

POO–Point of origin of an indirect fire attack**Post**–Guard post, sentry tower, gun position or any place a Marine defends

PRT–Provincial Reconstruction Team

PSYOPS–Psychological Operations

QJBR–The Al-Qaeda Organization for Jihad in the Land of the Two Rivers (*Tanzim Qaedat al-Jihad fi Bilad al-Rafidayn).* Another name for al-Qaeda in Iraq (AQI). Sometimes abbreviated TQJBR

QRF–Quick Reaction Force

R&S–Reconnaissance & Surveillance

RC–Reduced Communications, aka "River City"

RCT–Regimental Combat Team

RIP–Relief in Place

ROE–Rules of Engagement

RPG–Rocket Propelled Grenade. Soviet-designed shoulder-fired rocket

RPK–Soviet-designed light machine-gun used by insurgents

RTO–Radio Telephone Operator. The commander's radio man (the reference to telephones is archaic)

S3 – Staff designation for the Operations Officer

SATCOM – Satellite Communications

SASO – Stability and Support Operations. Modern version of counter-insurgency (COIN) operations

SAW – Squad Automatic Weapon, aka the M249 machine-gun

SF – U.S. Army Special Forces, aka Green Berets (not to be confused with SOF)

SOF – Special Operations Forces. Broad term for special mission units from several services. Includes Army Rangers, Navy SEALs, Army Green Berets, and other units

SSP – Scout-Sniper Platoon

SST – Scout-Sniper Team

SVBIED – Suicide Vehicle-borne Improvised Explosive Device

Task Force – A unit or organization specially organized for a task. Can refer to a wide variety of conventional military units and special operations forces, but in this book mostly refers to the conglomeration of elite U.S. special mission units known as Task Force 714

TOA – Transfer of Authority

TOW–BGM-71 tube-launched, optically-tracked, wire-guided anti-tank missile

Trac–Another nickname for an AAV

UAV–Unmanned aerial vehicle, aka remotely-piloted aircraft (RPA)

UH-1 Iroquois–Medium helicopter for multiple missions, aka "Huey"

UHF–Ultra-high frequency

VBIED–Vehicle-borne Improvised Explosive Device

VC–Vehicle Commander

VCP–Vehicle Checkpoint

VHF–Very-high frequency

VMA–Marine attack squadron. The "V" is a WWII-era designator for fixed-wing aircraft

VMFA–Marine strike fighter or fighter/attack squadron.

WIA–Wounded in action

WERV–Western Euphrates River Valley

XO–Executive Officer. The second-in-command in a tactical unit

ABOUT THE AUTHOR

Roger "Ajax" Trueblood is a retired U.S. Air Force intelligence officer, and former CIA analyst, who deployed twice to Southwest Asia and Iraq, in 2004/05 and in 2007. After being part of the 2007 surge and experiencing first-hand the positive effects of the tribal Awakening, he began a long search to understand what he had witnessed. That journey led his research efforts step-by-step back along the Euphrates River Valley where he discovered the amazing story of Al-Qaim and the Marines of 3/2. Today he lives, writes, and hikes in St. George, Utah, among the red rock canyons and picturesque mesas of the desert southwest.

CPSIA information can be obtained
at www.ICGtesting.com
Printed in the USA
BVHW040407031222
653334BV00004B/9/J

9 781950 794928